Performing Difference

Representations of "The Other" in Film and Theater

Edited by
Jonathan C. Friedman

UNIVERSITY PRESS OF AMERICA,® INC.
Lanham • Boulder • New York • Toronto • Plymouth, UK

Copyright © 2009 by
University Press of America,® Inc.
4501 Forbes Boulevard
Suite 200
Lanham, Maryland 20706
UPA Acquisitions Department (301) 459-3366

Estover Road
Plymouth PL6 7PY
United Kingdom

Library of Congress Control Number: 2008931105
ISBN-13: 978-0-7618-4154-8 (paperback : alk. paper)
ISBN-10: 0-7618-4154-7 (paperback : alk. paper)
eISBN-13: 978-0-7618-4267-5
eISBN-10: 0-7618-4267-5

Contents

Introduction

In his landmark work, *I and Thou,* Martin Buber claimed that "relation is reciprocity . . . Inscrutably involved, we live in the currents of universal reciprocity."[1] Emmanuel Lévinas, the Lithuanian-born Jewish philosopher who became one of France's most important intellectual figures of the twentieth century, went further by insisting that our ethical obligation to the other is the first truth of human existence, preceding any relationship. Despite their differences, the basic premise of Buber and Lévinas, that is to say, our primary duty to an "ethics of the other," undergirds the rationale for this edited volume on depictions of race, ethnicity, and gender in contemporary film and theater. Although a phrase like "performing difference," and words like "alterity," "the other," "otherness," and "othering" are strange and charged, reflecting invented language and a certain trendiness to academic research, they reflect the substantial changes in thinking about human relations which the markers of postindustrial society (technology, travel, and information access) have helped to effect.

This manuscript assesses diverse portrayals of groups and individuals that have been traditionally marginalized or excluded from dominant historical narratives. One of its aims is to complement the existing body of research which has begun to include these groups and individuals in existing histories or to create new narratives by and for them. A focus on representation on film and theater is a logical extension of this broader effort. Expressing one's racial, ethnic, and gender identity is first and foremost a performative act, that is to say, it is linked to a certain set of behaviors and practices that are synonymous with the performers. Moreover, roles for groups and individuals are very often reflected and created by the performing arts. David Román, professor of English at the University of Southern California, has argued for a rethinking of performance as central, rather than marginal, to the national imaginary. In his words, "performance's liveness and impermanence allow for a process of exchange—between artists and audiences, between the past and the present—where new societal formations emerge."[2] Cinema studies professor Ed Guerrero takes this sentiment further, writing in the forward of the compilation, *Reversing the Lens,* that we live in an "electronically mediated technoculture where one's screen image determines so much about one's political fortunes and collective fate."[3] On the issue of the Holocaust alone, films, television, and theatrical productions have been indispensable in helping to assimilate the genocide of the Jews into the American popular consciousness. It is no exaggeration to say that in an age of YouTube, countless cable TV options, and blockbuster films, performance media constitute an essential (if not the essential) access point for a broader, public discussion about race, gender, and class and the performance roles associated with each.

To some scholars, analytical assumptions such as these represent politicized academia at its worst. So why enter such a minefield? The answer goes to the core of my approach as a Holocaust historian, which rests on twin premises. One is a belief in the necessity of exposing and rooting out prejudice in its most benign forms, specifically antilocution and avoidance. The other belief comes from the likes of Jewish theoreticians like Isaac Deutscher, who suggested that there was something very Jewish about marginal Jews seeking a universal sharing of narratives:

> The Jewish heretic who transcends Jewry belongs to a Jewish tradition. You may, if you like, see Akher [the heretical Jew] as a prototype of those great revolutionaries of modern thought: Spinoza, Heine, Marx, Rosa Luxemburg, Trotsky, and Freud. You may, if you wish to, place them within a Jewish tradition. They all went beyond the boundaries of Jewry . . . Yet I think that in some ways they were very Jewish indeed. They had in themselves something of the quintessence of Jewish life and of the Jewish intellect. They were *a priori* exceptional in that as Jews they dwelt on the borderlines of various civilizations, religions, and national cultures. They were born and brought up on the borderlines of various epochs. Their minds matured where the most diverse cultural influences crossed and fertilized each other . . . Each of them was in society and yet not in it, of it, and yet not of it. It was this that enabled them to rise in thought above their societies, above their nations, above their times and generations, and to strike out mentally into wide new horizons and far into the future.[4]

Applying Deutscher's ideas to a discipline such as Holocaust and Genocide studies has serious implications. The focus on collective murder and ways to prevent this most heinous form of bigotry might shift to points on a continuum which do not necessarily end in physical annihilation. One might hail this as a broadening of perspective, but others might see this as moving too far off message, into the realms of tolerance or "diversity" studies, which have their own intellectual standard-bearers and constituents. Many Holocaust specialists already disapprove of the linking of the Jewish Holocaust narrative with the non-Jewish one, or claim that the Holocaust only applies to Jews. Others are just as uncomfortable with any association with other genocides, emphasizing the singularity of the "Final Solution." These concerns cannot simply be dismissed, but must be countered with a reasoned counter-argument, the most convincing of which is that there is strength in numbers. Countless groups have experienced persecution and genocide throughout the ages. By working together in a framework of empathy, they can weave a powerful narrative, one that might someday become as imbedded into our individual and collective consciousness as a most basic instinct. A discourse of comparative victimization, which pits out-groups against out-groups, not only perpetuates isolation, but it leaves intact the basic power dynamic which enables bigotry and hate to lead to genocide.

This compilation of essays is the result of my overarching philosophy. As a meeting point of several fields of study, it is organized around three meta-themes—race, gender, and genocide. The past few years has seen a flurry of books on the first two topics, among them Harry Benshoff and Sean Griffen, *America on Film: Representing Race, Class, Gender, and Sexuality at the Movies* (London: Blackwell, 2003), Lane Ryo Hirabayashi and Jun Xing, eds., *Reversing the Lens: Ethnicity, Race, Gender, and Sexuality Through Film* (Boulder, Colorado: University of Colorado Press, 2003), Norman Denzin, *Reading Race: Hollywood and the Cinema of Racial Violence* (New York: Sage, 2002), Sharon Willis, *High Contrast: Race and Gender in Contemporary Hollywood Films* (Durham, North Carolina: Duke University Press, 1997), and Jude Daves and Carol Smith, eds., *Gender, Ethnicity, and Sexuality in Contemporary American Film* (London: TF-ROUTL, 2000). Our proposed volume adds to this body of research in its breadth and focus.

Unlike Benshoff and Griffin's *America on Film,* which is an excellent textbook about race, gender, and class in cinema (and which scrutinizes one film per subcategory), this compilation is more global in orientation. Included are analyses of films and theatrical productions from the United States, as well as essays on cinema from Southern and central America, Europe, and the Middle East. Topically, the contributing authors write about the depiction of race (in articles about African Americans, Asian-Americans, Native Americans, Afro-Brazilians), ethnicities (Germans, Turks, Hispanics, Jews), gender and sexual orientation (women, gay men, and lesbians), and genocides.

In the volume's first segment, on race and ethnicity, I begin with an assessment of films from 20th Century Fox's post-World War II period of social

activism, while Dalton Anthony Jones focuses on how the more recent production, *Powder,* speaks to the cinematic construction of both whiteness and blackness. Subsequent articles in this section move from the "radically other" of Shylock (Paul Pfeiffer's essay) to the increasingly blurred worlds of other and
insider. Here we feature essays by Tia Malkin-Fontecchio, on Brazil's minority
of race and class (the *favelados),* Margarete Landwehr, on Turks in Germany,
Raz Yosef, on Jews of Middle Eastern origin in Israel (*mizrahi*), Jun Xing on
Asian-Americans, and Bonnie Morris, on her own mixed Jewish heritage.

The second large-scale segment of the book centers on others of gender
(i.e., women) and sexual orientation (i.e., gay men and lesbians), and here
there are dual interests. One relates to how stage and screen have depicted
these out-groups in situations when they are thrust into forums traditionally
associated with the male in-group (Melissa Ziobro's article on films about
women in the armed forces and John Clum's essay on gay men in professional sports.) The second area of concern is similar to that of our earlier
segment, the intersection of others of gender, race, and ethnicity. Geetha Ramanathan discusses mestiza feminism in the film *Frida*, while I examine the
interplay of gay and ethnic discourses in Eytan Fox's film *The Bubble.*

The final segment assesses how cinema visualizes the destruction of the
other. Ilan Avisar traces the evolution of the portrayal of the Holocaust in
films, while John J. Michalczyk and Susan A. Michalczyk look specifically at
representations of bystanders in Holocaust films and documentaries. For his
part, Christopher Thomas tracks the change over time in depictions of the
German "perpetrator." Focusing on memory and denial, Edward Hanes eval-
uates recent films on genocide, and William Hewitt concludes the volume
with an essay exploring themes of redemption and genocide in films about
Native Americans. The focus on genocide, a term which I interpret broadly,
perhaps controversially so, and the inclusion of Jewish voices into the narrative stand out as the major differences with other works on the subject. As
with *Reversing the Lens,* the point of reference here is that of the editor; so
whereas Jun Xing and Lane Hirabayashi include a number of entries on their
particular subject of expertise (Asian-American studies), this manuscript
bears my imprint—a focus on Jewish and Holocaust history. Yet this is not
solely or even primarily a work of Jewish studies, and the questions asked by
each author reveal a shared line of inquiry: Who or what groups are represented? Who is doing the representing, that is to say, who is in charge of the
portrayal? The out-group? The in-group? Who has historically been in charge
of the portrayal, and how has this changed over time? What is the forum for
the production? The large-scale feature, or the independent venue? What is
the intended audience? What is the audience reaction? Is the intention to
change audience perception? Has this been successful?

An overarching issue here is the extent to which the performing arts construct authentic and sympathetic visions of the "other." Two recent films provide a starting point for discussion—Paul Haggis' 2005 Academy Award winning picture *Crash,* and Israeli filmmaker Eytan Fox's 2006 film *The Bubble (Ha-Buah),* which I review in greater detail in chapter twelve. Both address the theme of racial and interethnic relations and the violence that so frequently accompanies the encounter with the other. Set in Los Angeles, *Crash* weaves together numerous storylines with multiple characters of different races and ethnicities, using the simple (some would say simplistic) metaphor of the car and the modern street as the window through which to offer social commentary. Heroes become villains and villains become heroes as *Crash's* numerous automobile accidents, carjackings, and traffic stops play themselves out. In *The Bubble,* set in Tel Aviv's bohemian Sheinkin District, two gay friends (Noam and Yali) and their female roommate (Lulu) have their lives radically transformed when a gay Palestinian (Ashraf) enters the picture. Noam and Ashraf begin a sexual relationship and fall in love, but the two are doomed by political events outside their control. By their very titles, *Crash* and *The Bubble* suggest the fragility and volatility of contact between "others," and yet, despite their attempts to move past stereotypes, neither film is able to undo them. They are in many ways less authentic and sympathetic than they intend—trapped by the very discourse which they seek to change. Black men remain carjackers and crooked cops; whites are either outspoken or closeted racists; same for Israelis, with the added dimension of childish optimism; and Palestinians are terrorists and suicide bombers. The question is, could the stories of *Crash* and *The Bubble,* and others like them, be told successfully without their foundational premises about the "other?" This is the ultimate issue which readers should ponder as they read through the essays. What constitutes an "effective" representation of the "other?" Are there criteria which we can devise in assessing such effectiveness?

NOTES

1. Martin Buber, *I and Thou*, Walter Kaufmann, trans. (New York: Touchstone, 1970), 67.

2. David Román, *Performance in America: Contemporary U.S. Culture and the Performing Arts* (Durham, North Carolina: Duke University Press, 2005), 1, 2.

3. Lane Ryo Hirabayashi and Jun Xing, eds., *Reversing the Lens: Ethnicity, Race, Gender, and Sexuality Through Film* (Boulder, Colorado: University of Colorado Press, 2003), xi.

4. Isaac Deutscher, *The Non-Jewish Jew and Other Essays* (London: Oxford University Press, 1968), 25–27.

Section One

RACE AND ETHNICITY

Chapter One

"A Conscience for Hollywood? The 'Social Issue' Films of Twentieth Century Fox, 1947–1950"

Jonathan C. Friedman, West Chester University

In the initial years after World War II, Twentieth Century Fox released a series of social issue films which confronted anti-Semitism, racism, and mental illness, among other themes, and which stood out from the standard dramatic and comedic fare of the time. These films were *Gentleman's Agreement* (1947) (which dealt with anti-Semitism), *The Snake Pit* (1948) (set in a psychiatric asylum), *Pinky* (1949) (about a bi-racial woman who appears white), *Broken Arrow* (1950) (with Jimmy Stewart and a redemptive storyline about Native Americans), and *No Way Out* (1950) (with Sidney Poitier as a black physician who treats a racist patient). The questions begged by this flurry of postwar social activism on the part of Hollywood are obvious: What was the impetus behind the production of these films? What was the paradigm guiding their representations of the "other?" And to what extent did they have an impact on their target audience?

As to the first question, it is clear that bringing Hollywood into the promotion of the Allied effort during World War II left the culture of the motion picture industry transformed. Prior to the war, as historians such as Neal Gabler point out, the largely Jewish studio moguls had muted their criticism of the Third Reich in favor of magnifying their Americanness, out of fear of stoking popular anti-Semitism. This changed with the U.S. entry into the Second World War, and the government's enlisting of feature films as part of its overall propaganda effort. According to Richard Maltby, the press releases of the Motion Picture Association after the war "bristled with statements of high . . . intentions to consolidate [the] wartime image of social responsibility."[1]

Yet the motive to turn out social issues films was certainly just as material in rationale. Hollywood could turn a profit by capturing foreign markets and continuing to use film as propaganda for non-American audiences. Such was the not-so-subtle intention of MGM executive Louis B. Mayer:

> The screen, in common with newspapers and radio, fights the battle for freedom of speech . . . A motion picture should not only afford entertainment, but be of educational value. It can portray fairly and honestly the American way of life and can be a powerful influence in the lives of millions in other countries who are either denied access to our way of life, or who have never had the opportunity of experiencing it.[2]

The intentions of Twentieth Century Fox's Gentile executive, Darryl Zanuck, were similarly driven by the bottom-line, and Zanuck had been no more critical than his Jewish colleagues of the Nazi regime prior to 1941. Yet some historians, like Gabler and Gerard Molyneaux, contend that Zanuck's desire to make *Gentleman's Agreement* in particular resulted from his own brush with anti-Semitism.[3] (He was apparently prevented from reserving a room at a luxury hotel and at least initially from gaining membership in the exclusive Los Angeles Athletic Club—in both instances because he was mistakenly regarded as Jewish.) Still, he did not refuse his eventual induction into the Club, and Elia Kazan, who directed *Agreement* and had a troubled working relationship with Zanuck, contends that the latter had no strong feelings about anti-Semitism but was interested in whatever would make a good story:

> This kind of story solution was the essence of Darryl's theory of how social issues had to be handled for the American film audience, always through a love story in which the lovers are involved in the issue under conflict. Any less personal treatment, Zanuck believed, would not hold his audience's attention.[4]

Gentleman's Agreement was based on the Laura Z. Hobson novel which appeared as a serial in *Cosmopolitan* magazine. Hobson, the daughter of the editor of the *Jewish Daily Forward,* decided that instead of having a Jew expose anti-Semitism, she would have a Gentile writer pose as a Jew to experience anti-Jewish prejudice first-hand. Zanuck spent $75,000 for the rights to the book, and he brought in Broadway playwright Moss Hart to do the screenplay, Kazan to direct the picture, and Gregory Peck to play the lead.

The studio encountered legal difficulties with the project from the very beginning. One of the issues that Zanuck was forced to confront before filming began was his decision to keep in the script references to anti-Semites such as Gerald L.K. Smith and John Rankin. The inclusion of Mississippi congressman Rankin was the more problematic citation, given that it involved a prominent politician, but screenwriter Hart claimed that he had merely quoted a direct passage from an article in *Time:*

John Rankin, Mississippi Democrat, stood up in the House to denounce the soldier's vote bill . . .'the chief broadcast for it is Walter Winchell, the little kike I
was telling you about the other day.' This was a new low in demagoguery—even
for John Rankin—but in the entire House, no one rose to protest.[5]

George Wasson, Fox's legal advisor, felt that by referring to specific names,
the studio opened itself up to a variety of slander and libel suits. He recom-
mended that Fox obtain the consent of *Time* to reproduce the relevant seg-
ments and then deal with the issue of defamation if and when it arose:

> . . . With respect to Smith, Rankin, and Bilbo, I believe that their appeal is solely
> with the 'weak minded,' the 'unconscious' and the 'non-conscience' people . . .
> My personal feeling is that if we are afraid of lawsuits, we should not make this
> picture, inasmuch as it seems obvious that the primary purpose of the making of
> this picture is to impart a 'most vital message' to the people of this country if
> not to the people of the world.[6]

Zanuck concurred in a memo to Wasson:

> We are definitely going to use the names of living individuals. Walter Winchell
> might be the most problematic. Let the rest sue. They won't dare and if they do,
> nothing would make me more happy than to appear personally as a witness or a
> defendant at the trial.[7]

In the end, only two individuals sued Fox—Smith, whose suit was dismissed,
and a man who protested the inadvertent mentioning of a phone number that
happened to be his.[8]

Despite resolution on the legal front, the production faced opposition from
some Jewish groups, like the American Jewish Committee, whose members
believed that the film threatened to trivialize a grave issue. Zanuck also had
to weather competition from studios pursuing their own socially conscious
projects. Indeed, *Gentleman's Agreement* was one of two films made in 1947
giving representation to social anti-Semitism in the United States. The other
film was *Crossfire,* an RKO picture which dealt with the murder of a Jewish
man. (The novel actually involved the killing of a gay man). Zanuck tried to
get RKO to withhold the film until after *Gentleman's Agreement* was released
but to no avail. RKO head Dore Schary replied to Zanuck that the Fox mogul
had not discovered anti-Semitism and that it would take more than two pictures to eradicate it.[9] With great anticipation, and a certain degree of anxiety,
Gentleman's Agreement was released on 11 November 1947.

The film centers on journalist Phil Green (played by Peck), who goes un-
dercover for a magazine, *Smith Weekly,* to expose anti-Semitism in everyday
American life. The brainchild of the project is the daughter of the magazine's

publisher, a young woman with liberal political leanings named Kathy, played by Dorothy McGuire. Deciding to pose as a Jew, Phil encounters firsthand subtle manifestations of prejudice: His mother's physician disparages Jewish doctors; a neighbor tries to erase Phil's assumed name of Greenberg from the mailbox; a restricted hotel refuses to admit him; his son Tommy is beaten up by his friends, who call him "dirty Jew;" and his Jewish friend, Dave Golden, an army officer played by John Garfield, is harassed by anti-Semitic thugs. Kathy, who is Phil's fiancée as well, evinces anti-Semitic tendencies too by refusing to sell Dave a home in her home town of Darien because of a restrictive housing covenant—a "gentleman's agreement." She also comforts Tommy after his altercation by saying, "You're not a Jew any more than I am," and, in an initial shoot, she worries that Phil might actually be Jewish. This latter query was a point of concern for Zanuck, who thought that if Kathy were played as an anti-Semite, Phil would clearly end his relationship with her:

> As now played, there is no question that Kathy is not only frightened over Phil's being Jewish—she is horrified. And she betrays herself so completely that it is difficult to know why Phil comes back to her and forgives her . . . Kathy is *not* anti-Semitic. Not a bit of it. But she makes the mistake that 99 percent of the people make by conforming to the custom and unconsciously observing the gentleman's agreement . . .[10]

At film's end, all is resolved happily (in stock Hollywood tradition); Phil gets the story; Dave convinces Kathy of her shortsightedness and is able to purchase the house in Darien; and Phil and Kathy find true love. It was this approach which brought success to the film at the box office, and *Gentleman's Agreement* went on to receive the Academy Award for Best Picture in 1948. Not all critics were pleased, however; John Mason Brown of the *Saturday Review* attacked the premise that people should be good to Jews because one never knows when they may turn out to be Gentiles, and the *New Yorker* was even more biting in its review:

> It seems to be Mrs. Hobson's conviction—and vicariously Hart's—that anti-Semitism can be defeated by renting Jews houses in 'restricted' areas and by not listening to dull jokes. The problem, I'm afraid is quite a bit bigger than Mrs. Hobson and Mr. Hart make it out to be. The setting which they have placed their charade is so extravagantly frivolous that any reference to a subject more serious than a peplum seems dragged in and even embarrassing . . . Maybe Hollywood ought to lay off until the boys can put a little meat on the bones of the idea.[11]

Even Kazan, who won the Academy Award for Best Director, came to characterize the picture as a series of clichés. In one of his harsher moments, he called the film "just a pleasant fucking picture:"

> It doesn't have what would have made it lasting in its effect: The intimate experience of someone who had been through the bitter and humiliating experience [of anti-Semitism . . .][12]

Perhaps Edwin Schallert of the *Los Angeles Times* said it best when he wrote that Nazi occupied Europe could furnish far more bitter, far more horrible examples of what real persecution meant.[13]

In December 1947, Gregory Peck declared that the movie industry was actually "leading public opinion" with the release of the film.[14] However, the effect of *Agreement* on audiences was as questionable as the value of its content. Sociologist Russell Middleton, writing for the *American Sociological Review* in 1960, and psychologist Irwin Rosen, writing for the *Journal of Psychology* in 1948, queried target audiences after a screening of the film to assess its overall impact. Middleton concluded that the proportion of subjects in the experimental group who showed a reduction in anti-Semitic sentiment after exposure to the film was significantly greater than those in the control group (that is to say, those who had not seen the film). He cautioned that the influence of the film may not have had a lasting effect and that it might have simply exerted pressure at surface conformity.[15] Rosen qualified his results in a similar fashion. Although his experimental group showed a significantly more favorable attitude toward Jews one day after seeing the picture, the change in attitude was slightly less dramatic two days later, suggesting a drop-off over time.[16] The problem with the film, as both Middleton and Rosen saw it, was precisely its inability to ensure that any changes in non-Jewish cognitive and behavior patterns would be permanent. And public opinion polls into the late 1940s showed that Americans continued to regard Jews as the chief menace in society, followed by African-Americans, Japanese, and Germans respectively.[17]

There is also the myth that *Agreement* somehow paved the way for the May 1948 Supreme Court ruling in *Shelley v. Kraemer* banning restrictive housing covenants.[18] In fact, the case had nothing to do with anti-Semitism: The Shelleys, the couple who had suffered discrimination, were black. Moreover, the court had agreed in June 1947, months before *Agreement's* release, to hear the case as part of its October term.[19] Jews did indeed benefit from the ruling, as did other ethnic and religious minorities, and yet the attempt to alter the American social landscape was brought about not by film or popular opinion, but by a Supreme Court that was amenable to such change.

One cannot overlook the added irony of *Agreement's* appearance two weeks before the blacklist of Hollywood directors and scriptwriters by leading Hollywood executives as part of the anti-Communist efforts of the House Un-American Activities Committee (or HUAC). On 25 November 1947, studio executives issued the now infamous Waldorf Statement following a meeting in the Waldorf Astoria, in which they agreed to fire ten Hollywood screenwriters, producers, and directors, who were accused of Communist sympathies and who stood charged with contempt of Congress because they refused to participate in the committee's inquest. Philip Dunne, a writer at 20th Century Fox, initially contemplated a vigorous anti-HUAC campaign, but quieted down after Zanuck told him not to "do anything foolish."[20] *Agreement* co-star John Garfield was blacklisted because he had been a member of the leftwing Group Theater in New York. Despite testifying before the HUAC to clear his name, he could not escape the label of subversive, and he ended up drinking himself to death.[21] This concurrent development will forever taint the legacy of Zanuck's social enterprise.

Zanuck followed up *Agreement* with the film *The Snake Pit,* one of the first American films to depict in a constructive way the state of treatment for people with mental illness. Based on a fictionalized autobiography by Mary Jane Ward, *The Snake Pit* involved the story of a woman (played by Olivia de Haviland) who is confined to a psychiatric hospital. Producer-director Anatol Litvak saw the galley pages to the book, paid $75,000 for the film rights, and eventually approached Zanuck to finance the production. Although leery about the subject matter, Zanuck green-lighted the project as an extension of his human interest stories, so long as it did not present itself as an indictment of the American psychiatric profession.[22] Released in November 1948, the film was lauded by film critics as "unflinching" and de Haviland's performance as "superb."[23] Even the usually skeptical Bosley Crowther of the *New York Times* called the film "fascinating and deeply moving."[24]

The main theme of the picture is expressed in its title. De Haviland proceeds through her treatment as though down an ever-spiraling nightmare. She recovers with the help of a physician (played by Leo Genn) who becomes obsessed with her case. The film went on to take in $4.1 million at the box office (Fox's third successful film of 1948), and de Haviland secured an Academy Award nomination for Best Actress. In the film's wake, twenty-six states passed legislation pertaining to procedures in state run mental institutions, although this may have been pure coincidence. Even before the end of World War II, many state hospitals began eliminating the more odious methods of psychotherapy. The number of patients in seclusion per hospital, for instance, was reduced from an average of twenty-nine in September 1946 to ten in January 1949.[25] It would be more accurate to suggest that far from changing the landscape of psychiatry, *The Snake Pit* gave a clearer impetus to a film about race which Zanuck had put on the back-burner. This was the film, *Pinky.*

Based on the novel *Quality,* developed by Cid Ricketts Sumner from a story she published in *Ladies Home Journal, Pinky* is about a bi-racial nurse who passes for white and who encounters racial prejudice because of her mixed white and African-American heritage. Similar to *Gentleman's Agreement, Pinky* features a white actress giving voice to a bi-racial character—adding two levels of distance to a more immediate other—the African-American, in order to maximize (perhaps only inadvertently) the palatability of the subject to a white American audience. Zanuck initially drafted the legendary John Ford to direct *Pinky,* but he quit during the first week of shooting, and Kazan was pressed into replacing him. Jeanne Crain was cast in the lead role of Pinky, and Ethel Waters played her black grandmother. In the novel and initial draft of the script, Pinky moves north to train as a nurse, and she falls in love with a young, white doctor. Terrified of telling him that her great-grandmother was black, Pinky flees to the south. There, she nurses a cantankerous white female aristocrat (Ethel Barrymore) who wills Pinky her plantation house, which Pinky considers turning into a clinic. In the meantime, Pinky's lover follows her south, but upon hearing her secret, he leaves in disgust. Zanuck was dissatisfied with the initial version of the script from Dudley Nichols:

> . . . I went ahead with *Gentleman's Agreement* because I firmly believed that in spite of the controversial subject matter it was a great *movie story . . .* The reason I have vacillated so much about *Pinky* is because in my heart I am certain that at this point it is not a good enough movie . . . This is not a story about how to solve the Negro problem in the South or anywhere else. This is not a story particularly about race problems, segregation, or discrimination. This is a story about one particular Negro girl, who could easily pass as a white and who did pass for a white. This is the story of how and why she, as an individual, finally decided to be herself . . . [26]

Zanuck brought in Philip Dunne to figure out a workable ending. Dunne suggested that Pinky's lover should not run away and that he should still profess his love for her but only on the condition that she would agree to pass for white. Then, according to Dunne, her dilemma would have both personal and political resonance: Should she deny her heritage or proudly acknowledge it, open her clinic, and devote her life to providing care for poor whites and blacks? Making her decision to stay, Pinky dismisses her love with the line: "You can't live without pride." Zanuck had Dunne complete the final script for the film, which used Nichols' title, *Pinky.* Zanuck sent Dunne's version to Nichols, who responded with a detailed critique, complaining that he could not conceive of a white man ever agreeing to marry a girl with "even a drop of African blood in her veins." Zanuck read the letter to Dunne, who was shocked by the hypocrisy of Nichols, an outspoken liberal. Zanuck merely shook his head, dropped the letter on his desk, and said, "I never could understand the liberal mentality."[27]

For his part, Kazan made every effort to create a film that was different from *Gentleman's Agreement,* altering mood and heightening psychological tension, but he had reservations about *Pinky's* content:

> I don't think anybody took the damn film too seriously. It was a pastiche. Taking a subject which has got dynamite in it and castrating it. At that time, that sort of liberalism paid off . . .[28]

Bosley Crowther of the *New York Times* also found much of the film disagreeable:

> With all its virtues . . . This scan of a social problem has certain faults and omissions which may be resented and condemned. Its observations of Negroes as well as whites is largely limited to types that are nowadays far from average. The 'old mammy' sentiment is extolled. And a passion for paternalism is very obvious at the picture's core. No genuinely constructive thinking of relations between blacks and whites is offered. A vivid exposure of certain cruelties and injustices is all it gives . . .[29]

Robert Hatch of the *New Republic* was even harsher; he called the film a "fraud" and a "mass market romance given a shot of social responsibility."[30] Despite the criticism, *Pinky* took in $4.2 million at the box office, following its debut on 29 September 1949, and was Fox's number one film for that year. Waters and Barrymore also won Academy Award nominations for Best Supporting Actress. Given that Hollywood at the time still operated under the infamous Production Code, which expressly prohibited depictions of interracial dating, and given the illegality of sexual relations between whites and "nonwhites" in a number of U.S. states, one could argue that *Pinky* was a bold step in chipping away at both censorship and social discrimination. Yet the film remains problematic, both for its content and its context.

In January 1952, and again in April, Kazan testified before HUAC that he had joined the Communist Party in the summer 1934 to protest Hitler and that he had been assigned to a unit whose members belonged to the Group Theater Acting Company. Kazan admitted that his primary responsibility was to turn the GTA into a Communist front organization. Weary of the party's police state tactics, he resigned his membership in 1936. Although he refused to implicate his former colleagues during his January 1952 testimony, he relented in April:

> . . . I have come to the conclusion that I did wrong to withhold these names before, because every secrecy serves the Communists . . . The American people need the facts and all the facts about all aspects of Communism in order to deal with it wisely and effectively . . .[31]

In his memoirs, Kazan claims that the decision to name names was a painful but necessary one:

> Darryl urged me to 'name names for chrissake. Who the hell are you going to jail for? You'll be sitting there and someone else will sure as hell name those people. Who are you saving?[32]

The last two films in the short-lived social conscience period at Fox were Delmer Daves' *Broken Arrow,* released in July 1950 and Joseph Mankiewicz's *No Way Out,* released one month later. The former, starring Jimmy Stewart, involves a white man's attempt to make peace with Apache chief, Cochise. The latter features, Sidney Poitier in his screen debut as a medical intern who is hunted by a bigoted gangster, played by Richard Widmark, after his brother dies on Poitier's watch.

Based on Elliott Arnold's 1947 novel, *Blood Brother, Broken Arrow* is a fictionalized account of war and peace between the Chiricahua Apaches and Arizona settlers in the 1870s. Apache chief Cochise, played by Jeff Chandler, is portrayed as an able strategist and wise statesman. However, many of Cochise's allies, particularly those who disagree with his peace-making efforts, continue to be portrayed as "savages." This troubling aspect of the film is compounded by the use of white actors in the roles of Cochise (Chandler was Jewish) and Stewart's love interest Sonseeahray (played by Debra Paget) and Native Americans (such as Jay Silverheels of Tonto fame) in roles as Cochise's followers who break ranks. At the same time, Stewart's character, Tom Jeffords, a frontiersman tired of fighting, is also painted as noble, but most of his white comrades in arms are not, and in the end, Sonseeahray is killed and Stewart is wounded by whites who oppose the peace process. The pattern of unease with interracial marriage (as in *Pinky,* and to a lesser extent *Gentleman's Agreement*) did not go unnoticed. Bosley Crowther pointed this out in his rejection of the picture, which he claimed offered Native Americans mere patronage rather than justice.[33] For all the criticism, *Broken Arrow* was the second most profitable film of 1950, taking in approximately $3.5 million.

No Way Out, by contrast, made the least amount of money of the afore-mentioned films at the time, for reasons about which we can only speculate. Was it because of its genre (a crime drama as opposed to a love story), or be-cause, of the five films, it was the only one to feature a minority in the lead-ing role, or because, again of the five, it was the only film to address more directly a social problem at hand? Director Mankiewicz is alleged to have welcomed the challenge to upstage Kazan and produce a film with a harder edge than either *Pinky* or *Gentleman's Agreement.* In *No Way Out,* Poitier plays Dr. Luther Books, an intern whose first case is to treat two brothers who have been shot while trying to hold up a filling station. Brooks discov-ers that one of the brothers is actually dying from a brain tumor, and when he dies, the other brother, an outspoken racist by the name of Ray Biddle, played by Richard Widmark, channels his rage into a revenge scheme against Brooks which culminates in an attack against the intern. In the film's ironic conclusion, Brooks helps Biddle to recover from his wounds suffered during their melee, despite himself being wounded by his racist pursuer. Tending to his adversary's injury, Brooks admonishes "Don't cry white boy, you're gonna live."

Mankiewicz has said that the film was the first honest depiction of racial violence on the silver screen, and whether or not this was in fact the case, *No Way Out* features a race riot and enough racial epithets to boil the blood of even the most contemporary observer.[34] In the wake of racial violence in Chicago, censors from the city demanded that Fox delete scenes showing African-Americans with clubs and whites with chains and broken bottles. Mankiewicz called the censors' request "absurd" and justified the film's bleak portrayal by arguing that Hollywood had no right to put a positive spin on the problem of race. The censors had their way, however, and *No Way Out,* found itself only in limited release. It made a paltry $1.3 million, barely breaking even, and was only the seventeenth most popular film for Fox in 1950. This was despite the film's centrist credo. Poitier's character was more than just reasonable, but, in the words of historian Donald Bogle, "the perfect dream for white liberals to have [over] for lunch or dinner."[35] Bogle argues in fact that Poitier's characters were consistently "mild-mannered toms, throwbacks to the humanized Christian servants of the 1930s. When insulted or badgered, the Poitier character stood by and took it . . ."[36] Yet the problem with Poitier's characters may stem less from their universalizing or mainstreaming ap-proach than from their creation in a medium constrained and dominated by the broader white culture of the time.

The tension between accessibility and authenticity is one of the key issues impacting the efficacy of media representations of the other, and it is perhaps the central issue shaping an evaluation of Fox's social issue films. If we look at sheer numbers, four of the five films qualified as a success for the studio, meaning that their intended and hidden messages at the very least reached a broad audience. It is unclear, though, what kind of impact they had in truly altering perceptions of and policy towards racial and ethnic minorities and other outcasts in American society. Most of the films resonated with critics as well, although here too, their reception was not universally positive, and many critics had similar problems with authenticity and message. The question is, is filtering the experience of the other through an in-group in a forum as popular as the large scale studio feature necessarily better or worse than a low-budget, independent film about an out-group by an out-group? I would argue that impacting as wide an audience as possible is desirable but that the content of the images is key. For in-group depictions of out-groups to be effective as education and as artwork, verisimilitude is crucial, whether the thrust is universalizing (we are all alike) or minoritizing (we are different, and that is inherently good).

The problems with Fox's social issue films were threefold. One, there was the obvious hypocrisy of calling for a more tolerant society at a time when Hollywood and government were engaging in a cultural purge of the liberal-left; and two, the mainstreaming message of the films was so calculatedly oblique. In three of the films (*Gentleman's Agreement, The Snake Pit,* and *Broken Arrow*), representations of the out-group are secondary or dependent upon redemption by an in-group hero. In the case of *Pinky,* structuring a story about racial identity around the issue of "passing" enabled the dominant representation once again to be outwardly white, and the identity crisis about blackness shaped through the filter of whiteness. The third problem was the lack of institutional follow-up and the quickness with which Zanuck abandoned the entire venture.

After *No Way Out,* the period of social activism on the part of Twentieth Century Fox came to an end. Diminishing cinema attendance due to the emergence of television forced studio executives to create new ways of sustaining an audience. In the case of Fox, this came in the form of light-hearted comedies (1955's *The Seven Year Itch*) and bible spectacles (1953's *The Robe*). Such films not only enabled cinema to compete with TV, but were also more reflective of the prevailing cultural conservatism of the time, providing an uncritical escape valve for American audiences in the context of the Cold War. While the social issue films and their chief advocate, Darryl Zanuck, were comparatively "progressive," neither were as visionary or seminal as their admirers believed. The films represent at best a transitional phase in the destabilization of the Production Code, paving the way for bolder representations of the "other." At worst, the period of social conscience at Fox was a conflicted, almost hypocritical experiment that had limited effects on both film and American society as a whole.

NOTES

1. Richard Maltby, "The Politics of the Maladjusted Text: Analysis of the *film noir*," *Journal of American Studies*, vol. 18, no. 1 (1984): 64.

2. *Motion Picture Herald*, 12 July 1947, 27, as cited in Maltby, "The Politics of the Maladjusted Text," 64.

3. See Neal Gabler, *An Empire of Their Own: How the Jews Invented Hollywood* (New York: Anchor Books, 1988), 349, and Gerard Molyneaux, *Gregory Peck: A Bio-Bibliography* (Westport, Connecticut: Greenwood Publishing, 1995), 87

4. Elia Kazan, *Elia Kazan: A Life* (New York: Da Capo Press, 1988), 332, 333.

5. *Time*, 14 February 1948, 17, 18.

6. George Wasson to Darryl Zanuck, 7 May 1948, Box FX-LR-184, Folder 6706, Twentieth Century Fox Film Corporation Collection, Records of the Legal Department, UCLA Theatre Arts Library.

7. Zanuck to Wasson, 8 May 1947, Box FX-LR-184, Folder 6706, Fox Collection, UCLA Theatre Arts Library.

8. "Court Denies Smith's Plea for Film Ban," *Tulsa Daily World*, 14 April 1948.

9. Schary as cited in Gabler, *An Empire of Their Own*, 349.

10. Darryl Zanuck to Elia Kazan, 18 June 1947, in Rudy Behlmer, *Memo from Darryl Zanuck* (New York: Grove Press, 1995), 133, 134.

11. "Just a Slap on the Wrist," *The New Yorker*, 15 November 1947, 117.

12. Kazan, *Elia Kazan*, 333.

13. Edwin Schallert, "Award Challenging Feature Makes Debut," *Los Angeles Times*, 26 December 1947, 6.

14. Philip Scheuer, "Peck Defers to Men Who Make Pictures," *Los Angeles Times*, 14 December 1947, III: I.

15. Russell Middleton, "Ethnic Prejudice and Susceptibility to Persuasion," *American Sociological Review* (October 1960): 686. Middleton used Theodor Adorno's ten item list of anti-Semitism, developed in *The Authoritarian Personality*, as part of his questionnaire, positing the following scenarios and asking for agreement or disagreement.

1. Anyone who employs many people should be careful not to hire a large percentage of Jews.

2. One trouble with Jewish businessmen is that they stick together and connive so that a Gentile doesn't have a fair chance in competition.

3. The Jewish districts in most cities are the results of the clannishness and stick-togetherness of Jews.

4. Persecution of Jews would be largely eliminated if the Jews would make really sincere efforts to rid themselves of their harmful and offensive faults.

5. Jewish leaders should encourage Jews to be more inconspicuous, to keep out of professions and activities already overcrowded with Jews and to keep out of the public notice.

6. I can hardly imagine myself marrying a Jew.

7. The trouble with letting Jews into a nice neighborhood is that they gradually give it a typical Jewish atmosphere.

8. No matter how Americanized a Jew may seem to be, there is always something different and strange, something basically Jewish underneath.

9. There may be a few exceptions, but, in general, Jews are pretty much alike.

10. There are too many Jews in the various federal agencies and bureaus in Washington, and the have too much control over our national policies.

16. Irwin Rosen, "The Effects of 'Gentleman's Agreement' on Attitudes Towards Jews," *Journal of Psychology* 26 (October 1948): 532-536.

17. See the polls in Charles Herbert Stember, *Jews in the Mind of America* (New York: Basic Books, 1966), 128, 129.

18. See Leonard Dinnerstein, *Antisemitism in America* (New York: Oxford University Press, 1994), 93.

19. *Shelley v. Kraemer* involved a grievance against the decision of the Supreme Court of Missouri overturning a lower court's ban on restrictive housing covenants. In a six to zero ruling on 3 May 1948, the Supreme Court rules that such restrictions violated the equal protection clause of the 14th Amendment. Conceding that the amendment was aimed at state action only and not private conduct, however discriminatory, Chief Justice Fred Vinson contended that judicial action for the enforcement of private agreements was in fact state action and therefore within the amendment's field of operation. Transcript of Record, Supreme Court of the United States, October 1947, No. 72, J.D. Shelley at al vs. Louis Kraemer et al, Certiorari Granted 23 June 1947, Microfilm Reading Room, Georgetown University Law Library.

20. Philip Dunne, *Take Two: A Life in Movies and Politics* (New York: McGraw Hill, 1980), 212.

21. Gabler, *An Empire of Their Own,* 384, 475.

22. *The Motion Picture Guide* (Chicago: Cinebooks, 1986), 2989, 2990.

23. *Life,* 29 November 1948, 71, and *New Republic,* 8 November 1948, 28, 29.

24. *Motion Picture Daily,* 14 November 1948, 8.

25. Don Martindale, et al, *Mental Disability in America Since World War II* (New York: Philosophical Library Inc., 1985), 90, 141, 142.

26. Darryl Zanuck to Dudley Nichols, 1 November 1948, in Behlmer, *Memo from Darryl Zanuck,* 162.

27. Philip Dunne, *Take Two,* 61, 62.

28. Michael Ciment, *Kazan on Kazan* (New York: Viking Adult, 1974), 60.

29. *New York Times,* 30 September 1949, 28.

30. Hatch, "The Failure to Cope," *The New Republic,* 3 October 1949, 23.

31. Among the names given by Kazan were: Lewis Leverett, co-leader of the unit, J. Edward Bromberg, another co-leader (who was already deceased), Phoebe Brand, Morris Carnovsky, Tony Kraber, Paula Miller, Clifford Odets, and Art Smith. "Communist Infiltration of the Motion Picture Industry, Part Seven: 10 April 1952," in *Hearings Before the Committee on Un-American Activities of the House of Representatives,* 82nd Congress, 2nd Session, 24, 28 January, 5 February, 20 March, and 10, 30 April 1952 (Washington: Government Printing Office, 1952), 2407, 2408, 2409, 2411.

32. Kazan, *Elia Kazan,* 455.

33. *The New York Times,* 21 July 1950, 15, Ralph Friar, et al, *The Only Good Indian . . . The Hollywood Gospel* (New York: Drama Book Specialists, 1972), 202, and Michael Walker, "The Westerns of Delmer Daves," in *The Book of Westerns,* ed. Ian Cameron (New York: Continuum, 1996), 124.

34. Mankiewicz as cited by Kenneth Geist, *Pictures Will Talk: The Life and Films of Joseph L. Mankiewicz* (New York: Da Capo Press, 1983), 156.

35. Bogle, *Toms, Ccoons, Mulattos, Mammies, and Bucks: An Interpretive History of Blacks in American Films* (New York: Continuum, 1989), 176.

36. Bogle, *Toms,* 176.

Chapter Two

"Grounding Race: *Powder* and the Shifting Terrain of Whiteness"

Dalton Anthony Jones, Yale University

> Yet for all these accumulated associations (of Whiteness,) with whatever is sweet, and honorable, and sublime, there yet lurks an elusive something in the innermost *idea* of this hue, which strikes more of panic to the soul than that redness which affrights in blood.
>
> Herman Melville, *Moby Dick*

"The baby?"

"The baby, I'm concerned, might have some abnormalities. Outwardly we can already tell that the child has no pigmentation. It's called albinism. It's strictly genetic."

"That's pale skin right?"

So begins Disney's 1995 film *Powder*. Its main character, Jeremy, whose nickname is also the title of the movie, is an albino male who emerges within a practically all White Texas town. On its own terms, this is a potentially innocuous scenario. As the movie unfolds, however, we find that in addition to his whiter than white skin, Jeremy also possesses literally Christ-like virtues and superhuman abilities. He is able to read the inner thoughts of other characters and uses telekinesis to move and bend metal objects with his mind. He has memorized every book that he's ever read and his IQ scores are said to be so far "off the charts," that "there isn't even a classification" for him. In fact, scientific experts describe Jeremy as being the "most advanced intellect in the history of humankind." With these powers he brings courage and ethical insight into an otherwise ignorantly brutal world and exudes a Zen-like, prophetic wisdom that is calm, centered and detached. To put it simply, *Powder* is a movie that envisions the loss of melanin as being the evolutionary height of humanity's moral and intellectual development. As such, the film becomes more than a simple exercise in commercial entertainment; it provides a unique portrait of how contemporary racial assumptions, and their accompanying notions of cultural identity, have so deeply embedded themselves within our nation's collective conscious that they often appear to be natural. *Powder* is an ideal vehicle through which we can analyze how historical constructs of racial identity have been culturally internalized and can be seen to express themselves within our public imagination. Furthermore, the movie belongs to a growing canon of films whose tendency is to dramatize the social alienation of supremely "gifted" working class White males.

This paper establishes the context of *Powder* by beginning with a brief historical overview of racial representations as they have functioned within the entertainment industry of the United States and then proceeds to offer an explication of how these representations are specifically continued and reflected within the movie itself. Throughout, I will stress the dialogical relationship, the interdependence, between our constructions of Black and White ideas of individual and social identity. The final section, therefore, addresses both the transformative potentials as well as the regressive dangers inherent to this dialogical relationship, or negotiation, as it takes place between Black and White voicings of their personal subjectivities.

One of the things that is most fascinating about *Powder* is that, despite the film's overtly White supremacist assumptions, its racial semiotics have gone almost completely un-critiqued within the public discourse. Hardly any reviewers of the film, for example, were able or willing, to place the narrative of *Powder* within a racial context, and when they were able to do so, they saw it not as an exaltation of a White ideal but as "a statement about tolerance against such societal ills as racism and homophobia." Ironically, their focus, almost exclusively, was on the emotional trauma of Jeremy's persecution by, and alienation from, a culture that was stubbornly intolerant and unaccepting of social difference. In addition, it is highly doubtful that anyone involved in the making of *Powder* or the millions of North American and European moviegoers who poured into theaters to witness the spectacle (and who continue to rent the film in substantial numbers), should be considered "racist" in the classical sense of the word simply because they failed to understand or analyze the movie's racial assumptions. Very few of them, I'm sure, would be willing to defend the biologically essentialist notions for locating racial difference which are the premise upon which the tale of *Powder* unfolds. It is therefore, by necessity, one of the functions of this paper to use *Powder* as a means to examine some of the ways in which Euro-centrically based notions of White supremacy have become legitimized within our nation's public discourse.

However, it is not my intention here to simply reiterate the claim, which has been made before, that Hollywood and the media system in the United States serve as mouthpieces for racist and stereotypical ideas of both Black and White constructs of subjectivity. Such a critique, in my opinion, would run the danger of being far too simplistic and one-dimensional. The media, like our perceptions of it, do not derive from a single source or origin. It would be a gross mistake for us to view the "media" as a monolithic structure which has the unified power to present visions of destructive racial imagery that are designed exclusively to oppress people of color and other minority groups. In fact the structure of institutions, as well as the structure of the ideologies which compose them, are much more complex than that. As Stuart Hall states in his essay, "The Whites of Their Eyes: Racist Ideologies and the Media," by "Simply reducing them (various media sources) to what we think of as their essential nature—pure instruments of ruling-class racist ideology—we will not be able to deconstruct the credibility and legitimacy which they, in fact, carry."[1] It is precisely this "credibility and legitimacy" which is perhaps most fascinating about the movie *Powder*, that is, just how easily its racial semiotics were (and are) able to go unquestioned and unexamined.

If our intention is to understand and critique the function of culturally defined categories such as race or personal identity then it becomes imperative that we find ways to locate and thoroughly scrutinize the focal points, or "points of origin," from which the manifestations of these ideological conceptions are derived. By "origin," I am not suggesting a "first cause," or primary essence in the genealogical meaning of the word. Instead, I intend only that we can find a temporally located space that exists in relation to, in juxtaposition to, our ideas of both a subjective and inter-subjective positionality. Reconstructing such positions allows us to highlight specific occurrences as they manifest themselves within culture and which serve as, or make evident, functional centers around which revolve key ideas concerning who we are and how we relate to others. In other words, it is imperative that we find where the semiology of racial objectification and consumption is located, defined, and promoted. Again, the movie *Powder* functions as a prime example of such a site. Finally, while *Powder* alludes to a multiplicity of divergent cultures and imagines itself to be committed to difference, it is instead firmly, and exclusively, rooted in an idealized vision of White identity. It presents us with a legitimized "new" racialism in which the illusion of difference is being produced within a White homogeneity. From the perspective of people of color, at least, this non-plural plurality is highly problematic.

To understand how this cultural "blind spot" (in terms of our ability to decipher the semiotics of racial representation) is able to exist, it is necessary for us to take a look for a moment at the film's historical precedents.

BLACKFACE AND IMPERIALISTIC COMMODITIZATION

Powder's use of whiteface as a vehicle for the expression of a racialized White identity is directly linked to the history of identification masking that was begun in 1605 when Queen Anne of England became "the first European in recorded history to black her face." This historical detail, among others, leads Michael Rogin to conclude that "Blackface is a product of European imperialism, the material and psychological investment in the peoples being incorporated into the capitalist world system of the sixteenth and seventeenth centuries."[2] While seemingly obvious, it is important to note that Rogin has used the capitalistic terms "product" and "investment" to characterize the relationship between the White dominated culture of imperialism and the people of color that it has colonized. The representation of Blackness is seen to be a product of, a "direct result of," or a "consequence of," an imperialistic investment. As such, it becomes an action which is taken in order to accrue a "financial return or benefit." It is not a neutral act of altruism or curiosity—a process of "free" exchange or sharing. In fact, the term investment is also defined as being a "state of military siege." Under contemporary political conditions, commercial representations of Blackness and Whiteness are therefore fundamentally linked to the psychological processes engendered by larger over-reaching imperialistic realities. Considering the role of the Disney Corporation in producing and distributing *Powder*—as well as the films *Phenomenon* and *Good Will Hunting*—and in light of the continuing atmosphere of a globalized commercial imperialism, the movie's racial representations must be understood and critiqued on these terms.

Our contemporary ideas of racial identity, then, are inherited from the process of racial abstraction that was begun as a psychological justification for imperialistic violence. The idea of Blackness, however, which was abstracted from the Black body and reflected within the European and European-American psyche necessitated the creation of a corresponding idea of Whiteness, and, like the idea of Blackness, the idea of Whiteness has been removed from the constraints of the lighter skinned European body. We can see this physical/meta-physical dichotomy reflected within *Powder*. Jeremy's super intelligence, physical powers and hypersensitivity are all a representation of an exalted imperialistic ideal of Whiteness. His physical Whiteness, like the concept of Whiteness, exists above and beyond the "White" body as such. But while it is an idea of an existential ideal of purity and difference, it is also an idea of difference that has become uniquely functional. It is precisely this idea/ideal of difference that has facilitated the commercial consumption of racial "Otherness" as both the idea of the body's essence and the body itself, are conceptually merged within the vehicle of ideology.

There is nothing in the history of blackface, from the eighteenth through twentieth centuries, which would indicate that the use of racial masking as a form of imperialistic investment has been altered since the time of Queen Anne. Some two hundred and twenty years after her performance, it was another English national, Charles Matthews, who would help give rise to the mass commercialization of the American vaudeville and minstrel traditions by staging, in blackface, his meticulously detailed observations of the dialects, songs, and mannerisms of African American slave culture.[3] Ninety-five years after Charles Matthews, Hollywood was officially born as D.W. Griffith, using blackface, depicted the birth of a reconstructed and reconciled national White identity in *The Birth of a Nation*.[4] And again, thirteen years after Griffith's vision of a new nation, the advent of sound solidified the role of film as a vehicle for disseminating popular culture, and with it national identity, when a black-faced Al Jolson sang, with teary eyes and on bending knee, "Mammy."

Due to the emerging political empowerment of African Americans, the use of blackface as a form of racial representation was eliminated shortly after the Warner Brothers' 1928 release of *The Jazz Singer*. The right of the Black body to portray itself in the presentation of its own voice (even if the means for producing such representations remained beyond its control) created a corresponding new set of standards by which Whiteness was forced to define and express itself. An example of these new standards can be witnessed in the historical rise of Walt Disney to national prominence. The Disney empire, or "magical kingdom," can be directly connected to the demise of the overtly stereotypical and derogatory depictions of Blackness which, in turn, threatened the political and ideological sovereignty of the colonial White empire. Disney was able to capitalize on the growth of Black empowerment by creating a whole new category of "Otherness" in the form of animated talking animals. Mickey Mouse, who not coincidentally debuted in 1928, the same year as "The Jazz Singer," was directly inspired by the figure of Al Jolson. Wearing white gloves, Mickey was depicted in such films as *The Jazz fool* (1929), *The Karnival kid* (1929) and *Blue Rhythm* (1931). Similarly, Disney films such as *Snow White*, ('Mirror, mirror on the wall, who's the fairest of them all?') *Sleeping Beauty*, and more recently, *Pocohantas*, must all be seen as belonging to an historical effort to preserve the mythology of the White idea/ideal. This is the legacy to which *Powder* belongs. The whiteface of *Powder*, while representing an extension of this tradition of blackface, is also an example of some of the creative ways in which what is understood to be "White" culture has responded to the effort to eliminate its control over the contextual presentation of the Black voice.

THE WHITE IDEA/IDEAL

In 1851, the year that Herman Melville's *Moby Dick* was completed, Europeans were in the midst of a frenzied colonial expansion that had them spreading essentially unchallenged around the globe. In his novel, Melville describes the idea of Whiteness as calling up a "peculiar apparition to the soul."[5] It is, significantly, a copy of this book which Jeremy will first use to illustrate the remarkable powers of his mind. The whiteness of Jeremy, like the whiteness of the whale, functions as the very embodiment of this "peculiar apparition." Just as the whale moves within the spiritual depths of the ocean, beyond the reach of mortal men, the figure of Jeremy similarly floats throughout *Powder* in an elusive and ghostly manner. Both the whale and Jeremy live on the boundary between the physical and the meta-physical and signify the corporeal presence of the frightening power and strength of the White idea/ideal. But even at the historical mid-point of imperialistic domination in which Melville wrote, we find that the self-conscious awareness of the vulnerability of the White ideal was beginning to "strike panic" within, and haunt, the White soul.[6] As an ideological tool of imperialism the function of constructing an idea/ideal of the White soul is that it serves to simultaneously maintain and justify the physical presence of the White body's material domination over both the idea and the body of the subordinate racialized "Other." But as we see in *Moby Dick*, it is Ahab, the Semitic presence of Blackness that has been physically and spiritually violated by the idea/ideal of white consciousness, who turns to hunt the elusive figure of the white whale with a single-minded and "maniacal" sense of purpose. The very presence of Ahab is, therefore, the Achilles heel of the White construct. If the ship of state (here symbolized by the Pequod) is manned by an "Ahab," the fear is that he will risk the very safety, indeed the very existence, of the ship in his pursuit of White consciousness. The fate of the White power structure therefore equals the fate of the idea/ideal of White consciousness and the two are, in fact, seen as being fundamentally intertwined. It is already clear by 1851, then, that the threat to the White ideal, which becomes synonymous with the threat to White colonial power, will come as a result of being directly challenged and confronted by the presence of the derogated "Other." As long as this challenge does not take place, Whiteness will be able to avoid confronting its own racial and social construction. It is precisely this presence of Ahab that the pluralistic homogenization of the new racialist vision of *Powder* has eliminated.

In his article, "The Souls of White Folk," Walter Benn Michaels appropriately indicates the period of reconstruction as a time in which the semiotics of White racial identity were raised to new levels. It is also, significantly, the period in which the United States was first politically forced to grapple with the newly unsubordinated (relative to the conditions of chattel slavery) presence of the Black embodied voice. The creation of a new exalted functioning of the White idea/ideal, an "invisible empire" of Whiteness so to speak, served as a unifying focal point around which the post civil war White south could rally. Michaels notes that the "stunning incoherence of *Plessy v. Ferguson*," in which the visual whiteness of Plessy's skin becomes merely a disguise for the Blackness of his blood, attested to the fact that skin color alone was an insufficient protection against the dangers of cultural miscegenation. The idea/ideal of Whiteness was therefore even further removed from its material vulnerability and placed more securely within the realm of a sacred spiritual trust. Whereas the spiritual ideal of Whiteness had once rested exclusively in the privilege of White skin, the emancipation of Blackness into American society created a fissure within the White psyche and brought to the surface an idea of Whiteness that transcended the color not only of Blackness, but also of its own Whiteness.

White skin, no longer a guarantee of one's racial purity and inclusion into the sacred trust of White brotherhood, now entailed the added requirement of being able to sufficiently demonstrate a specified set of cultural/spiritual ideals. According to Michaels, "The Klan wear sheets because their bodies aren't as white as their souls, because *no* body can be as white as the soul embodied in the white sheet."[7] Again, Jeremy's skin, which is whiter than white, can be understood to serve the same function as the white sheets of the Klan, that is, it represents not only the body of Whiteness, but also the potency of the conceptual idea/ideal of Whiteness. Jeremy's transcendent detachment from the screen of *Powder* is reminiscent of the rides of Griffith's mounted Klan in "The Birth of a Nation." His figure becomes the literal disembodied soul of Whiteness. It represents and preserves an ideal while at the same time making painfully evident the empirical, or biological, unattainability of that ideal.

When stripped of blackface as a means for racial representation in the late 1920s the only thing that was left for the White body to reflect itself off of was the glaring construction of its own ideal, an ideal that was rapidly becoming socially and politically dispossessed. As it became increasingly clear that the concept of the "White ideal" was beyond the means of the physical capabilities of the White body, the White psyche was left to function within the confines of an empirically based ideological crisis. This crisis, which has primarily been engendered by the liberation struggles of people of color, is the inheritance, the dilemma, and the conflict of *Powder*. Just as the struggle for the Black subject lies in asserting his or her social right to expand beyond the constraints of its culturally defined potential, the body of Whiteness, conversely, struggles to live up to, to attain, its own impossible idea/ideal of racial purity.

POWDER: THE CLEANSING OF VIOLENCE

Jeremy as Orphan

Although *Powder* grossed over 32 million dollars in 1995, it has clearly not had the broad based commercial and sociological repercussions that are associated with the releases of both *The Birth of a Nation* and *The Jazz Singer*. However the importance of the film lies not so much in how it has impacted itself upon society, but instead, in how society can be seen to have impacted itself upon the film. Beyond the overtly White supremacist assumptions of *Powder*, the transition from blackface to whiteface provides us with a uniquely fascinating opportunity to examine some of the ways in which Whiteness confronts its own construct. As I have mentioned, *Powder* (along with films such as *Little Man Tate, Phenomenon* and the Matt Damon trilogy) is a lens through which we are able to witness the psychological crisis which has emerged within White consciousness as the gap between the philosophical ideal and the materialistic limitations of Whiteness becomes revealed. It is through Jeremy that we witness how the idea of an ideological White essence, while continuing to assert itself, has become literally and symbolically orphaned since the time of *The Jazz Singer*. The central tension of *The Jazz Singer* is the generational fissure between the young jazz singer (Al Jolson) and his rigorously orthodox father. It is this theme of White patriarchal disenfranchisement that is repeated in both *Little Man Tate* and *Good Will Hunting*. *Little Man Tate,* is the story of a child prodigy born to a struggling single mother while *Good Will Hunting* revolves around an adolescent working class orphan from Boston's South End. In *Powder,* Jeremy's mother dies while he is still in her womb, and in the movie's opening sequence we find his father, upon seeing him for the first time, standing above the young child sobbing over and over again, "That's not my son." As he looks down upon the White racial ideal of Jeremy, the father rejects him as not his, or at least, not being of himself. This abandonment stands in stark contrast to the family unity that was depicted in the film's first close-up, a shot of the intertwined hands of Jeremy's parents. The question which *Powder* seems to be asking itself, and which we ought to ask ourselves as we view *Powder*, is how might the physical inheritance of Whiteness maintain its internal unity and cohesiveness, its sense of power and integrity, without the existence of a White supremacist ideal?

While being produced in the present Jeremy is depicted as being an unwanted, inherited, product of the past. He is a responsibility which belongs not to the current generation of his parents, but instead to their ancestors. We first encounter Jeremy as an adolescent hovering in the basement shadows of his dead grandparents' home. Upon their death, the first person to speak with him is a nurturing social worker, Jessie Caldwell, who is sent to coax him out from his dark seclusion and into the world of modern society. As Jessie gazes around the dimly lit room she takes a copy of *Moby Dick* from the shelves and asks him if he has read it. After he tells her to pick a page she replies, "Two hundred and Sixteen." Jeremy proceeds to recite from heart, "Where lies the final harbor whence we are no more, no more. In what rapt either sails the world of which the wearyth will never weary. Where is the foundling's father hidden? Our souls are like those orphans whose unwedded mothers die in burying them. And the secret of our paternity lies in their grave. And we must there to learn it." In this quote we see how the weariness of spiritual yearning is directly tied to the soul's inability to locate a biological origin—its inability to find a permanent earthly home. Again, the mourning of the White soul (as it exists as an ideal) is directly linked to its confrontation with the limitations of the White body. Similarly Jeremy, representing the physical and spiritual White ideal, cannot be at peace because he is separated, due to the restrictions of the corporeal form, from the socio-cultural body of Whiteness . Instead, he wanders throughout the film, alienated from other characters and seeking to escape the confines of their "new" society in which he, the White ideal, ostensibly at least, no longer has a place. It is therefore fitting that the primary setting of *Powder* is the orphanage where Jeremy is sent after being forced from his grandparents' home. In these scenes, the crisis of generational alienation, the struggle for identity inheritance, becomes abundantly evident as the frame is filled with the young orphaned victims of the White mind/body fissure.

Jeremy has been raised by his grandparents as a "family secret," on an isolated rural farm set off from the developments of modern society. He has lived his life in their basement, hidden from the light of day and rarely seen by the neighbors who describe him as being "some kind of phantom." When Jeremy is asked why he didn't call anyone after his grandfather died he replies, "Grandpa said that there would be a day, when he would die, like grandma died, and that people would come and see me and try and take me away." Jeremy fears that he will be "taken away" from his home, a home that lies within the heart and soul of the ancestral White body. *Powder* presents us with a world in which the construct of White racial purity is being isolated and confronted by modern forces. The grandparents' basement, like a Freudian representation of the inner conscience of White culture, is a place where the figure of modern psychiatry, the social worker, must descend in order to confront and resolve the fissure within its own psychological creation.

But it is Jeremy, and not the social worker, that ultimately functions as a mediator between the dispossessed White psyche and the alienated White body. Like Faulkner's Compsons, all of the families depicted in *Powder* are in a state of disintegration and internal conflict. In a major sub-plot of the film the wife of the town sheriff lies in a coma, at their home, slowly dying. The authoritarian cohesion of White society, symbolized by the sheriff's family, is coming apart. The Sheriff, Doug, is estranged from his only son, Steven, and returns from work each day exhausted by his efforts to enforce and contain Jeremy. We see him sitting by his wife's bedside try-ing to reach her, holding on to the slim hope that she will somehow be able to survive. He talks to her and rubs her dying lips with ice. Finally, in a last desperate effort, Jeremy is called to her bedside. Even though we have heard the doctor, who happens to be the only Black character in the film, telling the sheriff that, "She's past communicating. You can't get inside her head, and if you could, she'd probably tell you, 'let me go,'" Jeremy is nevertheless able to read her innermost thoughts by simply placing his hands on her forehead. In an emotionally charged scene, Jeremy allows the husband and wife to communicate by linking himself between them. "She believes in miracles now," Jeremy says, "and so should you. She thinks I'm an angel, come to take her home and to bring you and Steven together again, remind you of how much you are still in each other's hearts. He loves you more than any man in the whole world and she won't go, she won't leave this place, this room or this world until you know that you still have a son." In a clear appeal to White family heritage and unity, Jeremy tells Doug that she is remembering how hard he and their son had searched for her lost wedding ring, the bond of family solidarity, in the snow. She cannot die unless she knows that Doug and her son will reunite and recog-nize their eternal love for one another. It becomes evident that without the unifying ideal of an exalted White culture, one that is based upon the racially supremacist manifestations of Jeremy, it is feared that the White family unit will disintegrate. In the end it is only through Jeremy, the White ideal, that the White family is able to come together and maintain its internal unity and cohesiveness. Through Jeremy the mother is able to die in safety and peace and the father and son are able to find a common ground and reunite.

Just as Jeremy's birth broke the bond between his mother and father, sym-bolized in the opening close-up of his parents' gripped hands, it now func-tions as an indispensable element in uniting the White family.

Jeremy as "Other"

Jeremy's father, then, can be seen to have failed the White family by not having had embraced the White ideal of his child. The failure of White society lies, not in rejecting the idea of Jeremy, but instead in failing to accept and hold onto it firmly enough. It is the state, as represented by the sheriff, his deputy, the orphanage, and the social worker, who become the real threat to the White ideal of Jeremy who is constantly struggling to escape their oppressive restrictions and control. This scenario, as Michaels notes with reconstruction, "enables white men to imagine themselves as victims of imperialism, it enables them to imagine the imperial power as their own government."[8] *Powder* thus dangerously, albeit unintentionally, begins to play into the same "Whiteness as victim" psychosis which fuels the stridently racist and violent White nationalist militia movements of the United States and Europe. It is precisely this notion of a racial White identity victimized by state forces unsympathetic to the ideals of White supremacy and "free individualism" which have historically fueled the terroristic actions of the Klan and other White supremacist groups.

Clearly one of the things that is most disturbing about *Powder* is its almost complete absence of a Black embodied voice. As such, *Powder* ultimately maintains a rigid adherence to the ideals, however unattainable, of White supremacy. Throughout the film we find that the conflation of genetic origins with the peacefulness, or rest, of the White soul is repeatedly stressed. However alienated Jeremy may appear, *Powder* does not renounce the concept of racial superiority which he personifies; indeed, it undeniably creates a romanticized sympathy and longing for it. Perhaps it would be easier for us to understand the racial implications of *Powder* by reversing the identity of Jeremy. Viewers and critics of the film would not fail to reflect upon its racial semiotics if an African American called "Charcoal," with jet Black skin and the powers and insights of Jesus, were to be born into an all White southern town. This exclusion of the Black body from *Powder* is an indication that the confrontation between the body of Whiteness and its exalted ideological construction do not necessarily represent a significant evolution in White racial consciousness. It would be dangerous for us to simply interpret the father's rejection of Jeremy, or Jessie's willingness to confront Jeremy within the social psyche, as a repulsion at a racialism which they cannot accept. When viewed within *Powder's* overall adherence to the conceptual framework of White supremacy, these acts cannot be seen to be a process which is simply the function of its own progressive reformation. Instead, what we have is a world in which the exertion of racist premises can coincide quite comfortably with the denial that such constructs are either valid or good, and perhaps even more dangerously, that such constructs even exist at all. In other words, the

new racialism we find in *Powder* and other films of the genre, has created a
silent space through which racist premises can function while simultaneously
being denounced.

Powder raises the crucial issue of whether or not the Black voice will be allowed to address the White body through its own corporeal form. Corresponding to the ostensible demise of overtly racist biological and intellectual
theories of racial identity, there has been an effort to erase the person of color
from semiotic discourse entirely. Clearly genes and biology, as the basis for
life, are important, even *essential*, ingredients to human existence; otherwise
we as a culture wouldn't be so repulsed by the thought of eugenics or the horrors of genocide. What we find in *Powder*, however, is a form of genetic and
semiotic whitewashing that is reminiscent of the identity cleansing of Norman Bates in Alfred Hitchcock's *Psycho*. In *Psycho*, Norman Bates puts on
the clothes of his dead mother and literally begins to speak in her voice in an
effort to preserve the essence of her life and assuage his conscience for his
own complicity in her death. *Powder's* use of "racial cross dressing" or
"racial necrophelia" similarly functions to mollify the White conscience.
Guilty itself of cultural violence and genocide, the White conscience is able
to wear the voices of cultural difference without undertaking the cumbersome
task of negotiating with their physical bodies. One example of this within
Powder is the degree to which Jeremy displays a fundamental understanding
and relationship with nature that is reminiscent of Native American and Eastern spirituality. He sits in the woods with a noble and quiet presence which
acknowledges a deep rooted connection and interdependence of all living
things. As he communes with nature in one scene, salamanders come to him
and he allows them to crawl on his body. His philosophical insights are also
stereotypically Native American and/or Eastern. In another scene he actually
serves as a channel to pass the spirit of a dying deer into the body of the racist
poacher who has shot it. These culturally pluralistic qualities are brought out
again later when he begins to get close to a girl from town:

> What are people like on the inside?
>> Inside most people there's a feeling of being separate, separated from everything.
>> And?
>> And they're not. They're a part of absolutely everyone, and everything.
>> Everything? I'm a part of this tree? You're telling me that I'm part of some
>> fisherman in Italy on some ocean I've never even heard of? Some guy sitting on
>> death row? It's hard for me to believe all of that
>> It's because you have this spot that you can't see past.

As he utters the lines "this spot," Jeremy reaches up and touches her forehead
in an obvious reference to the third-eye that is fundamental to the spiritual

systems of Buddhism, Hinduism and Ancient Egypt. While it is, perhaps, problematic to link these permeable spiritual concepts to a form of "exclusive domain" which attributes them solely to the physical cultures with which they are traditionally associated, it is, however, important for us to note, particularly in light of the racial agenda for which *Powder* itself has set the tone, that absolutely no mention of these "originary" cultures is made in the film whatsoever.

This silence, or non-acknowledgment, of the Black embodied voice can in itself be a form of physical imperialism. The White body, responsible for the genocide and continued oppression of the Native American (there are, after all, Native Americans who could have played the role of Jeremy) and the colonization and exploitation of the North American and East Indian continents, now has the ability to enter and become that which it has dispossessed. It claims access to and controls the internal and external dialogue, the psychic space of Black "Otherness," through annexation and affectation. Ominously then it is death, which in addition to fetishizing difference marks the movement from voyeurism to possession. Death becomes a form of portraiture, a means to capture the alien identity by freezing it within time and space, establishing the significance of the dominant White identity while at the same time fixing the location of the Black "Other."[9] In doing so, the White mind/body dichotomy is able to assuage its historical conscience by keeping the idea of Black "Otherness" alive in a state of continually suspended animation. This process ingeniously avoids accountability for the cultural violence of imperialism by escaping the need for the direct negotiation with, and acknowledgment of, imperialism's victims.

Again, Jeremy's White mask of Blackness allows the very idea of victimization to be transferred away from the Black body and onto the White Psyche. By placing itself in the role of the ostracized racial "Other," the White ideal is thus able to reenact upon itself the very process of cultural degradation which is the hallmark of colonial imperialism. Jeremy is constantly referred to as "Boy" and "Son" and is subject to all of the classic taunts of White American Racism; "Why do you look like that?" "They kick you out of cancer camp?" "You got some kind of disease?" "Don't look at me." "What are you doing with my daughter." "You think you can be like us?" And so on. Jeremy is surrounded and taunted by the orphans who are the result of the socially displaced idea of Whiteness. Jeremy's cultural alienation continues and reflects the White myth of "burden" which has been so fundamental to perpetuating the western imperialistic tradition. It posits Jeremy as resisting the racism of his fellow Whites and anti-racism becomes the libratory virtue of the ideal White male. In a classic example of cyclical reasoning, colonialism thus establishes the notion, and expectation, that a libratory philosophy will emerge from within the very systems that have historically created and perpetuated racist oppression. We can see how the exaltation and promise of such "Western ideals" as "freedom," "individualism," "democracy," etc., can similarly function to encourage the Black subject, in the United States and abroad, to patiently sit back and await the perpetual reformation of Western ideologies.

This colonial saga is again replayed in a poignant scene between Jeremy and Jessie, in which the trauma of the trans-Atlantic slave trade that was inflicted upon the African American is dramatized:

> Jeremy please.
>   I want to go home. Do you understand that? I want to go home.
>   Look . . . Whatever you saw.
>   I saw that I don't like what you do. Any of you.
>   Jeremy . . .
>   No! You pretend to be my friend the way that you pretend everything. A friend doesn't lock you up. A friend doesn't take you away from your home and say that it's for your own good. How long do you really think I'll let you keep me here?

Again, it is Jessie, the contemporary figure of the psychiatrist, who is confronting the ghost of the White past. We can see how the residual guilt of imperialism is being played out within the White psyche as Jeremy confronts her with the crimes perpetrated upon the body and soul of Blackness. The final question, "How long do you really think I'll let you keep me here?" is an indication that the catalyst for this confrontation is not merely a sudden awakening of the White racial consciousness but, instead, a response to the cultural liberation of the racialized "Other," a response that the White ideal often seeks to avoid by, first isolating (even through death if need be) and then through actually becoming that very "Other."

Michel Foucault has stated that, "Science, the constraint to truth, the obligation of truth and ritualized procedures for its production have traversed absolutely the whole of Western society for millennia and are now so universalized as to become the general law for all civilizations."[10] In *Powder*, electricity and the laws of Western science have, indeed, achieved the status of a new divinity. In a modern reenactment of the Immaculate Conception, Jeremy is born after a bolt of lightning kills his mother while he is still in the womb. It is electricity which is both the product and the cause of his remarkably Christ like powers. While there may be a reluctance to mention Native American and Eastern influences within the film, there is no such hesitancy in paying reverence to the high priest of Western science and genius Albert Einstein. It is his theories and spiritual insights that are consistently referred to throughout the film. On one occasion, Jeremy's science teacher asks him; "did you ever read any Einstein? No? He said that he believed in life after death, only because energy can never cease to exist; it relays and transforms but it doesn't ever stop, ever. And he said that if we ever got to the point where we could use all our brain, that we'd be pure energy and that we wouldn't even need bodies." He later implies that Jeremy is "closer to that energy level than anybody has ever been." and that he "has a mind that we won't evolve to for, like, thousands of years." *Powder* ends as Jeremy races out into a storm with his arms outstretched, Christ-like, towards the sky. A rod of lightning comes down and strikes him on the chest, lifting him up into the air and vaporizing him into Einstein's state of pure energy. Jeremy has thus completed the evolutionary cycle and become the archtypical "man of the future."

The silent plurality of Jeremy's White skin obscures the fact that there are fundamental ideological differences in the ways in which various cultural modes of functioning define and prioritize what is understood to be "truth." We cannot escape the fact that people who have developed in different geographical loci have also developed radically different methods for conceptualizing and ordering empirical and meta-empirical data. Huge divergences exist between various cultural understandings of such seemingly basic concepts as, time and space, kinship patterns, human to environment relational constructs, etc. As long as the Black embodied voice remains silenced, the threat exists that there will be no negotiation with the Euro-centric definitions of cultural truth which we see universalized in *Powder*. While "our" ideas of race, or the cultural understandings of personal identity to which race belongs, may or may not be seen as "essentialist," (i.e. comprising predetermined traits based upon such qualifiers as the genetic differences that we find manifested in skin color or the locals of geographically specific "points of origin") they are nonetheless the site of conflict and the domain of struggle for the reinscription of culturally determined values. Crossing the racial divide and creating an intermingling of discourse between the White and Black bodies exposes the terrain of social, political and economic realities to the possibility of new transformations. Segregated discourse, on the other hand, in many ways allows the existence of *Powder* to go unchallenged: Whiteface protects the White discourse from an engaged Black critique.

Post-colonial theorists have often valorized the "interstices," or the "liminal" spaces said to exist between designations of identity (between the "you" and the "I" of interaction,) for comprising a form of vital "Third space" which functions as an arena for the exchange and negotiation of cultural discourses. They envision this point of contact serving as an ever expanding, merging, circle of culture, between individuals and sets of individuals, who otherwise have varying geographic and historical links to time and space. For better or worse, then, at the moment of contact, a new hybrid culture can be said to be formed in which the two parties, in essence, participate in the creation of a matrix of new extended and merged articulations. The mere process of communication breaches cultural sovereignty. For instance, in articulating a third space that is unified, independent and inter-textual, Homi Bhabha envisions a discourse that is "inter-rational" and therefore transformational.[11] While it may be true that cultural definitions are negotiated and transformed within this third space, we must not be too quick to assume that this space stands temporally beyond the hierarchical registers and assumptions which individuals carry into their discursive interactions. The so-called third space, while presenting us with unique opportunities to transform discourse, is neither "eternally fractured" nor horizontal. It does not exist beyond empirical realities, instead, it is directly tied to and dependent upon them, which is, of course, precisely why this space is so potentially transformative. It is within these "liminal," third spaces, that the struggle for definition and semiotic control can be most fierce. Thus, how we define *who* we are will directly affect the ways in which we negotiate our discursive interactions, or as Stuart Hall states, "How we see ourselves matters because it enters into and informs our actions and practices."[12]

If the designation of a sign is an intersubjective territory, indeed, if it can be viewed as a territory at all, then it is, potentially, a site of struggle and conflict. The third space, being linked to time and space, is therefore subject to the potential interjection of violence—a violence which can function to disconnect one's sense of cultural continuity and agency. When there is tension within a signification the sign becomes a battlefield in which the signifying content of the sign becomes the site of both oppression and resistance. Ultimately, the question of "who" one "is" is also a question of how one is perceived, both internally and externally, as a being who occupies and shares space. Identity, in addition to being self-defining, also reflects an external engagement, a point of social contact that can be simultaneously physical, metaphysical, spatial and temporal. It is never purely self-referential. In order to negotiate this shared space effectively, it follows that one must have at least some understanding of who and where they are. Otherwise there is a risk of becoming subjected to external manipulation and control within the discursive process, thus setting the stage for a cycle of cultural dominance and victimization. But how does one define the "I" and the "Am" in the statement "I am," which is a crucial stage in defining "who one is"? Is it to be reduced to "I think therefore I am?"

No one can doubt that a prisoner left in solitary confinement would possess for a time the capabilities of thought and could, using Descartes empiricism, be said to exist. But these capabilities of thought, without a social context, would deteriorate over time. It is the ability to assert a conception of being, not simply to conceive it, which defines the ability "to be." To not be, then, is to lose the power of assertion. Individual becoming cannot be reduced to thought. It is, instead, because an individual exists within an inter-relational framework vis-a-vis other people and a system of signs that one sees one's self as truly existing. Indeed, it is through signs that we are even able to formulate thought. The ability to control or participate in the creation of the signifying content of the signs that are used to define thought and existence is directly proportional to the subject's sense of authority over their conception of "who" they are. In other words, the subject needs to feel that they have some agency in the semiotics of their own experience.

The interjection of cultural violence into discourse transforms the subject's understanding of its own frame of reference. It raises the question as to who has agency over the individual's subjectivity. To what degree, the individual may ask, are the boundaries of my own semiotics a reflection of an oppressive overlaying? Once a subjective positionality has been shifted, how does one create a re-framing? The struggle to re-frame our own perspectives is integral to the process of personal growth. It is the effort to create a social space which makes room for the ideas that we think will benefit us and help us understand our relationships to other people. Acknowledging the wounds from acts of violence which disconnect one from a perceived cultural continuity is often healed by an external act of reconnection with cultural forces that one would deem to be either a) sympathetic to the positionality that was originally violated, b) transformative of the system of oppression which originally created the violation, or c) facilitating both of these options simultaneously. Cultural identity can therefore be a necessary component of imperialistic resistance.

Black subjectivity, however, has become increasingly equated with an "identity politics," a term that has ominous and fetishistic connotations. By claiming the right to assert itself in the form of resistance, the Black subject is often forced into defending a position that seems to border upon the essential. The Black subject, from the position of the homogenized present, is seen as representing a "special interest" and, therefore, as being antithetical to the "common" good as it becomes defined by the universalized terms "we" and "our." What is good for the nation, becomes synonymous with what is good for "us." But within the framework of an imperialistic cultural violence that threatens to subsume the Black body, the formation of a Black "identity politics" can be seen largely as a critical response to the threat of the type of erasure which we find evident in *Powder*. Notions of a subjective "Black" experience should not be deemed as *necessarily* a defense of essentialist positionalities. Instead, such alignments may be merely a defensive site of ne-gotiation that is resorted to in order to prevent absorption within constructs which it perceives as antithetical to the survival of its own body and cultural ideals. The notion of a "Black" identity which stands in contrast to "White-ness" only becomes fetishistic when viewed from the blinders of dominant paradigms of personal definition which have been transformed into cultural universals.

In fact, the trend of multi-culturalism itself is often little more than a "nor-mative pluralism" too often reflective of what theorist E. San Juan refers to as the "guilty conscience of petty suburban liberalism." San Juan notes that cultural pluralism "concerns the orthodox conception of the dominant culture as simply comprising lifestyles that one can pick and wear any time one pleases."[13] From this perspective, multi-culturalism becomes a sophisticated ruse with which Whiteness can delay the process of cultural negotiation while simultaneously preserving at arm's length a host of commodifiable "Other" cultures for the purposes of exotic consumption. Perhaps it is no mistake that academic multi-culturalism, in the form of "Afro-American" and "Ethnic Studies" programs, was created at precisely the moment in history where we see a corresponding rise of a Black power movement reflecting a vocal, politicized Black consciousness. When all is said and done, multi-culturalism often functions to distance an internal critique of Whiteness at the moment in which it arises by creating a space through which so-called "authentic" Black culture can define itself solipsistically. But as we have noticed from the his-torical development of Blackface and Whiteface, the reformation of White supremacy is most effectively challenged frontally. One of the dangers of multi-culturalism is that an uncritiqued ideology of Whiteness has a dispro-portionate effect upon structural systems which directly affect both White and Black bodies. The impetus for transforming these dominant White paradigms of discourse are primarily derived from the assertions of the Black voiced subject.

It is evident that even without blackface the attempt to cross boundaries through the depiction of the Black voice has continued to be a force in Amer-ican culture and that the White expression, or more appropriately, translation, of the Black voice remains entrenched within the public psyche. The imperi-alistic carnivalization of the Black "Other" can be witnessed in virtually every media outlet from the post-modern expressions of MTV to the more overt commodifications of the Black form which take place in multi-national corporate advertising campaigns where we are encouraged to simply "shop in the market place of difference." A recent advertisement by Benneton, for ex-ample, features three human hearts laid out side by side. Each heart wears the label of a different color, White, Black, and Yellow; the obvious implication being that, in an homage to the late Martin Luther King Jr., regardless of skin color we are all the same inside. That it is the content of our characters and not the color of our skin that matters. But despite the enthusiastic heralding of a "post-imperialist" and "post-colonialist" global society, brought about by the fall of the former Soviet Union and the successful creation, between the United States and the United Nations, of a militarily hegemonic "new world order," transnational corporate profitmaking continues to exert itself upon the modern, or, "postmodern" subject with unprecedented force and sophistication.[14] Within this context Western pluralism while seeming to celebrate difference, is instead simply inviting that difference to meld into the very forces of imperialistic violence which threaten to erase and subsume it.

The sheer volume of racial imagery and "cross-dressing" which assault the modern senses often makes it difficult to interpret whether the images such as the ones we find in *Powder* are actually functioning to change or to maintain the structures that support racist ideologies. The tribalization of White youth culture, for example, through body piercing, tattoos, Mohawks, and the liberal (re) appropriation of inner city fashion, can in some ways be understood to comprise a rejection, or critique, of its own culturally inherited value systems, racial or otherwise. However, these attempts on the part of Whiteness to transform its culture through entering the realm of the Black "Other," in an expression of social defiance and a seemingly cross racial unity, must still be framed by the White commodification of the Black body that continues unabated. The *idea* of Blackness continues to exist as an object to be bought, sold, traded, pushed, poked and even petted (visible in the rise of the commercial marketability of the "exotic" sexuality of the person of color) but very seldom to be taken in equally, holistically incorporated and negotiated with. Due to the social inequalities in which racial discourse takes place, the forces of boundary permeation, whatever their intent may be, very often do not significantly challenge, but instead serve to facilitate, the continued appropriation and exploitation of the racialized "Other."

While it is a common practice to scrutinize the nature and function of Blackness, to ask the question of it, "What does it mean to be Black?" it is still rare that this question is posed to Whiteness. It is precisely this social reluctance, or inability, to confront Whiteness that allows the White supremacist assumptions of *Powder* to masquerade as pluralistic objectivity. As the Black embodied voice finds new ways to assert itself into a shared cultural discourse, it is crucial to insure that old racist paradigms of identity are not merely being reinscribed within new, more sophisticated systems of oppression. Some of the most reactionary policies, from the perspective of people of color, of the Reagan and Post-Reagan era (anti-affirmative action, anti-multi-culturalism, the attack on welfare programs, the restructuring of voting districts, the war on drugs and the expansion of the Prison Industrial Complex, etc.) have been promulgated under the guise of a new found "political correctness" which has equated the end of racism with a sudden declaration of a color blind or race free society—a society in which all men and women are created equal. It is this idea that race "doesn't matter" that allows us as a society to stop questioning the implications of who is making an assertion and in what context they happen to be making it in. Under the new racial constructs in which we find the emergence of *Powder* and other films of its genre, it becomes more important to consider *what* Jeremy is saying from a purely existential standpoint, than it is to consider *how* what Jeremy is saying translates into socio-economic realities. When we consider the cultural context of Jeremy, his melanin-free skin becomes glaringly evident and directly impacts the ways in which we interpret the semiotic content of his discourse. The attempt to "homogenize the history of the present,"[15] so to speak, in truth threatens to sacrifice what is understood to be Black identity at the altar of a new found anti, or post-essentialism. So long as Jeremy doesn't utter such epithets as "nigger" or "spic" (or in other ways verbally espouse genetically based racial doctrines which can directly link him to an overtly racist discourse,) we do not question how his "clean" words relate to his position in relation to structures of functional oppression. The unwillingness, or inability, of Whiteness to analyze itself subjectively—to appraise and reform the function of its own position within the construct of White supremacy—is the primary reason why the "problem of race" as a global dilemma is carrying itself so confidently into the 21st Century.

NOTES

1. Stuart Hall, "The Whites of Their Eyes: Racist ideologies and the Media," in *Silver Linings,* ed. George Bridges and Rosalind Brunt (London: Lawrence and Wishart, 1987), 36.

2. Michael Rogin, *Blackface, White Noise: Jewish Immigrants in the Hollywood Melting Pot* (Berkeley, California: University of California Press, 1996), 19.

3. Robert C. Toll, *Blacking Up: The Minstrel Show in Nineteenth-Century America* (New York: Oxford University Press, 1974), 26.

4. Michael Rogin, "The Sword Became a Flashing Vision: D. W. Griffith's 'The Birth of a Nation," in *Ronald Reagan, The Movie: Another Episode in Political Demonology* (Berkeley, California: University of California Press, 1988).

5. Herman Melville, *Moby Dick; or, The Whale* (Baltimore, Maryland: Penguin Books, 1851), 292.

6. Mellville, 288.

7. Walter Benn Michaels, "The Souls of White Folk," in *Literature and the Body: Essays on Population and Persons,* ed. Elaine Scarry (Baltimore, Maryland: The Johns Hopkins University Press, 1990), 188–190.

8. Michaels, 187–188.

9. Robert Stam, et al. ed., *New Vocabularies in Film Semiotics: Structuralism, Post Structuralism and Beyond* (London and New York: Routledge, 1992), 13.

10. Michel Foucault, *Power/Knowledge: Selected Interviews and Other Writings, 1972–1977,* ed. Colin Gordon (New York: Pantheon Books, 1972), 66.

11. Homi K Bhabha, *The Location Of Culture* (London and New York: Routledge, 1994), 19–40.

12. Hall, 32.

13. E. San Juan, Jr., *Racial Formations/Critical Transformations* (New Jersey-London: Humanities Press, 1992), 106.

14. E. San Juan Jr., "Postcolonial Theory Versus Philippine Reality," Working Papers in Asian/Pacific Studies, Duke University, 1995, 1.

15. Bhabha, 9.

Chapter Three

"Shylock:
Shakespeare's Sympathetic 'Other'"

Paul Pfeiffer, Salisbury University

Shakespeare's motives for writing *The Merchant of Venice* are clearly set in the xenophobia of his times, yet his treatment of his Jewish characters is characteristically vague. Typical of his approach, he offers a moral middle ground creating, for his time, a rare portrait of a people forced to the role of villain. The social position of stigma attached to Shylock, therefore, becomes Shakespeare's means of dramatizing the claustrophobic position not only of Jews, but of all aliens as well. Set amidst the fears of invasion which traumatized late 16th century Englishmen, *The Merchant of Venice* seems, from our distance of years, a remarkably rational and multifaceted study of the catastrophic impact of such distrust of any unknown.

Until the late twentieth century Shakespeare's play has held an unhappy position in the canon. Almost entirely omitted from standard repertory in the seventeenth century, from the eighteenth century onwards the play was acted in such a way as to enforce Anti-Semitic feelings and, as such, possibly deny Shakespeare's original purpose. This approach to this enigmatic play coincided with a mass cultural attempt to define what, for lack of a better term, we shall call "Englishness." The national pride engendered in Elizabeth's reign had, by the mid-eighteenth century cried out for identity. The incorporation of Ireland, Scotland and Wales into Great Britain in 1607 had further fed this need for identity. Britain's impact, carried across the globe, by the 1750s required a center around which the cultural origins could be based. Shakespeare became that center. As national poet, Shakespeare became the measure of all things English.[1]

Additionally, this identity became as much a religious point as a political one. Prior to Henry VIII's break with the Roman Catholic Church, to be En-

38

glish was to be Christian. Non-Christians were clearly outside the circle. Yet the Protestant Reformation changed that irrevocably. Elizabethans struggled to identify themselves more and more as Protestant Christians, a movement cemented by the Gunpowder Plot of 1604 and which fed directly the Anti-Papist fears of the seventeenth and eighteenth centuries. Catholics were ranked among all other 'Outsiders' including Jews as simply refusing to belong. Drama touching on the nature of the 'Outsider,' therefore, must be seen to include at least, if not directly reference English Catholics, as the more common population in London and, after 1604, the more feared national threat.

By the mid-eighteenth century, as the focus on national identity sharpened, issues arose as to who among the diverse populations in Britain might qualify. In addition, in more liberal circles attitudes of 'Christian Benevolence' and the prevailing concepts of Natural Rights seemed to draw attention to these 'Other' populations so long ignored. In 1753, the Jewish Naturalization Act, or the 'Jew Bill' as it was commonly called, was proposed. This legislation, which was accepted by the House of Commons, relaxed the existing alien laws making the naturalization of resident Jewish peoples more feasible. Under conservative pressures the bill was quickly repealed. Yet, this proposal awakened long-held fears in the Protestant Christian community. Naturalization had required the Oath of Supremacy and the Oath of Allegiance, both of which recognized the monarch as Head of the Kingdom as well as of the Church. These oaths also required taking the Sacrament. Christians doubted the validity of such an oath taken by one of another faith. Ancient issues of Anti-Semitism arose.[2] However, the naturalization of Jews was not the only issue at stake. The standing laws of naturalization had been put in place in 1609 and had been directed not at limiting the social power of Jews then living in London, but at the power of English Catholics. Denied citizenship, both groups were held as outcasts and severely limited in social/ political position.[3] To pass this bill would, therefore, open Protestant England to Catholics as well as Jews.

As the debate over this bill waged, pamphlets, newspaper columns and public letters fueled the fear. Theatres, sensing the publicity value of such a mood, were quick to join the fray. Shakespeare, now seen as England's poetic voice, became a reference point. *The Merchant of Venice* was produced frequently for its debate on this very issue of loyalty and of belonging to a nation. Sadly, the play was rather used to argue against the bill and served only to fuel xenophobia and Anti-Semitism for the next two hundred years.

Slowly, the treatment of Shylock evolved from a comic villain, traditionally played in a red beard, to one of more sympathetic tones, however cruel his motives. When Charles Macklin played him in 1741, he spent much of his time amidst the Jewish merchants of London in close study of their habits, their dress and manner of speech. Thus, when he came to perform the role, he presented to his patrons a Shylock which if not authentic, at least conformed realistically to their impressions. Macklin's interpretation, however, won the accolade, (attributed to Alexander Pope) "This is the Jew / That Shakespeare drew.'[4] One might suspect that this implied Macklin's Shylock well matched the contemporary image of the devious Jew so popular in the streets. Yet, perhaps Pope saw the character more sympathetically and recognized, thanks to Macklin's acting, the duality of Shakespeare's moral stance in this play, a stance evident in all of his plays.

Only in post-Holocaust years do we find a willingness to examine Shylock from the stance of the victim. He may now be seen as dark and hard-driven, but is assuredly pushed to his actions. Shylock's actions are clearly motivated by external forces—by the cruelty of Christian law and by the cold nature of Christian competitors. These actions are clearly seen as arising from his desire to succeed as well as to seek revenge. Shylock is not a hero, yet neither is Antonio. In light of twentieth and twenty-first century approaches to characterization and the connected study of psychology, we may clearly see how Shylock's actions are driven by these dual motivations. Yet, these are also clearly stated in the play and, therefore, tell us much about Shakespeare's intended interpretation.

In order to determine Shakespeare's intentions with this play and, indeed, with Shylock, a proper examination of the play in the context of its time is required. This examination must trace two topics: first, the larger context of the play in Elizabethan culture of the 1590s, and secondly, as an expression of Shakespeare's personal life in that same period. The play surely represents Shakespeare's answer to the call for a profitable play to tap into the very real fear of Spanish invasion and the native xenophobia. This fear had become a reality when the Spanish Armada struck and was defeated in 1588. Yet the morally unsettled nature of this play also must stand as a quiet testament of his very private position.

THE PRIVATE AND SOCIAL CONTEXTS

The year 1596–7 for Shakespeare held a series of emotionally traumatic events that dramatically shaped his view of himself, his world and his writing. Shakespeare's work, therefore, provides invaluable insight when examined as a direct reaction to these external events. In addition, specifics about the lives of others in his circle and the effects of contemporary events on them are available and may also be applied to Shakespeare by association. The present scope does not allow a more complete biographical study yet through an examination of this single year, matching events to the writing, a man emerges whose private life and heritage were consistently at odds with the expectations placed on him by his professional and public life.

Between 1596 and 1597 Shakespeare wrote *King John, King Henry IV part two* and the rather mysterious *The Merchant of Venice*. The deeply personal sonnets, which may be seen as intimate confessionals, also date from this period and offer additional and important psychological detail. Examining Shakespeare's writing in conjunction with the external events of his life at the time of composition, the plays and the sonnets may be seen to contribute immensely to our understanding of him. In particular, *The Merchant of Venice,* composed at the culmination of a series of events beginning with the death of his only son, emerges as a complex yet seemingly disjointed comedy of conflicting ideologies which may be seen as Shakespeare's plea for tolerance.

Set against the fears of invasion and forced religious conversion traumatizing English Protestants of the 1590's, *The Merchant of Venice* seems a remarkably rational and multifaceted study of the catastrophic impact of such distrust. The morally unsettled nature of the play stands as a quiet testament of Shakespeare's very private position. What emerges is a portrait of a man whose own status as a secret outsider would enable him to create a character tortured between the obligations of faith and tradition and acceptance and social stability.

Taking a middle moral ground Shakespeare creates a rare portrait of an 'Outsider' forced by Christian prejudice to the role of villain. The social stigma attached to Shylock, therefore, becomes Shakespeare's means of dramatizing the claustrophobic position not only of Jews, but of all aliens. As recent scholarship has focused on the undercurrent homosexual bond between Antonio and Bassanio the dimensions of alienation in this play are further compounded.

Shakespeare has long been revered for his masterful presentation of opposing forces with equal sympathy placing audiences squarely in the middle, the implied victim of conflicting ideologies. Shakespeare's deft handling of this position of conflict between opposites may, finally, be our richest clue as to his inner world. This practiced neutrality may be more clearly understood given the strong impact of a rural childhood steeped in the traditions of Catholicism on his adult life in Protestant London.

SHAKESPEARE'S CATHOLICISM

The degree to which Shakespeare actually adhered to the 'Old Religion' is outside of the scope of this examination. However, his rural roots were clearly

Roman Catholic and as Protestantism did not, of course, take an immediate hold, we may well imagine that his childhood was steeped in the traditions of that faith. Reluctant to change, rural England remained true to the 'Old Religion' until strict enforcement of conformity began in the 1560s.[5] The Ardens, Shakespeare's mother's family, were known recusant Catholics. Town Council records for Stratford-upon-Avon indicate that John Shakespeare, the poet's father also resisted the change.[6] Many people of John Shakespeare's age would have remembered the fearful shifts of State Religion since the reign of King Henry VIII. The cycles of rural life had been tied for nearly one thousand years to the feast days and holy days of the Church calendar. Given the terror of damnation, farming folk would have clung to these rhythms for what psychological safety could be had. But threats from abroad were to make religious belief a political imperative. Matters of private conscience became issues of public security.

The fear of Spanish (Catholic) invasion and the uncertainty of the succession fed into public consciousness creating an atmosphere of intense racism and mistrust of 'Outsiders.' London Theatres quickly adapted to this mood providing, as the old morality plays had done, a vehicle for the promotion of a political/theological agenda. Londoners thrilled to a revival of Christopher Marlowe's *The Jew of Malta*, which pinned national fears to medieval anti-Semitism in its comic villain, Barabas. Shakespeare, as a playwright for the rival company, would also have been called upon to join the fray. Yet Shakespeare chose at this moment not to demonize 'Outsiders' but rather celebrate his country's past—a telling choice.

A RALLYING POINT FOR "OLD ENGLAND"

Shakespeare's histories answered this call, yet these he anchored not in fear but in nostalgia. He rallied his countrymen to the memory of an England all but lost to them.

A crucial aspect, which would not have gone unnoticed, was that the 'Old England' of Shakespeare's histories had also been a Catholic England—as yet undisturbed by the Reformers. Yet religion and nationalism were now intertwined. Spain threatened conquest and Catholicism. One can imagine the fine line Shakespeare must have felt compelled to walk. Shakespeare chose not to speak out directly. By not rallying clearly to the Protestant cause, as poets and dramatists had been challenged to do, Shakespeare may reveal his true beliefs.

One striking event very likely increased the pressure to produce a play to feed upon popular anti-alien sentiments and to balance the competition of

Marlowe's *The Jew of Malta.* Thus pressured at last, Shakespeare would create an 'Outsider' which far outstripped the ranting caricature of Marlowe's Barabas. This catalyst was the sensational trial and gruesome execution of the queen's personal physician. In 1594 the English fears of outsiders were galvanized to the fate of one 'New Christian,' Dr. Rodrigo Lopez. The impact of this event was not lost on Shakespeare.

Driven out of Portugal in 1559 as a converted Jew, Lopez had settled in London establishing himself as a physician eventually becoming House Physician to St. Bartholomew's Hospital. Despite racial prejudice and professional jealousy, he developed a large practice among powerful people including Sir Robert Dudley, Earl of Leicester, and Sir Francis Walsingham. In 1584, the year Lopez was admitted to the College of Physicians, a libelous pamphlet attacking Dudley suggested that Lopez distilled poisons for Dudley and other nobleman as well. In 1586 Lopez reached the pinnacle of his profession being made physician-in-chief to Queen Elizabeth. The Queen demonstrated her favor 1589 by granting him monopolies on the importation of aniseed and sumac. Lopez was wealthy, respected, owned a house in Holborn and had a son enrolled at Winchester College. He was viewed, at least outwardly, as being a dutiful and practicing Protestant.

However, in 1593 a complex web of conspiracy came to light against Don Antonio, the Pretender to the Crown of Portugal, then in protective exile in London. In October one Esteban de Gama was seized in Lopez's house on a charge of conspiring with Spain against Don Antonio. Soon two others, Gomez d'Avila and one Tincino were seized. By confronting the prisoners some vague evidence was elicited leading to the conclusion that a plot to poison the queen was underway. Lopez was implicated and subsequently accused by Robert Devereux, the Earl of Essex of conspiring with Spanish emissaries to poison the Queen. Lopez was arrested on January 1st 1594 and examined by Essex, who failed, however, to find any definite cause for suspicion. Later, put to the rack, Lopez confessed to having entertained suggestions as to poisoning the queen for the sum of 50,000 ducats, but, as he alleged, merely with the design of cozening the King of Spain. Lopez was convicted in February, and on June 7th along with D'Avila and Ticino, Lopez was subsequently hanged, drawn, and quartered as a traitor.[7] No clear evidence was brought against Lopez, yet he was condemned: a scapegoat to public fear. The Queen herself was uncertain of his guilt (hence the delay in his execution) and he maintained his innocence of treason and his being converted from Judaism to Christianity to the end. According to the Elizabethan historian William Camden, Lopez stepped forward on the scaffold and declared that, "he 'loved the Queen as he loved Jesus Christ.' Which," Camden adds, "coming from a man of the Jewish profession, moved no small laughter in the standers-by."[8] Traditionally, a prisoner's last statement was considered a moment of undoubted truth as the prisoner was speaking without hope of reprieve and in fear of damnation. The crowd had treated Dr. Lopez' final oath as a joke.

Shakespeare may very well have witnessed this dehumanizing event. If not, he certainly would have heard about it in grim detail. Indeed, given Shakespeare's circle of acquaintances at court, and amongst the Jewish quarter where he had lived a few years prior, (in Bishop's Gate) he very possibly may have known Lopez either professionally or personally.[9] In any case, the brutal denial of dignity in the face of ritualized slaughter would not have been lost on Shakespeare. The duality of this moment; the persecution of one who was 'outside' yet strove to belong, one whose last act protested his loyalty only to be met with derision must have stirred in Shakespeare a deep sympathy. This experience would, within two months, allow him to create an 'Outsider' of intense psychological realism— Shylock.

THE DEATH OF HAMNET

Two very private incidents in this year were to have a profound impact on Shakespeare's sensibilities and his reaction to his world, though on the surface, at least, these might be seen to have little influence on *The Merchant of Venice*. The first of these incidents was the sudden death of his only son, Hamnet.

In the summer of 1596, plague closed the Theatres forcing Shakespeare's company to tour. He was in Kent when word reached him that his only son, Hamnet, had died. Shakespeare was only thirty-two years old, yet he considered himself and his wife (four years his senior) too old for future children. Given this outlook, the death of his only son would have triggered in the father the grim reality of his own mortality and the end of his bloodline. Shakespeare thus entered into a period of his life, to which he would later refer in one of his sonnets as, 'a Hell of Time.' We may witness him working out his turmoil through his writing.[10]

Sometime in the same year (1596), Shakespeare was commissioned to rewrite an older play of *King John* in answer to the anti-Catholic fervor of London theatergoers. Curiously, however, Shakespeare systematically diffused the anti-Catholic sentiments in order to present the opposing ideologies with equal sympathy. No firm connection between the play's composition and the death of Hamnet can be established, yet how aptly Shakespeare makes such sorrow palpable through the voice of a grieving mother:

> Grief fills the room up with my absent child,
> Lies in his bed, walks up and down with me,
> Puts on his pretty looks, repeats his words,
> Remembers me of all his gracious parts,
> Stuffs out his vacant garments with his form.
>
> (*King John*, 3.4 Lines 93–97

What comfort might be offered for such a grief? In the Old England, Catholic England, the faithful clung fast to the belief that the soul of the departed could be assisted in its sufferings in Purgatory through the intercession of the living. Masses could be said; prayers offered; the departed might even be addressed and asked to intercede on the part of the living. The relationship between the living and the dead did not end at the grave. Centuries of English Catholics had lived and died in the hope of this care from the living. Yet all of this had changed within one generation as Protestantism stamped out such communion as heretical. The continuing relationship between the living and the dead had been eradicated. Worse, it had been made illegal.[11] Instead of the traditional ceremony committing "*thy* body to the ground," the new Protestant service committed '*the* body to the ground." A seemingly insignificant shift in semantics had totally negated the possibility of assistance either for or from the dead. Surely, this must have provoked desperation from those who clung to the old ways. Young Hamnet's funeral must have been intensely disquieting. Shakespeare's parents, older friends and relatives surely would have hoped for more. Shakespeare's immediate reaction is not known, yet soon, in his *Hamlet*, Laertes would protest the perfunctory nature of his sister's funeral demanding, "What ceremony else? (*Hamlet,* 5.1 205, 207)"

THE YOUNG MAN OF THE SONNETS

Following the death of his son, Shakespeare entered into an enterprise that was to yield a potent and intensely private insight through a powerful collection of sonnets. Michael Wood cites computer analysis of the language and vocabulary of the early sonnets placing their composition after 1596. If one accepts this dating, William Herbert, future Earl of Pembroke emerges as the likely candidate. Events in Shakespeare's life in comparison to the emotional content of the sonnets and his other plays strongly support this theory. Taken as such, the sonnets become more intensely autobiographical allowing a richly dramatic portrait of the turmoil of Shakespeare's London life.

In April of 1597, Shakespeare was introduced to young Herbert. Shakespeare was well known to the family, for the elder Herbert had been the patron of Shakespeare's company in the early 1590's. William's mother was an

especially enthusiastic supporter of poets and actors and is believed to have
commissioned Shakespeare to write seventeen sonnets for the young aristocrat's 17th birthday with the object of persuading him to marry for the family's sake. These earliest sonnets, written to the 'Young Man,' center on
themes of the achievement of immortality through both the traditional path of
marriage and procreation and through the more romantic illusion of literary
tribute. This immortality through verse offers, ironically, to preserve both
subject and the grieving poet. Here, the mature Shakespeare's often urgent
advice to his young subject emphasizes the inevitable effects of time on
beauty and, therefore, sexual attractiveness – and performance.

Thus began a relationship that was to have a traumatic effect on the poet
and his reputation. Shakespeare continued to dedicate sonnets to young Herbert on whom he had developed a most intense and complex fixation. Succeeding sonnets increased in intensity of feeling and passionate urgency. The
poems seem to have shocked the Herbert family who kept the two apart, for
Shakespeare's sonnets then take a turn towards the grief of enforced separation and distance.

THE SONNETS IN BRIEF

Shakespeare eventually had the sonnets printed as a collection in 1609. He no
doubt reworked them as was his custom, but arranged them to tell a story of
his journey from fascination to infatuation into passion, separation and the
deep despair of betrayal and loss.[12] There is a growing sense of mortality, futility, and guilt. For during the summer and autumn of 1597, Shakespeare was
not only involved in the complicated relationship with the 'Young Man,' but
was also drawn into what was to become an intensely sexual affair with a
married woman – the so-called "Dark Lady" of the later sonnets. Within these
few months, Shakespeare, as if a character in one of his plays, was to be taken
through the churning tide of homosexual passion; an intensely sexual affair
with another man's wife; the discovery of betrayal at the hands of these two
lovers; the scandal of his private poems published and made to face his own
fading youth and sexual power through rejection and dismissal: all revealed
through his sonnets.

Perhaps the most significant aspect of the sonnets, in terms of this examination, is the character of the "Dark Lady" on whom Shakespeare is clearly
transfixed in the later poems. Despite ten years away from his wife and family, Shakespeare does not seem to have been the womanizer one might have
expected. John Aubrey described him as 'not to be debauched' intending
Shakespeare as withdrawing from such opportunities, as other sources also

described him.[13] We are presented, therefore, with a man of rural conservative moral background struggling with the temptations of the 'naughty world' in which he made his fortune. We see Shakespeare struggling and winning, until he fell under the spell of Emilia Lanier, the "Dark Lady" of his sonnets.

Emilia Lanier, wife of a French musician at court, visited Simon Forman, an astrological physician, throughout the late spring, summer and autumn of 1597. Dr. Forman's notebooks reveal much of the private lives of many of Shakespeare's neighbors and friends. The wives of several actors of his company also consulted with Doctor Forman. Emilia was of the Bassano family, a Venetian family of musicians who had served at court since King Henry VIII. The Bassanos, interestingly, were also Separdic Jews and, therefore, of dark complexion. Emilia had also been the mistress of Lord Hunsdon, the patron of Shakespeare's Company. That they would have known one another is fairly certain.[14]

The later sonnets, beginning with 127, are written to this "Dark Lady." Mrs. Lanier was well known for her sexual attractiveness and appetites and Shakespeare seems clearly 'out of his depth' in tangling with her. Yet sometime in the early autumn of 1597 he must have entered into a sexual affair with her. Through the sonnets we learn of his growing sense of guilt over the affair, which seems to validate Aubrey's assessment that he had, hitherto, remained faithful to his wife. Shakespeare's sonnets reveal a man in the misery of weakness and guilt.

Through the final phase of Shakespeare's journey, he weighs out the corrupting power of lust and the guilt of infidelity echoing the old religious dramas of his youth. He chastises himself for his weakness and downfall with such as "The expense of spirit in a waste of shame is lust in action."[15] This heavy sense of the burden of his sins seems all the more explicable if we consider Shakespeare's Catholic background.

THE MERCHANT OF VENICE

As Shakespeare entered into this heated affair he was also at work on two plays. *Henry IV Part One*, in which the epitome of "Old England," Sir John Falstaff had been introduced, proved such an enormous success as to oblige a sequel. Whilst *Henry IV part two* most likely took his immediate attentions, Shakespeare also embarked on another, less polished but perhaps more intensely personal play, *The Merchant of Venice*. Poignantly, at the peak of the turmoil of his sonnets, Shakespeare addresses the issue of the 'Outsider.'

The Merchant of Venice is based on an Italian folk tale printed in 1558 as *Il Pecorone*. (*The Simpleton*) by Ser Giovanni Fiorentino. As there was no known English translation at the time, Shakespeare may well have read it in its original – which would speak to his continued learning and worldliness after Stratford Grammar School. One other source, which provides the concept of the 'pound of flesh,' is *The Orator*, by Alexander Silvayn. First translated into English in 1596, appearing so shortly before Shakespeare's composition, this was a clear precedent for the notion of a Jew castrating or circumcising a Christian as a penalty for a debt. This aspect of Shakespeare's plot is surely borrowed from Silvayn.[16] The majority of the plot and detail for *The Merchant of Venice* is owed to *Il Pecorone*. Very likely, Shakespeare was introduced to this story through Emilia Lanier. In addition to the later sonnets, Shakespeare's relationship with Lanier was to prove instrumental in the development of *The Merchant of Venice*.

Contemporary references place the play at the time of Shakespeare's affair. The most prevalent is Salarino's reference to the shipwreck of the Andrew.[17] This was one of Sir Walter Raleigh's ships returning from engagements fighting the Spanish that foundered on the infamous Goodwin Sands. Among the survivors was the husband of Emilia Lanier. As Shakespeare's affair with her took place during his absence, this event and his return would have been memorable, to say the least.

Described in its first printing as a comedy, *The Merchant of Venice* is an uncomfortable mix of romantic comedy—which is not light—and tragedy—which is not grave. Unwilling to commit to one ideology, the play presents neither in a convincingly positive light. Shakespeare thrusts upon us love poetry that rings insincere and creates sympathy for characters that later prove unworthy. Nothing is, as it seems. The lovers are false and self-serving. The 'villain' Shylock is obsessive and inhumane yet gains our sympathies. Yet, to some extent, he is driven to it 'by Christian example.' The 'hero,' Antonio, is subjugated by unrequited love—but for the young Bassanio.

ANTONIO AND BASSANIO

Much current scholarship has examined the homosexual nature of the relationship between Antonio and Bassanio.[18] As this paper focuses on Shylock principally, a more thorough treatment is out of its scope, yet a summary is required in order to place the play and its themes of tolerance in perspective with events in Shakespeare's private life.

The relationship between Antonio and Bassanio seems extraordinarily autobiographical given the conjunction of the play and the sonnets. Immediately upon his first entrance, Antonio's friends attribute his sadness to being in love. His sudden, "Fie! Fie!" seems an overreaction. Antonio, much panged by the confusion of his feelings, suffers from melancholy. This is a love much like Shakespeare's for the 'Young Man' without hope or future. The jaded Antonio is clearly in love with the younger Bassanio: of higher birth, sexually magnetic and morally bankrupt. Bassanio refuses to acknowledge the intensity of Antonio's love yet manipulates him for money needed to pursue a wife: "In Belmont is a lady richly left."[19] Antonio, unable to prevent his Adonis from finding a 'proper' mate feels unworthy and agonizes over the futility of his love. Shakespeare must have understood this intensely. Antonio ventures fortune, reputation and life for Bassanio. Only in the courtroom, when faced with the reality of Antonio's sacrifice, is Bassanio made to face his feelings. Moved by Antonio's public declaration of love, Bassanio reveals his love. Both have, in a sense, 'outed' themselves to their personal and professional worlds.

Shakespeare's depiction of Antonio and Bassanio may be seen, in light of now known elements of his private life at this time, as intensely personal. Yet, this interpretation may seem modern. Once more, we have only to examine the writing Shakespeare produced in this year alone to see the impact of his private affairs on his creative mind. Yet, as moving and intimate as this portrait of alienation is, Shakespeare centers his plot on a conflict much more familiar to his audiences: the conflict of faith.

SHYLOCK

On his first appearance in the play, Shylock enters with Bassanio deep in the contemplation of Antonio's bond for three thousand ducats. Shylock ends his first three lines with a simple, "well," implying deep and seemingly distracted thought. Yet, this is clearly an act as, after listing the many reasons against such a bargain, he quickly agrees to the arrangements. Bassanio is too thrilled at the prospect of wooing Portia to realize that Shylock is intending to lose his money. Here, Shylock is drawn in in such a way as to suggest the Machiavellian temper of Marlowe's Barabas, yet there is none of the overt barbarity or joy in his cruelty with which Marlowe treats his subject. Shylock is, justifiably, suspicious and acts as any man of business, indeed, should. Asking to speak with Antonio himself, he is invited to dinner by the rather dim-witted Bassanio.

Shylock takes this as an affront to his religion, yet he begins by citing the New Testament:

> Yes, to smell pork, to eat of the habitation
> which your prophet the Nazarite conjured the devil
> into: I will buy with you, sell with you, talk with
> you, walk with you, and so following: but I will
> not eat with you, drink with you, nor pray with you.[20]

Shylock is interrupted by Antonio's entrance. Yet, what we have come to
know of him thus far reveals a mind sharp enough to *use* the Christian prejudices to frame a worthy argument and one capable of manipulating rhetoric
to his advantage.

On sight of Antonio, Shylock retreats into a short aside, in which he offers
further reasons for his desire for Antonio's fall.

> How like a fawning publican he looks.
> I hate him for he is a Christian:
> But more, for that low simplicity
> He lends out money gratis, and brings down
> The rate of Usance here with us in Venice.[21]

Shylock's first reason cited is religious prejudice yet, he quickly reverses this
to place greater emphasis on profit. Here Shakespeare uses a standard convention of all Elizabethan theatre in that a character speaking alone confides
in the audience secret thoughts which are always taken to be true. In placing
this information as an aside, we know immediately how to interpret Shylock's
future actions: though religion may be cited, finance is always his first prior-
ity, at least at this point in the play. Herein lies an essential difference between
Shakespeare's Shylock and Marlowe's Barabas: Shylock is changed by the
events of the play and made to realize, especially through the loss of his
daughter, the value of his heritage, whereas Barabas has no such epiphany
and continues to the end as hateful as he began.

Immediately after this aside, Shylock cites as a parable an Old Testament
story, with which the Christians curiously do not seem familiar. His meaning
is lost upon them. Shylock seems to enjoy his momentary "upper-hand." As
he teases them with successful completion of the bargain with Antonio, however, Shakespeare has Shylock cite specific examples of what modern society
would label "hate crimes" of which Antonio and his fellows have been guilty.
These are quite specific and underscore the deep impact of such actions on
Shylock. At the same time, in his lawyer's method of framing an argument,
Shylock clearly establishes the sense of being the more charitable of the two
in seeming to forgive these injuries in order to come to Antonio's assistance,
ironically turning Christian virtue on its end. Eventually, Shylock agrees,
making light of past grievances and springs his trap, the seemingly ridiculous
insurance for the bond with a pound of Antonio's flesh. Thinking the old man
disordered in his mind, Antonio agrees.

The most famous of Shylock's speeches provides vital clues to his inner
life. Shakespeare reveals much of his creation's priorities in Act Three scene
one. Crucial to understanding Shylock's passion in this moment is to recall
that this follows immediately upon his learning of his daughter's betrayal; of

her rejection of her father and her heritage. He enters fuming over his humiliation and loss. After much teasing and mockery, Salarino finally asks Shylock of what use he would make of this pound of Antonio's flesh. Prompted by the taunting of the young men, Shylock erupts with:

> To bait fish withall, if it will feed nothing
> else, it will feed my revenge;[22]

The young men are clearly intimidated by the passion and the barbarity of Shylock's reply. Shylock builds on this moment by cataloguing the wrongs he (and his people) have received at Christian hands:

> He hath disgrac'd me, and
> hindred me half a million, laughed at my losses, mocked at
> my gains, scorned my Nation, thwarted my bargains,
> cooled my friends, heated mine enemies . . .[23]

This list is illuminating not only for the variety of the injustices but more so, for the order in which they occur to Shylock. He begins with matters of pride, but pride as found through his business dealings. Speaking specifically of Antonio but implying all Christians he implies that these are all done to thwart without just cause conjuring an air of persecution. Oddly, however, in the midst of this catalogue, Shylock adds that Antonio has "scorned my Nation." This is added in such a way as to almost discount religion as a source of his pain, though he has used this earlier and will return to this again as a source of his own hatred. Shakespeare concedes to the popular stereotype which Marlowe had provided in Barabas, yet provides richer psychological underpinnings with the hint of Shylock's hypocrisy. Lastly, he concludes with the assertion that Antonio has "cooled" his friends and "heated" his enemies — an image to which he will shortly return.

Coming in the midst of this tirade, one must wonder just what the nature of Shylock's Judaism might be? To what extent, then, is Shylock true to his faith? How important is tradition to him, or is this merely a ploy, a convenient cover for his more mercenary intentions? Obviously, Shylock suffers a great conflict between his traditional faith and his hopes for social inclusion and prosperity. Left here, one might conclude that Shylock is purely mercenary and superficial.

Yet, Shakespeare does not end there. Shylock continues in what is now the most famous of Shakespeare's pleas for tolerance. Yet the parallels Shylock draws between himself and his Christian adversaries carry a deeper significance and a darker threat.

> . . . And what's the reason? I am a Jew: Hath not a Jew eyes?
> Hath not a Jew hands, organs, dimensions, senses, affections,
> passions, fed with the same food, hurt with the same weapons,
> subject to the same diseases, healed by the same means,
> warmed and cooled by the same Winter and Summer as
> a Christian is: if you prick us do we not bleed? If you tickle us,
> do we not laugh? If you poison us do we not die? And if
> you wrong us shall we not revenge?[24]

Having drawn these vivid similarities, Shylock comes to the present point: racial prejudice and the double standard of Christian morality:

> If we are like you in the rest, we will resemble you
> in that. If a Jew wrong a Christian, what is his humility?
> Revenge. If a Christian wrong a Jew, what should his sufferance
> be by Christian example? Why revenge.[25]

Hard-driven, he concludes with a threat which is equally double-edged:

> The villainy you teach me I will execute, and it shall go hard
> but I will better the instruction.[26]

   With these words, Shylock's future motivations are made clear. He has at once made a logical argument for his equality with the Venetian Christians pointing out their likeness in all aspects of humanity save one: religion. Their prejudice is neatly determined to be one of faith. The burden for this tension is clearly set upon the Christians and the responsibility for any future hardships or cruelty Shylock claims will be merely his own imitation of themselves. As they so clearly seek his imitation of Christianity, he resolves to give it them. Perhaps, in a subtle turn of Christian practice, Shylock may be seen to absolve his future sins in this final turning of logic.
   The betrayal of a child, in particular a daughter, is a theme Shakespeare would return to—most famously in Lear: "How sharper than a serpent's tooth it is to have a thankless child. (*King Lear,* Line 312)." Yet Shylock's betrayal at the hands of his daughter runs deeper than we might immediately see as the wrong encompasses her rejection of his solitary paternal care (presumably as a widower) of his social position within their community and, more importantly perhaps, of their religion and cultural heritage. As Jessica is now a 'New Christian' Shylock would also know, in advance, the uneasy and fruitless path his daughter had chosen as one who would never truly be accepted by the faith which she chose to embrace. As a father, responsible for matching his daughter to a man who could provide as he had done, this betrayal from within would seem most treacherous on many levels. He curses her, cry-

ing out, "I would my daughter were dead at my feet and the jewels in her ear."[27]

This is a clear reference to fifteenth century sumptuary laws of Northern Italy requiring all Jewish women to pierce their ears and wear earrings as an identification mark.[28] In this scene, as Shylock curses her betrayal and the loss of his jewels, he seems to wish her return to her faith as well as her death. The most intimate moment and most revealing glimpse of the inner Shylock also is provided at the end of this same scene, when Tubal lastly confesses to Shylock the news of Jessica's pawning of his precious turquoise ring for a mere monkey. This clearly devastates Shylock, and that Tubal held this to the end indicates he knew of sentimental significance of this ring and anticipated the impact of such a frivolous loss. Shylock confides:

> Out upon her. Thou torturest me, Tubal, it was my Turquoise;
> I had it of my Leah when that I was a bachelor:
> I would not have parted with it for a wilderness of monkeys.[29]

This is a moment of intensely personal and intimate confession and the only mention of Jessica's mother. The significance of the ring, therefore, is used to heighten our perception of Shylock as a grieving man subject to injury and immediately recalls his comparisons of Christians and Jews made but moments before. The placement of this deeply felt moment immediately after such a logical and humanist argument for compassion clearly sets our moral judgment of Shylock on edge.

In Act Three scene three Antonio's ships are lost; his bond is due. Shakespeare provides a moment of confrontation as Antonio, bound for prison, pursues Shylock. That the Jailor accompanies Antonio and has clearly been advocating his case to Shylock is a telling aspect of this scene. The dialogue characteristically begins in mid-conversation as Shylock enters protesting their pleas for sympathy. His part in the scene is brief as he repeats his determination to pursue his bond. He reminds Antonio, once again, of past injuries and, repeats his warning of danger by Christian example:

> Thou calls't me dog before thou had'st a cause,
> But since I am a dog, beware my fangs.[30]

Shylock's sole argument seems to be that he swore an oath and must not relent, yet, of course, there is more. He turns to a question of his image on the Rialto, among his peers:

> I'll not be made a sot and dull eyed fool,
> To shake my head, relent, and sigh, and yield

To Christian intercessors: follow not,
I'll have no speaking, I will have my bond.[31]

On this, Shylock exits. His rushing out at first suggests impatience yet the mere repetition of his argument suggests a hidden fear that he will, in fact, relent. That he mentions this at all suggests his resolve is weakening. He has no further argument in his favor but one of honor and his oath.

In Act Four, Antonio is brought to trial. The Duke urges Shylock to be merciful asking for a "gentle answer" (playing perhaps unconsciously on the words "gentle" and "gentile.") Shylock begins his reply by restating his intention to pursue his bond furthering the argument by reminding the court that he has taken a sacred oath upon his Sabbath. He then launches into a long speech in which he equivocates rather than openly answers. Elizabethans would have immediately recognized this action as one of Catholic deviousness for equivocation was a tactic taught to all Catholic missionaries as a means of confessing information under torture without actual incrimination and the damnation of lying. Any form of such avoidance in discussion was rendered highly suspect, therefore, in Elizabethan England. That Shylock equivocates seems to demonstrate in him a measure of ill-fated hubris but also taps into popular fears, not of Jews but of Catholics.

When asked again for mercy, Shylock turns to a comparison between the newly revived Christian practice of slavery (and the treatment of such slaves as property having been purchased) and of this pound of flesh which, also having been purchased, Shylock argues he ought to be allowed to do with as he pleases. [Given credence with Renaissance interest in Classical ideas and practices, The slave trade had begun when Columbus imported Native American slaves to Spain but the true slave trade was to follow shortly as the first black Africans were brought to Central America in 1502. The business of slavery was, consequently, well under way by Shakespeare's time.[32] That Shakespeare, through Shylock, brings slavery into the argument is a subtle reminder of the cruelty and dispassionate mind-set of the Christian adversaries. That both sides of Shylock's example are based in the concept of humans as property is a sound argument. Finally Shylock returns to Venetian law pointing out the hypocrisy of legally finding against him in this case.

The Duke has no answer but to threaten to dismiss the Court unless a certain Bellario arrives in time. A letter conveniently excuses Bellario's absence, but introduces in his stead, a learned young lawyer, Balthazar. This is, of course, the disguised Portia who is promptly ushered in to hear the case. Portia shakes the Court's confidence by immediately asking "Which is the Merchant here, and which the Jew?"[33] This must be a ruse on her part to disarm the Court and give false encouragement to Shylock, yet it builds upon the very notion that Christians and Jews are distinguishable by appearances. After gaining an immediate confession of guilt from Antonio, Portia concludes that, "Why then the Jew must be merciful."[34] Shylock demands to know the reason, which prompts Portia's famous, though misinterpreted, speech on "the Quality of Mercy."

Taken out of context, this speech embodies the power of Christianity's principles and movingly sets the standard for Charity as a means towards Godliness. The speech draws on concepts of mercy as crucial attribute of Kings but also of God. To be God-like, one must be merciful. Also, taken out of context, the speech creates the image of the Christian heroine championing her faith. Yet, taken within the context of the scene, Portia's argument takes on a judgmental and callous tone. She urges Shylock to behave according to Christian standards. She concludes this plea with,

> Therefore Jew, though justice be thy plea, consider this,
> That in the course of justice, none of us
> Should see Salvation: we do pray for mercy,
> And that same prayer, doth teach us all to render
> The deeds of mercy.[35]

Her argument is solely in Christian terms, implying a form of forced conversion. Knowing this to be repugnant to men of his faith, Portia is quite safe in making this seemingly benign request. Also, at the same moment, she puffs up the vanity of her fellow Christians in making so eloquent a case for their own faith. The device may be seen in a moment to have been clearly a trick to force Shylock into solidifying his stance against Antonio.

The ruse succeeds. Shylock is lured into Portia's net with the promise of his bond. Antonio is made to prepare for the knife. Shylock, barbaric in his ecstasy, demonstrates his preparedness by producing balances and scales as well. Here, a traditional piece of stage business is to have Shylock salaciously whetting his knife upon a stone or strap in preparation for his intended butchery. Antonio is defeated and resigns himself to his fate. He refers to himself, curiously, as a "tainted wether of the flock, meetest for death."[36] On one level, he recalls Shylock's parable of the sheep early in the play, yet in describing himself as 'tainted' meaning "castrated" as he speak tenderly to Bassanio, Antonio refers to the powerlessness of both his physical state as a condemned prisoner and his emotional state as the hopeless lover of Bassanio. Antonio has bared his soul to Bassanio and to all the court as his breast is laid bare for Shylock's ready knife.

As Shylock is on the point of incision he is stopped by Portia. Here she springs her trap. The bond makes no mention of blood. Therefore, the flesh may be taken only without bloodshed. To shed Venetian blood would be a capital offence with lands and good confiscated and reverted to the state. Prior to this moment, Shylock has been offered thrice or even double thrice the value of his bond but had refused, seeking only the letter of his bond. This obstinacy now comes back upon him. He quits the case, accepting his principal in repayment but is denied. He will have only his bond, the pound of flesh. Unable to proceed without further danger to his life, Shylock relents and makes to quit the court. Yet Portia is not so merciful, after all. She calls Shylock back citing further Venetian law.

> If it be proved against an Alien,
> That by direct, or indirect attempts
> He seeks the life of any Citizen,
> The party against the which he doth contrive,
> Shall seize one half of his goods, the other half
> Comes to the privy coffer of the State,
> And the offender's life lies in the mercy
> Of the Duke only, 'gainst all other voice.[37]

Shylock is indeed trapped. The Duke, in a great display of Christian Charity, allows Shylock his life. Yet Shylock, deprived of his property, and thereby his livelihood, insists they take all leaving him nothing on which to live. Antonio offers a harsh compromise in relinquishing his hold on half of Shylock's goods in order that Shylock may have use of them (to increase his fortune) until his death at which point his fortune should go to Shylock's 'New Christian' daughter and her seducer/husband. While this *appears* more charitable it is, in the end, a slower and more painful punishment. Yet Antonio is not quite finished. He further requires that Shylock convert to Christianity—thus depriving him of property, livelihood, family, community and religion. But for his life itself, Shylock's destruction is complete.

From an Elizabethan Protestant standpoint, Shylock's treatment at the hands of Antonio would have seemed righteous. Yet, the undercurrent hypocrisy of these cruel and excessive punishments advocated and heartily cheered so soon after Portia's eloquent plea for mercy and the Godliness of forgiveness is not to be lost. The psychological no-man's land of those forcibly converted must have resonated deeply with Shakespeare's audiences, who, though cheering for Shylock's punishment, must have been taken aback by this sudden and final thrust.

In converting to Christianity, Jessica had cast off her cultural heritage, the very point upon which her traditional identity is hung. As vital part of that culture, there could be no worse crime than to go against family, tradition and faith. Conversion forced or otherwise, is a recurring theme in this play as

Shylock in the end is made to accept Christianity. As such, in losing his suit against Antonio Shylock loses all of his property, but he is forced to reject the one treasure he might retain—his traditional religion and his cultural identity. Finally, out-maneuvered of his property and of his livelihood, Shylock is stripped of his heritage; forced to embrace that which embodies all he fears and detests. Cast out from all he is a true 'Outsider' made to wander like Oedipus, in a cultural and emotional no-man's land.

ART IMITATES LIFE

Theatrical tradition, ironically, holds that Shakespeare acted Antonio himself. As Elizabethan playwrights wrote for the specific talents of the company, and there is much that is autobiographical in the relationship of the two male characters, Shakespeare surely wrote the role with himself in mind. In this case, one may easily imagine Shakespeare working out his own depression and psychological turmoil through his writing. For a man who was so carefully guarded, his private sonnets and *The Merchant of Venice* offer especial insight as we see his guard drop slightly in the midst of deep personal crisis.

Given the emotional turbulence of Shakespeare's life from the death of his only son through the futile passion for William Herbert and the self-effacing affair with Emilia Lanier, *The Merchant of Venice*, created at the climax of these events, reveals more of the private man than may have been imagined. Shakespeare's emotional attachments and his psychological reactions to them may be more completely understood if the sonnets and *The Merchant of Venice* are viewed together as forms of autobiography. One may well imagine the tensions he must have felt; the anguish over his confusion of emotion, the final recognition of his wrongs and his certainty of judgment.

THE PLEA FOR TOLERANCE

In *The Merchant of Venice* Shakespeare addresses the deep-seated fears of Shakespeare's countrymen. Though centered on the conflict between Christian and Jewish moral values, the play forces its audience to examine deeply personal issues. Shakespeare expands on a story of conflicting moral codes and rash actions creating characters whose motives are never as they appear and whose Faith, based in Love, is used as a rallying point for blatant brutality. *The Merchant of Venice* was not intended to address Anti-Semitism but rather one of much deeper concern for Elizabethan audiences, and for Shakespeare himself. The play's religious intolerance dramatized the turmoil faced by Elizabethan England. Yet, Shakespeare does not, as Marlowe had done, solidly endorse the status quo. All of the characters in *Merchant* (Christians and Jews alike) are singularly self-serving and unscrupulous. Neither faction— Christians nor Jews—emerges in a good light. Shylock, though he may be seen in a more sympathetic light, becomes (as he, himself promised) as inhumane as his Christian persecutors. In *The Merchant of Venice* Christian right triumphs. But, Shakespeare seems to ask, "At what cost?"

As a comedy, the play includes a seemingly traditional tale of romance ending in marriage. Yet this is no union of "True Love" as the lovers are clearly more interested in power and money. Their poetic declarations ring insincere. Shakespeare's view of love at this juncture seems dark indeed. Considering that he was writing this play at the peak of his disgrace at the hands of the "Dark Lady" this seems quite natural. Ironically, only one sincere love emerges in the play, the love of Antonio for Bassanio, and as this takes an untraditional form raises its own questions. The play "brings to the table" issues of love—genuine and unfettered by boundaries of gender—set against the love of money and power.

The title lends us a clue as to Shakespeare's intentions. The play is not about Shylock, the obvious "Other," though he is at the center of the play; nor is it about Bassanio and Portia, the ostensibly "happy couple." *The Merchant of Venice* is Antonio—the lone man who ventures all—money, reputation, even life—for his love of Bassanio. Yet just as, at the peak of Shylock's obsession with crushing Antonio, he is returned to a very human level through the loss of his daughter – and of his precious turquoise ring; Antonio, as his fate reverses, immediately turns to destroy Shylock. For all the cant of forgiveness, rational thinking and mercy, Antonio is not above the ruthlessness of his fellow Christians. His triumph over Shylock, therefore, is made hollow by the savagery with which he exacts his revenge.

Shakespeare has shifted attention from the obvious contest of religious ideologies to the more subtle limitations of our definition of love. What emerges as heroic, in this play, is a love that is faithful. Faith, therefore, takes on dimensions more intimate and more relative, than creed or dogma. *The Merchant of Venice*, seen as the culmination of a period of intense internal struggle, emerges as Shakespeare's plea for tolerance. Out of the pain of his own experience, Shakespeare argues that intolerance of any kind negates our Divine Spark. As a humanist, he asks us to become more humane.

That Shakespeare was a practicing Catholic cannot be proved, but the secret Catholic traditions of his rural upbringing surely shaped his life and work. A protest against religious intolerance seems clearly present in spirit. The sexual stance established in his sonnets, also plainly place him in a position of guarded neutrality and secret sympathy. Through his Art, Shakespeare published a recurring plea for release from fear and suspicion, advocating human decency and the private freedom of personal beliefs. In his age, as indeed in any of spiritual ambiguity, fear and distrust fused to create a social energy of directed hatred and religious hypocrisy. Through the living Theatre Shakespeare urged and continues ever strongly to urge the forging of a New World from within.

NOTES

1. James Shapiro, *Shakespeare and the Jews* (New York: Columbia University Press, 1996), 78.
2. Shapiro, 196.
3. Shapiro, 190.
4. Shapiro, 214.
5. Michael Wood, *Shakespeare* (New York: Basic Books, 2004), 7.
6. Wood, 11.
7. http://www.jewishencyclopedia.com/view.jsp?artid=544&letter=L
8. Stephen Greenblatt, *Will in the World* (New York: Norton Press, 2004), 277.
9. Wood, 124.
10. Wood, 165, 166.
11. Greenblatt, 312.
12. Wood, 305.
13. Wood, 180.
14. Wood, 195, 196.
15. "Sonnet 129," in William Shakespeare, *The Complete Works of William Shakespeare* (London: Spring Books, 1970).
16. Shapiro, 126.
17. William Shakespeare, William, The *Merchant of Venice, First Folio Edition of 1623*, Lines 31–33.
18. Seymour Kleinberg, *"The Merchant of Venice*: The Homosexual as Anti-Semite in Nascent Capitalism," in *Literary Versions of Homosexuality*, ed. Stuart Kellog (New York: Haworth, 1983); James O'Rourke, *Racism and Homophobia in the Merchant of Venice* (Baltimore, Maryland: Johns Hopkins University Press, 2003); and Steve Patterson, "The Bankruptcy of Homoerotic Amity in Shakespeare's *Merchant of Venice," Shakespeare Quarterly*, vol. 50, no. 1, Spring,1999.
19. *Merchant of Venice*, Line 170.
20. *Merchant of Venice*, Lines 355–61.
21. *Merchant of Venice*, Lines 364–368.
22. *Merchant of Venice*, Lines 1265–66.
23. *Merchant of Venice*, Lines 1266–70.
24. *Merchant of Venice*, Lines 1270–78.
25. *Merchant of Venice*, Lines 1279–82.
26. *Merchant of Venice*, Lines 12830–84.

27. *Merchant of Venice*, Line 1300–01.

28. Shapiro, 120.

29. *Merchant of Venice*, Lines 1331–33.

30. *Merchant of Venice*, Lines 1692–93.

31. *Merchant of Venice*, Lines 1700–03.

32. Paul Kuritz, *The Making of Theatre History* (Englewood Cliffs, New Jersey: Prentice Hall, 1988), 154.

33. *Merchant of Venice*, Line 2082.

34. *Merchant of Venice*, Line 2093.

35. *Merchant of Venice*, Line 2008–13.

36. *Merchant of Venice*, Line 2021–22.

37. *Merchant of Venice*, Line 1267–74.

Chapter Four

"The 'New Marginality:' Representations of the *Favela* in Recent Brazilian Cinema"

Tia Malkin-Fontecchio, West Chester
University of Pennsylvania

After reaching an all time low in 1992, when only two feature length films were produced, Brazilian cinema experienced a renaissance in the late 1990s. Film production boomed; Brazil produced 155 feature films between 1995 and 2000.[1] The number of first time directors and the size of the national audience increased dramatically. The international community recognized the high quality of Brazilian films with prestigious awards, including four Academy Awards nominations.

Despite the fact that Brazilian cinema started the twenty first century with new direction, many of the films produced since 1995 show clear roots in past Brazilian cinema, specifically in the socially conscious Cinema Novo (New Cinema) of the 1960s. Brazilian directors continue to focus on themes related to the Brazilian social reality—poverty, regional contrasts, urban violence, and criminality. In particular, Brazilian cinema has returned to the *favela* (or shanty towns) as a primary focus in recent years, addressing a complex set of issues related to *favela* life but mainly focusing on the violence of the *favelas* and the role that narco-trafficking gangs have played in the escalation of that violence.

In Latin American urban geography there is a tendency to concentrate the middle class and wealthy in the city center and relegate the poor to the geographical margins. This is true in Rio de Janeiro. The center of the city is ringed with suburbs and peripheral neighborhoods; while the rich are concentrated in the Zona Sul (the South Zone or Rio's beach area), the poor find themselves on the outer edge and in the hillside *favelas* of the city, creating a vertical and horizontal division of city. *Favela* is the Brazilian term for urban slums or irregular settlements that line the hills of Rio de Janeiro and other urban centers in Brazil. While there are competing estimates of how many *favelas* exist in Rio de Janeiro—some studies argue the number is as high as 752, but the official government Census of 2000 identified only 516—one thing is clear: the *favelas* are resident to an ever increasing share of Rio de Janeiro's population. Even if we follow the more conservative estimate of the 2000 Census, 1.65 million people or close to twenty percent of the urban population of Rio de Janeiro lives in the *favelas*. During every decade from 1950 to 2000, with the exception of the 1980s, the *favelas* grew at a much higher rate than the population of the "formal city" of Rio de Janeiro.[2]

While the *favela* is not a new subject for film, the way Brazilian film represents the *favela* and its residents has changed significantly over time. Early representations romanticized the *favela* and the poverty of its residents (*favelados*). These early films often focused on the culture of the *favela*—the music and dance of samba—linking samba, Afro-Brazilians and the *favela* with *brasilidade* or Brazilian national identity. The most notable examples of this representation are *Favela dos Meus Amores* (*Favela of My Loves*, 1935) and *Orfeu Negro* (*Black Orpheus*, 1959), the French-Brazilian collaboration, directed by Marcel Camus.

Significant changes came in the late 1950s. A new group of filmmakers who were interested in creating a "national" and "popular" cinema, began to focus on what they perceived to be more genuinely Brazilian themes rather than imitating Hollywood films. They produced independent, low budget films often times using nonprofessional actors.[3] Out of this movement came two productions about the *favelas* by director Nelson Pereira dos Santos, *Rio 40 Graus* (*Rio 40 Degrees*, 1954) and *Rio Zona Norte* (Rio North Zone, 1957). These films portrayed *favelados* and Afro-Brazilians in a new way; instead of the paternalistic representation of earlier films, dos Santos created a "sympathetic" portrait of the daily struggles of the urban poor.[4] The Cinema Novo of the early 1960s continued to engage the topic of the *favela*, further elaborating on this more critical approach to filmmaking. Brazilian filmmakers such as Glauber Rocha, Carlos Diegues, Ruy Guerra and Nelson Pereira Santos organized the Cinema Novo movement around the assumption that political, social, and aesthetic change was needed in Brazil. The movement was influenced by the political context in which it originated, first the increased leftist activity of the early 1960s and then the repressive military regime after 1964. At least in its early stage it was optimistic about transforming society through its critical gaze. As Carlos Diegues expressed it early in the movement: "Cinema Novo is a committed cinema, a critical cinema . . . Brazilian filmmakers . . . have taken their cameras and gone out into the streets, the country, and the beaches in search of the Brazilian people, the peasant, the worker, the fisherman, the slum dweller."[5] In his famous 1965 essay, "The Aesthetics of Hunger," Glauber Rocha looked back on the early years of Cinema Novo and noted the need for a cinematic style that would represent the real Brazil, the Brazil of hunger, frustration, lack of hope and violence. "Cinema Novo shows that the normal behavior of the starving is violence."[6] While Cinema Novo films primarily focused attention on the hunger and misery of the *sertão* (the Northeastern backlands plagued by drought), *Cinco Vezes Favela (Favela Five Times*, 1961), is an early example of Cinema Novo that specifically centers on urban poverty.[7]

As noted above, Brazilian cinema has returned to the *favela* as a primary focus in recent years. The main goal of this essay is to highlight the various ways in which recent Brazilian films have attempted to address the social reality of the *favela*. These new films are not just a response to the 1960s social reality of poverty and exclusion but to the violence that has erupted in the *favelas* since the expansion of drug trafficking in the 1980s. Social exclusion is well documented, but recently drug traffickers and *favelados* have called attention to the "new marginality" by symbolically bringing violence out of the *favelas* and suburbs and into the Zona Sul. The marginalized youth of Rio de Janeiro made themselves visible through the *arrastões* or "beach sweeps" of 1992. Groups, sometimes as large as 300, would descend on the middle- and upper-class beaches of the Zona Sul and steal everything in sight. These "sweeps" received much media attention and even made international headlines. Films directors such as Carlos Diegues and Fernando Meirelles have attempted to do the same by making films like *Orfeu* and *Cidade de Deus*.

These films are the cinematic response to the increasing violence in the *favelas* of Rio de Janeiro. Rio de Janeiro has one of the highest murder rates in the world; in the last ten years murder rates have averaged 50 per 100,000. However, if one considers just the *favelas* and poor neighborhoods, those rates are actually much higher—over 150 per 100,000.[8] Both the Brazilian media and cinema have devoted more space to the topic as violence has increased.

FAVELAS, MARGINALITY, AND THE CITY DIVIDED

When in the late 1990s Brazilian cinema became fixated on the filmic representation of Rio de Janeiro as a divided city, filmmakers were explicitly drawing on a conceptual framework developed by Brazilian journalist and writer Zuenir Ventura in his 1994 book *Cidade Partida*. Ventura painted a portrait of a city divided into two parts—the wealthy or middle class Zona Sul and the impoverished *favelas*.[9] This division is often described by *favelados* as the division between the *favelas* (*morros*) and the *asfalto* (literally the cement but used to refer to the rest of the city). This division is not necessarily one of physical geography as the *favelas* and middle class neighborhoods are often adjacent to one another. For most of the twentieth century this division could be conceptualized as one of social class and material deprivation. Traditionally, *favelas* have been defined as places of chronic poverty and traditional culture and values. They have also been defined by what they lack: title to property (most were squatter settlements), access to city services (electricity, water, garbage collection, schools), and jobs. In contrast, *O Globo*, Rio de Janeiro's most respected newspaper, could boast in 2003 that "a still incomplete study by the city government . . . shows that if the region formed by Ipanema, Leblon, Lagoa, Jardim Botânico, Gávea, São Conrado, and Vidigal [the Zona Sul] were an independent country, it would have the highest Human Development Index on the planet."[10] The *favelas* and the middle class neighborhoods are spatially near but socially distant from one another.

Ventura spent ten months researching in one of Rio's large favelas, Vigário Geral—a *favela* where in 1991 the military police had massacred 21 civilians. He documented that this exclusion was a long-standing problem in Rio de Janeiro, despite the myths that the city was characterized by conviviality stemming from the proximity of the *favelas* and the middle class neighborhoods of the Zona Sul. Indeed, the origins of the modern *favela* are in Brazil's Old Republic (1889–1930). Homeless veterans of the Canudos War established the first squatter settlement in Rio de Janeiro upon their return in 1897.[11] In order to protest the fact that the federal government had not paid them, the soldiers settled on the Morro da Providência near the War Ministry. The soldiers named their community *favela* because of the presence of a plant that grows in the same region as where they had fought the war (the northeastern state of Bahia).

Cortiços, slums or tenements located in the downtown area, were more common than *favelas* in turn-of-the-century Rio de Janeiro. However, the Brazilian elite deemed these tenements, and the city center as a whole, to be overpopulated, dirty and unhealthy. As a result they soon embarked on an urbanization project that hoped to remake Rio de Janeiro in the image of Paris. The Old Republic's civilizing campaign would bring "Order and Progress" by razing the tenements and forcibly relocating their residents to the periphery. Major removal schemes for *cortiços* and *favelas* began in earnest in 1902, when the city mayor Pereira Passos launched an urban project that widened the streets and razed over 1,600 tenements. These projects were expanded in the 1920s.[12] Thus, the first *favelas* were not only the result of soldiers protesting the failure of the state to pay them back wages, they were the result of a preexisting shortage of housing for the poor exacerbated by modernization schemes.

While the First Republic's civilizing campaign would dramatically increase the population in the informal *favela* settlements, the *Estado Novo*

(New State, 1930–1945) which followed, did nothing to improve the housing situation for the poor. It proposed removing *favelados* to *parque proletários* (state housing projects that were closely regulated) and eliminating the *favelas*.[13] The *Estado Novo* also continued to imagine the *favelas* as a social problem or disease, refusing even to locate them on maps. In fact, *favelas* were not located on maps of Rio de Janeiro until the 1970s; prior to that time they appeared as green spaces.[14] Under the Second Republic (1945–1964), Brazil returned to democratic rule. The government, however, maintained a weak presence in the communities and most improvements that were made were the result of community organizing. It is during this time that *favelados* began to organize local governance, including vigilante groups to maintain public order and settle disputes. They also began to cut illegally into city power lines to bring electricity to the communities. Populist politicians courted the popular vote in the *favelas* but offered relatively few improvements.[15] The military government of 1964–1985 did little to improve conditions in the *favelas*; instead they stepped up efforts to remove the *favelas*. Between 1968 and 1975, the government removed over 100,000 people and destroyed seventy *favelas*.[16] In conclusion, over the course of the twentieth century state policy towards the *favelas* changed little. Minimal effort was made to integrate the "informal city" with the formal one; proposals to solve the "social problem" of the *favela* almost exclusively focused on removal.

Despite the fact that the government did little to improve the quality of life in the *favelas,* the reality is that today many socio-economic groups live in *favelas*, and water, paved streets, electricity, and schools are typical as well. However, most of these improvements came, at least initially, as the result of community organized *mutirão* or self-help projects.

The one thing that all the *favelas* continue to have in common is crime and violence. When middle class residents refer to the *favelados* as *marginais* they do not mean to say the marginalized or socially excluded. *Marginal* stands in for criminal in current Brazilian Portuguese. Today the residents of the *favelas* (and suburbs) are isolated more by the violence and the control of drug trafficking gangs than their poverty.

Three gangs dominate Rio de Janeiro's *favelas*: the Red Command (*Comando Vermelho*), the Third Command (*Comando Terceiro*) and the Friends of Friends (*Amigos de Amigos*). These gangs are networks to distribute guns and drugs, particularly cocaine. Before the late 1970s, the drug trade in the *favelas* was local and mainly in marijuana. Change came because the Colombian drug cartels switched their transit routes for cocaine being sent to the United States and Europe. Cities like Rio and São Paulo became transshipment locations and as they increased in importance new consumer markets developed locally.[17] According to government estimates, these drug cartels send $15 million in drugs (cocaine and marijuana) through Rios *favelas* each month. Only 20 percent stays in the *favelas*; the other 80 percent is shipped to Europe and the United States.[18]

Some scholars, such as Brazilian sociologist Luiz Eduardo Soares, go so far as to argue that the drug traffickers have carved out feudal bases of power in the *favelas* where the State has no authority:

> The territorial control of the bandits subtracts the zones of urban poverty from the national State and creates an archipelago of independent areas, a species of clandestine feudal barony, nonetheless visible, that the law cannot reach, where democratic institutions, the Constitution, and the law do not operate.[19]

Other scholars argue that the drug traffickers have come to offer a parallel state structure, but emphasize the fact that the gangs offer the *favela* services that the national government cannot or refuses to provide. The gangs provide public security (no crime is tolerated within the areas they control), jobs and community support (paying for soccer fields and hosting large dance parties called *bailes funk*). However, it would be incorrect to argue that the Brazilian nation state maintains no presence in the *favelas*. Since the beginning of re-democratization in the 1980s the government has expanded the number of schools, improved the quality and supply of water, and increased its police presence in the *favelas*.

A discussion of the *favelas* and the "new marginality" would not be complete without some explanation of the role that the police play in the communities. The increase in the activities and overall strength of the drug gangs has led to more military and police interventions in the *favelas*. The Brazilian police force is divided into uniformed *Polícia Militar* (Military Police or PM) and the plainclothed *Polícia Civil* (Civil Police or PC). The PC carry out investigations while the PM play a more direct role in the day-to-day maintenance of order. Both the PC and PM are corrupt, and the PC play a direct role in the drug trade, arranging for the purchase of weapons and accepting payoffs to aid in the movement of drugs. In recent years, the Rio de Janeiro state government has organized an increasing number of police raids on the *favelas*. These raids, led by a special division of the PM called the *Batalhão de Operações Policiais Especiais* (Special Police Operations Battalion or BOPE), result in shootouts between the police and the drug gangs. While these raids have not broken the power of the drug gangs, they have resulted in the loss of civilian life and further decreased quality of life for those living in the *favelas*.[20]

I will now turn to a discussion of two recent cinematic representations of the *favela*, *Orfeu* and *Cidade de Deus*. The following section will explore whether the films employ the metaphor of the divided city and whether or not they reproduce past stereotypes (positive and negative) about the *favelas*. If the films employ the metaphor of the divided city, how do they represent the divide? Is it one based on simply on the violence of the drug economy? Or do they make visible the underlying structures of race and class that have historically divided Brazil? Do the films clearly distinguish between civilians and criminals in the film? Do the films represent all *favela* residents as criminals?

ORFEU

In Carlos Diegues's *Orfeu*, the myth of Orpheus serves as the backdrop for a story about violence and the drug trade in Rio de Janiero's *favelas*. Through the development of this story another story emerges, one that focuses on the cultural richness and diversity of the *favela*. While the film contests the old myth of marginality, it confirms the idea that drug trafficking and police corruption are responsible for the new marginalization of the *favelados*. In addition, the film does not explicitly engage in a discussion of the role that race plays in social exclusion and in fact does much to confirm Brazil's long-standing myth of racial democracy.

The film is a retelling of the Greek myth of Orpheus and Eurydice and specifically of Brazilian playwright and composer Vinicius de Moraes' play *Orfeu da Conceição*. This is of course not the first time a Rio de Janeiro *favela* has served as the setting for this myth. *Black Orpheus,* by French director Marcel Camus, was also set in a *favela* and involved an Afro-Brazilian cast. Despite the fact that Carlos Diegues, director of *Orfeu*, has denied that the film is in dialogue with the original, one can see clear connections.

Orfeu is a well-off samba composer, musician, and leader of a local *escola de samba* (samba school). He is a celebrity both in the *favela* and Rio in general. By contrast, the main character Lucinho, the drug lord, is white. The film is set on Carioca Hill, an imaginary *favela* in Rio de Janeiro. The story unfolds as the *favela* prepares for Carnival. Orfeu and his family are respected members of the community. Eurydice is a migrant from Acre, in Brazil's distant North, who comes to the *favela* in search of a distant cousin after the death of her father. For Orfeu it is love at first sight; soon after meeting Eurydice ends his relationship with his current girlfriend Mira, a beautiful and confident Playboy centerfold, to be with Eurydice. But of course things do not go well for Orfeu and Eurydice. As Carnival begins, a confrontation is brewing between the police and the local drug gang. The drug dealer, Lucinho, is a childhood friend of Orfeu. Orfeu asserts his role as a leader of the community and orders Lucinho to leave Carioca Hill. While Orfeu is

competing with the *escola de samba*, his image broadcast to millions on
Brazilian television, Lucinho accidentally kills Eurydice. After winning the
Carnival competition, Orfeu returns to Carioca Hill and discovers that Eurydice has been killed. He then proceeds to take vengeance on Lucihno. After
recovering Eurydice's body from below Carioca Hill, he returns to the Hill
where he encounters Mira and her friends. Mira then takes her revenge on Orfeu, mortally wounding him when she stabs him with a carnival prop.

Unlike other recent *favela* films, such as *Noticia de uma Guerra Particular* (*News from a Private War*, 1999) and *Cidade de Deus*, Diegues did not
film *Orfeu* on location. As a result, the film is a self-conscious recreation of
a *favela* and its residents. This fictional *favela* is represented as a positive
place despite the prevalence of violence and criminality. For Diegues, the
favela is a place of diversity and cultural productivity:

> I'm really trying to examine what's happening in this social environment that I
> know so well. The paradox in Rio's *favelas* today is that those slums are, at one
> and the same time, a social shame—the place where people excluded from reg-
> ular Brazilian society are ghettoized—but also a cultural treasure. They are cre-
> ating a new music, a new architecture, a new language, new customs.[21]

The diversity and cultural strength of the *favela* is represented in the film
through the population of the *favela* and the production of the *escola de
samba*. Orfeu and his family appear to be almost middle class. They live in a
multi-room house with a breath-taking view of Rio de Janeiro and Guanabara
Bay. The house is outfitted with all the trappings of modern life: sewing machines, televisions, laptop computers, cell phones and music equipment. The
samba that Orfeu composes for Carnival on a laptop computer is a modern
mix of samba, hip-hop and funk.

There is of course much truth in this representation of the *favela*. Orfeu is
part of an intact nuclear family, with strong relationship with both parents.
While his parents are divided on the issue of religion (his father is an evangelical Christian and his mother practices Candomblé, an Afro-Brazilian religion),
this only reaffirms the diversity of the Brazilian population. The film thus con-
tradicts the typical images of marginality—the favela as having a culture of
poverty (criminality, family breakdown, pessimism, and parochialism) that reproduces itself. Even Eurydice, who arrives from the parochial Northern state
of Acre, arrives by plane. Religiosity is also dealt with but again in a way that
emphasizes diversity and modern developments rather than traditionality.

The film purposely highlights Brazil's racial diversity, showing a wide variety of racial types. Orfeu and his family are black. Mira is biracial. Eurydice
is brown (*moreno* or *pardo* is Brazilian Portuguese). Lucinho, the police officer "Paraiba" and a significant number faces in the crowd are white (although

most members of his gang are black or mulatto). There is even a scene in the movie where a bar owner is shown to be Chinese (he is referred to as Mr. Fumanchu). The positive role models in the community are all dark skinned and the leader of the drug gang and the corrupt police officers are white. The film thus reproduces many of the stereotypes about race relations in Brazil that stem from Gilberto Freyre's *Casa Grande e Senzala* (*The Master and the Slaves*) and misses the opportunity to highlight the prevalence of racism in Brazil. While the cast of *Orfeu* may represent a microcosm of Brazil as a whole, it misrepresents the racial and ethnic make-up of the typical *favela* community. Brazil's system of racial classification is very ambiguous and often complicates North American understandings of Brazilian race relations. But according to the 1991 Brazilian Census the majority of Rio de Janeiro's *favelados* were nonwhite.[22] The typical understanding of Brazil's residential distribution is that there is not racial segregation only class segregation. Films such as *Orfeu* explicitly confirm this myth by overemphasizing that *favelas* are multiracial places where whites and non-whites are equally represented.

Orfeu debunks the original myth of marginality and engages in a discussion of the new marginality.[23] The films demonstrates that the *favela* is part of the urban fabric—connected to Rio but through carnival—and connected to a modern global culture and economy. In advancing this connection, it shows that *favelados* are not resisting modernity, but rather they are consumers and producers of modern Brazilian culture.

The film is also an answer to the media representation of the *favela* as a place inhabited solely by criminals. The film clearly distinguishes between "civilian" and "criminals" and shows how the vast majority of residents of the *favela* are for the most part victims of violence and criminality and not criminals themselves. It also attempts to explore the relationship between the "civilian" and the "criminals" within the community. The film shows how both children and young adults are drawn into the gangs by the promise of material reward. It further demonstrates that the larger community tolerates or even supports the gangs because of what the gangs offer to the community in return. Eurydice's cousin Carmen is quick to explain that Lucinho has helped her out on many an occasion, giving her money to get by when she was out of work and even buying her a television. Much has been written about the positive role that gangs play in creating a sense of personal security and maintaining order in Rio de Janeiro's slums in the absence of real policing. This issue is dealt with directly in the scene where Lucinho dispenses justice in the case of a man accused of raping an adolescent girl.

In conclusion, despite addressing the issue of narco-trafficking drug violence and police corruption, *Orfeu* is a highly romanticized portrayal of Rio's *favelas*, in particular with respect to race relations and cultural production.

The film's attempt to expose the brutality and violence of the drug wars is overpowered by the competing themes of the *favela's* diversity and its rich popular culture.

CIDADE DE DEUS

The *favela* depicted in *Cidade de Deus* stands in stark contrast to the Carioca Hill of *Orfeu*. *Cidade de Deus* is a real *favela* that originated as a public housing project in 1966. Furthermore, the film is based on the 1998 novel *Cidade de Deus* by Paulo Lins, a resident of the *favela*. The film charts the development of *Cidade de Deus* from its establishment in the 1960s to the 1980s. During this time this government housing project evolves from a place lacking in urban services (paved streets, electricity) and job opportunities, to a crime-ridden ghetto isolated from the rest of Rio de Janeiro. The situation inside the *favela* deteriorates as the drug trade takes off, inviting violence and police corruption. The movie clearly engages the metaphor of the city divided and suggests that the cause of the division is the expansion of the drug trade and police corruption.

As in *Orfeu*, the subject of the movie is gang warfare, drugs and criminality, but this time the film takes the insider's perspective. The film begins in the 1960s. Buscapé (Rocket), our narrator, is young boy in the *favela*. Meirelles's use of an internal narrator, while a departure from the novel that the film is based on, is critical to the movie's message. Despite the fact that the gang warfare described in the film results in the death or imprisonment of all the main characters, the movie ends with a small hint of hope in the character of Buscapé. An aspiring photographer, his photograph of Zé Pequeno (Li'l Ze) and his gang is published on the front page of a respected Rio de Janeiro newspaper. As a result, he finds himself awarded an internship at the newspaper and a means of escaping the *favela*. This escape is possible because Buscapé never becomes formally involved in the drug gangs. In the original novel (and real life) Buscapé is white; however, in the movie the director cast a black actor. Meirelles opted to cast a black actor for this role "so as not to give the idea that it is only white who turn out well."[24] Yet many scholars, such as Alba Zular, a noted anthropologist whose work in the City of God inspired Paulo Lins to write his novel, have criticized the depiction of race in *Cidade de Deus*. Zular, in particular, criticized the film for depicting the *favela* as if it were "a black ghetto." In the film, the main gang struggle is between the gang of Sandro Cenoura (Carrot) and Zé Pequeno. While Cenoura is white and Zé Pequeno is black, most of gang members on each side are black (preto) or brown (moreno). She suggested that this misrepresentation was part of an effort to market the film to an international audience, an audience already familiar with the concept of the black American ghetto.[25] This may be true, but just as likely is the possibility that Meirelles was over-compensated for the "racial democracy" depictions found in movies like *Orfeu*. The film tried to paint a more realistic picture of the *favelados*, the majority of whom are nonwhite, but it went a bit too far in this representation.

Buscapé begins the story of *favela* with the story of a group of "old-style" gangsters called the Tender Trio. The group, which includes Buscapé's brother, begins with robberies of the local gas delivery truck. They steal money from the driver but in Robin Hoodesque fashion, distribute the cooking gas to the community. The Tender Trio soon finds itself in serious trouble, however, when they organize an armed robbery of a local motel. After they have left the motel, an aspiring gangster, Dadinho (Li'l Dice) enters the motel and viciously murders everyone. The Tender Trio is blamed and the gang falls apart after the robbery. The group dissolves after they carry out an armed robbery of a brothel: Shaggy is killed by the police, Alicate (Clipper) finds religion, and Merreco (Goose) is killed by Dadinho (Lil Dice). This is the first point in the film where the question of escaping the *favela* and a life of crime is raised. It is made clear, though, that the youth of the *favela* have limited opportunities to break free of their geographical and social marginality, with conversion to Evangelical Protestantism presented early on as the only solution.

The film is divided into three parts. In the second part we find ourselves in *Cidade de Deus* during the 1970s. Zé Pequeno (Li'l Ze formerly Li'l Dice) takes over the drug-dealing business in the *favela* and expands his grip by killing all of his competition. Bené (the last of the old-style gangster or *malandros*) is accidentally murdered at a party; he had served as a moderating force in the gang. After Bené's death, Zé Pequeno moves to take over the last remaining competitor, Cenoura, and by the early 1980s gang warfare has engulfed the *favela*. At the end of the movie, everyone is either dead or imprisoned. Zé Pequeno, freed by corrupt police, is shot by a rising group of prepubescent gangsters.

Where does the average *favelado* fit into *Cidade de Deus*? While they are central to *Orfeu*, in *Cidade de Deus* practically all f*avelados* are connected to crime, violence and gangs, if not directly, then through family or romantic relationships. Thus, one must question the view of the *favelados* Meirelles conveys to middle class Brazil (as well as the global film consumer). Based on the images circulated in the media, middle-class Brazil already imagines the *favelados* as *marignais* or criminals, thieves and narco-traffickers. In various studies conducted in the last ten years, *favelados* note that the biggest problem they face in securing employment outside of the *favela* is the stigma attached to living in the *favela*.[26] While it is true that narco-trafficing is a major problem, the majority of the *favela* residents are working-class poor. It is not the violence and the criminal activity that marginalizes the *favelado*, rather it is poverty, social discrimination and racism.[27] The movie *City of God* does nothing to contest the image that *favelados* are all criminals; in fact it reaffirms this image.

Cidade de Deus also engages the issue of the drug gangs and personal security. Despite the fact that the war between the competing factions of Cenoura and Zé Pequeno (Lil Zé) end up engulfing the community in violence, Zé Pequeno insists throughout the movie that the gang helps maintain public order in the community and dispense justice. He repeatedly notes that there would be no robberies in his territory. In fact, his conflict with the child gang (the Runts), a conflict which ultimately leads to his death, stems from the fact that the Runts keep robbing members of the *favela*, despite being instructed not to. In one of the most disturbing scenes of the film, *Zé Pequeno* first shoots two of the Runts (one in the hand and the other in the foot). Then he forces a young member of his own gang, *Filé-com-Fritas* (Steak and Fries), to kill one of the two boys as a warning.

City of God presents a more realistic portrayal of the escalating gang wars over territory but not of the impact of those wars on the typical residents of the *favela*. Everyone in *City of God* is tied to crime and drugs. There is a clear conflation of *favelados* and criminals in the film. Even Buscapé the protagonist, flirts with crime; it almost seems that the only reason he does not end up in crime is that he is inept at it.

CONCLUSION

In various published interviews, filmmaker Fernando Meirelles has revealed his inspiration for making the movie. After reading the novel by Paulo Lins, Meirelles concluded that it was a story "all Brazilians should know."[28]He goes on to explain that "the book reveals a side of Brazil I didn't know. I've lived in Brazil for 45 years, and I never knew that's how things went on in the slums . . . I made City of God thinking specifically about middle class Brazilian audiences – people like me, my neighbors, my family, my friends – who want to pretend *favelas* are not our problem."[29] So in the end what do *Orfeu* and *Cidade de Deus* reveal to us about the *favelas* of Rio de Janeiro? And what remains hidden? The films demonstrate that *favelas* are places of cultural and social vitality. They also reveal that violence is increasingly part of the fabric of every day life and culture in the *favelas*. In doing so, the films repeat most of the familiar positive and negative stereotypes about the *fave-*

las. However, the underlying problem of racial and social discrimination that creates the conditions for the existence of the *favela* in the first place remains out of sight. This is the hidden problem that the Brazilian middle class want to deny and both of these films allow them to continue in a state of denial.

NOTES

1. This decline was the direct result of government reform. In the early 1990s the Brazilian President Fernando Collor de Mello closed Embrafilme, which served as a critical source of funding for Brazilian Cinema. After Collor de Mello was impeached in 1992, the government reintroduced state support with the Audiovisual Law of 1993. José Álvaro Moisés, "A New Policy for Brazilian Cinema" in *The New Brazilian Cinema,* ed. Lúcia Nagib (London and New York: I.B. Tauris & Company, 2003), 3.

2. The only reason that this was not true during the 1980s is that the government pursued an eradication policy that destroyed *favelas* and forcibly relocated over 100,000 residents during the 1970s. Janice Perlman, "The Myth of Marginality Revisited, The Case of *Favelas* of Rio de Janeiro: 1969–2003" in *Becoming Global and the New Poverty of Cities,* ed. Lisa M. Hanley, Blair A. Ruble and Joseph S. Tulchin (Washington, DC: Woodrow Wilson International Center for Scholars, 2005), 9, 11.

3. Robert Stam, *Tropical Multiculturalism: A Comparative History of Race in Brazilian History and Cinema* (Durham, North Carolina: Duke University Press, 1997), 157–158.

4. Ibid.

5. Carlos Diegues, "Cinema Novo" in *Brazilian Cinema,* ed. Robert Stam and Randal Johnson (New York: Columbia University Press, 1995), 66.

6. Glauber Rocha, "An Aesthetic of Hunger," in Stam and Johnson, *Brazilian Cinema,* 70.

7. For Cinema Novo films about the sertão see *Vida Secas* (Barren Lives, 1963) and *Deus e o Diablo na Terra do Sol* (*Black God, White Devil,* 1964). *Cinco Vezes Favela* was also unique because it was produced by the National Student Union's Centers of Popular Culture.

8. Enrique Desmond Arias, *Drugs and Democracy in Rio de Janeiro: Trafficking, Social Networks and Public Authority* (Chapel Hill, North Carolina: The University of North Carolina Press, 2006), 1.

9. The Zona Sul is made up of many of Rio de Janeiro's most famous neighborhoods including Leblon, Ipanema, Copacabana, Leme, Lagoa, São Conrado, Jardim Botânico, Gávea, (Botofogo is sometimes included but it is really in the Centro).

10. In the 2007/2008 Human Development Index rankings (http://hdr.undp.org/en/statistics/) Brazil placed seventieth or last in the list of countries deemed to have a High Level of Human Development. The title of the newspaper article cited below, notes that the Zona Sul would have ranked better than Norway if it was its own country. Norway is second only to Iceland in the current rankings. Luis Ernesto Magalhães,

"Em Plena Zona Sul, Um País Melhor do que a Noruega," *O Globo*, July 17, 2003 quoted in Arias, *Drugs and Democracy in Rio de Janeiro*, 18.

11. The Canudos War was a three-year war the fought between the Brazilian federal government and a messianic community in the interior of the northeastern state of Bahia. The government ended up sending over 12,000 soldiers to exterminate the community. Under the leadership of Antonio Conselheiro, the people of Canudos resisted tenaciously. In the end the government's victory came at a very high cost. Of the 12,000 soldiers, 5,000 were wounded or killed. Not a single male defender of Canudos survived; the few surviving women and children were forcibly relocated. Thomas E Skidmore, *Brazil: Five Centuries of Change* (New York: Oxford University Press, 1999), 80.

12. Zuenir Ventura, *Cidade Partida* (Rio de Janeiro: Cia das Letras, 1994), 13. Also see Teresa A. Meade, *"Civilizing Rio:" Reform and Resistance in a Brazilian City, 1889–1930* (University Park, Pennsylvania: The Pennsylvania State University Press, 1997).

13. Arias, *Drugs and Democracy in Rio*, 23.

14. Perlman, "The Myth of Marginality Revisited," 12.

15. For a first hand account of life in Brazil's *favelas* during this period see Carolina Maria de Jesus, *Child of the Dark: The Diary of Carolina Maria de Jesus*, trans. David St. Clair (New York: Signet, 2003).

16. Arias, *Drugs and Democracy in Rio de Janeiro*, 25.

17. Alba Zaluar, "The Paradoxes of Democratization and Violence in Brazil," 15. Paper presented at the Conferência Brasil e União Européia Ampliada, 2004. http://www.brasiluniaoeuropeia.ufrj.br/en/pdfs/the_paradoxes_of_democratization_a nd_violence_in_brazil.pdf

18. Robert Neuwirth, "Rio Drug Gangs Forge a Fragile Security," *NACLA Report on the Americas* 36, no. 2 (2002), par 3. http://web.ebscohost.com

19. Luiz Eduardo Soares, *Meu Casaco de General: 500 Dias na Front da Segurança Pública do Rio de Janeiro* (São Paulo: Companhia das Letras, 2000) quoted in Arias, *Drugs and Democracy in Rio de Janeiro*, 2.

20. A June 2007 raid on the *favela* Alemão, in which 1,300 police officers were sent into the community, resulted in nineteen deaths and many others being wounded. While the police maintained that the victims were all drug traffickers, stray bullets often hit innocent bystanders during the shootouts. "For the police, everyone is a drug trafficker, especially after they've killed you," said community organizer Edmundo Santos Oliveira. "Then it's up to the family to try to prove their loved ones were innocent." In October of 2007 at least a dozen people were killed on a raid in one of Rio's *favelas*; among the victims was a 4-year old boy. Michael Astor, "Rio Police Promise War on Drug Gangs," *The Washington Post*, June 28, 2007 and Monte Reel, "Celluloid Tale of Rio's Drug War, Told From Police Perspective, Is the Talk of Brazil," *The Washington Post*, October 22, 2007. http://www.washingtonpost.com.

21. Karen Backstein, "I Want to Make Films for Today: An Interview with Carlos Diegues," *Cineaste*, vol. 26, no.1 (2000): http://web.ebscohost.com

22. Luiz Cesar de Queiroz Ribeiro and Edward E Telles, "Emerging Dualization in a Historically Unequal City," in *Globalizing Cities: A New Spatial Order?* ed., Peter Marcuse and Ronald van Kempen (London: Blackwell Publishing, 2000), 88.

23. See Janice Perlman, *The Myth of Marginality: Urban Poverty and Politics in Rio de Janeiro* (Berkeley: University of California Press, 1976).

24. Perlman, *The Myth of Marginality.*

25. "Diretor de "Cidade de Deus" enfrenta críticas e minimiza a sua pretensão" Folha de São Paulo 30 of August, 2002. (http://www1.folha.uol.com.br/folha/ilustrada/ult90u26965.shtml).

26. Perlman, "The Myth of Marginality Revisited," 22.

27. Robin Sherrif, *Dreaming Equality: Color, Race and Racism in Urban Brazil* (New Brunswick, New Jersey: Rutgers University Press, 2001), 3–4.

28. René Rodríguez, "The Gangs of Brazil's Favelas" *Hispanic*, January/February 2003, 66.

Chapter Five

"Liminal Spaces in Fatih Akin's *Gegen die Wand/Head On*: Orientalism vs. Globalization"

Margarete Landwehr, West Chester University

The Turkish/German director Fatih Akin won the Golden Bear Award at the Berlinale Film Festival, for his film *Gegen die Wand/Head-On* (2004), which depicts a tragic love story between two second-generation Turks in Hamburg. The film garnered many accolades from critics, who claimed that it would revolutionize German cinema as well as the self-perception of the two million Turks living in Germany. The columnist Franz Josef Wagner, for example, stated that the film would "make us Germans and Turks into one country."[1]

The protagonists, Cahit (Birol Uenel), a middle-aged day laborer and alcoholic, and Sibel (Sibel Kekilli), a vivacious young woman, find themselves in a mental health clinic because they have both attempted suicide. Cahit has driven against a wall in a drunken stupor (hence, the film's title) and Sibel has cut her wrists. Sibel hounds Cahit to marry her so that she can escape the stifling atmosphere of her traditional family and enjoy her independence and sexual adventures. Cahit reluctantly agrees, they marry, and, eventually, fall in love. In a fit of jealousy, Cahit unintentionally kills Sibel's lover and goes to jail. Sibel leaves for Istanbul to escape her brother who wishes to avenge the family honor by killing her. Once Cahit leaves prison, he briefly reunites with Sibel in Turkey, but, the lovers fail to continue their relationship as Sibel has a child with another man and remains in Istanbul. At the film's conclusion, Cahit returns to his village. Thus, each character has chosen a different path, which offers only limited happiness. Cahit returns as a "foreigner" to a somewhat alien culture and unknown future; Sibel sacrifices her lover for the sake of her child.

The characters' straddling between two cultures not only constitutes the framework of their conflict, but also refers to a larger conflict—that between traditional, regional cultures and the globalized culture of an increasingly interconnected world. Thus, Cahit and Sibel's tragic love story also reflects the dilemma of Turkish *Gastarbeiter* (guest workers) in Germany as well as of immigrant groups struggling to cope with the culture of their host country.

Akin creatively manipulates cinematic techniques to underscore his protagonists' marginal status both in Germany as well as their Turkish community. For example, he reworks the classic Hollywood melodrama in his narrative and creatively employs the use of liminal and simulacral spaces, various languages (English/Turkish/German), and contrasting musical scores (traditional Turkish ballads/English pop songs) in depicting his characters' struggle between two cultures — a traditional Turkish culture with its arranged marriages and restrictions on women and the globalized culture of Hamburg and Istanbul with liberal attitudes towards sexuality and alternative lifestyles.

Furthermore, through this reinvention of the Hollywood melodrama, the self-conscious juxtaposition of contrasting music (and cultures), and the use of space, Akin, a German/Turk, deliberately underscores his own predicament as a filmmaker negotiating two cultures by foregrounding two oppositional discourses that "interpret" his story. In particular, if the tableau of a Turkish band whose songs of tragic love and fate represents traditional Turkish culture, then the pervasive TV images and English pop songs that infiltrate the sound track offer an opposing (western) narrative of free will and choice.[2] If the former takes place in a simulacral space, then the latter embodies the pervasive "space" of a globalized culture. Thus, Akin, aware of his own liminal status as director caught between two cultures, problematizes the choice of cultural discourses at his disposal in his work and, consequently, offers a complex, innovative film narrative. As Barbara Abrash and Catherine Egan note: "And it is precisely these non-mainstream productions that most consistently challenge traditional perceptions, question conventional wisdom, and posit alternative ways of representing and interpreting history and culture."[3]

LIMINAL SPACES: TRADITIONS VS. GLOBALIZATION.

Significantly, both characters' attempts to break through social conventions mark them as outsiders of their communities and, like the picaro, the outsider figure in a picaresque novel, their behavior questions the very validity of the traditional mores and gender roles of their culture. Appropriately, Cahit's crashing into a wall serves as a metaphorical reference not only to his sometimes violent breaking through social boundaries, but also, I believe, to the story's locale, Germany, noted for its wall and its historic, liminal space, straddling socialist (GDR)and capitalist (FRG) Europe. Thus, the spaces in which the characters dwell—Germany and Istanbul—constitute the liminal spaces in which eastern and western Europe overlap (Germany) and in which East and West meet (Istanbul). Moreover, both characters frequent locales such as seedy bars that harbor those who live on the fringe of society. Similarly, the clinic, like Cahit's prison, shelters many who might be regarded, however unfairly, as the misfits, the outcasts, of society. The film portrays their pariah status with numerous scenes in which they are literally cast out of a community space: Thus, Cahit is thrown out of a bar after he attacks a customer; both Cahit and Sibel are told to get off a bus by the Turkish conductor after a violent argument; and, later, Sibel gets kicked out of a bar in Istanbul.

Various languages—Turkish, German, and English—are spoken to underscore the protagonists' existence in a liminal space both geographically (Germany/Istanbul) and culturally/temporally (between a traditional Turkish culture [the past] and a cosmopolitan one [the present].) Moreover, both traditional Turkish songs and pop music with English lyrics serve as a point/counterpoint in interpreting Cahit and Sibel's love story. If the Turkish lyrics emphasize fate and an individual's helplessness in changing the course of his/her destiny, then the English pop lyrics extol freedom and free choice. For example, Cahit's German psychiatrist urges him to change his life by citing the lyrics of an English pop song: "If you can't change the world, change your world." In contrast, a Brechtian staged tableau of a traditional Turkish band with the minarets and mosques of Istanbul as a backdrop intercuts the various stages of Cahit/Sibel's story with commentary on events or predictions of their future, similar to a Greek chorus in ancient tragedies. Thus, the film begins with the Turkish singer lamenting the sufferings of unrequited love, which foreshadows Cahit's falling in love with Sibel, who is unaware of his feelings and seeking only trysts from disco encounters. At the film's conclusion, when the lovers reluctantly separate, the singer laments the agony of lost love. Thus, Akin employs English pop lyrics and Turkish ballads as a type of internal dialogue that offers two contrasting interpretations of Cahit and Sibel's love affair and which induce the viewer to participate in the film's narrative by negotiating between these two views of their love affair.

A popular concept in film studies, this "dialogism" originates from Russian scholar Mikhail Mikhailovich Bakhtin's study of race and ethnic representation. Bakhtin, regarded language, text, and media as simply utterances or voices rather than sentences or images. Bakhtin claimed that "Each cultural voice exists in dialogue with other voices."[4] Even if spectators do not speak from the film itself, they are drawn into a conversational process with it. Thus, Bakhtin's concept of dialogism bestows an active role onto viewers, who are not merely passive recipients of the film's message, but rather, in a

constant dialogue with the cinematic narrative. By offering contrasting interpretations of his work, Akin invites the spectator to engage in an inner dialogue with the film and, perhaps, even to experience vicariously the protagonists' struggle in negotiating their paths in life between two conflicting
cultures and world views.

Most importantly, the Istanbul tableau with its mosque and minaret also
represents a simulacral space of an idealized Turkey with its traditional customs and values such as a belief in fate. As the contrived and static *mise-en-
scène* suggests, the traditional world view depicted by the songs and images
no longer exists or, perhaps, exists only in the imaginations of emigrants who
nostalgically long for a country that they left behind, but that has radically
changed since their departure. Juxtaposed to this tragic depiction of their
love, an American pop song accompanies the film's credits with the lyrics
"Life is what you make it." Thus, the Turkish songs with their themes of
tragedy, irrevocable fate, and enduring suffering, and the English pop lyrics
with their exhortations to search for happiness, to remain optimistic about the
future, and to determine one's own destiny present opposing *Weltanschauun-
gen* and underscore the liminal space between two cultures in which the characters find themselves. (It is only in the Turkish clubs of Hamburg in which
both pop music and Turkish songs are played that the two cultures appear to
coexist in harmony.)

Another counterpoint to the Turkish tableau are the ubiquitous television
images that represent globalization as seeping into and eroding local cultures.
The film portrays this erosion in the undermining of traditional social and
gender roles. For example, Sibel views a female Turkish weight-lifter also
named Sibel successfully lift an enormous set of weights, an apt metaphor for
her own struggle to carry her burden and for the changing role of women all
over the world. Indeed, Selma, Sibel's divorced cousin, who manages a modern, luxury hotel in Istanbul and gives her a job as a maid, embodies this new
world. Her modern attire, use of English and exercise equipment, and prestigious position attest to the new social and sexual freedom of the liberated
woman, but, as Sibel viciously points out to Selma, her success has come at
a high price. Sibel claims that her husband left Selma because she has become
a workaholic, which allows no room for a personal life.

In short, the film presents both literally and metaphorically three spaces.
Firstly, the imaginary or simulacral space of the Turkish tableau with its
mosques and minarets represents the past, or alternatively, immigrants' idealized memory of their homeland and its traditions. Secondly, the liminal
spaces, represented by the bars, discos, prison, and clinic, depict Sibel's and
Cahit's marginalized status in society as foreigners and unconventional outsiders both in Germany and within their own Turkish community. Finally, the

cosmopolitan space of a globalized culture is represented by modern Istanbul and, in particular, by the hotel in which Selma works. The liminal spaces dominate the film as the plot focuses primarily on Cahit's and Sibel's struggle between two cultures and their search for a new identity.

A brief discussion of the concept of liminality will clarify this discussion of the search for identity and transitional passages in life. Originating from the Latin word "limen" or "threshold," liminality has been used primarily by the anthropologist Arnold Van Gennep and Victor Turner "to describe the nebulous social and spiritual location of persons in ritual rites of passage."[5] Moreover, "liminality denotes an indeterminate existence between two or more *spatial or temporal* realms, states, or the condition of passing through them."[6] A popular concept in literary studies, the term is often employed to describe the life phases of the immigrant, exile, border or ethnic identities. Related themes are those of dislocation and identity/selfhood.

I would like to suggest that these three spaces also trace the trajectory of Sibel's search for a new identity. Sibel breaks away from the confining strictures of traditional Turkish culture and her past, embodied by the claustrophobic space of her family's apartment, by refusing to accept her family's conventional expectations of her as a daughter. Most of the film portrays Sibel (and Cahit) in liminal spaces, which suggest the transitional phase of their development. In particular, the frequently staged scenes in modes of transportation such as cars, planes, buses, etc. underscore this state of transition. Finally, Selma's fate as a divorced woman living alone in the antiseptic atmosphere of a chain hotel depicts a "modern" lifestyle in which family ties and traditional gender roles are broken and, to some extent, foreshadows Sibel's future life—her casual arrangement with a live-in boyfriend and child.

In particular, Sibel's journey of self-discovery constitutes a radical transformation of her sexual and social identity, and consists of three stages: escape, transition, and reintegration into society. These three stages resemble Van Gennep's classic three phases of such rites of passage as initiation rites that places Sibel's process of maturation in a larger context. The rites of passage include:1. the separation stage; 2. liminal (threshold) rites and 3. postliminal incorporation rites. Each phase has its symbols. The separation phase incorporates death symbols such as sacrifices and cutting rituals, such as shaving the head or body mutilation including circumcision or clitoral excision that permanently mark the novice as a member of his/her clan and differentiate him/her from other tribes. Thus, Sibel's suicide attempt, her cutting her wrists, marks her first separation from her family, literally and metaphorically. It results in her first escape from her home, albeit to a mental clinic, as well as a rejection of her family. (Both parents interpret her suicide attempt as an affront to them). When her adultery is discovered, she is literally and symbolically cast out of her family. She is banned from their apartment and her father's burning of her photos symbolizes her "death" as a daughter.

Gennep discovered that the liminal stage can be represented by trans-vestitism and mock death. If the former suggests an ambiguous sexual iden-tity, then the latter marks the break with one's former life. In her transition from Hamburg to Istanbul, Sibel has cut her hair and wears androgynous clothes, a mark of her newly found freedom, and shortly afterwards suffers a mock death of sorts. After having left Selma's hotel to seek a free lifestyle for herself, Sibel, in despair, taunts some street thugs enough to have them beat her up and leave her for dead. The viewer doesn't know if she has survived the ordeal until Cahit's visit to Istanbul. Finally, the incorporation stage can be marked by threshold crossings. Cahit's return to his Turkish hometown, constitutes a reintegration into another society and Sibel's establishment of her own modern home with boyfriend and child in Istanbul symbolizes her own crossing into a new life. Furthermore, Sibel's symbolic "death," the beat-ing, and her daughter's birth can be perceived as the death of Sibel's old per-sona and the birth of a new self.

Thus, Sibel and Cahit's journey from the claustrophobic space of the Turkish immigrant household, through the liminal spaces of bars, prisons, and clinics, to a reintegration into society also marks their journey of self-discovery and creation of a new identity. For Sibel, the journey consists of re-jecting the role of obedient daughter, experiencing both the freedom and suf-fering of being a sexual and social renegade and reintegrating into society as a mother. Cahit evolves from social outcast, to reluctant and, later, devoted, husband, to a wanderer, who eventually returns to his roots.

Despite their arduous journeys, the film presents an open-ended and rather bleak view of their future. The two choices depicted in the film appear to be either a return to the traditional Turkish lifestyle with its confining gender roles or an escape from these conventional roles into the cosmopolitan lifestyle of a globalized world. Whereas the former provides meaning, it is also portrayed in the film as oppressive, especially for women; although the latter is the dominating culture, it is depicted, in Selma's case, as offering a meaningless freedom, devoid of intimate relationships or spiritual values. Cahit, who leaves Istanbul alone to face an uncertain fate in his hometown, may find it difficult to return to the narrow confines of village life. With his limited knowledge of Turkish and of the culture, he may not be able to adapt to a radically different lifestyle. Selma, Sibel's alter-ego, who embodies the media ideal of the independent professional, indulges in the body culture of modern life with her relentless exercising in front of the television set, her only companion, and a symbol of the forces of globalization that destroy tra-ditions and family ties. The spectator is privy neither to the life that awaits

Cahit in his hometown nor to Sibel's partner and the nature of their relationship. Thus, this rather unsatisfactory, inconclusive conclusion invites the
viewer to imagine the protagonists' lives beyond the screen perhaps somewhere in a liminal space between the two extreme choices presented.

COGNITIVE MAPPING IN A GLOBALIZED WORLD?

Akin's film delineates not only the tragic trajectory of Cahit and Sibel's love
affair, but also a collective narrative—the insidious infiltration of a global
culture in every corner of the world through mass media and the subsequent
eroding of traditional cultures. With this in mind, I would like to suggest that
the ubiquitous television images and the English pop lyrics that infiltrate
many scenes, rather than the vast open spaces of the non-descript, anonymous
hotel or the cityscape of Istanbul's skyscrapers, best depict the omnipresence
of globalization. Consequently, the film, like its characters, has broken out of
the confining boundaries of defined spaces to a more fluid, amorphous space
of media images and sound. This depiction of globalization reflects Gayatri
Spivak's non-space based post-colonial world. Spivak, along with others,
concludes that "We are moving toward a planetary capitalism. . . . In that
sense the whole world is postcolonial."[7] Thus, cultural colonization, not territorial conquest, marks the globalization of traditional cultures. In a similar
vein, the German director Wim Wenders succinctly described the colonizing
force of American cinema through one of his characters who proclaimed that
"America has colonized our [German] subconscious."[8] Wenders elaborates:
"I am convinced that the most important industry for mankind, even more important than the defense ministry, will be the entertainment industry. This in-
fernal form of entertainment production will eventually trounce down all
sense of cultural identity and every chance of self-determination."[9]

Frederic Jameson's discussion of "cognitive mapping" in *The Geopolitical
Aesthetic: Cinema and Space in the World System* will shed light on Akin's
cinematic depictions of globalization. Taken from Kevin Lynch's *The Image
of the City*, "cognitive mapping" serves as a metaphor to describe "the phenomenon by which people make sense of their urban surroundings."[10] Thus,
it describes the intersection of the personal and the social, which allows individuals "to function in the urban spaces through which they move."[11] In his
preface to Jameson's book, Colin MacCabe explains that cognitive mapping,
a metaphor for the political unconscious, constitutes "*the individual's successful negotiation of urban space* (my emphasis)."

Furthermore, in his introductory chapter, "Beyond Landscape," Jameson
discusses "the disappearance of specifically national cultures and their re-

placement, either by a centralized commercial production for world export or by their own mass-produced neo-traditional images" and points to "a geopolitical unconscious" that "attempts to refashion national allegory into a conceptional instrument for grasping our new being-in the-world."[12] In other words, Jameson argues that the particular and regional is being replaced either by global, mass—produced images or pseudo-traditional ones. This collective transition from a national to a supranational consciousness represents a radical shift not only in *Weltanschauung*, in a group's view of the world, but also in its own relationship to the world. Thus, Jameson furnishes a theoretical framework that elucidates the transitions of Akin's film between portrayals of national allegory (the traditional Turkish songs in the tableau) to a globalized worldview (the television images and pop songs). As we have seen, this transition portrays not only the shift from local to global, but also a significant shift in world view (a belief in fate and order to unlimited freedom and self-determination).

Jameson raises the issue of the non-representability of our place within the globalized, post-modern world and concludes that a clearly demarcated social space by which we can define ourselves no longer exists. In his essay, "Postmodernism and Consumer Society," Jameson offers a rather bleak prognosis of the individual's sense of dislocation in this "hyperspace":

> . . . this latest mutation in space—postmodern hyperspace—has finally succeeded in transcending the capacities of the individual human body to locate itself, to organize its immediate surroundings perceptually, and cognitively to map its position in a mappable world. And I have already suggested that this alarming disjunction point between the body and its built environment . . . can itself stand as the symbol and analog of that even sharper dilemma which is the incapacity of our minds, at least at present, to map the great global and decentered communication network in which we find ourselves caught as individual subjects.[13]

Accordingly, cognitive mapping, that is to say, the need to orient ourselves in a new global space, will be experienced primarily through media representations. As Jameson claims the "world system of late capitalism (or post-modernity)" cannot be conceived independently of media experience which "*eclipses its former spaces* and faxes an unheard of *simultaneity* across its branches (my emphasis)."[14] Thus, in any discussion of a globalized culture, particularly in cinematic narrative, any definition of space and the related concept of culture will have to be radically revised to embrace the postmodern situation of an all-pervasive media that transcends both time and space with its simultaneity and omnipresence. Louis Althusser succinctly sums up this situation when he wrote: "Space without places, time without duration."[15] The ubiquitous media images and songs that infiltrate Akin's film depict this "colonization" of local cultures into one globalized "megaculture," in which traditions are forgotten or rendered meaningless, and the individual can no longer orient him/herself in the contemporary world. Thus, Selma, who lives the media ideal of the independent professional finds herself alone, cut off from family, in the sterile spaces of a modern western hotel and surrounded by television images, both symbols of the forces of globalization.

Furthermore, in "Postmodernism and Consumer Culture," Jameson claims that the ubiquity of media images will not only undermine our attempts at cognitive mapping, of orienting ourselves in a space, in the present, but also has destroyed our sense of history, of the past. He states that ". . . we seem condemned to seek the historical past through our own pop images and stereotypes about that past, which itself remains forever out of reach."[16] In a similar vein, Akin's film demonstrates that cinematic images are replacing local narratives of a nationality's history. To paraphrase Jameson, Akin cinematically depicts the transformation of reality into images, in particular, the reduction of Turkish history to stereotyped images, with his staging of the Turkish band in front of the minarets and mosques of Istanbul. Thus, this tableau can be regarded as a self-referential statement on the role of the media, particularly film, to alter or even create the images by which we "remember" our collective past. Jameson claims that this "disappearance of a sense of history" is "the way in which our entire contemporary social system has little by little begun to lose its capacity to retain its own past, has begun to live in a perpetual present and in a perpetual change that obliterates traditions of the kind which all earlier social formations have had in one or another to preserve."[17] Jameson concludes that two central features of a postmodern world are: "the transformation of reality into images" and "the fragmentation of time into a series of perpetual presents."[18] In short, the relentless penetration of the media through advertising, television and internet images shapes our sense of both our present reality and our past.

To sum up thus far, *Gegen die Wand* refers cinematically to these two contemporary dilemmas discussed by Jameson—the inability to orient ourselves in a clearly delineated space or to return to our roots, our history, for identity. Consequently, Akin's cinematic narrative constitutes not only the individual stories of two social outcasts, but also a "national allegory" of the plight of Turkish *Gastarbeiter*, who can no longer wholeheartedly embrace the past, the traditions of an increasingly alien (Turkish) culture nor find a niche in the alienating globalized culture that glorifies the freedom of the individual at the expense of a communal identity.

OPPOSING DISCOURSES?:
ORIENTALISM VS. GLOBALIZATION

Finally, Jameson's discussion of third-world literature and national allegories will further elucidate Akin's role as a Turkish/German filmmaker working within an essentially "western" medium, cinema. In "Third-World Literature in the Era of Multinational Capitalism," Jameson argues that all third-world texts, even those that are seemingly private "necessarily project a political dimension in the form of national allegory: *the story of the private individual destiny is always an allegory of the embattled situation of the public third-world culture and society.*"[19] If the texts of "capitalist culture" such as western realist and modernist novels emphasize "a radical split between the private and the public, between the poetic and the political, then the third-world text demonstrates the inversion of this relationship: psychology, or more specifically, libidinal investment, is to be read in primarily political and social terms."[20] Jameson claims that the collective, political nature of third-world texts results from the artist's sense of "subalternity," a term coined by Gramsci, which refers to "the feelings of mental inferiority and habits of subservience and obedience which necessarily and structurally develop in situations of domination—most dramatically in the experience of colonized peoples."[21] In other words, the third-world artist's awareness of his/her subaltern position as dominated economically and socially by a first-world, globalized culture, compels him/her to link the personal with the communal. As Jameson explains: "When a psychic structure is objectively determined by economic and political relationships, it cannot be dealt with by means of purely psychological therapies."[22] Thus, Akin, a German/Turk in western, cosmopolitan Germany who is creating within a "western" art form not only depicts the national allegory of his fellow second-generation German/Turks, but also his own aesthetic crisis as an artist straddling two cultures and their respective narratives.

In particular, Akin foregrounds an aesthetic dilemma, a crisis of representation, that is, his predicament as a German/Turkish director caught between two narrative discourses that are portrayed as extremes in order to underscore the dilemma—the traditional Turkish narrative of a tragic love story, determined by fate and embodied by the Turkish tableau and its songs, or a contemporary soap opera, whose characters make foolish choices and bring about their own demise. Indeed, the lovers' violent behavior, their plunge into disaster, and the plot of betrayal and reconciliation, loss and redemption, constitute all the trappings of a Hollywood melodrama.

Although at first glance, these radically different narratives appear to offer diametrically opposed worldviews, upon closer examination, one discerns that they actually spring from the same source, from a western perspective. On the one hand, the Turkish tableau set against the backdrop of the mosques and minarets of historical Istanbul does not reflect a contemporary Turkey, but rather, idealized, Orientalized stereotypes. Coined by the influential literary critic Edward Said, Orientalism refers to the Western image of the "Orient" as portrayed in novels, political language, and the media. Thus, according to Said, Orientalism reveals more about the West and its fantasies than about the actual people or culture of the East. Originating in nineteenth-century European colonialism and its distinctions between an "inferior" Orient and a "superior" Occident, Orientalism, according to Said also functions as a type of Western discourse, a "Western style for dominating, restructuring, and having authority over the Orient." Thus, the relationship between East and West is one "of power, of domination."[23]

Could not children of immigrants absorb this western discourse of their cultural past? Akin's use of the Turkish tableau with its easily recognizable visual signifiers—the minarets and mosques—and the "Orientalist" motif of fate in the love songs—imply that these stereotypes belong to his reservoir of images of Turkey as the "Orient" both as an émigré and filmmaker. The almost surreal staging of the tableau in an unrecognizable, simulacral space suggests that the image and the stories belong to an imaginary, romanticized past that exist now only in the nostalgic memories of Turkish emigrants. Could Akin be insinuating, what Jameson has clearly articulated, that our past is forever out of reach and that we can only seek the historical past through media images and stereotypes? Perhaps this state of affairs is particularly acute for a second-generation émigré who has learned about his parents' culture in western schools and films.

On the other hand, contemporary media images such as stereotypes of fulfilled "westernized," independent women that Selma and, to a lesser extent, Sibel, try to emulate are equally illusory as their emulation clearly does not bring the happiness they promise, but rather short circuits it. If Selma finds herself alone and lonely in an empty hotel room, then Sibel discovers that sexual freedom doesn't offer the happiness she seeks. Rather, this freedom has brought expulsion from her family and much suffering. Moreover, as Sibel realizes at the film's conclusion, complete freedom doesn't exist as she must choose between her child and her lover.

In short, both the Orientalist stereotypes and the westernized media clichés are products of a western discourse. If the former dominated the portrayal of the East during the colonial period, then the latter dominates the postcolonial period and has "colonized" the regional cultures through images. In short, Jameson's claim that reality—both past and present—has been reduced to images appears to hold true in Akin's cinematic world and constitutes a self-referential theme in the film.

Finally, both discourses are equally untenable options, because they both fail to capture the true nature of the characters and their reality and cannot provide a meaningful narrative. Thus, neither the semantically charged but outdated, Orientalized sterotypes of a beautiful, but elusive woman and her valiant, but doomed lover of some idealized, "Oriental" past nor the reductive melodramatic cliches of Hollywood accurately depict Akin's characters. If the Orientalist narrative is obsolete, then the contemporary, globalized alternative lacks all specificity, and, therefore, meaning. Indeed, the shots of Hamburg and modern Istanbul lack any references to local landmarks. Istanbul's generic, contemporary skyline suggests that Selma's and Sibel's stories are repeatedly occurring in urban settings all over the world. The endless repetition of their stories renders their individual suffering virtually meaningless. Akin appears to suggest that the repertoire of images available to him as a Turkish émigré in western Europe are either a romanticized, Orientalist view of Turkey's past or the clichés provided to him by the Hollywood melodrama and soap opera. Thus, like Sibel, Akin is caught between two cultures and their discourses, neither of which offers satisfying alternatives as cinematic narratives. Consequently, he attempts to achieve a creative compromise, to form an uneasy truce by perpetually shifting in the liminal space between the two.

NOTES

1. Dietmar Kanthak,"'Gegen die Wand': Eine Liebesgeschichte im deutsch-türkischen Milieu," *EPD Film* 4 (2004): 34.

2. Of course, there are more than two "cultures" portrayed in the film. With the intercutting of scenes, Akin, for example, deliberately contrasts how Turkish women relate to each other much differently than the men do. Also, the vast difference in attitudes towards sexuality is evident. In the case of Sibel's family, her relationship to her mother, who is more tolerant of her independent daughter, contrasts sharply with her father's and brother's attitude towards her. The "western' culture portrayed here is both German and American as American dominance of German cinema and German popular culture in general has existed since the American postwar occupation of West Germany and its control of the German film industry in the immediate postwar years. Clearly all the characters exist in both cultures to a greater or lesser degree. The binary opposition between two "extremes" offered here is for the sake of the argument I am attempting to present.

3. Barbara Abrash, and Catherine Egan, ed., *Mediating History: The Map Guide to Independent Video by and about African American, Asian American, Latino, and*

Native American People (New York: New York University Press, 1992), 3, as cited in *Reversing the Lens: Ethnicity, Race, Gender, and Sexuality through Film,* ed. Jun Xing and Lane Ryo Hirabayashi (Boulder, Colorado: University Press of Colorado, 2003), 12.

4. For a discussion on dialogism and Bakhtin see: Robert Stam, "Bakhtin, Polyphony, Ethnic/Racial Representation," in *Unspeakable Images: Ethnicity and the American Cinema*, ed. Lester Friedman (Urbana, Illinois: University of Illinois Press, 1991), 251–76, 353, and Xing and Hirabayashi, *Reversing the Lens,* 14.

5. Lisa Ortiz, "Liminality," in *Encyclopedia of Postmodernism*, ed. Victor Taylor and Charles E. Winquist (New York and London: Routledge, 2001), 218.

6. Ortiz, "Liminality," 219.

7. Gayatri Chakravorty Spivak, *The Postcolonial Critic: Interviews, Strategies, Dialogues* (New York and London: Routledge, 1990), 94, 95.

8. Roger Cook, and Gerd Gemuenden, ed., "Excerpts from Interviews with Wenders," *The Cinema of Wim Wenders: Image, Narrative and the Postmodern Condition* (Detroit, Michigan: Wayne State University Press,1997), 12.

9. Cook, "Excerpts, 84.

10. Frederic Jameson, *The Geopolitical Aesthetic: Cinema and Space in the World System* (Bloomington, Indiana: Indiana University Press, 1995), xiv.

11. Jameson, *The Geopolitical Aesthetic,* xiv.

12. Jameson, *The Geopolitical Aesthetic,* 3.

13. Frederic Jameson, "Postmodernism and Consumer Society," in *The Norton Anthology of Theory and Criticism,* ed. Vincent E. Leitsch (New York/London: W. W. Norton & Co, 2001), 1960–1974.

14. Frederic Jameson, *The Geopolitical Aesthetic,* 10.

15. Louis Althusser, *Montesquieu, Rousseau, Marx* (London: Verso: 1972), 78.

16. Jameson, "Postmodernism and Consumer Society," 1967.

17. Jameson, "Postmodernism and Consumer Society," 1974.

18. Jameson, "Postmodernism and Consumer Society," 1974.

19. Frederic Jameson, "Third-World Literature in the Era of Multinational Capitalism," *Social Text* 15 (1986): 69.

20. Frederic Jameson, "Third World Literature," 69, 72.

21. Frederic Jameson, "Third World Literature," 76.

22. Frederic Jameson, "Third World Literature," 69, 72.

23. Edward Said, "From Orientalism," *The Norton Anthology of Theory and Criticism*, 1992, 1994.

Chapter Six

"Fantasies of Loss: Melancholia and Ethnicity in Israeli Cinema"[1]

Raz Yosef, Tel Aviv University and Sapir College

[. . .] Sephardim, trapped in a no-exit situation, have been forbidden to nour-
ish memories of at least partly belonging to the people across the river Jordan,
across the mountains of Lebanon, and across the Sinai desert and the Suez Canal
. . . In a sudden historical twist, today it is to the Muslim Arab countries of their
origins to which most Middle Eastern Jews cannot travel, let alone fantasize a
return—the ultimate taboo. . . . This desire for 'return of the Diaspora' is ironically underlined . . . [in] . . . a kind of reversal of the biblical expression: 'By the
waters of Zion, were we sat down, and there we wept, when we remembered
Babylon.'[2]

In her article, *Taboo Memories and Diasporic Visions*, Ella Shohat writes a
melancholic eulogy of a lost past in Babylon, of the refused desire of Mizrahi
Jews in Israel to remember the loss of Arab-Jewish culture. Zionism positioned the Jew and Arab as polar opposites, thereby denying the existence of
an Arab-Jewish identity and history. Oriental Jews were represented in Zionist discourse as belonging to the local Semitic space of Islamic countries or to
the Mediterranean basin, while at the same time they were perceived as me-
diators between the Arab world and Hebrew-Jewish world. As Middle Eastern "locals," they brought Zionist nationalism closer to the Arab sphere and
legitimized it. However, at the same time, they also had to be uncompromis-
ingly Jewish and eradicate any Arabness from their identity.[3] Shohat writes,
"The Sephardi Jew was prodded to choose between anti-Zionist 'Arabness'
and pro-Zionist 'Jewishness.' For the first time in the Arab-Jewish history,
Arabness and Jewishness were posed as antonyms."[4] This discourse fore-
closed any possibility of remembering and missing the Arab home and homeland. Such memories became taboo—forbidden reminiscences. Mizrahim
were forbidden from publicly mourning their lost Arab-Jewish identity, from

transforming from grief to grievance—"from suffering injury to speaking out against it," as Ann Chang puts it.[5] This is the source of Shohat's melancholic writing, which challenges the Jewish State's cultural and political prohibitions against mourning the trauma of Mizrahi uprooting and loss of Arabness.

In his important article from 1917, "Mourning and Melancholia," Freud distinguishes between these two proximate mental states. Similarly to melancholia, "mourning is regularly the reaction to the loss of a loved person, or to the loss of some abstraction which has taken the place of one, such as one's country, liberty, and ideal, and so on. In some people the same influences produce melancholia instead of mourning and we consequently suspect them of a pathological disposition."[6] Melancholia is pathological because, unlike the mourner who comes to term with his loss and painfully adapts himself to a world in which the dead no longer exist, the melancholic denies the loss of the love object and resists replacing it with another: "In mourning it is the world which has become poor and empty: in melancholia, it is the ego itself."[7] But Freud also describes melancholia as a kind of identification and consumption:

> An object-choice, an attachment of the libido to a particular person, had at one time existed: then, owing to the real slight or disappointment coming from this loved person, the object-relationship was shattered. The result was not the normal one of withdrawal of the libido from this object and a displacement of it on to a new one, but something different . . . [T]he free libido . . . was withdrawn into the ego . . . to establish an identification of the ego with the abandoned object. Thus the shadow of the object fell upon the ego . . . The ego wishes to incorporate this object into itself, and the method by which it would do so, in this oral or cannibalistic stage, is by devouring it.[8]

In this purportedly pathological process, in which the melancholic consumes and appropriates the lost object, loss plays an important role in the construction of the ego. Melancholia designates a sequence of loss, denial and identification through which the ego is formed. It is not clear from "Mourning and Melancholia" whether the ego precedes melancholia, as it is only constructed as a psychic object once "the shadow of the object [has fallen] upon the ego." In other words, the ego is shaped through identification with the ghost of the other—the lost object.[9] Judith Butler argues that melancholia "produces the possibility for the representation of psychic life."[10] According to Butler, in *The Ego and the Id*, Freud revises his previous distinction between mourning and melancholia as he discovers that the ego itself is comprised of abandoned object-cathexes internalized as constitutive identifications. She writes: "Freud himself acknowledges that melancholy, the unfinished process of grieving, is central to the formation of identifications that form the ego. Indeed, identifications formed from unfinished grief are the modes in which the lost object is incorporated and phantasmatically preserved in the ego."[11] If the ego comprises a series of lost attachments, then the ego itself cannot be created without the melancholic internalization of loss. It follows that the process by which the ego is formed can be read as a series of losses. Or, in other words, melancholia does not signify loss, but rather complex relationships with loss.

Freud adds that "The loss of a love-object is an excellent opportunity for the ambivalence in love-relationships to make itself effective and come out into the open."[12] That is, when feelings of love that were formerly directed at the lost object return to the ego, they are accompanied by guilt and anger, emotions that were directed at the object and that, following its disappearance, are turned towards the ego in the form of admonishment, rebuke and self-punishment. Thus, according to Freud, consumption of the object is accompanied by ambivalence: not only nostalgic love, but also rage and anger. The source of anger and rebuke is directed toward the lost object. However, because they are by now both interwoven and assimilated into one another, it could be said that these grievances are directed neither at the subject nor the object. As Chang puts it, "At this moment *loss* becomes *exclusion* in the melancholic landscape."[13] The melancholic must exclude and deny the lost object in order to create a situation of lost-not lost. One could think that the melancholic would want the lost love object back, but his ego does not allow it. This dilemma of the melancholic sharpens his ambivalent attitude toward the lost object.

This psychodynamic may well be relevant in describing the situation of the Mizrahim in Israel. The Ashkenazi national ideal melancholically created itself through the ghost of the lost Mizrahi other. Ashkenazi Zionism constructed itself by excluding the Arabness of Jews from Arab countries, and simultaneously by assimilating Mizrahi otherness. The Arab past of the Oriental Jews threatened to destabilize the imaginary coherence of the homogenous Israeli nation and to blur the boundary between Jews and Arabs. Disrobed of his Arabness, the Mizrahi was nationalized as part of the construction of the purportedly universal national subject, and, via the ideology of the melting pot, was dissolved into the modern and ostensibly neutral Jewish collective, though which was actually distinctively Ashkenazi. But the Mizrahi Jews' affinity with their Arab past could not be entirely wiped out. The Mizrahi subject marked the border between Jewish nationalism and the neighboring Arabs, and legitimized Zionist presence in the Middle East. The Mizrahim were physically settled along the borders and in "abandoned" Palestinian urban neighborhoods, thus providing the State with a living barrier against Arab military attacks as well as with a means of thwarting the attempts of Palestinian refugees from returning to their land. The notion that the melancholic ingests the lost object, thus preserving the loss via its distancing and exclusion, could describe the process by which the Mizrahi subject belongs and does not belong; he is one of us while also being a stranger to the nation. The Mizrahi Jews were internalized and consumed into Jewish nationalism through a flattening of ethnic differences, while they were simultaneously marked as problematic, as a different group within Israeli society. The history of Jewish nationalism can thus be read as caught in a melancholic bind, between assimilation and rejection. Ashkenazi identity in Israel works in a melancholic fashion, as a system based simultaneously on consumption and identification, and on the psychological and social denial and exclusion of the Mizrahim.

A cinematic expression of this psychological ethnic drama can be seen in the film *Ariana* (1971), by the Jewish-Iranian director George Ovadia. The film is a social allegory that represents the melancholic appropriation and expulsion on the part of Ashkenazim of the Mizrahi other. The dramatic climax of *Ariana* takes place in a court scene, in which the lawyer Gabriel Shamir (Yitzhak Shilah) announces to the astonished audience that he is Ariana's father. Twenty years previously, he had a romantic affair with her mother, Kochava (Rachel Tarry), a young, innocent and pretty Mizrahi woman. When she became pregnant by him he held her in contempt, proposed she abort the pregnancy, and, when she refused to do so, threw her out of his well-to-do offices in disgrace. Kochava found warm refuge in the home of her good friends, Zohara (Tova Pedro) and Abood Mizrahi (Arieh Elias), a poor, childless couple from Jaffa, with whom she lived until her tragic death during the birth of her only daughter, Ariana (Dessy Hadari). Ariana grew up to be a beautiful young woman, remarkably similar to her mother. In the course of time, she fell in love with Gadi (Avi Toledano), an army officer and the son of a successful Ashkenazi businessman, Arthur Danieli (Avraham Ronai). Their interethnic and cross-class affair was met with disapproval by Gadi's father, who had been grooming him to marry the rich heiress of a respectable Jewish-Polish family, and so he nipped it in its bud by sending his son to France on business. Ariana, like her mother before her, finds herself abandoned by the man whose child she is bearing. When Gadi returns from France, the Mizrahi family sues him in court for reneging on a promise to marry Ariana. Ironically, the Danieli family is represented by Shamir, who discovers that Ariana is not the Mizrahis' biological offspring. When asked about the identity of Ariana's real father, Zohara relates that a few seconds before dying, Ariana's mother told her that her daughter's father was a successful lawyer called Gabriel. At this point the respectable Ashkenazi lawyer understands that he is Ariana's biological father. He calls off the case, declares his love and says he is willing to legally adopt Ariana, thereby paving a legitimate way for the interethnic marriage of Ariana and Gadi.

The film describes the melancholic expulsion of the Ashkenazi lawyer, who banishes his love object, Kochava, the woman he loved but could not accept because of her ethnic origin and low social status. From that moment on he is restless, tormented by her lost memory, haunted by her final words: "One day you'll regret this." Shamir condemns himself to a melancholic life of loneliness and alienation (he never married or had children). In his final speech in court, he says: "Today you see me a very miserable man, whose conscience is tortured by doubts and whose heart is riven with remorse. A man who is prepared to ask that you have mercy on him." His anger, which had previously been directed at the lost object, is now turned on his own ego in a mode of rebuke and self-recrimination. He adds: "Forgetting my selfish and base behavior, I rose through high society surrounded by prestige and respect." The Ashkenazi subject constructs itself through the melancholic rejection and incorporation of the Mizrahi other; he expelled the ethnic other, but could not forget its ghostly presence. In the film, the Ashkenazi melancholic repudiation also takes on a social and national dimension on account of the location of this Ashkenazi melancholic drama in the public-legal sphere of the courtroom. Perhaps it is no coincidence that the judge, behind whom we see the symbol of the state of Israel, is astonishingly similar in appearance to Israel's first Prime Minister, David Ben-Gurion.

The film also gives a cultural expression to this Ashkenazi melancholia. Ariana and Gadi first meet at a party where Mizrahi musicians are playing Arab music. The Ashkenazi Gadi approaches Ariana and asks her to dance the Hora with him, a dance with roots in Russian folklore. In this scene, the Mizrahi music is disavowed and expelled by the Hora dance and assimilated into Zionist-Ashkenazi ritual. In this sense, the Mizrahi music is the absent-present lost object appropriated into homogenic Ashkenazi-Israeli culture (this melancholic expulsion of Mizrahi music is very common in Israeli society, especially in folk dance events when participants dance the Hora to Mizrahi music). Ovadia's film, then, shows how Ashkenazi national cultural identity is constructed through the melancholic repudiation and internalization of the Mizrahi other. The boundaries of Ashkenazi subjectivity cannot be constructed without the Mizrahim and their constant disavowal. This is an entirely melancholic process.

Ariana belongs to the "Bourekas" genre (1964-1977), which dealt with interethnic tension in Israeli society. In most "Bourekas" films the tension between Mizrahim and Ashkenazim is resolved through the erotic union or marriage of a mixed couple. Through its deployment of the notion of the melting pot, this imagined ethnic integration both denied and silenced any representation of a

Mizrahi social struggle.[14] In these films, the Mizrahi subject is compelled to forgo his Arab cultural identity, if he is to be deserving of an Ashkenazi girl and to be part of "Western" Israeli society. In fact, the "Bourekas" films in general can be read as melancholic allegories of the nationalization and appropriation of the Mizrahi subject while eradicating his ethnic difference. The Ashkenazi national ideal in "Bourekas" movies is simultaneously shaped by the melancholic rejection of Mizrahi identity and its incorporation into the new Jewish nationalism. The Mizrahi is always the nation's lost other.

However, what is the subjectivity of the melancholic Mizrahi object? The migration experience of Mizrahim is based on a structure of mourning and melancholia. When a person leaves his country of birth he has a wide range of things for which to grieve, such as family, language, identity, standing in the community, and assets. In the context of Mizrahim in Israel, the national narrative of simultaneous expulsion and assimilation meant that Mizrahi mourning was forbidden and invisible, and led to an ethnic melancholia. Mizrahi melancholia is double: the Mizrahi subject was required to negate and eradicate his Arab identity, but was also forced to reidentify with that loss, because he or she was prevented from fully participating in the Ashkenazi national ideal. These layers of loss were censored, forbidden and silenced in Israeli culture.

These losses have recently been afforded cultural visibility through feature films by second generation Mizrahi directors, such as *Shchur* (Hana Azoulay-Hasfari and Shuel Hasfari, 1994), about how a thirteen year old Israeli-born girl copes with the traditions of her Moroccan family in the southern town of Be'er Sheva in the 1970s; *Lovesick on Nana Street* (Shabi Gavison, 1995), which describes the Mizrahi hero's melancholic yearning for Ashkenazi whiteness represented by an Ashkenazi girl with whom he falls in love; *Desperado Square* (Benny Toraty, 2001), which tells of the lost love for Indian cinema among the residents of a Mizrahi neighborhood; *The Barbecue People* (David Ofek and Yossi Madmoni, 2003), about the complex relations between a Mizrahi second generation and their parents' generation, which is detached from local life and attached to its youthful past in Iraq; and documentary films such as *Takasim* (Duki Dror, 1999) and *Chelry Baghdad* (Eyal Halfon, 2002), which expose the magnificent yet undocumented musical heritage of Jewish musicians in Arab countries and their reception Israel; *My Fantasy* (Duki Dror, 2001), which, through the eyes of the son-director, tells the repressed story of his father, who spent many lost years in an Iraqi jail; *Cinema Egypt* (Rami Kimchi, 2002), in which the filmmaker examines his mother's Arab-Jewish past in Egypt; *Kaddim Wind: Moroccan Chronicle* (David Ben Shitrit, 2002), the story of Moroccan Jewry in Israel as told through six second generation characters who relate personal stories of the racism and oppression that accompanied Moroccan Jews' absorption in Israel; *Mother Pazia* (Sigalit Banai, 2002), which focuses on the loaded relations between the Jewish-Arab singer, Pazia Rushdi, who was very successful in her native Egypt, and later found fame as the legendary star of Arab-language radio in Israel, and her Israeli-born actress daughter, Yaffa Yossia Cohen; and many others.

In this article I shall focus on Kimchi's *Cinema Egypt*, and on Toraty's *Desperado Square*. Through an analysis of these cinematic texts I shall examine how Mizrahi immigrants cope with their various losses. What is the relation between the Mizrahi second generation and their parents' cultural loss? In what way does this generation inherit that loss and work it out? David Eng and Shinhee Han argue that "immigration and assimilation might be said to characterize a process involving not just mourning *or* melancholia but the intergenerational negotiation between mourning *and* melancholia. Configured as such, this notion begins to depathologize melancholia by situating it as the inherent unfolding and outcome of mourning process that underwrites the loss of the immigration experience."[15] If the losses suffered by the first generation of Mizrahim are not resolved and mourned for during the process of assimilation—in other words, if the libido does not renew itself by investing in new objects—then the melancholia derivative of this situation is liable to be transferred to the second generation. The loss experienced by the parents following the erasure of their ethnic identity, while at the same time being prevented from fully assimilating into Israeli society, is transferred to their children, who try to deal with it in their films. I argue that these films are fantasies of loss through which the Mizrahi second generation attempts to "solve" the enigma of the origin of the melancholic identification and identity of both their parents and themselves. Through the fantasy of cinema, the sons restage their parents' loss, with which they identify, in order to search for a lost desire, to talk of a repressed love, and thus to try and redefine their (male) Mizrahi identity.

In Kimchi and Toraty's films this crossgenerational melancholic transfer is expressed through the relationship between the mother and her son(s). The sons do not retrieve the "original" object of desire to their mothers, if only because they are unable to do so. For their mothers, the distance between the past and present, between "there" and "here," has made the lost object both spatially and temporally remote, such that a return to it is only possible through an act of imagination. Memory of the Mizrahi past is a place that cannot be revisited, even if one can travel to the geographical territory that appears to be a place of "origin." Therefore, "home" is a mythic place of desire in the imagination of the Mizrahi immigrant. As members of the second generation who were born in Israel, the sons cannot reclaim the Mizrahi past of which they were never really a part, and with which they only identify through their mothers' melancholy. Members of the Mizrahi second generation have no clear roots in their heritage, and so they devise cultural routes that take them, via cinematic fantasy, to places and encounters with people they have never met. This forges a relationship between the past, present and future but does not presume an even, continuous passage through time and space. The grounded certainty of their Mizrahi roots is replaced in the films by the contingencies of the routes of fantasy.

In his documentary film, *Cinema Egypt*, director Rami Kimchi describes the story of how his mother, Henriette Ezer, arrived in Israel from Egypt in 1950. Using family photographs, documentaries about the migration of Mizrahim to Israel, old Egyptian feature films, still photographs, and video footage filmed by the director in contemporary Egypt, Kimchi, who also narrates the film, sets out with his mother on a journey to her Arab-Jewish past. His mother has been suffering from depression for some time, to the detriment of her health. As a child, he would tell those who took an interest in her condition: "Mother has heartache." What is the source of his mother's depression? She grew up in the town of Mit-Ghamr at the time of French colonial rule in Egypt. The earliest trauma she underwent was being separated from her home and father, a patriarchal and authoritative man whom she loved and admired. At the age of six he forced her to leave her hometown so that she would study French at the convent, and not Arabic at her school. But she refused to adapt to her studies at the convent. "I wanted to go home," she says. Her most meaningful positive childhood memory is of the Arabic films she used to watch at the only cinema in town, called Cinema Mazre— "Cinema Egypt." Her bedroom window adjoined the cinema's projection room, and at night she would fall asleep to the sound of Arabic songs from the movies: "Such lyrical songs, sad, I loved them." Eventually, Henriette was sent to her grandfather's brother in Westernized Alexandria where she was distanced from anything Arab. Thus, even as a child, Henriette was detached from her father and the Arab culture into which she was born.

After migrating to Israel and marrying, she set up house with her husband in the settlement of Binyamina, populated mostly by Ashkenazi Jews. The local cinema did not show Arabic films, and she rarely visited it. Arab culture was marginalized and almost completely forgotten: "There were new things, and new things make you forget the old," she says. "The Oriental Jews," argues Yehouda Shenhav, "cooperated with the Israeli project of modernization and de-Arabization on account of the negative standing of Arabness in the Israeli-Zionist public sphere."[16] It is therefore hardly surprising that Henriette's new model of masculinity, as she herself points out, was the cinematic Zionist figure of Ari Ben-Canaan played by Paul Newman in the film *Exodus*.

Given the influence of French colonialism in Egypt, and later on that of Zionism in Israel, the mother's Arab cultural identity was excluded. Kimchi recalls that at home "mother made sure only to speak Hebrew with the children. French was the language of the grown-ups. Ladino was the language of secrets, and beneath them all was Arabic, a language that was never spoken at home, the language of dreams." The melancholic, says Freud, "knows *whom* he has lost but not *what* he has lost in him."[17] Henriette knows that she lost her father, but denied that which was identified with him and that she lost within herself, her Arab-Jewish identity.

As the years in Binyamina passed, Henriette's depression deepened. Her marriage to Kimchi's father failed, and though they never divorced they lived separately for many years. Kimchi grew up with his mother while his younger brother lived with his father: "I remember that mother was sad. Aimlessly walking around the empty rooms in our house." In one of the scenes, Kimchi asks his mother if his father was similar to her father, and she answers firmly in the negative. Her husband, a short and gray English teacher, was an unsatisfactory object that could not take the place of her patriarchal father and return to her that which she had lost. He promised her a house with a garden in Binyamina, but was unable to keep his word. The husband, who had also immigrated from Alexandria, did not identify with his wife's loss. He succeeded in renewing his libido by investing in a new object, the Zionist-Ashkenazi ideal. The main scene devoted to him in the film describes a ceremony conducted by the Binyamina municipality in honor of his dedication to the teaching profession. When Kimchi shows his mother video clips that he filmed at the "Antoinette" café in Alexandria, she nostalgically remembers a romantic date she had been on there before she met her husband. She had a young suitor, but because he was a distant relative she rejected him, which today she regrets: "I was stupid. I could have had a different life today . . . I regretted it after I married." Her description of this idealized Egyptian bachelor reverberates with the extolled image of her father. In her fantasy, the romantic wooer could, perhaps, take her father's place, return to her that which she had lost, and give her a "different life." These are losses that she never forgot or stopped grieving for, and she installed them within her ego. Her anger, which was originally directed against her father for denying her of himself and her Arab identity, is internalized as melancholic depression.

The mother remained silent about her loss, just as she was left mute by the particularly biting depression that overcame her after separating from her husband. Butler writes:

> The melancholic would have *said something*, if he or she could, but did not and now believes in the sustaining power of the voice. Vainly, the melancholic now

says what he or she would have said, addressed only to himself, as one who is already split off from himself, but whose power of self-address depends upon this self-forfeiture. The melancholic thus burrows in a direction opposite to that in which he might find a fresher trace of lost other, attempting to resolve loss through psychic substitutions and compounding the loss as he goes.[18]

Kimchi is interested in turning Henriette's melancholic silence into an external dialogue between him and her, between mother and son. He wishes to give voice to her lost desire, not only for her sake, but also for him, as he too identifies with his mother's melancholic loss. He says: "I am making this film in order to identify with her, to understand her . . . I want to take her back to the scenes of her childhood, to the place of love." Kimchi identifies with his mother's unfinished grief. The melancholia is recycled and finds a new agent in the form of the son who tries to deal with it both for himself and his mother. At the beginning of the film he tells of his mother: "They called her Henriette, a French name. As a Sabra, I always thought they were calling her Orient. I castrated her name like this for years, and she didn't even bother to correct me." The son imagined his mother as belonging to another time and place, alien to the Ashkenazi Israeli identity he adopted for himself. She never told him what she had lost as a girl in Egypt; he knew nothing about the town of her birth, about her repressed Arab history. Kimchi feels guilty for castrating his mother's identity by getting her name wrong. As a child he criticized and judged her for accepting her lot. The guilt and self-recrimination felt by Kimchi today are, in fact, rebukes originally directed at his mother and the Arabness identified with her. He relates that as a child he was ashamed of his mother's ethnic origin and when asked where his parents came from would unenthusiastically answer, "My mother is from Cairo and my father from Alexandria." "But you can't see it on you," would be their complimentary reply. Every Friday evening Israeli television would show old Egyptian films; the films that were his mother's lullabies in Mit-Ghamr. Sometimes they would watch them together, and afterwards his mother would anxiously ask if he thought they were good. As an arrogant film student at university who had been brought up on Eurocentric culture, he would coldly reply that they were bad films. "Now I know," he says regretfully, "that mother had exposed to me her most vulnerable emotions, the love of her childhood which she had to turn her back on all those years, that she hesitantly tried to recruit my assistance so that she could find release." The loss never spoken of at home—Arabness—was melancholically uprooted from his external into his internal world. The rage felt toward the lost object was internalized as his own depression.

In his film, Kimchi tries to reply to his mother's mute plea, to release her repressed desire. "Cinema Egypt" in Mit-Ghamr had by now closed down and

Kimchi could not reopen it; instead, he reopens the "Armon" ("Palace") cinema in Holon, his birth town, where, among others, Arab and Turkish films
used to be screened when he was a teenager. Kimchi uses the technology of
cinematic projection to cope with his mother's and his own ethnic melancholy: if the melancholic "projects" the image of his loss onto the ego, the
cinema projects the lost object onto the screen, back into consciousness. It is
in this cinema that he shows his mother the footage he filmed in Mit-Ghamr,
Alexandria and Cairo—the scenes of his mother's youth—and in particular
excerpts from the Egyptian film, *Layla the Country Girl* (1941). The film tells
the story of Layla, an expressive and innocent girl, who, unbeknownst to her,
is betrothed to a rich groom, whom she marries before being uprooted to the
big city. In the city they mock this poor village girl, and even her husband
turns a cold shoulder on her until she adopts a Western appearance so as to
win his love anew. Throughout the film, Kimchi weaves his mother's story in
with that of Layla, and continually draws parallels between them. His choice
of the film *Layla the Country Girl* is not accidental. It is not just another
Egyptian film. It was directed by one of Egypt's most successful directors,
Togo Mizrahi, an Egyptian Jew, and Layla was played by Layla Murad, one
of Egypt's greatest actresses and singers, who was also Jewish (she later converted to Islam). Therefore, not only does Kimchi link his mother's story with
that of the cinematic Layla, but he also restages his mother's history in the
context of her lost Arab-Jewish culture.[19]

Similarly to *Cinema Egypt*, the melancholic figure of the Mizrahi mother
also stands at the center of Benny Toraty's feature film, *Desperado Square*.
Seniora (Yona Elian) is a widow who lives with her two sons, Nissim (Nir
Levy) and George (Sharon Raginiano) in an anonymous neighborhood on the
outskirts of Tel Aviv. As a young woman, before she got married, she had had
a secret affair with a young man, Avram Mandabon (Mohammed Bakri),
whose family owned the only cinema in the neighborhood. The two would
meet clandestinely, mostly in the cinema, where they would enjoy late-night
romantic viewings of the Indian film, *Sangam* (1964), starring the famous actor, Raj Kapoor. The only people privy to this secret affair were the projectionist at the cinema, Aron (Uri Gavriel), and Yisrael the Indian (Yosef
Shiloach), who would peep at the two from the roof and watch the film together with them until the break of dawn. However, their romance was nipped
in the bud when Seniora was betrothed against her will to none other than
Avram's brother, Morris, who was oblivious to his brother's affair with his future bride. Avram promised Seniora that he would tell his brother of their love
but could not find the courage to do so, instead fleeing the neighborhood under the cover of darkness. Seniora waited for him until sunrise, but he did not
return. With a broken heart she was forced to marry Morris and subsequently

gave him two sons. When Morris found out about her secret he closed the cinema, vowing that its doors would never reopen. Seniora loved her husband,
but never got over the loss of her first love, who had abandoned her. She
never finished grieving his departure, never told a soul about her pain and
loss. Wrapped in melancholia, she condemned herself to silence. The memory of her lost desire thus remained only in her broken heart, locked behind
the sealed doors of the cinema, dusty and torn like the rolls of celluloid left
scattered around the projection room.

By relating Seniora and Avram's affair with the movie *Sangam*, the film
ties Seniora's romantic loss to the loss of Mizrahi culture. *Sangam*, like many
other Indian, Turkish and Arab films, was extremely popular among
Mizrahim in the 1960s.[20] These films, which were mostly screened in cinemas in Mizrahi neighborhoods and towns, constituted a relatively legitimate
replacement for their forbidden Arab culture, thereby forming an alternative
to the Eurocentrism of the Ashkenazi cultural hegemony in Israel. *Sangam*
tells of two close friends, Gopal and Sunder, who are both in love with Radha,
though each is unaware of the other's love for her. When Gopal finds out that
Sunder also loves Radha, he decides to relinquish her for his good friend's
sake. *Desperado Square*, then, draws parallels between the trinity of lovers
comprised of Avram-Seniora-Morris with that of Gopal-Radha-Sunder. The
cinema's closure—that is, the expulsion of Mizrahi culture—parallels the
cessation of the love affair between Seniora and Avram. In one of the scenes
Seniora says, "The end has already been"—the end of the past love affair but
also the end of Mizrahi culture in the neighborhood. In another scene, Avram
says in Arabic: "Illi Fat Mat"—"The past is dead."

The film also emphasizes the notion that Seniora's cultural and romantic
melancholy does not only represent a personal loss but also a communal one.
As Jose Esteban Munoz argues: "Communal mourning, by its very nature, is
an immensely complicated text to read, for we do not mourn just one lost object or other, but we also mourn as a 'whole'—or, put another way, as a con-
tingent temporary collection of fragments, that is experiencing a loss of its
parts."[21] Sadness descends upon the whole neighborhood following the closure of the cinema. The cinema, as well as Seniora herself, became a lost object of desire for all the neighborhood's inhabitants ("everybody was in love
with their mother," says Aron to Nissim at one point in the film). The neighborhood's central square—called "The Square of Dreams," and which was a
Mizrahi cultural and communal meeting space—is renamed "Desperado
Square," and turned into a derelict place. Even though only Aron and Yisrael
the Indian knew the true reason for Avram's disappearance and Morris' closing of the cinema (it was rumored that the brothers had fought over the cinema), Seniora's secret loss indirectly became everybody's loss, as it led to the

removal of Mizrahi cinema from the neighborhood. When the guests cried at Seniora's wedding (one of them says: "I remember that wedding. Everyone had tears in their eyes,") they were indirectly identifying with her personal tragedy, which had been combined with their communal tragedy. In other words, the entire Mizrahi community shared Seniora's grief.

Of all the neighborhood's inhabitants the melancholic figure of Yisrael, the Indian voyeur, stands out in particular. It was he who sprayed the graffiti "Desperado Square" after the cinema was shut down. With a Raj Kapoor style wig on his head, and dressed in colorful clothes as befitting the peak of 1960s fashion, Yisrael drives around the neighborhood on an old sidecar motorbike, tape recorder on the handlebars, singing songs from old Indian movies. He conspicuously lives out the fantasy of loss. He denies and refuses to accept the expulsion of the love object and melancholically celebrates his victory over it. Freud describes in most negative terms the melancholic's inability to get over his loss, but he also tells us that this is how "love escapes extinction."[22] Yisrael militantly and melancholically refuses to allow the love object to disappear into oblivion. In contrast to the mourner, who is entirely satisfied with the death of the object and declares that it is dead in his soul, Yisrael the melancholic resists its elimination by making himself the lost object, by totally identifying with the loss. In fact, other residents of the neighborhood also live the fantasy of loss. Despite their advanced age, they occupy themselves with childish games (such as nonsensical card games; they tie one of their friends to a lamppost and kick a football at him; they argue over who will put one of the girls' hair into a ponytail; they build a wooden cart in order to collect planks of wood for a Lag Be'Omer bonfire) and impersonations of characters from the movies, such as Hercules and Machiste, and of movie actors, such as Lee Van Cleef and Giuliano Gemma, who starred in old Italian action films, which were also very popular with the Mizrahi public in Israel in the sixties. They rebel against the expulsion of their love objects from Israeli cultural space; they confront the social truth of their disappearance head on and resolutely refuse to deny them. As melancholics, they teach us, as Freud said, that "in the last resort we must begin to love in order not to fall ill."[23] In a certain sense, their oppositional melancholy becomes a kind of communal activism, a collective identification with loss, a militant refusal to abandon the lost object. Indeed, through communal loss, *Desperado Square* points to the political potential of melancholia.[24]

The Mizrahi second generation, Seniora's sons, has internalized its mother's melancholy. The film opens with a dream dreamt by Nissim a few days before the first anniversary of his father's death. In the dream, his father appeared before him and asked him to "break the vow" and reopen the neighborhood cinema. Nissim thus unconsciously identifies with his mother's loss.

On the very same day Avram makes a surprise return to the neighborhood after an absence of twenty-five years. He did not attend his brother's funeral, but has returned to say Kaddish (the Jewish mourning prayer) in his memory. The neighborhood's residents are astonished to see this ghost from the past ("He hasn't changed, he has stayed just the same," says Aron). The return of Seniora's lost love object parallels the return of the lost Mizrahi culture, for Avram has possession of the only copy of *Sangam*. For Seniora, the return of the lost object is accompanied by feelings of rage and anger that stress her ambivalent attitude toward him. She refuses to meet and talk with him, hating him for having abandoned her. Her anger toward him is incorporated as melancholic depression. Aron urges her to talk to him: "What will we talk about," she asks—"About life," he replies—"Whose life?" she retorts bitterly. Since he left she has had no life. This is also why she objects to Nissim and George's idea of screening *Sangam* at the cinema's gala reopening. Her revulsion of Avram is tied to her rejection of the idea of rescreening the Indian film. When Nissim finds out about the love affair between Avram and his mother he refuses to allow him to say Kaddish for his father in the synagogue. It would seem that more than Nissim is angry that his mother was in love with Avram instead of with his father, he identifies with her melancholy and anger toward the lost object. But it is precisely because of this melancholic identification with their mother that he and his brother George ultimately insist on rescreening *Sangam*, and not any other film. They want to project, and not introject, the image of loss in order to reconstruct the lost desire.

In both of these films, the mother is the signifier of the loss, the lost Mizrahi identity, and she herself is lost to her sons. Like the mother, the Mizrahi second generation "knows whom he has lost but not what he lost in him." They have memories, but no history. The mother has a history, but refuses to remember it. For both parents and children, the loss appears as a story, fragments of memories and experiences, which are distant from their lives in the present. They experience the loss through old films, dreams and fantasies. But these fantasies of loss are crucial resources that can serve as landmarks in paving a way to the future.

In contrast to the popular understanding of fantasy as illusion, as antithetical to reality, psychoanalysts Jean Laplanche and Jean-Bernard Pontalis, following Freud, argue that fantasy is reality for the subject—psychical reality—like the material world, that it shapes his or her existence as much as any other "external" force. They refute the distinction between unconscious and conscious fantasy (such as daydreaming), and point to the continuity between them. They mention three primal fantasies—the primal scene, seduction and castration—and term them "original" fantasies, original in that they are bound up with the subject's history and origins: "Like myths, they claim to provide a representation of, and a solution to, the major enigmas which confront the child. Whatever appears to the subject as something needing an explanation or theory is dramatized as a moment of emergence, the beginning of history."[25] Therefore, "the primal scene pictures the origin of the individual; fantasies of seduction, the origin and upsurge of sexuality; fantasies of castration, the origin of the difference between the sexes."[26] These primal fantasies precede and shape the subject's fantasy production. However, they are not a transcendental structure, but rather a "prestructure which is actualized and transmitted by paternal fantasies."[27] This distinction is important for a discussion of intergenerational relations. Primal fantasies precede our individual fantasies—they are transmitted through the culture we are born into—but at the same time they rely on and are enacted and shaped by our parents' fantasies, by specific historical discourses, "the history or the legends of parents, grandparents and ancestors: . . . this spoken or secret discourse, going on prior to the subject's arrival, within which he [*sic*] must find his way."[28] Laplanche and Pontalis focus less on the content of the fantasy and more on its structural role, its function in constructing and defining psychic processes. For them, fantasy is not simply wish-fulfillment, an imaginary space in which the subject acts out his desires. On the contrary: fantasy stages the subject's desire by giving it form. Through fantasy we narrate our desire. Fantasy is a mechanism by which desire is constructed and played out. They write:

> Fantasy . . . is not the object of desire, but its setting. In fantasy the subject does not pursue the object or its sign: he appears caught up himself in the sequence of images. He forms no representation of the desired object, but is himself represented as participating in the scene although, in the earliest forms of fantasy, he cannot be assigned any fixed place in it . . . as a result, the subject, although always present in the fantasy, may be so in a desubjectivized form, that is to say, in the very syntax of the sequence in question.[29]

In other words, the fantasy does not represent the attainment of the desired object, but rather provides a "mise-en-scène" of the desire. The subject's libidinal investment is in the entire script and not only in a certain object, and his or her identifications are liable to move between various positions.

When Kimchi screens old Arab films for his mother, and especially the film *Layla the Country Girl*, which he intertwines with his mother's history, he is using cinema to restage her childhood memory in which she listened from her bed to the Arab songs emanating from the projection room in the cinema in Mit-Ghamr. This event, which is part-dream, part-reality (the dimension of fantasy is also stressed when Henriette describes the "dreamlike music" that she used to hear) is structured as a primal scene for the mother:[30] She is watching her own history, witnessing the origin of self in the Egyptian family melodrama that becomes her own, the mise-en-scène of her desire. She sees herself through the cinematic mise-en-scène, caught in a "sequence of images," identifying with the image of Layla in a "desubjectivized form," as put by Laplanche and Pontalis, "in the very syntax of the sequence in question." The son tries to "return her to the place of love," to the site of her primal fantasy that constituted and shaped her desire. By reproducing her fantasy of origin, the son enables his mother to learn to desire once more, to love again that which she repressed and buried in her depression. By restaging her loss in fantasy, the mother's desire is rekindled.

This mother's fantasy, as reproduced by her son, is that "secret discourse, going on prior to the subject's arrival, within which he must find his way." Recycling his mother's history enables Kimchi to discover the origin of her lost desire that he identified with via the process of crossgenerational melancholy. In fact, the film *Cinema Egypt* itself is Kimchi's own family melodrama through which he tries to "solve" not only the enigma of the origin of his mother's loss but also, and mainly, his own loss. He imagines himself and his mother watching her fantasy together, which, as its author, is actually his as well. The mother's fantasy of origin is intertwined with the fantasy of origin of the son; the film *Layla the Country Girl* is joined together with *Cinema Egypt*. This integration can be seen as early as the film's opening sequence, when Kimchi's mother's name—Henriette Ezer—appears alongside that of Layla Murad, with Kimchi casting them both as the female stars of his cinematic fantasy. In this way, the son is also caught in a "sequence of images," appears "in the scene" through which he is also constructed as a desiring subject. Kimchi does not realize his mother's and his lost desire—because it cannot be fully satisfied—instead he sets out with his mother on a hesitant search for it. "The fulfillment of desire" is expressed by transposing it into the fantasy, into a state that will produce the loss constitutive of desire.

In the fantasy, the Mizrahi subject's identifications are not fixed, but rather fluid and shifting. Kimchi concurrently identifies with both his mother and her Arab-Jewish culture, as well as with Israeli culture. As a member of the second generation, he simultaneously identifies with "Cinema Egypt" and the "Armon" cinema, Mit-Ghamr and Holon, Israel and Egypt. As an Israeli filmmaker, he identifies with Israeli cinema, mainly with the "Bourekas" genre and its representation of Mizrahim. In the "Armon" cinema he sticks up posters from "Bourekas" movies such as *Aliza Mizrahi* (Menahem Golan, 1976), *Queen of the Road* (Menahem Golan, 1971), and *Charlie and a Half* (Boaz Davidzon, 1974). Furthermore, the film ends with a shot of a poster written in Hebrew of the film *Layla the Country Girl*, which he also puts up in the cinema. Thus, in the fantasy that the film constructs Kimchi is able to identify with Israel and the Middle East, Jewishness and Arabness—an identification that was oppressed, repressed and denied to the Mizrahim by the Zionist narrative. Unlike the disavowal of the object of desire — the Arabic language — from the private space of the home in particular and from Zionist space in general, in the film we hear Arabic all the time, mostly in excerpts from the film *Layla the Country Girl*. The director chooses not to add subtitles to the Egyptian film, instead translating and telling the story to the viewers himself. Throughout the film, Kimchi emphasizes the very act of narration, the narration of lost Mizrahi desire — not the attainment of the love object but the phantasmatic restaging of the origin of loss via cinema, which constructs the desire.

Seniora and Avram's viewing of the film *Sangam*, whose plot parallels their own affair, can also be seen as a symbolic version of the primal scene of origin: together they watch a cinematic dramatization of their own romantic encounter, their own history, the moment at which their desire originated. The fantasy of the Indian family romance gave form to their desire and thereby constructing it. They saw themselves "in the scene," identifying in a "desubjectivized form" with the cinematic images of Radha and Gopal. This desire, shaped by the film's fantasy, was lost with the closure of the cinema, and was internalized by Seniora as melancholic depression. At the same time, just like the child in the Freudian primal scene watching his parents' love act, so Aron the projectionist and Yisrael the Indian observed the intertwined spectacles of desire of both Radha and Gopal and Seniora and Avram. They too, and in fact all the residents of the neighborhood, are caught up in the "sequence of images," identifying with the fantasy that formed their desire, and which was lost and melancholically internalized when the cinema's doors were locked. The cinematic space functions as an ideal location for restaging the primal scene in that the very act of film viewing, as argued by Christian Metz, reproduces for the spectator the infantile experience of the scene of origin.[31] It is in this context that we can understand Aron's wish to return to the "dreams of yesteryear," Yisrael's uncompromising refusal to give up on his cinematic fantasy, and the childishness of all the inhabitants of the neighborhood — to see once again the infantile phantasmatic event in which their desire was constructed.

Nissim's dream, in which his father requests of him to open the cinema, is a wonderful cinematic expression of Laplanche and Pontalis' assertion that the parents' fantasies shape those of the second generation. This generation is represented not only by Nissim and George but also by the filmmaker himself (in the dedication at the end of the film, Toraty explicitly writes: "For the parents' generation with love.") The gala screening of *Sangam*, organized by the sons, reflexively refers to Toraty's own cinematic work. This Mizrahi second generation is trapped in the "sequence of images" of its parents' fantasies, which constitute its desire and identity. Toraty is attempting to restage the mise-en-scène of the parents' desire so that they can once more love the thing that they lost and with which he and his generation identified. And indeed, towards the end of the film, the residents of the neighborhood gather for the new screening, once more caught in the fantasy of the Indian film that constituted their desire. The only people not to come to the screening are Seniora and Avram, who stay in their houses, but who can hear the film's magnificent soundtrack, listening from afar to their own scene of origin. Only later, after the crowd has dispersed, do they arrive separately at the empty cinema, where Aron screens for them, and only them, the fantasy of loss that formed their desire. And Yisrael the Indian also watches from the roof for one last time the primal scene of origin, the restaging of loss that constructed his lost love. The film *Desperado Square* is therefore a fantasy of the sons' generation, setting out on a phantasmatic journey into the mother's past in order to seek out the origins of its melancholic identifications and identity. This cinematic fantasy restages the loss that constructed the desire of both generations. In this filmic fantasy the identification of the subject crosses the boundaries between generations and cultures, the personal and the communal, the psychic and the social. Thus it is no coincidence that the Indian word "sangam" means encounter.

The rescreening of *Layla the Country Girl* and *Sangam* does not represent a yearning for the mother's ideal past, a longing for "the good old days" of the "authentic" Mizrahi "home." Those films are not nostalgic fetish objects of an "original" Mizrahi culture. Rather, the sons restage them in order to change the present, to create a new Mizrahi standpoint that will allow multiple positions of identifications with and between Jewishness and Arabness, Israel and Arab countries, West and East. In Homi Bhabha's words, Kimchi and Toraty "restage the past," thereby introducing "other, incommensurable cultural temporalities into the invention of tradition. This process estranges any access to originary identity or 'received' tradition."[32] The "here" and "there," the past and present intersect in the directors' cinematic fantasies, thus subverting the Zionist distinction between the Jewish West and the Arab East, as well as resisting the hegemonic demand for the deletion of Arab otherness.

Kimchi and Toraty's melancholic fantasies can also be read through a gender perspective. They are Oedipal fantasies of heterosexual second generation Mizrahi men who restage their mother's cultural loss by appropriating the place of the father. The Mizrahi father appears in Kimchi and Toraty's films as someone who failed or who held back the mother's lost desire from her. The reconstruction of the mother's desire through the restaging of the fantasy of loss is necessarily an attempt to take the father's position and to right his historical injustices. This Oedipal desire should be understood in the context of the representation of the father figure in male Mizrahi discourse in Israel. In the 1970s, the Mizrahi "Black Panther" movement, dominated by men, called for a rebellion that would destroy the oppressive Ashkenazi establishment and demanded that the legitimate rights of Israeli society's oppressed be recognized. At the same time, the Mizrahi "Black Panthers" movement was also a rebellion against their Mizrahi parents, and especially the Mizrahi father, who was perceived as having been passively humiliated and defeated by the Ashkenazi hegemony. The Mizrahi Panthers, and male Mizrahi activists up to the present day, constructed the narrative of the docile and castrated Mizrahi father in order to forge their resistance to Ashkenazi superiority and to produce an image of a new heterosexual Mizrahi man. The yearning for Mizrahi phallic masculinity was perceived as an affront to Ashkenazi hegemony, but was itself based on an ideology with repressive characteristics, especially toward women and gays.[33]

In the film *Desperado Square*, the Oedipal fantasy of taking the father's role corresponds with this phallocentric Mizrahi sexual politics. In order to reconstruct themselves as normative heterosexual Mizrahi men, the sons desire to repair and rewrite their history, to be reborn, to take fatherhood of themselves. Throughout the film, Nissim and George take on a paternal role, not only with regard their mother, of whom they take care and whose honor they preserve, but also with regard to other residents of the neighborhood (for instance, they defend a female neighbor from a thief who is trying to steal her gas canisters; they look on with paternal authority at their neighbors' childish games, and they mediate between them when they fight). Although the brothers are represented as more mature than the other residents of the neighborhood, they are still perceived as not yet having fully entered the male heterosexual Oedipal order. This notion is exemplified in a scene in the neighborhood nightclub: George has failed in his attempts to court Gila the waitress (Ayelet Zorer), whom he loves but who consistently rejects his approaches. The film gives us no information about Nissim's romantic circumstances. The only reference to his sexual subjectivity is made in the same scene, when he seems scared of a threatening "erection" displayed by David (Leon Hasapar), the neighborhood crazy, who had stuffed a lady's tights shaped as a penis into his groin. During a Greek dance, in which he smashes plates on the floor, David turns his "erect penis" in the direction of Nissim's astonished face. Violently and homophobically, Nissim kicks him out of the club.

The appearance of Nissim's father in his dream, asking him to reopen the cinema, is an Oedipal fantasy on the part of the son who, by taking the position of the failed father, tries to "solve" the origin of his mother's melancholia and his own melancholic male identity in order to reconstruct it. In the screening of the film *Sangam*, the sons restage the fantasy of their mother's origin, her mise-en-scène of desire, enabling her to love again, thereby rectifying the injustices perpetrated by their father. Avram's appearance, Seniora's lost love object, is essential for the recreation of the mother's desire, but also comprises an obstacle for the sons in taking their father's place. This explains why Seniora and Avram do not come to the rescreening of the Indian film. Were they to be present, Nissim and George would have to observe their mother's desire for a stranger; they would be watching a kind of primal scene in which their father has no role. The complete exclusion of their father from the fantasy is impossible, for it would also negate the sons' very existence, and so they would not have been able to reproduce the Oedipal narrative and reconstruct their heterosexual male identity. Therefore, the film requires that Seniora and Avram be absent from the event so that Nissim and George can take their father's place. For the very same reason the film also requires that Avram ultimately leave the neighborhood. Were he to renew his affair with Seniora it would threaten Nissim and George's male domination. He has to clear the stage to allow the sons to appropriate their father's position. Therefore, the sons' melancholic identification with their mother is replaced by their identification with paternal authority.

Following Freud, Judith Butler argues that the male child's first lost object of desire is his father. She claims that heterosexual masculine subjectivity is formed melancholically by first relinquishing the father as an object of desire and then internalizing him as a primary and essential identification. She says that heterosexual identity is thus

> purchased through a melancholic incorporation of the love it disavows: the man who insists upon the coherence of his heterosexuality will claim that he never loved another man, and hence never lost another man. And that love, that attachment, becomes subject to a double disavowal: a never-having-loved and a never-having-lost. This 'never-never' thus founds the heterosexual subject, as it were; this is an identity based upon the refusal to avow an attachment and hence, the refusal to grieve.[34]

Nissim and George's identification with their father is essential in order for them to establish their melancholically constructed heterosexual male identity. The film, then, renounces the sons' *ethnic* melancholic identification with their mother for the sake of their *gender* melancholic identification with their father. Seniora and Avram are not the only ones to be excluded from the cinema: so is David, the queer pervert, who is kicked out of the theater by his friends after making a nuisance of himself during the film. His violent expulsion (the second of the film) removes the sexual threat that he represents not only for Nissim but also for the childish male residents of the neighborhood, thus establishing and reconstituting their heterosexual subjectivity. George's heterosexual male identity is also ratified when, after the screening, and perhaps unsurprisingly, Gila accepts his proposal of marriage. Toraty's film, therefore, is a fantasy of a Mizrahi male second generation setting out to discover the origin of their ethnic melancholic identifications and identity so as to finally reconstruct a heterocentric, patriarchal Mizrahi manhood.

Rami Kimchi in *Cinema Egypt* also takes on the role of the father, his mother's father and his own, and restages his mother's loss that constitutes the lost desire. This is undoubtedly an Oedipal fantasy on the part of a son hoping to replace the failed father. However, unlike in *Desperado Square*, the film does not exclude the father so that the son can take his place and construct a phallocentric Mizrahi masculinity. The father is present throughout the film and Kimchi tells his story too, though without this detracting from his full identification with his mother. The reconstruction of his mother's desire enables her to imagine the romantic figure of the young Egyptian courtier whom she met in the café in Alexandria. Hearing his mother say that after she married she regretted having rejected the young Egyptian's advances ("I could have had a different life,") Kimchi is hurt and diverts his gaze from her. In the life she fantasizes, there is no place for Kimchi and his father. However, despite the pain, Kimchi does not divert his identification with his mother and incorporates her melancholic loss within it. In his cinematic fantasy, for the sake of his melancholic identification with the maternal he relinquishes his identification with the phallic power and control that have characterized masculine Mizrahi discourse from the seventies to the present day. And so maybe it is no accident that at the end of his film, in a childlike gesture, Kimchi almost warily asks his mother: "Mommy, can I give you a kiss?"

NOTES

1. This essay was originally published as Raz Yosef, "Restaging the Primal Scene of Loss: Melancholia and Ethnicity in Israeli Cinema," *Third Text,* vol. 20, no. 3-4 (2006). Reprinted by permission of Taylor and Francis, Ltd.

2. Ella Shohat, "Taboo Memories and Diasporic Visions: Columbus, Palestine and Arab-Jews," in *Performing Hybridity,* ed. May Joseph and Jennifer Natalya Fink (Minneapolis and London: University of Minnesota Press, 1999), 146, 148, 150.

3. On this subject see Ella Shohat, "Columbus, Palestine and Arab-Jews: Toward a Relational Approach to Community Identity," in *Cultural Readings of Imperialism: Edward Said and the Gravity of History*, ed. Keith Ansell-Pearson et al. (New York: St. Martin's Press, 1997), 88-105; Ella Shohat, "The Invention of the Mizrahim," *Journal of Palestine Studies*, vol. 29, no. 1 (Autumn 1999), 5-20; Hannan Hever, Yehouda Shenhav, Pnina Motzafi-Haller, ed., *Mizrahim in Israel: A Critical Obser-*

vation into Israel's Ethnicity [in Hebrew], (Tel Aviv: Hakibbutz Hameuchad Publishing, 2002); Yehouda Shenhav, *The Arab-Jews: Nationalism, Religion and Ethnicity* [in Hebrew], (Tel Aviv: Am Oved Publishing, 2003).

4. Ella Shohat, "Sephardim in Israel: Zionism from the Standpoint of its Jewish Victims," in *Dangerous Liaisons: Gender, Nation and Postcolonial Perspectives*, ed. Anne McClintock et al. (Minneapolis and London: University of Minnesota Press, 1997), 47.

5. Ann Ahlin Cheng, *The Melancholy of Race: Psychoanalysis, Assimilation and Hidden Grief* (Oxford and New York: Oxford University Press, 2001), 3

6. Sigmund Freud, "Mourning and Melancholia" in *The Standard Edition of the Complete Psychological Works of Sigmund Freud*, ed. James Strachey, vol. 14 trans. (London: Hogarth Press, 1953), 243.

7. Freud, "Mourning and Melancholia," 246.

8. Freud, "Mourning and Melancholia," 248, 250.

9. Dianna Fuss, *Identification Papers* (New York and London: Routledge, 1995), 36-40.

10. Judith Butler, *The Psychic Life of Power: Theories in Subjection* (Stanford: Stanford University Press, 1997), 177.

11. Butler, *The Psychic Life of Power*, 132

12. Freud, "Mourning and Melancholia," 250-251.

13. Cheng, *The Melancholy of Race*, 9.

14. For different critical views on the "Bourekas" genre see Judd Ne'eman, "Zero Degree in Film" [in Hebrew] *Kolnoa* 5 (1979): 20-23; Ella Shohat, *Israeli Cinema: East/West and the Politics of Representation* (Austin: University of Texas Press, 1987); Nurith Gretz, *Motion Fiction: Israeli Fiction in Film* [in Hebrew] (Tel Aviv: The Open University of Israel Press, 1993); Nitzan S. Ben-Shaul, *Mythical Expressions of Siege in Israeli Films*, (Lewiston, New York: The Edwin Mellen Press, 1997); Yosefa Loshitzkey, *Identity Politics on the Israeli Screen* (Austin: University of Texas Press, 2001).

15. David L. Eng and Shinhee Han, "A Dialogue on Racial Melancholia," in *Loss: The Politics of Mourning*, ed. David L. Eng and David Kazanjian (Berkeley, California: University of California Press, 2003), 353.

16. Yehouda Shenhav, "Jews of Arab Countries Decent in Israel: The Split Identity of Mizrahim in the National Memory Milieu," in *Mizrahim in Israel: A Critical Observation into Israel's Ethnicity*, ed. Hannan Hever, Yehouda Shenhav, Pnina Motzafi-Haller [in Hebrew] (Tel Aviv: Hakibbutz Hameuchad Publishing, 2002), 109.

117. Freud, "Mourning and Melancholia," 245.

18. Butler, *The Psychic Life of Power*, 182.

19. Togo Mizrahi and Layla Murad were part of the rich Arab-Jewish cultural community that existed in Egypt until the 1950s, which also included such famous musicians as Zaki Murad (Layla Murad's father), Da'ud Husni, and Sayyid Darwish who had revitalized Egyptian music in the early part of the century and was responsible for the production of Egypt's first full-length opera, *Cleopatra's Night*, in 1919. On this subject see Ted Swedenburg, "Sa'ide Sultan/Danna International: Transgender Pop and the Polysemiotics of Sex, National and Ethnicity on the Israeli-Egyptian Border,"

in *Mass Mediations: New Approaches to Popular Culture in the Middle East and Beyond,* ed. Walter Armbrust (Berkeley, California: University of California Press, 2000), 88-119.

20. The film *Sangam*, Raj Kupoor's first color movie as actor and director, was the most popular Indian film to be screened in Israel, almost as popular as the successful "Bourekas" film, *Sallah Shabati* (Efrayim Kishon, 1964).

21. Jose Esteban Munoz, *Disidentifications: Queers of Color and the Performance of Politics* (Minneapolis: University of Minnesota Press, 1999), 73.

22. Freud, "Mourning and Melancholia," 257.

23. Sigmund Freud, "On Narcissism: An Introduction", in *The Standard Edition* vol. 14, 85.

24. On the political potential of melancholia see Douglas Crimp, "Mourning and Militancy," in *Melancholia and Moralism: Essay on AIDS and Queer Politics,* (Cambridge, Massachusetts: The MIT Press, 2002), 149; Butler, *The Psychic Life of Power,* 167-200.

25. Jean Laplanche and Jean-Bertrand Pontalis, "Fantasy and the Origins of Sexuality," in *Formations of Fantasy,* ed. Victor Burgin et al. (London: Methuen, 1986), 19.

26. Laplanche and Pontalis, "Fantasy and the Origins of Sexuality," 19.

27. Laplanche and Pontalis, "Fantasy and the Origins of Sexuality," 17.

28. Laplanche and Pontalis, "Fantasy and the Origins of Sexuality," 18.

29. Laplanche and Pontalis, "Fantasy and the Origins of Sexuality," 26. Recent film theory has emphasized the analogy between this theorization of fantasy and the process of film viewing. See, for example, James Donald, ed., *Fantasy and the Cinema* (London: BFI Publishing, 1989); Elizabeth Cowie, *Representing the Woman: Cinema and Psychoanalysis,* (Minneapolis: University of Minnesota Press, 1997), 123-165; Teresa de Lauretis, *The Practice of Love: Lesbian Sexuality and Perverse Desire,* (Bloomington, Indiana: Indiana University Press, 1994), 81-148.

30. This memory of Henriette's reverberates with the "wolf man's" primal fantasy. Freud writes: "*It was night, I was lying in my bed.* This latter is the beginning of the reproduction of the primal scene." Sigmund Freud, "From the History of an Infantile Neurosis," in *Three Case Histories* (New York: Collier Books, 1963), 228.

31. Metz constructs an analogy between the primal fantasy and psychic processes involved in the experience of cinematic viewing: like the child passively yet raptly watching his parents' lovemaking, the viewer sits alone in the darkened cinema and is compelled to look in the direction of the screen; he peeps at the representation of absent people who disappear from him and remain distant (the cinema is characterized by a segregation of spaces, a distance between the viewer and the spectacle). He writes: "For its spectator the film unfolds in that simultaneously very close and definitively inaccessible 'elsewhere' in which the child *sees* the amorous play of paternal couple, who are similarly ignorant of it and leave it alone, a pure onlooker whose participation is inconceivable." Christian Metz, *The Imaginary Signifier: Psychoanalysis and the Cinema*, Celia Britton, Annwyl Williams, Ben Brewster and Alfred Guzzetti, trans. (Bloomington: Indiana University Press, 1982), 64.

32. Homi K. Bhabha, *The Location of Culture*, (London and New York: Routledge, 1994), 2.

33. For a full analysis for this discourse see Raz Yosef, *Beyond Flesh: Queer Masculinities and Nationalism in Israeli Cinema*, (New Brunswick, New Jersey: Rutgers University Press, 2004), 84 -117.

34. Judith Butler, "Melancholy Gender/Refused Identification," in *Constructing Masculinity*, ed. Maurice Berger, Brian Wallis and Simon Watson (New York and London: Routledge, 1995), 28.

Chapter Seven

"Cinematic Asian Representation in Hollywood[1]"

Jun Xing, Oregon State University

Starting in the late 1960s and early 1970s, there has been an explosion in literary and historical writing on Asian and Asian American film representation.[2] However, most works on Asian film representation, like literature on general ethnic representation, focus on image analysis, overlooking other dimensions of media. To help address this problem, Chicano film historian Carlos Cortés identifies three categories in the historiography of ethnic film analysis: content analysis (films as visual texts), control analysis (process of film making), and impact analysis (influence of films over the audience and vice versa).[3] These studies of Asian representation in cinema can easily be grouped along these lines. Essentially, scholars have attempted either to construct a typology of images, focusing on stereotypes as ideological phenomena, or to examine the institutional aspects of racism. Using Cortés's model as a theoretical framework, this chapter is divided into three sections. Each section critically engages one aspect of cinematic Asian representation: film as celluloid imagery, film as a political process, and film's institutional dimension.

REPRESENTATION AS IMAGE

Over the years, particularly since the 1960s, a large, if somewhat uneven, literature has been produced on Asian film images. Dorothy B. Jones's *Portrayal of China and India on the American Screen, 1896–1955* is often credited as the pioneering work.[4] Jones sampled over 300 feature and short-subject movies and traced the changing screen images of China and India from the turn of the century to the mid-1950s. A large number of scholarly essays followed this model of Asian "stock character" analysis.[5] These

studies uniformly focus on identifying ethnic stereotypes. Jones, for example
has categorized specific character types for both groups. The evil mandarin,
the pirate or bandit, the warlord, the detective, the peasant, the houseboy, the
cook, and the laundryman were the major Chinese stock characters. For the
Indians, there were the primitive tribesman, the rajah, the benighted native,
and the Bengal soldier.[6] In a similar fashion, Christine Choy, a prominent Korean American documentarian, grouped Asian American images into four
main stereotypes: the "stock" image, the "mysterious villain," the "china
doll" or "geisha," and the "Banzai war crime" image.[7]

All images are created as a matter of specific setting and particular timing.
Because Asian screen images are historical constructs, they do not remain
static. Some scholars have traced the changes of those images and grouped
them along certain historical lines. Harold Isaacs, in his seminal study of
Asian images, *Scratches on Our Minds: American Images of China and India*
(dealing not merely with film images), has classified American imagery of
China into six historical periods. They are: (1) the Age of Respect (eighteenth
century); (2) the Age of Contempt (1840–1905); (3) the Age of Benevolence
(1905–1937); (4) the Age of Admiration (1937–1944); (5) the Age of Disen-
chantment (1944–1949); and (6) the Age of Hostility (1949–).[8] Focusing
partly on genre conventions and partly on international politics, Dick Stromgren has conveniently placed the history of Asian screen images into four periods: (1) the Silent Era: Exotic Melodrama; (2) the Burma Road and Beyond;
(3) the Red Menace; and (4) a New China and Fiendish Old Plots.[9]

In this section, instead of summarizing film character types or repeating the
historical timelines, I will organize my survey of Asian images, based loosely
on three formulaic traditions: the "yellow peril" formula, the "Madame Butterfly" narratives, and the Charlie Chan stories. These three Hollywood for-
mulations represent the staples of America's popular imagination of the "Orientals." As narrative conventions, they are noted for their incredible staying
power and their wealth of sexist and racist clichés.

THE "YELLOW PERIL" FORMULA

In their perceptions of Asians, nothing is more ingrained in American popular consciousness than the "yellow peril" image. A term first used mainly for
Japanese and Chinese in the United States, it soon collapsed all of Asia into
one yellow horde and became a catchword signifying the "yellow menace" to
Western Christian civilization. As Harold Isaacs noted, the yellow peril concept originally came to America from Europe, rooted in medieval fears of
Genghis Khan and his Mongol hordes.[10] By the late nineteenth century, the

growth of the Chinese presence in California gave birth to the anti-Chinese movement that was partly based on the threat of the yellow hordes of invaders. The germ theory, intermixed with racial, anti-immigrant, and xenophobic rhetoric, provided theoretical and political support for the yellow peril thesis. In the twentieth century, the Boxer Rebellion in China and Japan's 1905 victory over Russia appalled the Western world, giving further proof of the threat from the "bloodthirsty hordes" of Chinese fanatics and warning that the "rejuvenescent Japanese race [had] embarked on a course of conquest."[11] The call to protect the national body politic from the attack of the impending yellow peril proved especially potent during World War II, the Korean War, and the war in Vietnam.[12]

The yellow peril image has spawned two of Hollywood's favorite genres: the rape narratives, and the "Banzai" type war films. By the same token, Gina Marchetti, in her study of the various strategies deployed by Hollywood to influence the American public perception of Asia, has found the fantasy of miscegenation in three kinds of narratives: the rape stories, captivity tales, and seduction narratives.[13] Indeed, in Hollywood films, images of race and sexuality are always intimately intertwined, and sexual aggression against white women has become a metaphor for the racial threat posed to Western culture by the "other." Gary Hoppenstand described the significance of this strategy:

> The threat of rape, the rape of white society, dominated the action of the yellow formula. The British or American hero, during the course of his battle against the yellow peril, overcame numerous traps and obstacles in order to save his civilization, and the primary symbol of that civilization: the white women . . . The yellow peril stereotype easily became incorporated into Christian mythology, and the Oriental assumed the role of devil or demon. The Oriental rape of the white women signified a spiritual damnation for the woman, and at the larger level, white society.[14]

The rape narratives also found their way into Hollywood cinema during the silent era. One of the first feature-length films to exploit the image of the sinister Oriental rapist was Cecil B. DeMille's highly acclaimed *The Cheat* (1915), described by Kevin Brownlow as "one of the most sensational films of the early cinema."[15] The sadistic Burmese ivory king Arakua (originally a Japanese money lender named Tori), played by Sessue Hayakawa, best exemplifies the classic Asian male image. He is mysterious, exotic, and sinister. But ultimately, the libidinous Arakau represents a sexual threat to the Christian social order through his desire to possess the body of Edith Hardy, a white social butterfly. This symbolic miscegenation is intended to arouse a white-supremacist fear: Asian males pose a racial threat to white womanhood. The emotional grip on the viewers climaxes in the notorious branding scene, when

Arakau tears the gown from Edith's shoulder and brands her like an object in his collection. It was reported that audiences screamed and some women even fainted in their seats.[16] The famous courtroom sequence at the end illustrates the solution to the racial threat: mob lynching. Not as blatantly racist was D. W. Griffith's classic *Broken Blossoms* (1919), a film commonly described as "sensitive and humanitarian," in which the fantasy of rape and the possibility of lynching form its subplot.[17] The film features Lillian Gish as Lucy, the daughter of a murderously brutal prizefighter, and Cheng Huan, a "Yellow Man" from China. Intended as a sympathetic treatment of the Asian character, the film displays the Yellow Man as dreamy, frail, but lustful. After a vicious beating by her father, Lucy collapses before the "Chink" storekeeper. The sequence of Lucy's first night at the Chinese man's house raises the tantalizing suspense of rape. Robert Lang describes the details of the following scene: "We see in the shots of an increasing intimacy between the Yellow Man and Lucy, an extreme close-up of the Yellow Man's face . . . and Lucy drawing away from the Yellow Man in wonder tinged with fear."[18]

As a pervasively displayed stereotype in popular culture, Asian men were routinely portrayed as gangsters or rapists with perverted sexual appetites for white women. Often, the white women victims would eventually be rescued by a white male hero and the Asian rapist lynched by white male vigilante groups. As Tom Gubbins recalled, "You remember, back in the old days of serials, the spectacle of the heroine being snatched by villainous Orientals and dragged into a den of vice. It was quite common. The truth of the matter is that fewer white girls have been attacked by Chinese than by any other race of people."[19]

Since the beginning of this century, another mainstay of yellow peril discourse has been linked to war. "The majority of white Americans," John Dower wrote in his book *War Without Mercy*, "have been intimately introduced to Asians in the context of war and violence on the motion picture and television screens."[20] Two of the earliest and most durable Asian villains were Ming the Merciless and Fu Manchu. Together, they represented the incarnations of the yellow peril in the Oriental crusade to conquer the world. The prototype of Emperor Ming, the Merciless, appeared in the *Flash Gordon* movie series in the 1930s. The character was delineated as a sharp contrast to the pure and honest Flash Gordon and Miss America, Dale Arden. Fu Manchu, the arch-villain of the Sax Rohmer novels, was cruel, vicious, and a throwback to Genghis Khan. To paraphrase Richard Oehling, the diabolical Fu Manchu symbolized for the American audience three main strands of racial fears: Asian mastery of Western knowledge and technique (denoted by his degrees from three European universities in chemistry, medicine, and physics); his access to mysterious Oriental "occult" powers (his eyes can hypnotize victims); and his ability to mobilize the yellow hordes.[21] In the war narrative, sometimes an evil dragon lady (for example, Fu Manchu's various female companions) is paired with her male counterpart. Often sexy, sly, and terribly cruel, the dragon lady has a notorious penchant for white men. Other early yellow peril movies include *Limehouse Blues* (1934), *Chinatown Squad* (1935), *She* (1935), *China Seas* (1935), *Secret Agent* (1936), *The Soldier and the Lady* (1937), *Lost Horizon* (1937), and *Shadows of the Orient* (1937).

The three wars fought in Asia—World War II, the U.S. intervention in Korea, and the American fiasco in Vietnam—have left an important legacy for the war stereotype of Asians. "Pearl Harbor enabled Hollywood to revive all the old 'Yellow Peril' characteristics," wrote William Everson. "The Jap [was] as screaming, unshaven, wizened fanatic, crouched low over his machine guns, bombing Red Cross ships."[22] Hollywood practically developed a subgenre around World War II: *Destination Tokyo* (1943), *Guadalcanal Diary* (1943), *The Purple Heart* (1944), and, most important of all, *The Bridge on the River Kwai* (1957). Within the war narrative, a subgenre of tong wars or crime melodramas has utilized the same yellow peril theme. Chinatowns, known as isolated, sordid, violence-ridden urban ghettos, have long been the ideal stock settings for gangster movies, from *The Hatchet Man* and *The Mysterious Mr. Wong* in the 1930s to *Big Trouble in Little China, China Girl,* and *Year of the Dragon* in the 1980s.

The yellow peril formula may not be as blatant now as in the past, but stories of "white slavery" and war continue to haunt the silver screen. More recent movies like *Girls of the White Orchard* (1985), made-for-television exposé of white slavery in contemporary Tokyo, *Year of the Dragon*, and the *Karate Kid* series all have the threat of rape as their subplots. Yellow peril representations of Japan have also taken a new twist in the late 1980s and 1990s. Economic competition with Japan is often analogized to World War II battles. Flippant suggestions of using the *Enola Gay* to drop another atomic bomb as the final solution to trade frictions provide further evidence of this point. For example, in 1992 Senator Ernest Hollings of South Carolina suggested "jokingly" that a factory's employees "draw a mushroom cloud and put underneath it: Made in America by lazy and illiterate workers and tested in Japan."[23] Screen images of the yellow peril continue to feed this Japan-bashing movement. Productions like *Gung Ho* (1985) and *Rising Sun* (1993) are two better-known examples. The latter, a Michael Crichton novel-turned-blockbuster movie, is a clear reincarnation of the Fu Manchu who competes with whites in a fashion not unlike the incarnation of evil.[24] "Business is war," declared Eddie Sakamura in the movie of *Rising Sun*. The recent controversy over the re-release of a World War II-era cartoon, *Bugs Nips Nips,* testifies how such a war mentality is alive and well today. One scene shows

Bugs Bunny giving ice cream cones, with hidden bombs to a crowd of Japanese as he remarks, "Here's you go bowlegs, here you go monkey face, here
you go slant eyes, everybody gets one."[25] Only after strong protest by Japanese American Citizens League (JACL) did MGM-UA Home Video reluctantly pull the tape from the shelves.

THE MADAME BUTTERFLY NARRATIVES

David Henry Hwang's 1988 Tony Award winning play *M. Butterfly* tells an
incredible story. In his twenty-year-long affair with Beijing Opera performer,
including the birth of a child, the French diplomat Rene Gallimard had
learned nothing at all about his lover — not even the truth of his sex. Gallimard
had never seen his "girlfriend" naked, and is quoted saying, "I thought she
was very modest. I thought it was a Chinese custom." At Gallimard's trial it
is revealed that his lover was not only a Chinese spy but also a man. This baf-
fling true story of a Frenchman duped by a Chinese man masquerading as a
woman serves as a perfect footnote on *Madame Butterfly,* the best-known cinematic inscription of Asian women. Disruptive of naturalized gender categories, Hwang's *M. Butterfly*, as Jessica Hagedorn observed, tells "more
about the mythology of the prized Asian women and the superficial trappings
of gender than most movies that star real women."[26] As a direct reversal of
the miscegenation threat presented in the yellow peril stereotypes, Asia (in
these yellow fever narratives) ceased to be a place of peril, becoming instead
a place of tropical beaches, magical cultures, exotic landscapes, and sexual
encounters, where "Asian women are objects of desire, who provide sex,
color and texture in what is essentially a white man's world."[27]

It has long been Hollywood tradition for a white male lead to freely con-
duct liaisons with any nonwhite women. East-West romances in particular
have sparked many literary and theatrical works in the West, perhaps the most
enduring of which is *Madame Butterfly*, the archetype of Oriental femininity.
First written as a magazine short story by John Luther Long in 1898, *Madame
Butterfly* was adapted into a one-act play by David Belasco two years later.
Giacomo Puccini's opera, at first a fiasco in its 1904 premiere at La Scala,
Milan, quickly became one of the most widely preformed and long-lasting in
the repertory.[28] The story of Madame Butterfly is well known. Pinkerton, a
bored U.S. naval officer stationed in Nagasaki, fakes a wedding to develop a
liaison with Cho-Cho-San, a local Japanese prostitute. After he departs, she
gives birth to his child and then anxiously awaits his return. Several years
later, Pinkerton returns with his elegant American wife, but only to claim his
child, not his abandoned lover. Heartbroken, Cho-Cho-San commits suicide.

Madame Butterfly, as Endymion Wilkinson observes, became a master narrative in Orientalist discourse:

> In recent centuries the rich tradition of Oriental exoticism took a new form as colonial conquest and rule provided the opportunity in the form of readily available girls, and encouraged Europeans and Americans to think of the West as active and masculine and the East as passive and feminine.[29]

Various Hollywood versions of the Butterfly tale have been set in Japan (Mary Pickford's drama [1915], Sessue Hayakawa's "sequel" to *Madame Butterfly, His Birthright* [1918], *Sayonara* [1957], *The Crimson Kimono,* [1959]), China (Anna May Wong's *Toll of the Sea* [1922], and *Sand Pebbles* [1966]), Vietnam (*China Gate* [1957]), and several Chinatowns (*Daughter of the Dragon* [1931] and its contemporary sequel *The Year of the Dragon* [1985]). As Marchetti has observed, in the Western vision of Asia, the entire continent becomes exotic, beckoning woman, who can always satisfy white males' forbidden desires.

In numerous Hollywood films, Asian women were routinely depicted in film as spoils of war and objects of pleasure for lonely soldiers. In *The World of Suzie Wong*, for example, the sexy and pretty Suzie (played by Nancy Kwan) works out of a bar frequented by white sailors. William Holden plays a white "nice guy" painter. Suzie falls madly in love with him. She and the other prostitutes in this movie are cute, giggling, dancing sex machines. In all these stories, the Asian-white love must be illicit, and, because it breaks taboos, it offers forbidden pleasures for the audience. In the early 1990s, this Asian whore image was perpetuated in a British musical megahit *Miss Saigon* (1991). A slight reworking of the Butterfly construction, its plot cannot be more familiar. Cho-Cho-San has become Kim, a Saigon prostitute, while Lieutenant Pinkerton now is an enlisted man named Chris. He goes away. She has his child. He returns with an American wife. She kills herself. The producers themselves have *Miss Saigon* as an updated adaptation of *Madame Butterfly*. Replete with "Orientalist" touches, exotic costumes, and peculiar actions, the musical renews the stereotype of the destitute, helpless, and ultimately disposable Asian woman who is foolish enough to pin her hope on a white lover.

Unlike Black women, who are consistently reduced to mammies by Hollywood, Asian women find their bodies are more often fetishized as objects of sexual conquest and seduction, as casualties of war, as mail-order items.[30] These Lotus Blossoms, as Renee Tajima calls them, are utterly feminine, delicate, and quiet, a rare antithesis of their often allegedly loud independent American counterparts.

THE CHARLIE CHAN GENRE

Asian and Asian American screen representations are often classified into good guys and bad guys, with some slight variations. A new order of "good" Asian representation is created in the Charlie Chan stories. As early as the 1930s, a "Good boy, Charlie" character, the Asian manservant, began to appear in Hollywood movies. Based on a derogatory term for Japanese houseboys, like the fawning houseboy in *Auntie Mame* (1958), this domestic servant character was often known as Charlie.[31] With his typical traits, such as submissiveness, loyalty, and lack of sexuality, Charlie would soon become the prototype for another reigning Asian stereotype, the famous Oriental detective Charlie Chan.

Beginning in the 1930s the "inscrutable Oriental detective" stories were developed by 20th Century Fox and Paramount, including the films about Mr. Moto and Mr. Wong. However, Charlie Chan, based on Earl Derr Biggers's novels, was the best-known. "Chan was the epitome of the 'damned clever Chinese,'" as Harold Isaacs wrote, "blandly humble in the face of Occidental contempt and invariably confounding all concerned by his shrewd solution of the crime."[32] Created at almost the same time in Hollywood, the benevolent Charlie Chan balanced out the diabolical Fu Manchu. The two are inextricably intertwined in Hollywood fiction. John Stone (the producer of the original Chan films at Fox Studios) was quoted saying that the Chan characterization "was deliberately decided upon as a refutation of the unfortunate Fu Manchu characterization of the Chinese, and partly as a demonstration of his own idea that any minority group could have been sympathetically portrayed on the screen with the right story and the right approach."[33] Having appeared in forty-six films, the Charlie Chan character became institutionalized as the nonthreatening Asian (read: a physical wimp, a sexual deviant, and a political yes-man).

Evidently Charlie Chan films have developed the narrative tradition of depicting Asian males as stealthy and nonassertive, devoid of all the traditional masculine qualities associated with Anglo-American males. Frank Chin compared this Asian image to the "house nigger" stereotype for African Americans. "House niggers is what America has made of us," Chin wrote, "admiring us for being patient, submissive, aesthetic, passive, accommodating and essentially feminine in character . . . what whites call 'Confucianist,' dreaming us up [as] a goofy version of Chinese culture to preserve in becoming the white male's dream minority."[34] If we put this stock Asian male character in a comparative perspective with the portrayal of other ethnic groups, Frank Chin's observation seems quite true. Hispanic males, for example, are often presented as extremely macho individuals, who are subject to uncontrollable fits of temper, drinking, and violent outbursts.[35] The earliest "greaser" movies were typical examples of this character type. And black male film images have been changing drastically over the years, in Donald Bogle's words, from "toms, coons and servants to bucks and heroes." The earlier submissive image of the 'good negro" Uncle Tom has largely been replaced since the 1960s by Black tough guys, in the so-called blaxploitation films. The full-grown tough, arrogant, and very decisive John Shaft in the early 1970s helped to create what Bogle called a period of Buckmania. In a sense, the emerging Black tough guy "seemed to be avenging all those earlier black males who had to bow and kowtow."[36] (Interestingly, *kowtow* is well-chosen, coming from a Chinese word for obsequious difference.)

In sharp contrast, Asian male characters have been and continue to be feminized. Chiung Hwang Chen, for example, has located a cinematic castration, so to speak, in the 1993 movie *The Ballad of Little Jo*. The plot of the movie, writes Chen, portrays Asian men as effeminate and "devoid of the typical American maleness."[37] Peter Feng, for another example, addresses Asian masculinity (or lack of it) through a comparative analysis of Steven Okazaki's *American Sons* (1995) and mainstream media.[38] It is also interesting to note that in the last couple of decades the Asian sissy male image in heterosexual relations has spread into homosexual relations. In the gay community, the derogatory term "rice queen" has often been used to refer to a gay Caucasian man primarily attracted Asian men. In their relationships, the Asian virtually always plays the role of the "woman" and the so-called "rice queen" is the "man" both culturally and sexually. "This pattern of relationships had become so codified," David Henry Hwang noted, "that until recently, it was considered unnatural for gay Asians to date one another."[39] The symbolic meaning of this pattern is well-articulated by bell hooks in *black looks*:

> Within white supremacist, capitalist patriarchy the experience of men dressing as women, appearing in drag, has always been regarded by the dominant heterosexist cultural gaze as a sign that one is symbolically crossing over from a realm of power into a realm of powerlessness.[40]

In the 1960s, a new rendering of the "model minority" entered the long Hollywood Charlie Chan tradition. Intended to be read as a positive and sympathetic portrayal of Asians, the model minority image is a new variation of the old Charlie Chan genre. *Flower Drum Song* (1961), the first and possibly only all-Asian-cast Broadway musical, portrayed the Chinese community as humble, quiet, and successful. As Renee Tajima commented, *Flower Drum Song* "gave birth to a whole new generations of stereotypes—gum chewing Little Leaguers, enterprising businessmen and all-American tomboys of the new model minority myth."[41] The model minority image represents "a new bent on racist representations of Asian Americans," as Marchetti points out, and it can also be traced to the Charlie Chan prototype.[42] This deliberate social positioning is grounded in a kind of white paternalism. Historian Roger Daniels has perceptively pointed to overt racist comparisons by neoconservatives between the Black underclass and more upwardly mobile Japanese and Chinese Americans.[43]

What is more, the female Asian newscaster image (modeled after Connie Chung) "has [also] come to embody a new bent on racist representations of Asian Americans as the 'model minority.'"[44] Representations of Asian broadcast anchorwomen have lately appeared even in some mainstream movies and TV series like *The American President* (1995), *Hard Copy* (1994), and *Quantum Leap* (1994). However, the best footnote to this new twist of Asian cinematic representation is Miramax Film's plan to resurrect the Charlie Chan movie.[45] In sharp contrast to the portly hero of the past, the new Chan, according to Gary Granat, senior executive vice president at Miramax, will be a "more well-rounded character" who is hip, slim, cerebral, sexy, and (naturally) a martial arts master. Best of all, this new Chan of the 1990s will be played by Russell Wong, a Chinese American, instead of a white man. "Clearly, by the casting of Russell Wong as the new Chan," Granat promises, "our efforts are to make him into a real role model for Asian and non-Asian audiences."[46]

In the twenty-first century, these Asian images are still alive and thriving in the media. To any careful observer it is no secret that with very little variation the same racist and sexist fantasies about Asians and Asian Americans continue to flourish and to command the popular consciousness. As Herbert Schiller describes in his book *The Mind Managers*, the recycled or reinscribed screen stereotypes of Asian Americans in television and film are constantly consumed by the general population.[47] Thanks to new conceptual studies (for example, in psychology and linguistics) on ethnicity in film, media's impact on spectators' attitudes towards others, particularly with regard to prejudice and stereotyping, is beginning to receive more critical attention. Scholars in social psychology, for example, have applied a social-cognitive approach to the film-viewer relationship. Film audience members as social cognizers "actively select, organize, transform, and interpret film information at times in a biased or distorted way, guided by their needs, values and beliefs, especially those concerning 'self' and 'others.'"[48] This alternative reading of the spectator's role is further developed in the field of linguistics. Film scholars have also borrowed the critical concept of "dialogism" from Russian scholar Mikhail Mikhailovich Bakhtin in the study of race and ethnic representation.[49] For Bakhtin, language, text, and media are essentially a matter of utterances or voices rather than sentences and images. "Each cultural voice," he claims, by nature "exists in dialogue with other voices."[50] Even though listeners, readers, and spectators do not speak from the film itself, they are already in the conversational process with it. Thus, the Bakhtinian formulation of dialogism posits an active role for the audience members, who are not passive recipients of the film message but rather are constantly in internal dialogue with the film they are viewing. This politics of representation is the subject of the second section of this chapter.

POLITICS OF REPRESENTATION

Many audiences in the United States resist the idea that images have an ideological intent . . . image making is political—that politics of domination informs the way the vast majority of images we consume are constructed and marketed.[51]

Bell hooks makes this insightful comment in her book *Black Looks*. She argues that images and representation can most usefully be understood as a specific signifying practice. In the same vein, Stuart Hall calls for our critical attention to the "politics of representation." "There is no escape from the politics of representation," he argues, "and we cannot wield 'how life really is out there' as a kind of test against which the political rightness or wrongness of a particular cultural strategy or text can be measured."[52] But it is Edward Said's theory of Orientalism that allowed film historians and scholars to make the shift from the former simplistic notion of imagery to representation in films as a means of political discourse. The concept of Orientalism has become a powerful analytical tool in the study of racial, ethnic, and gender representation in visual media (especially with regard to Asians and North Africans).[53] To put it simply, *Orientalism* helped to raise discussions on racism, colonialism, and Asian representation to new levels, concerning the question of power and systems of representation. According to Said, Orientalism is less about the Orient, as a particular geographical area, than about the historical experience of confronting and representing the other. "The Orient was Orientalized not only because it was discovered to be 'Oriental' . . .," Said wrote perceptively, "but *made* Oriental."[5] As a Eurocentric idea, Orientalism promotes the differences between the familiar (Europe, the West, "us") and the strange (the Orient, the East, "them").

In his book, Said pointed out that "the Orient helped to define Europe (or the West) as its contrasting image, idea, personality, and experience."[55] The Orient became a sort of surrogate self for the West. That is where the

conventional East/West dichotomy came from. Under this East/West, self/
other polarity, Orientals are what Occidentals are not. In public perceptions
(people's minds) Orientals and Westerners are binary categories defined always in reference to each other. For "Orientalism to make sense at all depends
more on the West than on the Orient," Said argued,

> and this sense is directly indebted to various Western techniques of representa-
> tion that make the Orient visible, clear, "there" in discourse about it. And these
> representations rely upon institutions, traditions, conventions, agreed-upon
> codes of understanding for their effects, not upon a distant and amorphous
> Orient.[56]

As a colonial master discourse, Hollywood's movies perpetuate examples of
Orientalism in their generic formulas, narrative conventions, and cultural assumptions. Hollywood's representation of Asians follows Rudyard Kipling's
famous saying, "East is East and West is West, and Never the Twain Shall
Meet."

Although Edward Said drew his primary evidence of Orientalism from academic writing, travel literature, and novels, there has been a growing body
of literature on Orientalism in film published in the 1980s and 1990s.[57] As
Matthew Bernstein stated, "In *Orientalism*, Said expressed the hope that additional studies of other aspects of the phenomenon would follow his own,
and indeed cultural critics and theorists have take up Orientalism as an in-
triguing and compelling paradigm for the representation of race, ethnicity,
and gender in the media, and particularly in film."[58] Three recent books on
Asian visual representation are exemplary works in this growing body of literature: Gina Marchetti's *Romance and the "Yellow Peril": Race, Sex, and
Discursive Strategies in Hollywood Fiction* (1993), James Moy's *Marginal
Sights: Staging the Chinese in America* (1993), and Darrell Y. Hamamoto's
Monitored Peril: Asian American and the Politics of TV Representation
(1994). Marchetti examines "the way which narratives featuring Asian-Cau-
casian sexual liaisons work ideologically to uphold and sometimes subvert
culturally accepted notions of nation, class, race, ethnicity, gender, and sexual orientations."[59] Similarly, tracing the history of representations of the Chinese, both on Broadway and in Hollywood, Moy's book "consists of ten readings, each a treatment of Euro-American strategies deployed in the staging of
the Chinese in America."[60] Hamamoto contextualized the "symbolic subordination" of Asian Americans on television, in the historical systems of racism,
such as the ideology of "manifest destiny," U.S. military action in Asia, and
the Japan-bashing movement in the 1980s and 1990s. He writes: "Popular
cultural forms such as network television programs are especially effective
vehicles for the transmission of a racialized discourse that confers legitimacy

to white supremacist social institutions and power arrangement."[61] Hamamoto skillfully frames the history of the representation of Asians on American television in a political, economic, and psychosocial color-caste system.

In this section, I will briefly discuss the representational strategies of Hollywood and how they operate and function as a powerful tool of social control with regard to Asian Americans.

REPRESENTATIONAL STRATEGIES

The late film historian James Snead once wrote about Hollywood's strategies of Black representation. "My work on Hollywood film analyzes film stereotypes in terms of codes they form, and makes these codes legible, inspecting their inner working as well as the external historical subjects they would conceal."[62] Specifically, he identified three devices used in Hollywood fiction on Black Americans. "Whenever you see blacks, in Hollywood movies especially," Snead suggested, "you should be looking for three kinds of operation: mythification; marking; and omission."[63]

A careful analysis of their formal properties reveals that similar schemes are deployed by Hollywood in representing Asian Americans. In Hollywood fiction Black mythification easily becomes Asian inscrutability. Indeed, Asians have long been stereotyped as "inscrutable Orientals." Asian characters in film can be good or bad, but they are always mysterious. "The anthropological gaze," as Moy explains, "the look that seeks to dominate, subjugate, and colonize," represents the mythification device Hollywood uses on Asians. Moy argues that the imperialistic gaze, as a representational practice, provides the means for the Anglo-American construction of "Chineseness." The gaze assumes authority of pseudoscientific objectivity and authenticates the self/other differences. In films, often the gaze translates into manipulation of the mise-en-scène. DeMille's silent film *The Cheat*, shot on black-and-white film stock, is a good case in point. Lighting and shadows were skillfully manipulated to highlight Arakau's mysterious qualities. The kimono, the statue of Buddha, the rich silks, the figurines, and the incense burning created a perfect mise-en-scène of Oriental inscrutability. While it is difficult to describe inscrutability, some of the key elements are racial features (body shapes, facial features, and skin color), peculiar dress and hair styles, exotic eating habits, weird customs, and grotesque language accents.

In turn, marking (distinguishing racial traits), for Asian Americans, has been largely achieved by their racialization. The longtime Hollywood practice of racialization is played throughout what Eugene Wong has called "yellow-facing," or racist cosmetology. This tradition not only allows the white actors and actresses to steal the show, but, like blackface, it helps dramatize Asian racial features (such as "slanted" eyes), to the extent of absurdity. For example, the title character in the Charlie Chan series was always portrayed by a white actor. Before his sudden death in 1938, Warner Oland performed the lead in some sixteen Charlie Chan films. He established the "good Oriental" detective type with his mysterious crime-solving ways. Oland's successors included Sidney Toler and Roland Winters. These white actors played the inscrutable Oriental detective Charlie Chan with taped eyelids and a singsong, "chop suey" accent. James Wong Howe, the famous Chinese American cameraman, was reported to call whites in Chinese roles "adhesive tape actors" because of this practice.[64]

This discourse of racialization also exists in the real world. A World War II-era *Time* magazine cover story provided the following "helpful" guide for the difference between the Chinese and Japanese:

> Japanese are likely to be stockier and broader-hipped than the short Chinese. . . . Chinese, not as hairy as Japanese, seldom grown an impressive mustache. . . Although both have the typical epicanthic fold of the upper eyelid (which makes them look almond-eyed), Japanese eyes are usually set closer together . . . the Chinese expression is likely to be more placid, kindly, open; the Japanese more positive, dogmatic, arrogant . . . Japanese are hesitant, nervous in conversation, laugh loudly at the wrong time . . . Japanese walk stiffly erect, hard heeled. Chinese, more relaxed, have an easy gait, sometimes shuffle.[65]

In addition to the physical features, heavy Asian accents become another way of marking their differences. Elaine Kim, for example, did a careful analysis of the dialect of Charlie Chan, which is characterized by high-pitched, singsong tones; tortured syntax; the confounding of "l's" and "R's"; the proliferation of "*ee*"-endings; and the random omission of articles and auxiliary verbs.[66] This Charlie Chan dialect has become a recognizable feature of stereotypical "Asian" racial traits.[67]

"The death of Asia," a key narrative device in Hollywood fiction, has been discussed by several scholars as a way of omission (by killing off Asian characters). Dorothy Jones named the relationship between suicide, death, and sex "the death syndrome," while Maxine Hong Kingston called it the Oriental "suicide urge and suicide mode."[68] "There are a whole series of films," wrote Jones, "in which one of the lovers meets a tragic death before the match can be consummated."[69] James Moy describes "the death of Asia on the American field of representation" as a continuing motif in popular American culture.[70] Eugene Wong suggests that Asian life is portrayed by Hollywood as "cheap," or as less valuable than American life. In war genre movies between

1930 and 1975, according to Wong, an average of ten Asians were killed for every white.[71] The death syndrome is a constant Western-Asian theme and can be found as early as Cho-Cho-San in *Madame Butterfly*, around the turn of the century, and as recently as *Miss Saigon* in the 1990s. The device seems to provide the only possible ending to early love stories between an Asian and a Caucasian. In *The Bitter Tea of General Yen* (1933), for example, Megan (a captured missionary wife) falls in love with the general, but their love is never consummated, because Megan tells Yen how she feels only after he has poisoned himself and is dying. In *My Geisha* (1962), an American man praises Japanese women for "jumping into volcanoes" instead of suing for alimony like American women do.

Asian stereotypes and misrepresentations are not an incidental collection of innocent lies, but rather are by-products of a particular social order controlled by the "mind managers," a term invented by Herbert Schiller to describe media moguls and leaders of the educational establishment.[72] Thus, we should not only address how characters are depicted in our media, but also consider how they fit into social and ideological structures along the lines of race, class, gender, and ethnicity.

CONTROLLING IMAGES

In *Monitored Peril*, Darrell Hamamoto developed the concept of "controlling images"[73] when looking at the ideological context in which television images of Asian Americans are produced. For him, a controlling image is the practice of political, economic, and "psychosocial dominance" of subordinate groups through objectification.[74] Indeed, the most seductive and perhaps most powerful part of "the mind management industry," Hollywood images operate as powerful means of social control. Recently, the relationship between media stereotypes and their social impact has been a main topic of scholarly research on Asian film images. One useful approach scholars have taken lately has been to analyze the relationship between screen images and public prejudices. For example, when children in Georgia were asked their opinions about Japanese, the "majority who had never seen a Japanese before used the adjective 'sneaky,' no doubt strongly influenced by old Hollywood movies recently shown on TV about World War II."[75]

Stereotypes generated by the media serve the dual function of satisfying white self-fulfilling fantasies and blaming the victim. For example, Hollywood's glamorization of interracial romance between white males and Asian females serves some important ideological purposes. Gina Marchetti made an astute comment on the phenomenon: "Although Hollywood films have dealt with a range of interracial relationships between Caucasians and African Americans, Native Americans, and Hispanics, the industry, throughout its history, seems to have taken a special interest in narratives dealing with Asians, Pacific Islanders, and Asian Americans."[76] There is ample evidence to support the argument that sexual practice has been used repeatedly to enforce hierarchies of gender, race, and class in Hollywood industry. The assumption that Blacks are oversexed has served to justify their racial oppression. The similar idea that all Oriental women are utterly feminine and delicate has legitimatized their subordination. This Hollywood-promoted fantasy easily translates into the real world. For example, when Japanese synchronized-swimming star and Seoul Olympics medalist Mikako Kotani dressed in a Kimono to attend an International Olympic Committee meeting in Birmingham, Alabama, she was promptly described by a local reporter as a "geisha girl serving tea."[77] White men have also bought into the so-called yellow fever, with their fetish for exotic Oriental women. This fantasy has actually spawned an entire marriage industry. The Oriental mail-order bride trade has flourished over the past decade, with the Filipina wife particularly in vogue. American men order Asian brides from picture catalogues, just as they might buy a tool from Sears. It appears that many American men are seeking old-fashioned, compliant wives—the type of women they feel are no longer available in the United States.

Recently, several interesting studies have been done on the societal effects of media representation. It was discovered that the media's representation of the characteristics of a particular people helped to explain and excuse social problems in light of those characteristics (read: blaming the victim). A causal relationship between mass media stereotypes and anti-Asian violence has been persuasively articulated in a note in the *Harvard Law Review* entitled "Racial Violence Against Asian Americans."[78] According to statistics collected, Asian Americans suffer a higher per capita rate of hate crimes than any other racial minority. In the note, the author argues that stereotypes function as catalysts to violent crime committed against Asian Americans. "Despite the conventional wisdom that Asian Americans no longer face discrimination, many racial stereotypes continue to inform society's views of Asian Americans."[79]

Specifically, the note identified five major stereotypes. It points out that the perception that Asian immigrants are submissive, physically unaggressive, and politically docile may invite crimes. Asian Americans often become choice victims of street crime because they are deemed as unlikely to resist. Another stereotype of Asian Americans is that they are seen as foreigners, and this "animated a territorial response." "Because Asian Americans are different," the note suggests, "and because the difference is conceived as foreign—

not in a cosmopolitan sense, but in the aberrant, un-American sense they are denied the respect granted to fellow members of our national community."[80] This supposedly intrinsic foreignness promotes the "nativist" response. In the turf war against outsiders, a scapegoating response against Asian Americans goes hand in hand with turf protection. The tactic of classifying Asian Americans both as unfair competitors and as the model minority "amounts to interracial baiting that heightens resentment against Asian Americans."[81] Finally, the dehumanization of Asian Americans removes the social and psychological inhibitions against committing violence on a fellow human being. "For Asian American victims," the author notes, "the psychological process of dehumanization is achieved via the stereotype of foreignness, which denies them 'in-group' status, and that of fungibility, which strips them of individual dignity."[82] Indeed, the "foreigner" and the "fungible" (racial lumping) stereotypes "transmogrif[y] Asian Americans into a faceless, deindividualized horde" and also "[bridge] national boundaries holding Asian Americans culpable for the deeds of Asian governments."[83] Clarence Spigner, in his article, "Teaching Multiculturalism from the Movies: Health and Social Well-being," finds a correlation between Hollywood stereotypes about Asian Americans and the 1983 real-life death, at the hands of two assailants, of Vincent Chin in Detroit.[84]

Japanese American clinical psychologist Herbert Horikawa looks at the sociofilmic control from a clinical point of view.[85] As indicated by the title of his article, "Psychological Implications of Asian Stereotypes in the Media," Horikawa explores how racist stereotypes, as a special form of abuse, contribute to Asian Americans' developing "learned helplessness" (a psychological theory).[86] Because of the discriminatory information received from the mass media, Horikawa argues, Asian Americans develop the expectation of not having control over their lives. Accordingly, they tend to be less likely to try to exert control and power. Despite its limitations (for one, assuming the audience is a passive and uninformed Asian American one), the essay calls our attention to racism in visual media "as a special form of abuse in which the abused feel powerless."[87]

Misrepresentations not only justify the status quo by rationalizing racism, but they also create harm through "colonization of the imagination." Jessica Hagedorn, a Filipina American, wrote in *Ms.* Magazine:

> Colonization of the imagination is a two-way street. And being enshrined on a pedestal as someone's Pearl of the Orient fantasy doesn't seem so demeaning, at first; who wouldn't want to be worshipped? Perhaps that's why Asian women are the ultimate wet dream in most Hollywood movies; it's no secret how well we've been taught to play the role; to take care of our men.[88]

Stereotypes also help develop cognitive associations between race and aesthetics. For Asian women, judgments of physical beauty and self-worth are sometimes internalized from culturally imposed expectations. Asian female's anatomy has always been subjected to imposed ideals of physical beauty. Body shapes, facial features, and skin fairness are assigned value in a hierarchical manner. This mystique of Asian women is based on Western standards of exotic beauty, because the standard of beauty is not usually Asian, African, or Latino. The superstars in show business remain white and usually blond, though sometimes a brunet. A different reading of the Nancy Kerrigan/Tonya Harding soap opera on ice proves the point. In the media glitz on the incident, Kerrigan was uniformly described as a "classic American beauty." Lucrative business deals were piling up for her. The skater reportedly flew to Disney, for an advertising contract, without attending the closing ceremony for the winter Olympics in 1996, in which she won the silver medal. In contrast, four years ago, Kristi Yamaguchi, who won two world championships and an Olympic gold medal in Albertville, France, in 1992, was never able to cash in on her championship. Yamaguchi was "cold-shouldered" by American advertisers because she looked Japanese, and not blue-eyed and blond-haired.[89]

John Fiske, in his analysis of Michel Foucault's *Discipline and Punish*, incisively wrote, "Foucault has revealed in detail the ways in which western societies have made the body into the site where social power is most compellingly exerted. The body is where the power-bearing definitions of social and sexual normality are, literally, embodied."[90] The ideologies of gender and race often place the Asian female body under the burden of conformity. Eugenia Kaw's essay, "Medicalization of Racial Features: Asian American Women and Cosmetic Surgery" is a solid case study of the cosmetic alterations found among Asian American women in the San Francisco Bay Area (which includes nine counties).[91] Kaw presented well-documented findings on the most popular types of cosmetic surgery among Asian American women: eyelid restructuring, nose bridge buildup, and nose tip altering. Her research suggested that these women had internalized not only a gender ideology like other women, but also a racial ideology that associated their natural features with negative connotations. What was more, she discovered that the media industry and the industry of medicine had joined forces in promoting these racial and gender stereotypes.

This process of internalization does not stop here. It leads further to "flawed self-representation" (to borrow a term from James Moy). In his spirited analysis of "the establishment of a new order of stereotypes, authenticated by its Asian American authorship," Moy has found that Asian American artists unconsciously participate in perpetuating and even institutionalizing Hollywood's false cinematic images. Moy makes the valid point that stereotypes have infiltrated and transformed the consciousness of Asian American artists as much as they have transformed the consciousness of the Anglo-American audience.[92] "Unfortunately for Asian America," Moy wrote, "most recent playwrights have located the struggle under the sign of greater racial authenticity. What better way to get behind the façade of the Chinese stereotype than to have a Chinese American guide?"[93]

Although his criticism is seriously undermined because of his reductive reasoning, in attributing popularity to a "complicitous desire" to "cater to Anglo-American expectations," Moy's argument brings to the forefront an important dimension of internalization. The dominant systems of representation have the power to represent and, by extension, to shape the consciousness of those who are the subjects of representation. Mira Nair's film *Mississippi Masala* (1991), for example, was criticized for its caricatures of Indian characters. Their mannerisms, "such as the bobbing of the head from side to side (an Indian way of saying yes)," to paraphrase Erika Surat Andersen in *Film Quarterly*, are exaggerated to the point of ridicule. "The Indian community is shown to be greedy, petty, and ridiculous," Andersen wrote. The men are drunks and the women are gossips. The hotel owner is greedy and hypocritical—paying lip service to people of color, displaying solidarity in one moment and disapproving of interracial romance the next. The bridegroom is depicted as effeminate, impotent, and ludicrous. In one of several bedroom scenes, he checks under his pajamas for an erection, and then hops on top of his bride (who emphatically rejects him), so finally he puts on headphones and watched TV instead. "If a non-Indian film-maker had portrayed such characters," Andersen speculated, "there would have been public outcry at the racist stereotypes. What does it mean for a film-maker to make such a film about her own people?" she asked indignantly. "Is it that she feels privileged to poke fun at her own kind? Are these scenes included purely for comic relief?"[94]

On the small screen, some critics have accused *All-American Girl* of being merely a multicultural spectacle for a white audience. This ABC domestic comedy, which premiered on September 28, 1995, was about a Korean American "Valley Girl" torn between her family's traditional values and the mall culture of Southern California. Gary Jacobs mentioned that *All-American Girl* was watched by 25 to 30 million people every week. "For many of them," he said, "this is probably the first time they are meeting an Asian American family."[95] However, the show caused some heated debates among its defenders and detractors. Guy Aoki, President of MANAA (the Media Action Network for Asian Americans), a media watchdog organization, was one of the show's star Margaret Cho's strongest supporters. "We feel 'All-American Girl' is positive," Aoki declared at an Achievement Awards dinner in honor of Cho, Janet Yang (the president of Ixtlan), and Russell Wong (star of the television series *Vanishing Son*), "because it is the first television series to feature an Asian American family. It is important for people across the country to see Asian faces every week, because in the past, we have been invisible or just purveyors of stereotypes."[96] Given the essentially conservative nature of network programming, most Asian Americans appreciated the first prime-time network series in television history with a primarily Asian American cast. But despite its stated goal to "crush Korean stereotypes (and find Cho a man)," the show was often cited by Asian American critics as an example of flawed self-representation.[97] In an interview Cho stated that "my character breaks all the stereotypes about Asian Americans. She's not good at math, she's lazy, she's rebellious, she's very outspoken. That sort of shatters all the stereotypes."[98] Many Asian American viewers and critics, though, regarded the show as offensive and misleading, for it emphasized cultural conflict instead of racism as the major theme, and it reinforced the model minority image. Their point is very well taken. Cho herself has compared her Asian American sitcom to the *Bill Cosby Show*. "The only thing I can possibly compare it to is the debut of 'The Cosby Show.' I'm Bill Cosby."[99] All in all, the small business-owning Kim family in the Cho show is presented as a showcase of the Asian success story. The show avoids any references to race and racism. As a reader of *AsianWeek* wrote, "'All-American Girl' is a banana — yellow on the outside, and white on the inside. It tries too hard to be all-American. And it fails because it relies too heavily on stereotypes, while taking few risks."[100]

Although the postscript at the end of each episode credits the show as being based on Margaret Cho's standup comedy, critics believe the critical Asian American perspectives of the actress's routines is lost in the sitcom. Bill Wong observes that "none of Cho's razor-like observations on race, ethnicity and culture were included in her character's dialogue with her parents, siblings or workmates. Except for the obvious physical features of most of the cast, one would be hard pressed to even know this show had Asian sensibilities."[101] Even though Touchstone TV made a last-ditch effort to rescue the show from poor ratings (including firing both executive producer Gary Jacobs and the show's writers, and replacing most of Cho's TV Korean American family), it went off the air after only one season.

Because of the lack of specific data concerning public and individual responses to specific movies, much work still needs to be done to determine precisely how audiences receive, distill, and believe Asian film images. In short, the effect of cinematic Asian representation remains an elusive matter hidden in the biographies of many men and women, which calls for new research and interpretations. What is more, film texts should be viewed as sites of ideological struggle and contestation. Their reception is a dynamic and dialogic process. Stuart Hall, among many others, calls for critical attention to the operation of resistance and alternative readings among ethnic groups. In fact, ethnicity can function as "both imprisoning stigma and potentially liberating identity."[102] Independent Asian American cinema, as alternative media, serves as a good example for this struggle with mainstream media in contesting Asian film representation. As a result, replication of hegemony by the mainstream media is disrupted, and oppositional narratives provide important alternatives to Hollywood representation of Asians and Asian Americans.

ROLE PLAYING IN REPRESENTATION

When we discuss racial stereotypes, we tend to think about them in either a cultural or an ideological sense, and rarely do we give serious thoughts to mass media's institutional aspect of representing people of a certain race. Using ideas from Russian formalists and neo-Marxists, Eugene Wong's dissertation-derived book *On Visual Media Racism: Asians in the American Motion Pictures* provides a much-needed perspective, relating textual practices to the institution of production. Wong argues that although the motion picture industry's racism against Asians has its definitive individual and cultural proponents, it was the institutionalized nature of the industry's racism against Asians that was particularly humiliating.[103] Drawn from studio archives and personal documents, Wong's work points directly to Hollywood's institutional modes of representation. While Wong touches on all three aspects of cinema, including production (capital, talent, and creation), distribution (marketing, promotion, and reviews) and exhibition, I will focus on three industry wide racist practices in casting as a particularly important dimension of the racism embedded in institutional representation: role segregation, role stratification, and role delimitation.

ROLE SEGREGATION

Segregating actors by roles seems to be reasonable, sometimes even desirable, when ethnic characters are cast. But the major problem is not role segregation per se, but the double standards used in casting. In the film industry, as Wong has carefully documented, Asians cannot cross into roles that are designated as white, yet Caucasian actors have the right to break the barriers of role segregation and cross freely into Asian roles (or Hispanic roles, and so on). This represents the discriminatory practice of one-way cross-over. Two historical reasons can be given for the persistence of this practice against Asian Americans. First, Asians cannot play white roles because of the two-tiered racial system in America. Contrary to our understanding as a people, America in the movies is not every color, but basically Black and White. This bifurcated system of representation is one of the root causes for Asian segregation on screen. Secondly, Asians cannot play white roles because of the East/West dichotomy. Asians could play their "ethnic" or foreign roles, but not those of general Americans. The film industry will be reluctant to cast Asians as part of the mainstream of American life until Asians are accepted by the society at large.

It is interesting to note that, to maintain this double standard, Eurasian characters have become Hollywood's favorite creations. These mixed-race characters obviously allow white actors and actresses, with minimum makeup, to steal major roles from Asians. The best example is the Eurasian role in the TV series *Kung Fu*. Bruce Lee was rejected by Warner Bros. for the leading role despite his awesome martial arts expertise and Chinese ethnicity. Hollywood deemed it legitimate for the Eurasian role to go to white actor David Carradine. "This racial rejection by Hollywood," as Tiana (Thi Thanh Nga) recalls in a recent article, "Bruce told me, made him furious. It impelled him to leave the United States and return to Hong Kong, where, in two dizzying years, he became an international legend." The week before he died, Tiana remembers, Lee vowed to "outgross Steve McQueen and James Coburn," and so he did. Both McQueen and Coburn were Lee's students, and yet "each had told him that he [Lee] could never reach their star status because he was Chinese."[104]

The controversy over the musical *Miss Saigon* is probably the most recent example of this "Asian drag" practice. In the Broadway production of the musical, the furiously debated decision of casting Jonathan Pryce (a white British actor) as the lead role of Eurasian male character allowed the British producer, Cameron Mackintosh, to literally practice the same tradition Hollywood had established for Asian characters. Under the guise of artistic freedom, Mackintosh's argument for color-blind casting could only serve to reinforce inequalities already in existence. Angela Pao's critical essay added one interesting dimension to the debate.[105] She drew our attention to how the cultural process worked in this case, specifically concerning gender and race. She argued that color-blind casting was impossible in *Miss Saigon*. The producer's decision to cast an Asian woman and a Caucasian man was *not* accidental. Rather, it had to do with the genre and the theatrical parameters: East/West tragic romance. Like *Madame Butterfly*, this Western maternal melodrama carried the following imperatives: the Asian prostitute, the "fallen woman," the maternal devotion to the child and to the lover, the desertion, and finally the suicide. To stick with these genre imperatives, the Eurasian role had to be played by a white man.

As for the implications involved when using cosmetics and wigs to "produce" a different race, Wong wrote:

> The industry's use of racist cosmetics is important in discussing institutional racism against Asians for three reasons: 1) The film industry has demonstrated its racist propensities by concentrating upon external racial differences, in this case the epicanthic fold. 2) The use of racist cosmetics has been instrumental in the establishment of race freedom for white actors in the systems of role segregation and major/minor role stratification. 3) Racist cosmetology has been utilized as a means of justifying the continued displacement of actual Asian actors in the industry as a whole, particularly on the major role level, thereby preventing them from developing professionally within the industry.[106]

Furthermore, Wong emphasizes that, although this cosmetic treatment is not unique to Asians, "no one in this country would dare to put on 'black face' anymore," thereby offending Black racial sensibilities, causing a public scandal, and jeopardizing employment opportunities in the process. Yet, white "producers do not hesitate to allow non-Asians to used 'yellow face' (racist cosmetology)," even to this day.[107]

ROLE STRATIFICATION

Eugene Wong calls role stratification the vertical counterpart to role segregation in the racial politics of casting. While Asian actors and actresses are often cast primarily as background fillers and to create cinematic atmosphere as extras and "racials," he claims they are not considered competent enough to play leading roles. As indicated by D. W. Griffith's curious casting decision in *Broken Blossoms* (1919): "Most of the background characters are Chinese, but a role such as Evil Eye, which required acting talent, was entrusted to Edward Piel, who was all too obviously Caucasian."[108] Thus, opportunities for Asian American performers become fewer and the roles' scope even more minimal, as the importance of the Asian roles rise. The practice of role stratification is more pervasive in casting, but it is even involved in role creation. For example, as Wong has shown in the introduction to his book, the movie industry imposed a system of double standards with regard to interracial romance.[109] Antimiscegenation laws and restrictive Motion Picture Production Code (which held sway from 1934 through the mid-1950s) had long forbade "scenes of passion," and expressly prohibited the filming of interracial sex or marital scenes and themes. However, the industry's double standards are based on the traditional racist assumptions in the white community concerning the "threat" of interracial sex and marriage. Despite such fears, white males are shown to easily transgress interracial sexual prohibitions on-screen. Such duplicitous stands have developed into the so-called phenomenon of "sexualization of racism."

In recent years, we have seen a new twist in the practice: leading roles are created for white actors or actresses in Asian American-themed productions. For example, when Alan Parker's *Come See the Paradise* (1990) was first released, some Asian Americans accused Dennis Quaid, a white actor, of stealing the stardom. The movie was about the internment of Japanese Americans during World War II. Quaid played a guard who fell in love with a Nisei woman interned in the camp. Regardless of the moviemakers' intentions, the message conveyed was very clear to Asian Americans: a white lead was critical to make the movie acceptable for a mainstream audience. Mira Nair, director of *Mississippi Masala*, experienced similar problems with Hollywood in making her film. "People were disconcerted that we had no white characters [among the seventy-nine speaking parts] in the film," she recalls. One [executive] asked if I couldn't make room for a white protagonist. I said, sure, all the waiters in the film could be white," she recounted, laughing at her suggestion of casting whites as peripheral characters. Not bowing to the pressure, Nair made the movie independently with only $7 million and an independent crew—"an epic on a peanut," as Nair puts it. "We felt the story had to be told in the voices of the people it was about," she insisted. "It's about time one can see the world not necessarily through a white person's point of view."[110]

This phenomenon is perhaps not unique to Asian Americans. In a similar situation, Native American critics raised the same issue with Kevin Costner's blockbuster *Dances with Wolves* (1990). A drastic departure from the old "noble savage" image, the movie offered a more sympathetic portrayal of Native American peoples. But Indian media activists asked why the movie needed a white guide into Native American culture. Was it a white surrogate for the movie audience? To push the argument a bit further, were the Native communities merely offered up as a larger-than-life racial spectacle (in the same vein as graphic violence, alien encounters, car chases, and sex scenes) for the narrative development of the white male lead?

ROLE DELIMITATION

In addition, according to Eugene Wong, Asian Americans have experienced two kinds of role delimitations in the movie industry: numerical and dimensional. Looking over the entire history of mass media, in fact, one sees very few Asian roles in the first place. If we consider the airwaves today, Asians are almost absent, with some important exceptions. In the fall of 1991, the

Media Coalition of Minorities and Women monitored fifty-eight TV shows, and reported that out of 555 characters whose race was identified, only three were Asian (or Asian Pacific) Americans. This lack of employment opportunities has often forced talented Asian Americans to change their careers early. So, to correct this wrong, in 1992 the Media Action Network for Asian Americans (MANAA) launched its so-called "Operation Primetime" campaign in an effort to increase the representation of Asian Americans on TV.

Besides the problem of invisibility or underrepresentation, the roles that Asian Americans have been offered come from a limited number of stereotypes—largely a patchwork of clichés. In on-screen portrayals, white actors and actresses have been depicted as representing the entire spectrum of social and human types, whereas the professional horizons for Asian actors are very limited. Very rarely are the Asian roles fleshed out as fully developed characters. This system of stereotypical delimitations has successfully prevented dimensional development and aesthetic continuity in the creation of Asian characters on the screen. Unfortunately, Asian American actors and actresses have to confront the moral dilemma between reinforcing stereotypes of their people and maintaining their own professional and sometimes economic survival. As Ruthanne Lum McCunn wrote, "These are the images casting directors have in mind at auditions, and they are so powerful that Chinese American actors and actresses sometimes become doubtful about who they are, affecting phony [Asian] accents and using eyebrow pencils to make their eyes more slanted."[111] Adrienne Telemaque, a Chinese American actress, recalled in an interview, "Finally, I did get myself a Suzie Wong wig. I hated doing it, but it's what they want. After buying the wig, I got the job I went out for."[112] This practice reminds us of Robert Townsend's autobiographical *Hollywood Shuffle* (1987), where the filmmaker satirizes Hollywood racial conventions by having white directors "teach" Black performers how to conform to white stereotypes about Black characters.

Left with little choice, some Asian Americans try to make the best of a bad situation. Lauren Tom, who played one of the daughters in *The Joy Luck Club*, said, "I don't want to be Pollyannaish about it, but my attitude is that you're aware of inequalities and the racism that goes on in the world of casting, but to just keep focusing on the positive has enabled me to get parts that are cross-over." Tom's latest role, in *Mr. Jones* (1993) with Richard Gere, was not originally written for an Asian American. It remains to be seen whether this practice is the rule or the exception.

In the past three or four decades, an increasing body of literature has accumulated on Asian cinematic representation. Scholars have approached the subject from various perspectives. While it is beyond the scope of this chapter to present a full-blown account of those works, a limited sampling of the literature has been given here to look at three distinctive but interrelated dimensions of Asian representation in Hollywood: the "Oriental" image embodied in the "yellow peril" formula, the "Madame Butterfly" narratives, and the "Charlie Chan" genre; "politics of representation," the ideological functions of stereotypes as powerful means of social control; and the institutional aspect of representation in the industry, the "yellow-facing" tradition where Asian roles were played by "adhesive tape actors" in Hollywood.

NOTES

1. This essay is a revised version of a previously published chapter in my 1998 book *Asian America trough the Lens: History, Representations, and Identity* (Walnut Creek, CA: AltaMira Press, 1998).

2. Four major books and numerous articles deal with Hollywood stereotyping of Asians and Asian Americans. The four books are: Stuart Creighton Miller, *The Unwelcome Immigrant: The American Image of the Chinese. 1785–1882* (Berkeley, California: University of California Press, 1969); Dorothy B. Jones, *The Portrayal of China and India on the American Screen. 1896–1955* (Cambridge, Massachusetts: Center for International Studies, MIT, 1955); Harold R. Isaacs, *Scratches on our Minds: American Images of China and India* (New York: John Day Company, 1958); and Eugene F. Wong, *On Visual Media Racism: Asians in the American Motion Pictures* (New York: Arno Press, 1978).

3. Carlos E. Cortés, "What is Maria? What is Juan? Dilemmas of Analyzing the Chicano Image in U.S. Feature Films," in *Chicanos and Film: Essays on Chicano Representation and Resistance*, ed. Chon A. Noriega (New York: Garland Publishing, 1992), 83–104.

4. Jones.

5. The better-known works include Christine Choy, "Images of Asian-Americans in Films and Television," in *Ethnic and Racial Images in American Film and Television*, ed. Randall Miller (Philadelphia: Balch Institute, 1978); Richard A. Oehling, "The Yellow Menace: Asian Images in American Film," in *The Kaleidoscopic Lens: How Hollywood Views Ethnic Groups*, ed. Randall Miller (Englewood, New Jersey.: Jerome S. Ozer, 1980); Dick Stromgren, "The Chinese Syndrome: The Evolving Images of Chinese and Chinese-Americans in Hollywood Films," in *Beyond the Stars: Stock Characters in American Popular Film*, ed. Paul Loukides and Linda K. Fuller (Bowling Green, Ohio: Bowling Green State University Popular Press, 1990); and Renee Tajima, "Asian Women's Images in Film: The Past Sixty Years," *In Color: Sixty Years of Minority Women in Film: 1921–1981* (New York: Third World Newsreel, 1993).

6. Jones, 28–36 and 63–65.

7. Choy, 149.

8. Isaacs.

9. Stromgren, 61–77.

10. Isaacs, 63.

11. American writer Jack London, recently revealed to have had white supremacist views, worked as a war correspondent during the Russo-Japanese war. He wrote an influential essay entitled "The Yellow Peril" for the Hearst newspapers (which, perhaps not coincidentally, became tarred with the label "yellow journalism," implying stereotypes and unfair treatment), which helped advocate the yellow peril thesis. For more information, see Frank Gibney, *The Pacific Century: America and Asia in a Changing World* (New York: Maxwell Macmillian International, 1992), 479–511.

12. For a good overview and history of this yellow peril theme in Hollywood, see Oehling, 182–206.

13. Gina Marchetti, *Romance and the Yellow Peril: Race, Sex, and Discursive Hollywood Strategies in Hollywood Fiction* (Berkeley, California: University of California Press, 1993), Chapters 2–4.

14. Gary Hoppenstand, "Yellow Devil Doctors and Opium Dens: A Survey of the Yellow Peril Stereotypes in Mass Media Entertainment," in *The Popular Culture Reader*, ed. Christopher D. Geist and Jack Nachbar (Bowling Green, Ohio: Bowling Green University Popular Press, 1983), 174.

15. Kevin Brownlow, *Behind the Mask of Innocence* (New York: Alfred A. Knopf, 1990). 347.

16. Brownlow., 348.

17. Marchetti, 10.

18. Robert Lang, *American Film Melodrama: Griffith, Vidor, Minnelli* (Princeton, New Jersey: Princeton University Press, 1989), 102.

19. Brownlow, 334.

20. John Dower, *War without Mercy: Race and Power in the Pacific* (New York: Pantheon Press, 1986), 9.

21. Oehling, 204.

22. William K. Everson, *The Bad Guy: A Pictorial History of the Movie Villain* (New York: Citadel, 1964), 130.

23. Colin Nickerson, "Senator's Comment Ignites Fury in Japan," *Boston Globe,* 5 March 1992, 2.

24. Lan Nguyen, *"Rising Sun* Presents Damaging Portrayal of Japanese, Asians," *Rafu Shimpo,* 1 July 1993, 3.

25. For more information, see "Japanese Offended by Bugs 'Toon," *Fort Collins Coloradoan,* 5 February 1995, C1.

26. Jessica Hagedorn, "Asian Women in Film: No Joy, No Luck," *Ms.,* Jan./Feb., 1994, 77–78.

27. Hagedorn, 78.

28. For more information on the history of that opera, see *International Dictionary of Opera* (Detroit: St. James Press, 1993), 784–786.

29. Endymoin Wilkinson, *Japan versus the West: Image and Reality* (London: Penguin, 1990), 113.

30. Renee Tajima, "Lotus Blossoms Don't Bleed: Images of Asian Women," in *Making Waves: Anthology of Writings By and About Asian American Women*, ed. Asian Women United in California (Boston: Beacon Press, 1989), 300–17.

31. I owe the idea about this Charlie character to Amy Kashiwabara's online essay "Vanishing Son: The Appearance, Disappearance, and Assimilation of the Asian-American Man in American Mainstream Media" [http://www.lib.berkeley.edu/MRC/Amydoc.html], 6–8.

32. Isaacs, 119.

33. Jones, 34.

34. Frank Chin, "Confessions of the Chinatown Cowboy," *Bulletin of Concerned Asian Scholars*, vol. 4, no. 3 (Fall 1972), 67.

35. See Randall Miller, *Ethnic and Racial Images*, 243.

36. Donald Bogle, *Toms, Coons, Mulattoes, Mammies, & Bucks: An Interpretive History of Blacks in American Films* (New York: Continuum, 1994), 223.

37. Chiung Hwang Chen, "Feminization of Asian (American) Men in the U.S. Mass Media: An Analysis of 'The Ballad of Little Jo,'" *Journal of Communication Inquiry,* vol. 20, no. 2 (1996), 57.

38. Peter Feng, "Redefining Asian American Masculinity: Steven Okasaki's 'American Sons,'" *Cineaste,* vol. 22, no. 3 (1996).

39. See David Henry Hwang, *M. Butterfly* (New York: Plume Books, 1988), 98.

40. bell hooks, *Black Looks: Race and Representation* (Boston: South End Press, 1992), 146.

41. Tajima, "Asian Women's Images in Film," 27.

42. Marchetti, 216.

43. Roger Daniels, *Asian America: Chinese and Japanese in the United States Since 1850* (Seattle: University of Washington Press, 1988), 317–320.

44. Christine Choy, "Cinema as a Tool of Assimilation: Asian Americans, Women and Hollywood," *In Color*, 25.

45. Somini Sengupta, "Charlie Chan Retooled for the 90's," *New York Times*, 5 January 1997, sec. 2, pg. 20, col. 1.

46. Sengupta.

47. Herbert Schiller, *The Mind Managers* (Boston: Beacon Press, 1973).

48. Paul S. Cowen, "A Social Cognitive Approach to Ethnicity in Films," in *Unspeakable Images: Ethnicity and the American Cinema,* ed. Lester Friedman (Urbana and Chicago: University of Illinois Press, 1991), 353.

49. Robert Stam, "Bakhtin, Polyphony, and Ethnic/Racial Representation," *Unspeakable Images*, 251–76.

50. Stam, 258.

51. hooks, 5.

52. Stuart Hall, "What is this 'Black' in Black Popular Culture," in *Representing Blackness: Issues in Film and Video*, ed. Valerie Smith (New Brunswick, New Jersey: Rutgers University Press, 1997), 131.

53. Edward Said, *Orientalism* (New York: Pantheon Books, 1978).

54. Said, 5–6.

55. Said, 2.

56. Said, 22.

57. *Visions of the East: Orientalism in Film*, ed. Matthew Bernstein and Gaylyn Studlar (New Brunswick, New Jersey: Rutgers University Press, 1997) has a selected bibliography at the back of the book, which is very helpful as a starter.

58. Bernstein, 4–5.

59. Marchetti, 1.

60. James S. Moy, *Marginal Sights: Staging the Chinese in America* (Iowa City, Iowa: University of Iowa Press, 1993) 5.

61. Darrell Y. Hamamoto, *Monitored Peril: Asian Americans and the Politics of TV Representation* (Minneapolis: University of Minnesota Press, 1994), xi.

62. James A. Snead, *White Screens/Black Images: Hollywood from the Dark Side* (New York: Routledge), 2.

63. Snead, 143–149.

64. Brownlow, 325.

65. "How to tell Japs from the Chinese," *Time,* 22 December 1941, 81–82.

66. Elaine Kim, Asian American Literature: An Introduction to the Writings and Their Social Context (Philadelphia: Temple University Press, 1982), 12.

67. Anyone watching the O.J. Simpson trial would agree that Judge Lance Ito spoke perfect unaccented English; still, some people felt free to assign him an exaggerated Japanese accent. On April 4, 1995, New York Senator Alfonse D'Amato, for example, used a distorted Japanese accent during an appearance on a radio talk show to criticize the presiding judge's handling of the Simpson trial. Replacing his R's with L's, D'Amato quipped, "He is making a disgrace of the judicial system. Little Judge Ito. For God's sake, get them in there for 12 hours; get this thing over. I mean, this is a disgrace. Judge Ito with the wet nose. And then he's going to have a hung jury. Judge Ito will keep us from getting a televise[ed] for the next year." D'Amato's use of the mock Asian accent testifies to the power of this marking scheme. See Sam Fulwood III, "N.Y. Sen. D'Amato Apologizes for Using Japanese Accent in Parody of Judge Ito," *Los Angeles Times,* 6 April 1995, Section Part A.

68. Maxine Hong Kingston, *Tripmaster Monkey* (New York: Vintage Books, 1990), 319.

69. Jones, 17.

70. Moy, 82–94.

71. Wong, 241.

72. Schiller, 1.

73. I borrowed the term from Hamamoto's book. See page 1.

74. Hamamoto, 2–3.

75. Wong, 9.

76. Marchetti, 5.

77. As quoted by Karen Ma in *The Modern Madame Butterfly* (Rutland, Vermont and Tokyo: Charles E. Tuttle Company, 1996), 17.

78. *Harvard Law Review,* vol. 106, no. 8 (1 June 1993): 1926–1943.

79. *Harvard Law Review,* 1930–1931.

80. *Harvard Law Review*, 1934.

81. *Harvard Law Review*, 1936.

82. *Harvard Law Review*, 1937.

83. *Harvard Law Review*, 1938.

84. Clarence Spigner, "Teaching Multiculturalism from the Movies: Health and Social Well-being," in *Shared Differences: Multicultural Media and Practical Pedagogy*, ed. Diane Carson and Lester Friedman (Urbana, Illinois: University of Illinois Press, 1995), 106.

85. Herbert Horikawa, "Psychological Implications of Asian Stereotypes in the Media," in *Ethnic and Racial Images in American Film and Television,* ed. Allen Woll and Randall Miller (New York: Garland Publishing, 1988).

86. Horikawa.

87. Horikawa, 162.

88. Hagedorn, 78.

89. Arthur Webb, "Not Quite Gold, The Strange Case of Kristi Yamaguchi," *The Journal of the American Chamber of Commerce*, vol. 30, no. 4 (1 April 1993): 56.

90. John Fiske, *Television Culture* (New York and London: Routledge, 1987), 248.

91. Eugenia Kaw, "Medicalization of Racial Features: Asian American Women and Cosmetic Surgery," *Medical Anthropology Quarterly,* vol. 7, no. 1 (March 1993): 75–89.

92. Moy, 126.

93. Moy, 20.

94. Erika Surat Andersen, "Review: Mississippi Masala," *Film Quarterly*, vol. 46, no. 4 (Summer 94): 25–26.

95. Carlos Mendez, "Melodramatic Margaret Minces the Media Mavens," *AsianWeek*, 23 December 1994), 24.

96. See "MANAA's Media Awards Dinner to Honor Cho, Yang and Wong," *AsianWeek,* 4 November 1994, 15.

97. Monika Guttman, "One-Woman Cho," USA *Weekend,* 16–18 September, 1994, 8.

98. Guttman.

99. John Carmen, "Margaret Cho Breaks Ground in Sitcom Role," *San Francisco Chronicle,* 10 May 1994, E-1.

100. Joann Faung Jean Lee, "Margaret the 'All-American Bust' of TV," *AsianWeek*, 2 December 1994, 6.

101. As quoted by Darby Li Po Price, "'All American Girl' and the American Dream," *Critical Mass: A Journal of Asian American Cultural Criticism,* vol. 2, no. 1 (Winter 1994), 138.

102. Gina Marchetti, "Ethnicity, the Cinema and Cultural Studies," *Unspeakable Images,* 284.

103. Wong, 1–55.

104. Tiana (Thi Thanh Nga), "The Long March—From Wong to Woo: Asians in Hollywood," *Cineaste*, vol. 21, no. 4 (1995): 39.

105. Angela Pao, "The Eyes of the Storm: Gender, Genre and Cross-Casting in Miss Saigon," *Text and Performance Quarterly* 12 (1992): 21-39.

106. Wong, 40.

107. Oriental Actors of America to Actors Equity Association of New York, "Asian Roles for Asian Actors," *Bridge*, vol. 3, no. 3 (June 1974): 4.

108. Brownlow, 327.

109. Wong, 21–29.

110. David Gritten, "Salaam Mississippi," *Los Angeles Times*, 9 February 1992, Calendar Section.

111. Ruthanne Lum McCunn, "Adrienne Telemaque," in *Chinese American Portraits: Personal Histories*, 1828–1988 (San Francisco: Chronicle Books, 1988), 133.

112. McCunn, 133.

Chapter Eight

"Passing: A Reading on a Jewish Woman's Identity"

Bonnie Morris, George Washington University

"Passing" is a story about my experiences as the daughter of a Jewish-Gentile intermarriage. I wrote the script in autumn of 1989, at age twenty-eight, just three months after I had completed my Ph.D. in women's history with a focus on Jewish women's identity in America. I was having little success in publishing my dissertation research or being invited to present my work at academic conferences: Judaica scholars thought my work was "too feminist" and feminist scholars thought it "too Jewish." Frustrated, I decided to write a more personal storyline on Jewish identity, articulating my experiences as someone who cares passionately about Jewish culture and survival but *does not look* Jewish. Perhaps I'd be welcomed at conferences if I could provoke audiences with performance art about my own legacy of ethnic identity/white privilege in America. And lo! I constructed the script as a dramatic reading with scenes based on very specific turning points in my life, and during the lively Q & A which always followed, I invited audiences to write their own dramatic narratives. The bare-bones production, which required only a chair and no other technical support, made it possible for me to give presentations in any venue, particularly for groups with limited funds/ facilities. I was soon touring college campuses, feminist conferences, synagogues, women's music festivals, prep schools, and community center basements, giving workshops from Cornell to Colby, from Andover to the National Women's Studies Association. I received letters from all over the world, and became instrumental in forging Jewish women's networking at several major lesbian festivals. These experiences gave me the confidence, after four years, to write a more sophisticated one-woman show about teaching women's history, which I've performed around the globe since 1993. Thus, "Passing" launched nearly two decades of performance art activism that allowed me to turn scholarship into dialogue. Although to my 45-year-old self, "Passing's" original script looks like work from a much younger pen (as it was), I'm delighted to reproduce it here for first-time publication.

WHITE OUT

Once upon a time in Brooklyn, a Jewish daughter was born to a family of immigrants who had fled violence and debtors' prison in Eastern Europe. They yearned to give their newborn American daughter a beautiful, free life far from tenements. And so the family moved to faraway California, where the Jewish daughter might grow and play in the sunshine and sea air.

The Jewish daughter grew up clever and pretty, but clever and pretty enough to see that her people were not welcome or well-thought of in many places. Their different faces, different coloring, languages, holidays, customs, the pickled tongue and radishes were a barrier to acceptance, to success. The Jewish daughter felt hurt and betrayed, excluded by California's pretty people, who told her that her beauty was "exotic." She turned her inward pain into an ulcer. She changed her outer person to fit in: and dared the world to take her in that mask. She refused the tongue and radish and asked for green American salads. She smuggled a dime-store Christmas tree into her bedroom. She dyed her hair blonde, told people her name was *Jean.* The more her tribe pressed upon her, the more her curiosity led her to take every forbidden risk, until she dared to tell people she was Christian, and began to date the gentile surfer boys she saw on the beach.

Finally she made her choice. She would marry out, create anonymity and freedom for her own children, far from her immigrant kinfolk. She would give her own children the all-American world she had not quite belonged to. They would not be kept out of swimming pools like her own, darker-skinned nephews, her own sister's children.

And so the woman now grown and calling herself Jean married a handsome, fair-haired surfer, an athlete and movie model she met walking on the beach. And many of their relatives turned away in shame. "Why have you disgraced us so?" they shrilled. "How will you raise the children?" they taunted. Neither church nor synagogue performed the marriage ceremony. "Forget religion, forget ethnicity," the woman cried over her shoulder as she drove away in the handsome surfer's sportscar; they were married by a judge in a hotel full of movie stars.

On mother's day in 1961, a baby was born to this outcast couple—a baby girl as blonde as the mother's dreams, as white, as American, as gentile in appearance as her Christian daddy. The mother rocked the little baby in her arms, vowing that this would be the baby who had everything, the little golden girl, who could even be a cheerleader, someday. This baby daughter would be spared the weight of immigrant languages and their odd foods, their Yiddish curses, radishes. This baby daughter would have Christmas all December and a white hat every Easter, and know not the generations haunting her mother's childhood.

That was how gently, and so delicately, my mother brushed white-out across her past, across her adult life, across the map of my own future. I was a blond white baby fed on white-out, learning white-out, crawling toward a mirror called white privilege. that mirror said, go anywhere, be anything, for no one will suspect you are a Jew.

PASSING

Shalom! I am bonnie Jean; the baby fed on white-out to soothe my mother's fear. I learned my history when I grew old enough to ask, wise enough to observe, and educated enough to read. I learned to claim the heritage that was mine; to wear my natural Jewishness like a pearl. For I AM a Jewish woman, born of a Jewish woman, and mother from mother before her, beautiful generations skimming back to Boro Park, Warsaw, Minsk, Sinai and Egypt. I feel blessed by those matriarchs, their lands and languages and rituals and work. I am a daughter of Rachel, Miriam, Rebekah and Sarah, and in my blood runs the blood of tribeswomen who cut brick for Pharoah and then danced out of the Red Sea. But I have the straight, light hair of my Nordic father, not the desert colors of my mother. When I stand up to declare I am a Jew, no one believes me. I am doubted. I am questioned. Jews and non-Jews alike look me up and down with ethnic scrutiny, reducing me to the nakedness of those who fit no boundary of stereotype. "How can YOU be Jewish? you don't look Jewish," people say, guarding with their suspicion a legacy of limitation. I say: this is what Jewish looks like, for you, today, meeting me; Jews shall be dark and light, breathing from the corners of the earth and the roundness of the earth, from the multitude of breasts that fed a lineage that made me, a lineage brimming with knowledge and ritual that has nothing to do with the shape of one's nose.

But how the world loves a nametag! Thus, as a child, I am called (by others) half and half, half breed, half Jew (never "half Protestant".) Heathen. Atheist. Other children demand to know if I believe in God. Teachers separate children into Jews and Christians at holiday time, forcing us to make holiday artwork for either Hanukah or Christmas. Therefore the anonymity my mother sought for me becomes, instead, an endless round of decision-making in terns of my identity.

THE PAPER CANDLE

Teacher: And now, class, it's time for our holiday crafts! David, Sheldon, Debbie Katz, I want you Jewish children over there at that table making blue cardboard candles. Everyone else will stay at their regular desks and make red cardboard Santas with real arms and legs! Let's get started now—quickly and quietly. No talking!

Oh—I'd forgotten about you, Bonnie. What are you going to make this time? Please decide. We only have half an hour to make our holiday crafts. After that, it's time to practice our holiday songs: "Away in a Manger," "O Little Town of Bethlehem," "Silent Night," "O Come All Ye Faithful," and— "I Have a Little Dreidel."

Bonnie: But I can't decide. Sometimes we have Christmas AND Hanukah at our house. And you know what? Sometimes, when my teacher talks to me that way, I really wanna say the F word! Every December it's like this. The three Jewish kids are stuck over against the wall making paper candles that are supposed to hold holiday greeting cards. But who ever heard of a paper candle? It would just burn right up! I know what a real menorah looks like. It has eight candles. That's the whole point of Hanukah. The oil burned for eight days and nights and it was a miracle. I could make a menorah if she let us use enough art paper. No one sends Hanukah cards in L.A., anyway—not my mom's relatives. They just show up at the house. They use Yiddish words because they think I won't understand, but I know all those words. *Tsimisht, tzidrait, mishpocha, meshugena, schlemiel, goyishe kop.* On Christmas Eve we go to my other grandma's house. We just talk English there. Well, I'd better make a Santa. Everyone mostly is making Santa. I don't want to have to sit with Sheldon. If I make a Santa I can stay at my regular desk with Sheila. Her Santa is always *perfect.* Hmm . . . mine looks awful. This is too hard! I hate art. I'm the best writer in second grade but I can't do the pictures until the story is right. And this story is all wrong. It's *tzidrait.* It's *Meshugena.* My daddy says my teacher's a bat. That if she never has to leave class to go to the bathroom it's because she's on drugs. Here! I'm done! I MADE SANTA, OKAY?

Teacher: Well! Let's see. I want to show this to everyone in the class.

Bonnie: You do?

Teacher: May I have everyone's attention, please? Someone is talking! I want everyone to stop, look, and listen. Now, do you see Bonnie's Santa? I hope none of you made your Christmas art work as carelessly as this girl did!

HOW WE CHANGED OURSELVES: A BRIEF LIST

When I reached puberty, we moved to North Carolina. Here, born-again missionaries knocked on the door; children at day camp asked to see my horns; the preacher's daughter warned me I would burn in hell. My new friends signed letters to one another "Stay white." There were Ku Klux Klan signs everywhere: "Fight communism and integration; support your local Klan!" Before the first day of school, my parents sat me down on their bed and explained that the South was not Los Angeles. There would be different kinds of playground name-calling. My father said to me, "Don't ever let anyone get away with calling you a kike." He did not explain exactly how I should fight. With fists? With words? With dueling swords? But others fought by giving in and changing.

My aunt changed her nose. My mother asked people to call her Jean. My aunt dyed her hair blond. My mother put a blonde streak in her hair. My mother married out. My mother took my name from Brigadoon. My mother plucked my eyebrows. My mother shaved my legs. My mother suggested, shave your bikini line. My mother suggested, dress a little more conventionally. My mother suggested, don't speak so loudly. My father suggested, lose twenty pounds if you ever want to get a boyfriend in junior high. My Jewish friends had their legs waxed. My Jewish friends had their noses changed. My Jewish friends bought blue-green contact lenses. My Jewish friends had breast reduction surgery. My Jewish friends starved themselves to lose those twenty pounds.

My parents said, don't ever let anyone call you a kike. For a while, I plucked my eyebrows and shaved my legs and lost weight and streaked my hair with lemon juice and Sun-in; restrained my voice and signed my Celtic name, and all throughout those years, no one ever thought I was a kike.

DICTIONARY DEFINITIONS

Passing: (from Webster's Third New International Dictionary.)

The act of one that passes. A means of crossing. The act of identifying oneself or accepting identification as a white person. moving past. Having a brief duration. Quickly vanishing. Marked by haste, inattention, or inadequacy.

Given upon successful completion of an exam. A difficult, dangerous, or unfortunate state of affairs. Written permission to move about freely, or to enter an area enclosed to others. Gesture of a magician; a transference by sleight of hand or other deceptive means. Manipulation. The mark of certification. refusal to bid or bet in a game. The combination of dice that wins. To move on. to take a specific course. To go away from a place, from a person. To depart from life. to glide by. To come to view without hindrance or opposition. To go uncensured or unchallenged. To render a judgment. To go from the possession or control of one group. To become falsely held, regarded or identified. To serve as a substitute. To go beyond in some degree. To advance or develop. To leave others behind and transcend the range of limitations. To leave out of an account or narration. To live through; have the experience of. An effort. A sexually inviting approach. Counterfeit so good it is capable of being freely circulated. An opening, road, or other ways that is the only means by which a barrier may be passed or access gained to a particular place. A navigable channel, an opening between two peaks. A position that must be maintained, usually against odds. A chute from one level to another. To secure approval, sanction or acceptance. To go through satisfactorily, attaining the required standard. To approve as valid or proper. To let go unnoticed. To emit from the body. To gain entrance. To shift the responsibility to someone else. To vanish. To be accepted at face value. To take no action. To hand over. A free ticket. a written leave of absence. In music, a transitional, unaccented note, no a part of the harmony.

THE NUREMBERG LAWS

Lest we forget, David Duke won nearly 40% of the vote in his 1991 bid to be Governor of Louisiana. Two days after losing the election, the smiling former Klansman appeared on the CBS Evening News and spoke of running for President someday. Questioned by Dan Rather about his attitude toward Jewish and African Americans, Duke replied, "Well, I would encourage Jewish people to become Christians. I think that's the best way. But I also think Jews have been harmed by affirmative action. Why, the closest thing we have to the Nuremberg laws in this country are affirmative action laws."

But the Nuremberg Laws, introduced by Adolf Hitler in September 1935, declared Jews ineligible for a new form of German citizenship. Only persons of "pure" blood could hold Reich citizenship papers. Jews thereafter became subjects owned by the state. They could no longer vote or hold public office. Under the new Law for the Protection of German Blood and German Honor, Jews were forbidden to intermarry with Aryans or to have sexual relations with Aryans. Race defilement, or *Rassenschande*, became a transgression worse than murder. Persons with one Jewish parent, *Mischlinge*, were subject to these same laws. In drafting the Nuremberg laws, William Stuckart suggested that half-Jews be sterilized or killed; that they were dangerous enemies: "I prefer to see the half-Jews die."

David Duke calls affirmative action as harmful to Jews as the Nuremberg Laws; yet in 1980, he wrote in the Klan's *Crusader* magazine that "The Holocaust is primarily an historical hoax, and the greatest Holocaust was not against Jews, but perpetrated on Christians by Jews." And when he worked as a Klan leader with the White Student Alliance during the 1970s, Duke suggested that "Jews are filled with more hatred and rage for our race, for our heritage, for our blood than perhaps you can imagine. And we're losing our culture to Jewish degeneracy. The United States was founded by White Christians and intended to be a White, Christian, Western civilization."

Of course, during his interview with Dan Rather, Duke suggested his own Final Solution: simply convert all American Jews into Christians. Would one half of my body then slide into the other? The only act of "integration" men like Duke approve? My parents live in joyful *Rassenschande*, and I am an American *Mischling*, the half-Jew William Stuckart called the enemy.

The strength in my mother's backbone is that for forty years she has loved someone forbidden to her. She was called a traitor by her own people, and a racial threat by the white supremacists—yet she has faith in the ideal of the melting pot. She dared to cross over into another group as a teenager in the 1950s. I realize that my mother's daring, her ability to exist in another culture out of love, is her strongest Jewish characteristic: "Whither thou goest, I will go." My identification as a Jew stems in large part from admiration of my Jewish mother, and I long to protect her from the hate that still exists in a post-Nuremberg world, the hate of David Duke, the hate she hoped I would not experience.

STUDENTS COME TO MY OFFICE HOURS

Student number one: (pleasant, honest tone)

Hi, Dr. Morris; I'm really enjoying your class. I was wondering if I could do my paper on women who become born-again Christians, involved in fundamentalist churches. For research, I've been to several revival meetings in our county, and they're fascinating! You ought to come with me! Oh, don't feel self-conscious about being Jewish. No one would ever know. You don't look so bad, you can pass.

Student number two (aggressive, pre-professional tone)

No, thank you, I'll stand. Dr. Morris, I'll come straight to the point. I'm pre-med and I need an A in this course. So I thought I'd stop by and get to know you better because you're not like any professor I've ever had and I'm not sure what I have to do to do well. You're very young. Where did you do your graduate work? Have you published? Jewish history! So, I take it you're a Jew. I would never have guessed—I mean, looking at you, your nose really isn't that bad.

Student number three: (Valley Girl accent)

Hi, Dr. Morris, I'm not even in your class, but like my roommate is? And she, um, thought you could help me with my paper on the psychology of prejudism? I was thinking, like, maybe Adolf Hitler? Didn't he want everyone to have blue eyes, or something? So, would you know when all that was?

AT MY GRANDMOTHER'S BEDSIDE

My father's mother lies paralyzed in her nursing home bed. Throughout her life, she has distrusted Jews, has never understood why her beloved son had to marry one. Through his choice she became an in-law to dozens of Jews. She resented my mother for this, but was always loving toward me, the golden-haired granddaughter. I knew her as a generous, funny, high-spirited woman; it was a well-kept secret that she drowned her doubts in alcohol. Now a stroke has left her dazed, yet content, her mind wandering. She is seemingly without hate.

I travel for many hours and for thousands of miles to see her, knowing it may be the last time. I have not seen her for eight years, and prepare myself for the possibility that she may not recognize me. And she does not. I am a smiling stranger. But she does not mind my company. Her talk is filled with stories of my father, the son whom she adores. I agree that he is a wonderful man. She is thrilled that I have heard of him, and tells me confidentially, "You know, I used to be so proud of Roger. He was high class, high brow material! But he had to fall in with all those Jews, those low-class Jews! I asked him, Why? Is it their money you're after?" I remain silent, feeding her chocolates. It seems I will never stop hearing the story of how my mother disgraced my father's family. Once again I am an invisible creature, the product of an intermarriage. And yet it is only my grandmother's journey out of this world and into the next that allows her to speak honestly at last. I am just another grown-up to her in this conversation, not a golden-haired granddaughter any more.

MY INHERITANCE

I am a two-sided coin. On one side is written the story of the great American melting pot; on the other, the story of face value and American obsession with knowing exactly how white each person is. I am the face my mother dreamed of becoming, but because of that, I hear how those around me really feel about the tribe that is my mother. Because no one checks their words in front of me. No one assumes I'll be offended. It falls upon me to startle them, to educate them, to come out as a Jew in the midst of every casual instance of public and private anti-Jewish comment. This is the job I have been training for since birth, but alas, there is now a paycheck attached to it. My mother felt her greatest gift to me would be simply anonymity, the ability to pass. But in fact, it has merely made me a better witness to oppressions that exist.

Skinheads look right past me; I'm spared their street harassment. But according to their pamphlets, I am not white. I'm a "mud person," able to breed dark-skinned children, which makes me a threat to their vision of a racially pure America. I walk warmly with my secret. My dangerous blood pumping through my veins.

Mom, I am your daughter, fighting. I won't deny my Jewishness, my woman-love, my Otherness. I say: I am a woman without a man, yet formed of the mystic pietists and their male God; and linked to Amazons, to mothers hiding children, survivors of all slaughters. I am a trick of survival that permits a next generation while hiding it well. I could have said, "I'm not"; I chose, "I am." There's no need to apply a coat of white-out. And thus when people think to praise me with those words, "You look great, you pass," I have to say, "But not by my design."

Section Two

GENDER AND
SEXUAL ORIENTATION

Chapter Nine

"'This Manifest Indignity:' Hollywood's Portrayal of the Gender Integration of the Armed Forces in the World War II Era"

Melissa Ziobro, United States Armed Forces

Military necessity compelled the Armed Forces of the United States to recruit women during World War II. The public often showed little to no support for the gender integration that that entailed, perceiving it as "a radical inversion of the traditional roles of women as the passive sweetheart/wife/sex object whose ultimate mission was to wait for their virile menfolk to return from their masculine mission of fighting and dying."[1] Many, threatened by this inversion, labeled women in uniform comical, promiscuous, or mannish. Hollywood's portrayals of women venturing out of the feminine sphere and into the *über*-masculine military often irresponsibly reinforced the public's most serious misconceptions about women in uniform, misconceptions potentially detrimental to the American war effort if they threatened recruitment. This paper explores the gender integration of the Armed Forces and the public's response thereto, and analyzes Hollywood's portrayal of women in uniform and its potential ramifications.[2]

Prior to World War II, the Armed Forces occasionally used women in what they considered gender appropriate roles.[3] For example, civilian women cooked and mended for soldiers during the Revolutionary and Civil Wars, much as they had done for their men in times of peace. A few women acted as nurses during the American Revolution and continued to do so after the country gained its independence, despite some initial concerns about the close contact with men that this work required. The Army Nurse Corps, however, did not become a part of the Medical Department until 1901. The Corps became a military organization at that time, though the Army did not award nurses rank, pay, or benefits equal to those offered to male soldiers.[4] To equate women's work to men's work would have questioned male superiority. Such restrictions on the employment of women also pervaded the civilian economic sector during this period.[5]

The exigencies of World War I created additional opportunities for women in the military. The Marines allowed 305 women to serve as contracted administrative clerks during the war, and the Navy had enlisted eleven thousand "Yeomannettes" by December 1918. These women served most often in secretarial and clerical roles, though some occasionally became translators, drafters, fingerprint experts, ship camouflage designers, and recruiting agents. Some even deployed in support of the war effort.[6] The Army Signal Corps utilized just over two hundred civilian women as telephone operators, many of whom deployed as well, and all of whom received glowing praise from the Chief Signal Officer.[7] The services summarily released these women following the cessation of hostilities, despite their admitted usefulness during the conflict.

What, then, made the Armed Forces, "the most prototypically masculine of all social institutions," enlist women again during the Second World War?[8] In a word, necessity. Let us examine the case of the Army, which was the first of the services to employ women in uniform during the conflict. Historian Russell Weigley explains that the Army, by mid-1943, was approaching "the limit of the numbers it could remove from the economy without endangering a basic conception of the Allied war effort, that America was to be the industrial arsenal for all the Allied powers."[9] The Army could scarcely spare those men already in the service for non-combatant duties, with Dwight Eisenhower remarking,

> The simple headquarters of a Grant or Lee were gone forever. An Army of filing clerks, stenographers, office managers, telephone operators, and chauffeurs had become essential, and it was scarcely less than criminal to recruit these from needed manpower when great numbers of highly qualified women were available.[10]

The utilization of women in an organization such as the Women's Army Auxiliary Corps (WAAC) offered a "golden opportunity" to solve labor shortages such as those noted by Weigley.[11] So recognizable was the opportunity that Army Chief of Staff General George Marshall himself told the War Department in November 1941, "I want a women's corps right away, and I don't want any excuses!"[12]

A Republican Congresswoman from Massachusetts, Edith Nourse Rogers, introduced a bill to establish the WAAC on May 28, 1941. She cited two rationales for such an organization: to ease the shortage of able-bodied men and "to answer an undeniable demand from American women that they be permitted to serve their country, together with the men of America, to protect and defend their cherished freedoms and democratic principals and ideals."[13]

WAAC/Women's Army Corps (WAC) veterans later reaffirmed this second reason, with Mary Robinson, for example, saying of her service, "I just thought it was the sensible thing to do. The British had done it in two wars." WAC Carol Levin stated, "I wanted to end the war all by myself."[14] Emma Dale Love, who served with the Signal Corps, declared, "I was just doing my part."[15]

The predominantly Democratic 77th Congress eventually did establish the WAAC with Public Law 554 on May 14, 1942, after much heated debate over whether or not "women generals would rush about the country dictating orders to male personnel and telling the commanding officers of posts how to run their business,"[16] and "who then will do the cooking, the washing, the mending—the humble home tasks to which every woman has devoted herself?"[17] Bipartisan objections abounded, with Republicans and Democrats alike denigrating the idea of women in the military.[18] One opposing senator went so far as to claim that the bill "cast a shadow on the sanctity of the home."[19] Senators Francis T. Maloney (D, Connecticut) and John A. Danaher (R, Connecticut) led the dissenters, with Maloney protesting, "There has been no strong clamor for the plan from women's groups."[20] On the contrary, many organizations, including the New York State Federation of Republican Women's clubs, went on record to support Ms. Rogers's bill.[21]

After ninety-eight columns worth of debate in the *Congressional Record*, the WAAC bill finally passed the House by a vote of 249 to 86. The Senate approved the bill 38 to 27.[22] Not surprisingly, Senator Hattie W. Caraway (D, Arkansas), the only female Senator, voted to pass the bill.[23] It was amid this type of turmoil that the Army became the first of the services to enlist women during WWII, with the legislation calling for 150,000 female auxiliaries by the end of June 1943. The Navy, Coast Guard, and Marines followed the Army's lead, admitting women in July 1942, November 1942, and February 1943, respectively.[24]

Many shared the Senators' consternation over the gender integration of the services. Soldiers' attitudes towards women in uniform found in letters written home to loved ones included, "You join the WAVES or the WACs and you are automatically a prostitute in my opinion," "Velva, please don't join the WACs. I have good reason for not wanting you to . . . Some day I'll tell you why;" "I think it is best that he and Edith are separating, because after she gets out of the service she won't be worth a dime . . .;" "Any service woman-WAC, WAVE, SPAR, Nurse, Red Cross—isn't respected;" "I think it is enough to say I am not raising my daughters up to be WACs;" "Darling for my sake, don't join them. I can't write my reasons because the censors won't let them through;" "I don't want you to have a thing to do with them. Because they are the biggest houres (sic). I hope this gets through the censors;" "If they really need service women let them draft some of the pigs that are running around loose in every town;" and "Get that damn divorce. I don't want no damn WAC for a wife."[25]

Women in uniform often suffered disdain from the general public and loved ones, as well as from politicians and soldiers. For example, Emma Love stated, "I just about killed my mother because I said I was going to join the WAC. They tell me after I got over there that she cried for six months."[26] Dorothy Austell, who worked with classified intelligence, remembered telling her mother, "I'm going into the WAC," to which her mother stood up and said, "Not you."[27] Violet Caudle shared, "It was a disgrace to join the military. If you were a woman, it wasn't the thing that was done. He (her father) was afraid of what the neighbors would say."[28] Selene H.C. Weise, who served in the Southwest Pacific, recalled in *The Good Soldier: The Story of a Southwest Pacific Signal Corps WAC* that her mother was appalled when she joined "those women" in the WAC and would ask her to change out of her uniform whenever she visited home. Historians consistently corroborate this animosity, which, while for some reason concentrated against the WACs, touched women in all of the services in one way or another.[29]

Clearly not every female experienced this resistance. Carol Levin, for example, who sent her application to the WAAC a year to the day after the bombing of Pearl Harbor, recalled in a 1998 oral history interview that her mother actually envied her decision to enlist.[30] Dottie Gill recalled that her WAC uniform acted as an all-access pass to the "fashionable places" where "we would never have passed the 'velvet rope' had we not been in uniform."[31] Elizabeth Pollock noted, "The community (around her installation) is really showing a deep interest in our welfare" and "The people in town are doing more for us all the time, it seems."[32]

Salacious gossip and negativity, however, outweighed such positive responses. This "slander campaign," as it sometimes is known, especially with regard to the WAC, gained such notoriety during the War that both First Lady Eleanor Roosevelt and Rep. Edith Nourse Rogers publicly denounced the rumors as a "Nazi-inspired" attempt to undermine the American war effort.[33] Dorothy Austell recalled her understanding that Hitler was "putting propaganda out saying that all the women are getting pregnant, discouraging women to go into the military, and they're making the people believe that that's really happening."[34] Secretary of War Henry L. Stimson addressed the issue, too, saying, "My attention has been attracted to sinister rumors aimed at destroying the reputation of the WAACs. I refer to charges of immorality . . . I wish to state that these rumors are absolutely and completely false . . . I emphasize that I have made a thorough investigation of these rumors. They are completely false."[35] Even General George Marshall entered the fray, declaring:

I returned from Africa two weeks ago to find the most atrocious, if not subversive, attack being directed against an organization of the Army, one of the finest we have ever created. I refer to the WAAC. There was no foundation for the vicious slander, though some of it was given wide publicity. Some seem to be intent on the suicide of our own war effort, not to mention the defamation of as fine a group of women as I have ever seen assembled. Such a procedure to me appears inexcusable. If we can't be decent in such matters we at least should not be naïve enough to destroy ourselves.[36]

Attuned individuals from the average woman in uniform to the Army Chief of Staff recognized the danger slander posed to recruitment, and the danger stalled recruitment posed to the war effort.

Those who did not question the morality of women in uniform often questioned their femininity instead. According to historian Leisa Meyer, "the definition of the military as a masculine institution and the definition of a soldier as a man with a gun who engages in combat both excluded women."[37] Many thought women donning uniforms were trying to be men. The women themselves, however, were not necessarily looking to invert gender roles. They embraced their femininity, valuing their makeup and fashionable hairdos in addition to the work at hand. They refused to accept their femininity and their service as incompatible; they were determined to make the two co-exist. WAC Betty "Billie" Oliver, for example, wrote home to ask for a negligee to wear on her wedding night because she wanted "to let my boy know he's got a woman, not a soldier."[38] In fact, Elizabeth Pollock observed, "Everyone around here is terrified for fear she'll lose her femininity. I haven't heard so much talk about ladies in all my life as I have since I got into the WAAC."[39] A preoccupation with or need to assert their femininity shows that women in uniform recognized what their opponents did—that their military service might upset, or be perceived as an upset to traditional gender roles. Despite desiring and striving to retain their femininity, they placed a high value on service to their country. Women in uniform thus set out on the unenviable task of reconciling the two, a chore that could discourage women from joining the Armed Forces, as could a fear of being perceived as ridiculous or immoral.

Though manpower shortages necessitated the gender integration of the Armed Forces during World War II, many in the military and much of the public feared the concept and denounced women in uniform as comical, promiscuous, or mannish. Recruiters struggled to meet their goals, frustrated by the prevalence of these patently false rumors. For example, WAAC Lieutenant Mary E. McGlinn admonished college women that

The manpower of America is needed in the field and women must step into the non-combatant jobs now being filled by soldiers. American women have accepted all the privileges enjoyed by men in this Democracy; now they are being called on to share some of the responsibilities. I can't conceive of the girls in our colleges refusing to follow their brothers into the service at a time like this . . .[40]

Yet public disdain for women in the military reinforced the perceived inappropriateness of women's involvement. As one journalist observed,

Of the problems the WAC has, the greatest one is the problem of morals . . . of convincing mothers, fathers, brothers, Congressmen, servicemen, and junior officers that women really can be military without being camp followers or without being converted into rough, tough gals who can cuss out the chow as well as any dogface . . . [41]

Hollywood failed to help this problem, despite the industry's influence on the populace, or, as film critic Bosley Crowther deemed it, the industry's ability to "work a subtle chemistry on men's minds, imparting vicarious experiences which mold their psychic attitudes."[42] The U.S. government even recognized Hollywood's power, with President Roosevelt designating a "coordinator of motion picture affairs for the government" just eleven days after the attack on Pearl Harbor. The government reminded the film industry that there "were certain responsibilities and obligations arising from war, and that the studios were expected to make the best possible use of the motion picture as a weapon of democracy, as morale vitamins, and for the presentation of the government's message here and elsewhere."[43]

Executive Order 9182 soon established the Office of War Information (OWI; June 13, 1942), an agency dedicated to the consolidation of government information services.[44] The OWI included an arm called the Motion Picture Bureau, which governed "original creation and production of war films; coordinating the motion picture activities of other government agencies, and liaison with the motion picture industry in order to obtain the greatest possible distribution of government war films and assist the industry in making its own films significant to the prosecution of war."[45] OWI director Elmer Davis recognized and admitted that "the easiest way to inject a propaganda idea into most people's minds is to let it go in through the medium of an entertainment picture when they do not realize they are being propagandized."[46] Much has been written about the OWI and its dealings with Hollywood. For the purpose of this paper, suffice to say that the government and Hollywood worked together in both official and unofficial capacities and that the government's numerous official endorsements of Hollywood acknowledged the industry's undeniable influence.[47]

The motion picture industry released 1,313 feature films in the three years after the U.S. entered the war. Of those films, 374 directly addressed some aspect of the conflict, though not officially commissioned by the Armed Forces. Ninety-five of those depicted the "fighting forces," as opposed to explaining, "why we fought, the enemy, our allies, American production, or the home front." The large majority of those ninety-five films about the "fighting forces" focused on men, with just 5.3 percent focused on women in uniform.[48]

Those films that did feature women in uniform during and just after the WWII period stereotyped them horrendously. Many films attempted "humor" in doing so, consequently reinforcing the belief that service women were comical, petty, vain, and ineffective, sending the clear message that they did not belong in uniform. For example, the title of *Keep Your Powder Dry* (1945), a film about women adjusting to life in the Women's Army Corps, manipulated the word "powder."[49] Did it refer to literal gunpowder, general preparedness, or perhaps to a female penchant for makeup? Apparently, the latter, as *New York Times* critic Thomas Pryor lamented, "Metro's cheap and undignified fiction about the WAC had Lana Turner, Laraine Day, and Susan Peters perpetually appearing as though they spent all their time in the beauty parlor."[50]

Fellow critic Bosley Crowther complained, "This manifest indignity . . . makes the distaff members of our Army look like cats in a Hollywood boarding school." Crowther took issue with the fact that the film blatantly stereotyped WACs. Turner acted as a former "night club hound," looking "very come-onish" and handling her "neatly stacked torso in a plainly unmilitary way;" Day as a "wised up general's daughter" displaying "ramrod severity;" and Peters as a "humble soldier's wife" sitting on the sidelines "sweetly" and acting "very noble now and then." The critic concluded, "If they do anything to people for maligning the WAC, they will certainly do whatever it is to Metro (Metro-Goldwyn-Mayer, motion picture studio) for *Keep Your Powder Dry*."[51]

Never Wave at a WAC (1953), another comedy, received a less scathing review in the *Times*. The paper actually applauded the producers for shooting footage at Fort Lee in order to "depict the true military maidens in action."[52] However, the fact that the central character, a divorcé, entered the Army in pursuit of her boyfriend begs reproach. Veteran WACs rarely, if ever, cite such superficial motivation. Recall Carol Levin, who stated, "I wanted to end the war all by myself."[53] Other women sought opportunities denied to them in civilian life, such as Annie McNeil McCarthy, a WAC who stated, "I think before I went into the service; I wouldn't say I led a sheltered life but I was very limited."[54] One would be hard-pressed to find a real life female veteran confessing that she followed a man into the service like a lovesick puppy.

The *Never Wave at a WAC* divorcé's fickle nature created another negative perception of women in uniform, when she eventually disavowed her boyfriend and reconciled with her husband. Her capricious dating habits reinforced the on-going slander campaign against women in uniform. Further, her ignorance of Army protocol mocked WACs' earnestness and capability.[55] The most reluctant of real life male soldiers often succumbed to this capability when faced with it, as evidenced by comments such as, "Like most of my contemporaries, I wasn't much impressed by the thought of women in uniform . . . Today, after watching some 40,000 or more . . . I've been completely converted . . . There are no better soldiers on earth."[56] Fortunately, the soldier making this comment had encountered women in uniform on whom he could base his opinions. However, many soldiers who objected to women in uniform had never even met one.[57] They formed their opinions based on standard issue gender notions, influenced by outside sources, such as films like *Never Wave at a WAC*.

The women in *Ladies Courageous* (1944), a film actually sanctioned by the U.S Army Air Force as the "official motion-picture story of the Women's Auxiliary Ferrying Squadron, now known as the WASPS, Women's Air Force Service Pilots," displayed "hysterics, bickering" and other "unladylike" and "unpatriotic" conduct. The film portrayed them, in the words of the *New York Times*, as "a bunch of irresponsible nitwits." Indeed, one character crashlanded twice: once for attention and once while flying erratically in a fit of temper! Another woman committed suicide because of her husband's wandering eye. This emotional, unstable behavior disparaged the patriotic and courageous women who earned their wings in real life. Even the *Times* lamented, "*Ladies Courageous* will give many moviegoers a very bad impression of our women pilots."[58]

In addition to films that presented service women as foolish or comical, others called into question their character. *White Christmas* (1954), for example, featured a song called "Gee, I Wish I Was Back in the Army," in which two women dressed as WACs (Rosemary Clooney and Vera-Ellen) sang the following lyrics:

> Gee, I wish I was back in the Army
> The Army was the place to find romance
>
> Soldiers and WACS
> The WACS who dressed in slacks
> Dancing cheek to cheek and pants to pants

There's a lot to be said for the Army
A gal was never lost for company
A million handsome guys
With longing in their eyes
And all you had to do was pick the age, the weight, the size
Oh, gee, I wish I was back in the Army.[59]

While tongue in cheek, the words parody serious and persistent public perceptions of female soldiers as oversexed.

The WAC was not the only service so maligned in films. One of the taglines for *The Navy Way* (1944) read, "Filmed at Great Lakes Naval Training Station . . . with 70,000 of Uncle Sam's fighting Bluejackets . . . and a ship-shapely WAVE who makes the boys behave!" Other advertisements for the film promised movie-goers that they would be "ANCHORS AWEIGH . . . for thrills and action!" The movie posters, which prominently featured actress Jean Parker's crossed legs, made the sexual undertones in that tagline undeniable.[60] This objectification of Navy women could only encourage those real life sailors who lasciviously joked that they entered the Navy to "ride the WAVES."[61]

Here Come the Waves (1944) and *Skirts Ahoy!* (1952) also focused on the romantic trials and tribulations of their female leads. *Here Come the Waves* featured two sisters named Susie and Rosemary. Susie joined the Navy to get close to a certain male singer, Johnny. Johnny happened to be in love with Rosemary, etc., etc.[62] The three women in *Skirts Ahoy* joined the Navy because of man troubles. Writer Isobel Lennart's decision to perpetuate falsehoods about why women joined the Armed Forces was bad enough, but she then proceeded to have the women spend their time in boot camp scouting mates! [63] Not only did these films question the motives of women in uniform, they portrayed them as preoccupied with the opposite sex. This sent the wrong message to a public already concerned about the morality of women in uniform.

This Above All (1942), at its heart a love story, featured a society woman who joined the Women's Auxiliary Air Force (WAAF). Though set in Great Britain, an American studio released *This Above All* in the United States.[64] The film thus held the same potential to influence an American audience as any movie about women in the U.S. military. Posters for the film that asked, "When a woman goes to war, has she the right to live a soldier's life" surely gnawed at American film-goers who fretted over the same question, from the floor of Congress to the living rooms of the average household.[65]

Films that portrayed women in uniform as mannish presented the gender integration of the Army no more favorably than those that mocked or denigrated them. Such films directly lampooned the public's very real fear of gender role reversals. *I Was a Male War Bride* (1949), for example, spoofed the trials and tribulations of a male French Captain entering the U.S. under the War Brides Act. This law, enacted by the 79th Congress in 1945, allowed "spouses and adopted children of U.S. military personnel to enter the U.S. after World War II."[66] Cary Grant, as the beleaguered "bride," met the ultimate emasculation when confusion over his "bride" status finally forced him to dress as a woman in order to board a U.S.-bound ship with other war brides.[67] This cross-dressing scene warned of the imminent feminization of any man with a "mannish" military wife.

Similarly, *The Lieutenant Wore Skirts* (1956) followed the "plight" of a man trying to extract his wife from the military. The film, though released fourteen years after women first entered the Armed Services in World War II, lampooned the supposed incongruity of a woman being a wife as well as a soldier. This situation emasculated her husband, and at one point viewers even see a man don an apron (gasp!), just to highlight the "hilarity" of such inverted domestic arrangements. Interestingly, producers originally called this movie *I Lost My Wife to the Army,* something many men actually feared.[68] The producers of this film disrespected women in uniform when they suggested that those women could not fulfill their traditional feminine roles as wives and mothers, as well as their new, meaningful roles as soldiers if they so chose. In all, these movies echoed the public's most serious misconceptions about the gender integration of the Armed Forces: that women in uniform should be mocked and ridiculed, that they possessed suspect morals, and that they sought to invert gender roles.

It should be noted that Hollywood stereotyped and subtly belittled other groups of women, as well as those in the Armed Forces. Films often painted female nurses, for example, as bumbling, gamboling, selfish, or preoccupied with the opposite sex. *Four Girls in White* (1939), a film about female nursing students, featured the following repartee:

Pat: Oh, Norma, you look lovely!

Norma: Not in this uniform. But wait until I get into white. That's supposed to be irresistible.

Pat: Irresistible?

Norma: To men, kitten! This hospital has the richest patients and the highest paid doctors in the city. A girl has to get married sometime!

Pat: That's NOT what you're here for!

Norma: Oh, isn't it? (Laughter)

The nursing students cannot so much as make a bed at the onset of their training, and the focus of the film soon shifts from their schooling to their romantic entanglements. This lone example shows that Hollywood often portrayed nurses, like women in the Armed Forces, as inept, materialistic, and/or man-crazy.[69] This characterization, while unfair, held less potential danger for two reasons. One, the public saw nursing as a more traditionally feminine role and, by World War II at least, did not attach a stigma to nurses. No slander campaign against them abounded. Thus, no, or at least fewer, negative public perceptions existed for the films to reinforce. Secondly, recruitment of nurses did not directly relate to the number of men freed to fight on the front lines, as did recruitment of military women.

Did Hollywood maliciously target women in uniform? Not necessarily. Writer Lewis Jacobs reveals that Hollywood presented inaccurate, irreverent, and satirical versions of war in general during the first year of the conflict. He points out that many films displayed "little respect for the war's gravity," and that the "majority" of films made during that first year "were flagrantly puerile."[70] However, no stigma against men in uniform existed, so false, comedic or satirical treatment posed no serious threat to their enlistment. Further, films became more accurate in their portrayals of war as the conflict progressed, and more "dignified portrayals" of men in uniform emerged in films such as *Bataan* (1943*), With the Marines at Tarawa* (1944), *Guadalcanal Diary* (1944), *The Battle for the Marianas* (1944), and *Attack: Invasion of New Britain* (1944).[71] Unfortunately, increasingly dignified portrayals of women in uniform did not appear.

Movie critic Bosley Crowther warned Hollywood as early as 1940 of the dangers of "producing war films while the war is going on." He expressed his sincere hope that "film-makers . . . will steer fairly clear of war pictures, come whatever may, and that those they do produce (as they inevitably will) may be reasonably free of wild sensationalism, hysteria, and hateful fury."[72] Crowther's concerns stemmed from the fact that he, correctly, recognized film as "a medium which, however incidental some may think it, is still a forceful influence on human life."[73] Two years later, he railed against films of such poor quality that "such obtuseness . . . in wartime, is downright dangerous" and declared, "Hollywood must not make such pictures that foster misconceptions and complacency, else unwittingly it will contribute to a degeneration of morale."[74] Mr. Crowther, however, failed to specifically address Hollywood's treatment of women in uniform. Much of the historiography of World War II films falls short in this regard as well.

This paper begins to rectify that situation, first by highlighting the Armed Forces' need for women in uniform and the threat to recruitment posed by prevalent negative opinions of women integrating into the services.

Hollywood's undeniable and government recognized power over public opinion is then established. Finally, the industry's failure to portray women in uniform responsibly and accurately is examined. Hollywood contributed much to the American war effort, but fell woefully short of its potential to ease the plight of women in uniform. It might have done this merely by portraying them realistically and in a manner worthy of respect, a manner that might have encouraged greater public acceptance of women in the military.

NOTES

1. D'Ann Campbell, "Women in Combat: The World War II Experience in the United States, Great Britain, Germany, and the Soviet Union," *The Journal Of Military History* 57 (April 1993): 302–303, 321.

2. This paper, in the interest of time, focuses only those aspects of plot relevant to a film's portrayal of gender integration. The sources cited contain more information on the plots of these movies, and should be consulted if more details are desired.

3. Hanson W. Baldwin, *What You Should Know about the Navy* (New York: W.W. Norton and Company, 1943), 64; Rudi Williams, "Wartime posters drew men, women to patriotic duty," *Monmouth Message,* 16 April 1999, 6; Naval Historical Center, "WWI Era Yeomen (F)," *Naval Historical Center Homepage*, 6 May 2000, http://www.history.navy.mil/photos/prs-tpic/females/yeoman-f.htm; Olga Gruhzit-Hoyt, *They Also Served: American Women in World War II* (New York: Birch Lane Press, 1995), 125; Mattie Treadwell, *United States Army in World War II: Special Studies-The Women's Army Corps* (Washington, D.C.: Office of the Chief of Military History, Department of the Army, 1954), 10.

4. "Nurse Corps Role Vital," *Monmouth Message*, 3 March 1976, 12; Gruhzit-Hoyt, *They Also Served:*, 1; Mike Wright, *What They Didn't Teach You About World War II* (Novato, California: Presidio, 1998), 40; Treadwell, *The Women's Army Corps*, 6.

5. Judith A. Bellafaire, *The Women's Army Corps: A Commemoration of World War II Service* (Washington, D.C.: U.S. Army Center of Military History), 27.

6. Baldwin, *What You Should Know*, 64; Rudi Williams, "Wartime posters drew men, women to patriotic duty," *Monmouth Message,* 16 April 1999, 6; Naval Historical Center, "WWI Era Yeomen (F)," *Naval Historical Center Homepage*, 6 May 2000, http://www.history.navy.mil/photos/prs-tpic/females/yeoman-f.htm; Gruhzit-Hoyt, *They Also Served*, 125; Treadwell, *The Women's Army Corps*, 10.

7. "Signal Museum Acquires 'Hello Girls' Uniform," *Monmouth Message*, 23 March 1972, 14; Bettie J. Morden, *The Women's Army Corps, 1945–1978* (Washington, D.C.: Center of Military History, United States Army, 1990), 4; Rebecca Robbins Raines, *Getting the Message Through: A Branch History of the U.S. Army Signal Corps* (Washington, D.C.: Center of Military History, United States Army, 1996), 170, 184–185, 302; Oveta Culp Hobby, "The Signal Corps WAC," *Radio News* 31

(February 1944): 246–247, 406. U.S. Army Communications-Electronics Life Cycle Management Command Archives, Fort Monmouth, New Jersey.

8. Mady Wechsler Segal, "Women's Military Roles Cross-Nationally: Past, Present, and Future," *Gender and Society* 9 (December 1995): 757; Laura L. Miller "Not Just Weapons of the Weak: Gender Harassment as a Form of Protest for Army Men," *Social Psychology Quarterly* 60 (March 1997): 32–51; Kathryn Abrams, "Gender in the Military: Androcentrism and Institutional Reform," *Law and Contemporary Problems* 56 (Autumn 1993): 217–241.

9. Russell F. Weigley, *Eisenhower's Lieutenant's* (Bloomington, Indiana: Indiana University Press, 1981), 13; Campbell, "Women in Combat," 313.

10. Doris Weatherford, *American Women and World War II* (New York: Facts on File, 1990), 98; Dwight D. Eisenhower, *Crusade in Europe* (New York: Doubleday, 1948), 132–133; Elizabeth R. Snoke, "Dwight D. Eisenhower: A Centennial Bibliography," *U.S. Army Command and General Staff College*, 1990, http://www-cgsc .army.mil/carl/resources/csi/Snoke/SNOKE.asp; Treadwell, *The Women's Army Corps*, 393. While evaluating Eisenhower's positive response towards women, one must note that Kay Summersby Morgan, a British woman commissioned to the WAC over WAC Director Hobby's protest, recounts her romantic relationship with Eisenhower during the War in *Past Forgetting: My Love Affair with Dwight D. Eisenhower* (New York: Simon and Schuster, 1976). Summersby served under Eisenhower for three and a half years, first as his driver and later as his secretary and military aide.

11. Karen Kovach, *Breaking Codes, Breaking Barriers: The WACs of the Signal Security Agency, WWII* (Fort Belvoir, Virginia: U.S. Army Intelligence and Security Command), 5.

12. Carol Stokes, "Women in yesterday's Signal Corps," *Gordon.army.mil*, August 22, 2005, http://www.gordon.army.mil/AC/WWII/WOMEN.HTM; Wright, *What They Didn't Teach You About World War II*, 40; "More WACs asked by GEN Marshall," *New York Times*, 14 May 1944, 27; Campbell, "Women in Combat: The World War II Experience in the United States, Great Britain, Germany, and the Soviet Union," 302.

13. U.S. Congress. House of Representatives. *Sixteenth Anniversary of the Women's Army Corps: Extension of Remarks of Hon. Edith Nourse Rogers*. 85th Cong., 2nd sess., 14 May 1958. U.S. Army Communications-Electronics Life Cycle Management Command Archives, Fort Monmouth, New Jersey; Treadwell, *The Women's Army Corps*, 18.

14. Mary Robinson, interview by G. Kurt Piehler, Linda Lasko, and Bruce Chadwick, New Brunswick, NJ, 28 October 1994. Rutgers University Oral History Archives; Carol Levin, interview by Chris Hillary and Laura Micheletti, New Brunswick, NJ, 1 April 1998. Rutgers University Oral History Archives.

15. Emma Dale Love, interview by Eric Elliot, Charlotte, North Carolina, 4 June 1999. Jackson Library, The University of North Carolina at Greensboro.

16. U.S. Congress. House of Representatives. *Sixteenth Anniversary of the Women's Army Corps: Extension of Remarks of Hon. Edith Nourse Rogers*. 85th Cong., 2nd sess., 14 May 1958; Morden, *The Women's Army Corps*, 5; Treadwell, *The*

Women's Army Corps, 45; *The Army Almanac* (Washington, D.C.: Government Printing Office, 1950), 167.

17. Carol Stokes, "Women in yesterday's Signal Corps," *Gordon.army.mil,* August 22, 2005, http://www.gordon.army.mil/AC/WWII/WOMEN.HTM; Christopher J. Anderson, "Editorial," *World War II* (May 2006): 2; Deborah G. Douglas, "WASPs of War," *Aviation History* (January 1999).

18. "Senate sends back new bill for WAAC," *New York Times*, 28 April 1942, 18.

19. Nona Baldwin, "Bill to put women in the Army is passed," *New York Times*, 13 May 1942, 21.

20. Nona Baldwin, "Bill to put women in the Army is passed," *New York Times*, 13 May 1942, 21.

21. Nona Baldwin, "WAAC will begin recruiting soon," *New York Times*, 14 May 1942, 16; "Clubwomen back Army Corps plan," *New York Times*, 31 May 1942, 27.

22. Bellafaire, *The Women's Army Corps*, 4–5; Nona Baldwin, "Bill to put women in the Army is passed," *New York Times*, 13 May 1942, 21.

23. Nona Baldwin, "Bill to put women in the Army is passed," *New York Times*, 13 May 1942, 21.

24. Congresswoman Rogers and auxiliary corps Director Oveta Culp Hobby drafted a bill in early 1943 to make the WAAC a part of the Army, as opposed to an auxiliary thereof. Six months passed before both houses approved the bill. President Roosevelt signed it on July 1, 1943, giving birth to the Women's Army Corps (WAC). Winifred Quick Collins, *More Than a Uniform: A Navy Woman in a Navy Man's World* (Denton, Texas: University of North Texas Press, 1997); Carol Stokes, "Women in yesterday's Signal Corps," *Gordon.army.mil,* August 22, 2005, http:// www.gordon.army.mil/AC/WWII/WOMEN.HTM; Nona Baldwin, "Bill to put women in the Army is passed," *New York Times*, 13 May 1942, 21; Treadwell, *The Women's Army Corps*, 123. 217; Morden, *The Women's Army Corps,* 11–12.

25. WAVES refers to "Women Accepted for Volunteer Emergency Services" with the U.S. Navy; SPARs to the U.S. Coast Guard Women's Reserve. Treadwell, *The Women's Army Corps*, 212–213; William Friedman Fagelson, "Fighting Films: The Everyday Tactics of World War II Soldiers," *Cinema Journal* 40 (Spring 2001): 94–112.

26. Emma Dale Love, interview by Eric Elliot, Charlotte, North Carolina, 4 June 1999. Jackson Library, The University of North Carolina at Greensboro.

27. Dorothy B. Austell, interview by Hermann Trojanowski, Raleigh, North Carolina, 18 September 2000. Jackson Library, The University of North Carolina at Greensboro.

28. Violet K. Caudle, interview by Eric Elliot, Statesville, North Carolina, 20 April 1999. Jackson Library, The University of North Carolina at Greensboro.

29. Selene H.C. Weise, *The Good Soldier: The Story of a Southwest Pacific Signal Corps WAC* (Shippensburg, Pennsylvania: Burd Street Press, 1999) 8, 23–24, 60, 206–207, 212; Gruhzit-Hoyt, *They Also Served: American Women in World War II*, xv–xvi.

30. Carol Levin, interview by Chris Hillary and Laura Micheletti, New Brunswick, NJ, 1 April 1998. Rutgers University Oral History Archives; Gruhzit-Hoyt, *They Also Served: American Women in World War II*, xv-xvi.

31. Dottie Gill, *A Secret Place in My Heart: A Diary of a World War II WAC* (Lincoln, Nebraska: Writer's Club Press, 2000), 21.

32. Elizabeth Pollock, *Yes Ma'am! The personal papers of a WAAC private* (New York: Lippincott Company, 1943), 91, 113.

33. "Stimson Condemns Gossip About WAAC," *New York Times,* 11 June 1943, 6; Janann Sherman, " 'They Either Need These Women or They Do Not': Margaret Chase Smith and the Fight for Regular Status for Women in the Military," *The Journal of Military History* 54 (January 1990): 61; Weatherford, *American Women and World War II*, 91; Emily Yellin, *Our Mother's War* (New York: Free Press, 2004), 130; Violet K. Caudle, interview by Eric Elliot, Statesville, North Carolina, 20 April 1999. Jackson Library, The University of North Carolina at Greensboro.

34. Dorothy B. Austell, interview by Hermann Trojanowski, Raleigh, North Carolina, 18 September 2000. Jackson Library, The University of North Carolina at Greensboro.

35. "Stimson Condemns Gossip About WAAC," *New York Times,* 11 June 1943, 6.

36. Eleanor Darnton, "WAACs fight back," *New York Times*, 27 June 1943, x9.

37. Leisa D. Meyer, "Creating G.I. Jane: The Regulation of Sexuality and Sexual Behavior in the Women's Army Corps during WWII," *Feminist Studies*, 18 (Fall 1992) 581– 602.

38. Judy Barrett Litoff, *We're In This War, Too: World War II Letters from American Women in Uniform* (New York: Oxford University Press, 1994), 31; Campbell, "Women in Combat," 302–303, 321.

39. Pollock, *Yes Ma'am! The personal papers of a WAAC private*, 25.

40. "WAAC Talks to Coeds at Davis," *Sacramento Bee*, 16 December 1942. Signal Corps Publicity Item, U.S. Army Communications-Electronics Life Cycle Management Command Archives, Fort Monmouth, New Jersey.

41. Meyer, "Creating G.I. Jane," 581– 602.

42. Bosley Crowther, "Semi-Annual Report," *New York Times*, 28 June 1942, X3.

43. Lewis Jacobs, "World War II and the American Film," *Cinema Journal, 7* (Winter 1967–1968), 1–21; Dickran Tashjian, "Art, World War II, and the Home Front," *American Literary History* 8 (Winter 1996): 715–727; Robert Shaw, "New Horizons in Hollywood," *The Public Opinion Quarterly* 10 (Spring 1946): 71–77; Cedric Larson, "The Domestic Motion Picture Work of the Office of War Information," Hollywood Quarterly, 3 (Summer 1948): 436; Clayton R. Koppes, "What to Show the World: The Office of War Information and Hollywood, 1942–1945," *The Journal of American History* 64 (June 1977), 89.

44. Koppes, "What to Show the World," 87–105.

45. Larson, "The Domestic Motion Picture Work of the Office of War Information," 434–443.

46. Koppes, "What to Show the World," 87–105.

47. George Raynor Thompson and Dixie R. Harris, *The Signal Corps: The Outcome* (Washington, D.C.: Office of the Chief of Military History, Department of the Army, 1957), 547; Dulany Terrett, *The Signal Corps: The Emergency* (Washington, D.C.: Office of the Chief of Military History, Department of the Army, 1956), 82, 225–226; George Raynor Thompson, et al, *The Signal Corps: The Test* (Washington, D.C.: Office of the Chief of Military History, Department of the Army, 1957), 22, 389, 396.

48. Dorothy Jones, "The Hollywood War Film," *Hollywood Quarterly* 1 (October 1945), 1–19; Jacobs, "World War II and the American Film," 1–21.

49. *Keep Your Powder Dry*, directed by Edward Buzzell (MGM, 1945).

50. Thomas M. Pryor, "Ten that failed," *New York Times*, 30 December 1945, 21.

51. Bosley Crowther, "The Screen," *New York Times*, 12 March 1945, 22.

52. "*Never Wave at a WAC* at Astor," *New York Times*, 24 April 1953, 30.

53. Mary Robinson, interview by G. Kurt Piehler, Linda Lasko, and Bruce Chadwick, New Brunswick, NJ, 28 October 1994; Carol Levin, interview by Chris Hillary and Laura Micheletti, New Brunswick, NJ, 1 April 1998.

54. Annie McNeil McCarthy, interview by Molly McLean, University of Maine, 17 November 2000.

55. *Never Wave at a WAC*. Dir. Norman Z. McLeod. Writ. Fred Bardy, Ken Englund and Frederick Kohner. Perf. Rosalind Russell and Andrew McBain. 1953.

56. Weatherford, *American Women and World War II*, 97.

57. Weatherford, *American Women and World War II*, 96; D'Ann Campbell, "Women in Combat," 320–321.

58. "At Loews Criterion," *New York Times*, 16 March 1944, 17; *Ladies Courageous*, directed by John Rawlins (Universal, 1944); "Ladies Courageous," *Internet Movie Database*, http://www.imdb.com/title/tt0036529/.

59. *White Christmas*, directed by Michael Curtiz (Paramount, 1954).

60. "Taglines for 'The Navy Way'," *Internet Movie Database*, http://www.imdb.com/title/tt0037121/taglines; *The Navy Way*, directed by William Berke (Pine-Thomas Productions, 1944).

61. Gruhzit-Hoyt, *They Also Served: American Women in World War II*, xvi.

62. *Here Come the Waves*, directed by Mark Sandrich (Paramount Pictures, 1944); "Here Come the Waves," *Internet Movie Database*, http://www.imdb.com/title/tt0036912/.

63. *Skirts Ahoy!*, directed by Sidney Langfield (MGM, 1952); "Skirts Ahoy!," *Internet Movie Database*, http://www.imdb.com/title/tt0045155/plotsummary.

64. *This Above All*, directed by Anatole Litvak (Twentieth Century Fox, 1942); "This Above All," *Internet Movie Database*, http://www.imdb.com/title/tt0035431/.

65. "This Above All," *The Tyrone Power Pages*, http://tyforum.bravepages.com/post/thisabove.jpg.

66. U.S Supreme Court, "Knauff v. Shaughnessy, 338 U.S. 537 (1950)," *U.S. Supreme Court Center*, http://supreme.justia.com/us/338/537/case.html.

67. *I Was A Male War Bride*, directed by Howard Hawks (Twentieth Century Fox, 1949).

68. *The Lieutenant Wore Skirts*, directed by Frank Tashlin (Twentieth Century Fox, 1956); "The Lieutenant Wore Skirts," *Internet Movie Database*, http://www.imdb .com/title/tt0049443/; Bosley Crowther, "Screen: Lieutenant Wore Skirts," *New York Times*, 12 January 1956, 22.

69. Other excellent examples include *Women in War*, directed by John H. Auer (Republic Pictures, 1940); *Four Girls in White,* directed by S. Sylvan Simon (MGM, 1939); *So Proudly We Hail*, directed by Mark Sandrich (Paramount Pictures, 1944).

70. Jacobs, "World War II and the American Film," 1–21.

71. Ibid.

72. Bosley Crowther, "Proceed with care: A sober discourse upon the subject of pictures about the war," *New York Times*, 2 January 1940, 123.

73. Bosley Crowther, "Semi-annual report," *New York Times*, 28 June 1942, X3.

74. Ibid.

Chapter Ten

"Batting for the Other Team: Masculinity, Homosexuality, and Sports in Contemporary Drama and Film"

John M. Clum, Duke University

I have to admit at the outset that I have no great investment in sports. I was one of the Americans unpatriotic enough to avoid the Super Bowl telecast. I worry about any television program in which people get excited about watching commercials. So why are the sexual politics of athletics important to me? Because there we see the policing of normative masculinity that affects gay men—and women. My interest in this paper is twofold: first, in the connection between athletics, traditional norms of masculinity and homophobia; also, in the ways in which drama, film and television have problematized the athlete and introduced homosexuality as part of a critique of traditional norms of American masculinity.

In Richard Greenberg's award-winning 2002 play, *Take Me Out*, a baseball star goes through an identity crisis and falls out of love with baseball as a result of the fallout from publicly coming out. Greenberg's hero, Darren Lemming, does something "real life" major athletes only feel they can afford to do after they retire from professional sports, often through highly publicized memoirs like the current volume written by pro basketball player John Amaechi, *Man in the Middle*. Like Greenberg's Darren Lemming, Amaechi is of mixed race and from a middle class background. Like Lemming, Amaechi's race, social status and sexual orientation didn't seem to be big problems for him, though in retrospect it seems they were factors in his being traded from team to team by homophobic coaches or managers. As Amaechi notes toward the end of his memoir: "I'd been sent packing because [New Orleans Jazz coach Jerry] Sloan couldn't comprehend me, especially my sexuality."

Though he was not a major pro star and his career in the NBA was short, Amaechi's memoirs have become big news. The public coming out of a pro athlete is always major news because it breaks the myth that there are no gay athletes, a myth that is crucial to the maintenance of certain prevailing norms of masculinity.

The fictional Darren Lemming, who believed above all in his invincibility, discovered that he was profoundly disturbed by being publicly called a "half breed faggot" by a white Southerner and by receiving a vitriolic rejection from the Black man he thought was his friend. After John Amaechi's book was released, another NBA player, Tim Hardaway, publicly announced "I hate gay people" and went on to proclaim that homosexuality "shouldn't be allowed in the world or in the United States"—an interesting geographical distinction. Hardaway announced that if he knew a teammate was gay, he would insist that the teammate be fired. Clearly Hardaway felt that he would be supported in making this kind of comment and that he was speaking for the majority of players.

Much has been written recently on the ways in which athletics in their celebration of traditional masculinity support misogyny and homophobia. The problems for gay men in athletics have been well documented. This is not to say that the United States is the only country with codes of masculinity that subordinate anyone and anything not manly. While the United States is well behind Europe in developing a civilized attitude toward its sexual minorities, one doesn't see out European soccer stars anymore than one sees out NFL or NBA stars in America. Though on the BBC television series, *Footballers' Wives*, a show that proves that not everything on British television is as classy as *Masterpiece Theatre*, there are occasional gay athletes baring their bums just like their straight counterparts, *Footballers' Wives* is part soap opera, part soft core porn aimed at a female audience and not a reflection of the real attitudes of British soccer players or their famously loutish fans.

I got the idea for this paper after an incident in London last summer. After a performance by the Bolshoi ballet, my partner and I were on a train back to our flat in the London suburbs. Two young men who were somewhat chemically altered sat across from us. When one saw the ballet program in my partner's lap, he asked, "Do you bat for the other team?" My partner had no idea what the phrase meant. When he finally figured out the meaning of the phrase after it was repeated about twenty times, he answered yes which opened the door to various forms of verbal harassment. This being London, some of the other people on the train began getting vocally angry at the young men who soon sulked to another part of the train, surprised and angry that the crowd rallied against them. The greatest offense for our fellow passengers was that these young men didn't mind their own business and treat their neighbors with civility. Homophobia in England isn't government sanctioned as it is in the United States.

Despite the unpleasantness of this encounter, that phrase, "batting for the other team," which I hadn't heard in years, fascinated me. Gay men were included in a sports metaphor. Granted we were on the "other team," but perhaps that team had as good a chance of winning whatever game was being played as the team these young louts were on.

One 2007 Super Bowl commercial has been in the news and all over the internet. Two auto mechanics are working on a car. One has a Snickers bar in his mouth. The other can't resist and starts chewing on the other end of the bar. Eventually their lips meet and the men go into a fit of homosexual panic

"I think we just kissed."

"Quick, let's do something manly."

They then scream in pain as they start ripping out their chest hair. In this new century, every event, however trivial, is grist for the internet mill, and this Snickers commercial has been analyzed and critiqued on a number of blogs. Many on the gay left, sometimes too eagerly looking for offense, railed at the homophobia the ad demonstrated. I see it as a funny commentary on some men's fear of homosexuality as a threat to their masculinity. In their desperation to do something manly to rid themselves of the stigma of homosexuality, these men perform the ludicrous and painful act of pulling out body hair. The ad is, perhaps unintentionally, a satire on the very assumptions that make it impossible for gay professional athletes to come out. Football is manly, homosexuals are not. Inflicting pain on oneself or others is manly, kissing is not. The Super Bowl itself is the most publicized annual contest of manliness. And when one considers the issue of homosexuals in athletics, masculinity is the issue.

The "other team" for which some of us bat just isn't considered masculine. And the stereotypes gay writers and producers reproduce on television emphasize our sissiness. In the 2000 film, *The Broken Hearts Club*, written and directed by a gay man, Greg Berlanti, best known for television shows like *Dawson's Creek*, *Everwood*, and *Brothers and Sisters*, a group of otherwise healthy, virile West Hollywood men are forced by their boss to play on a baseball team that can't even win against senior citizens. Somehow the idea of a major team sport throws these otherwise virile young men into a fit of stereotypical, old fashioned sissiness. Since *The Broken Hearts Club* was made for a gay audience (straight men do not go to films about gay men), creator Greg Berlanti believed that this was a picture of ourselves that gay men could recognize and laugh at. Somehow on the playing field, gay men lose all vestiges of traditional manhood—or the playing field is the place where any pretense of masculinity drops away to reveal the sissy within. So who would want a gay man on their team? These guys in *The Broken Hearts Club* who fail so miserably on the diamond aren't genetically incapable of playing baseball. They have just given up on the idea of sports as a masculine rite of passage that doesn't include them. Unless, as in this case, their boss forces them to play.

In his book, *The Arena of Masculinity: Sports, Homosexuality and the Meaning of Sex*, Brian Pronger observes:

> For boys, sports is an initiation into manhood, a forum in which they can realize their place in the orthodoxy of gender culture. Sport gives them a feel for masculinity, a sense of how they are different from girls . . . For some, becoming adult men is more a matter of learning how they are estranged from masculine culture than it is one of becoming smug in its orthodoxy . . .[1]

And the ethos surrounding big time athletics is a reflection of that "masculine culture" which is pervasive. In his book, *In the Game: Gay Athletes and the Cult of Masculinity*, Eric Anderson writes:

> Hegemonic masculinity not only requires that a male maintain 100 per cent heterosexual desires and behaviors, but that he must continually prove that he is heterosexual. In a homophobic culture this is best accomplished through the sexual objectification of women and the public discussion of heterosexual 'conquests.' But this is also accomplished through the use of homophobic discourse.[2]

John Amaechi observes: "Over time, I became convinced that anti-gay prejudice is more a convention of a particular brand of masculinity than a genuine prejudice." It isn't just that many straight males believe homosexuals are not manly enough to be athletes. Evidence that there are champions who are gay would dispel that idea and many men do not want their definition of masculinity challenged.

At the same time, the gym, which used to be an all male bastion, has changed enormously. For years, gay fiction and memoirs presented the gym, and particularly the locker room, as a site that was both enticing and terrifying. One still sees the old fashioned men's gym, with its emphasis on boxing, on some violent television shows like *The Wire*. Ironically the dark, sweaty, "manly" gym was central to a film about a woman boxer, *Million Dollar Baby*. The old fashioned gym was a bastion of masculinity where men trained for violent sport. For many gay men, the gym was that scary place in high school. The pleasure of a space filled with barely or unclad men was vitiated by the awareness that one's difference was felt here more than anywhere else and by the fear that one would be caught looking or, even worse, become sexually excited at what one saw. It was in the locker room that gay men most urgently learned how to act straight or at least how to hide one's sexuality. So one was either drawn more strongly toward those sites or one learned to keep away.

Now, in our age of narcissism, the gym is no longer about athletics and athletes: It is about looking right. On a recent episode of the television reality show, *Gay, Straight or Taken*, a female contestant decided one man was gay because he belonged to the same gym she went to "and all the men there are gay." Whether that was true or not, there is now a perception that contemporary gyms are full of gay men. On the gay written and produced ABC series, *Brothers and Sisters*, gay Kevin meets his lover, a closeted soap opera star, at the gym where they engage in grueling workouts. On the long running *Queer as Folk*, the gay friends met and gossiped and admired the scenery at the gym. The gym is no longer a safe space for heterosexual men. However, spectator sports are still supposed to be just that. Perhaps the fact that the gym is no longer a gay free space makes some men all the more devout about the heterosexuality of big time athletics. Then there's the other big fear—that gay men will eroticize what should be a sex free space. And part of the homophobia associated with athletics is based on keeping sex out of certain masculine preserves since the compartmentalization of sex is part of masculinity.

In the film *The Broken Hearts Club,* the only time we see the awful gay baseball team score is when the gay Lothario on the team, the one who is always on the make and who has the best gaydar, figures out that the catcher for their opponent, a team of macho fireman, is gay:

> 'How likely is it that I can get you to write down your phone number?' he asks. The cute fireman answers, 'As likely as it is that you will hit a home run.' At which point, the batter hits the ball over the outfield fence. Before running, he hands the catcher a pen and piece of paper and says. 'Print neatly.'

Thus dramatizing the second reason gay men are alienated from the world of sports. Gay men, supposedly, can't keep sex out of everything and would hit on their fellow athletes. If manly men know how to control their sexual urges (and the lives of many star athletes suggest that they can't), unmanly gay men, lacking masculine control, will hit on anyone at anytime. Cole, the gay Don Juan in *The Broken Hearts Club*, is no different from most young men eager to hook up with the attractive women who come their way, except that he is flirting with a man in an all male bastion that is supposed to be a sex free zone.

Yet how in control of their sexuality are some of our heterosexual athlete heroes? In a recent episode on the NBC series *Crossing Jordan*, a closeted baseball star is willing take the rap for rape a friend committed, rather than defend himself and point the finger at the real culprit. Why not? Because he witnessed the crime in the company of his boyfriend and to assist the police would be to out himself. He tells the investigating officer that a heterosexual football star can get away with murdering his wife and a boxer can get away with rape, but a star athlete cannot get away with loving another man. In other words, crimes against women are bad, but manly, while sex with a man is a crime against masculinity, which is far worse.

Nonetheless, the threat is perceived to be the gay man in the locker room. Men are supposed to do the looking, not be looked at with desire or, perhaps, lack of desire. But this is placing rationality on something that is greatly irrational. In *Man in the Middle*, Amaechi notes:

> Homosexuality is an obsession among ballplayers, trailing only wealth and women. They just didn't like 'fags'—or so they insisted over and over again. It soon became clear that they didn't understand 'fags' well enough to truly loathe them. Most were convinced, even as they sat next to me on the plane or threw me the ball in the post, that they had never met one.[3]

As Amaechi points out, "fag" can be a vague term and may have little to do with sexual orientation. The Lifetime cable channel now has a reality show called *Gay, Straight or Taken*, on which a single woman must decide which of three men she meets is Gay, which already has a girl friend and which is straight and available. The publicity for the show claims that it is making a game out of what single women go through all the time. The female contestant rarely correctly identifies the gay man because she depends on stereotypes of gayness which don't pertain these days outside of television sitcoms. The moral of *Gay, Straight or Taken* is that even hip straight women can't tell who is gay, that those stereotypical "faggy" signs of gayness that television fosters in shows like *Will and Grace* and *Ugly Betty* simply don't help outside the world of sitcoms. And if you can't tell who is gay, anybody might be gay, even a football star.

Fags, then, are unmanly men. Anne Coulter recently called presidential candidate John Edwards a fag, then claimed this was not accusing him of homosexuality. She was merely claiming that Edwards wasn't man enough to be president. So one can be a fag without being a homosexual, but can one be a homosexual without being a fag? Athletes are in the business of manliness, particularly athletes in the most profitable team sports, and fags in either sense of the word are violations of manliness.

The first commercially successful works about homosexuality in athletics, Patricia Nell Warren's novel *The Front Runner* and the film, *Personal Best* were about gay and lesbian track stars, not football players. And, it turns out, Hollywood was eager to make a film about lesbian runners, but *The Front Runner* never was turned into a film. And, while it is possible for some

figure skaters and tennis players to be open about their sexuality, it is virtually impossible for players in the big three sports. Eric Anderson notes in his
book, *In the Game: Gay Athletes and the Cult of Masculinity*, "In a time of
decreasing cultural and institutional homophobia, institutions of sport have
remained steadfast in their production of a homophobic and conservative gender ideology."[4] This is why gay college and professional athletes carefully
hide their gayness. This is why great professional athletes don't come out until after they retire. Their careers ride on their maintaining the appearance of
being "real men" and "real men" are heterosexual.

What's really at stake here is an ideal of asexual manly comradeship. In
J.R. Ackerley's 1925 play, *The Prisoners of War*, set in World War II, the homosexual military officer who is the central character sees as his ideal the
Theban band of soldiers who both fought and loved together. "Each man used
to take his intimate friend to war with him, didn't he? And they'd protect each
other. It gave a man something *real* to fight for." Ackerely in England in 1925
was trying to detach male-male desire from the aesthete-dandy stereotype that
prevailed in England since the Oscar Wilde trials thirty years before. Homosexuals could be manly and heroic. Moreover, one could fight alongside one's
lover. However, if one sees the ideal masculine relationship as asexual and
competitive, homosexual love is impossible. In Ackerley's plays, male-male
love, manliness and heroism are combined here in a way that seems impossible in American culture.

In the United States, the intense bonding and loyalty of teammates represent another masculine ideal that one can see throughout American literature,
the sexless masculine bond as the ideal relationship. Once sex enters the picture, the masculine ideal is threatened. We see this all over the genre known
as the "buddy picture," a genre that became in the late 1960s prevalent just as
feminism was beginning to have some clout. These films have two men who
cross the country together as they do in Peter Fonda's *Easy Rider*, or share a
life of crime, as in *Butch Cassidy and the Sundance Kid*. No bond with a
woman is as close as the bond between men. Often this bond has to end in
death because the pure male bond is always under threat and/or one of the
men has to grow up intro the fallen world of heterosexual relationships. This
relationship cannot be put into words. As soon as Robert DeNiro's Michael
says "I love you " to Christoper Walken's Nick in that ultimate buddy film,
The Deer Hunter, made in 1978, Walken dies. We are not to assume that this
love had a sexual component, that it was anything other than an ideal, asexual male bond, though there are hints that Walken has sold himself in a number of ways. It is putting the feelings into words that leads to Walken's death.
What are the two guys doing at this moment? Playing Russian roulette, an exercise that has a number of political and sexual meanings in the film. The ad-

mission of love can only take place in the middle of a life or death contest between friends. If a gay character should find his way into a buddy film, he is mocked or beaten up. These are real men, and real men may love each other, but they can't have sex. Real men show that love through violent competition or sharing violent activity.

That ideal male-male relationship was at the heart of dozens of buddy films and of the classic 1971 television film, *Brian's Song*, which chronicles the friendship of football stars Brian Piccolo and Gayle Sayers. Assigned to room together in training and on team trips, Southern white Piccolo and African-American Sayers become best friends. At the beginning of the film, a narrative voice tells us, "This is a story about two men. How they come to know each other, fight each other, help each other." Here is a definition of male friendship: "know" (in the non-Biblical sense, of course), "fight" and "help." Friendship involves fighting— rivalry. When Sayers is not doing the necessary work to recover from a knee injury, Piccolo gets him to exercise properly by telling him: "I'm going to whip you, Sayers, but you gotta be the best or it don't mean a thing." Real masculine friendship involves rivalry, competition, the need to "whip" your best friend. When Piccolo is diagnosed with terminal cancer, the inarticulate Sayers tearfully tells an audience, "I love Brian Piccolo and I'd like all of you to love him too." Both Sayers and Piccolo are happily married, so there's no threat of homosexuality lurking in that word "love". However both men's wives realize the power of the bond between these men, realize that their bond is stronger than their marriages. The wives, however doting, seem more ornamental than integral parts of the men's lives. They sit silently in restaurants while the husbands regale them with their exploits. Part of the force of the film in 1971 was built on the fact that Brian Piccolo was white and Gayle Sayers African-American. In the rough and tumble, manly world of athletics, race was just something for them to joke about. The real issue is the force of homosociality, which takes precedence over heterosexual bonds in part because it does not involve sex. The telefilm is careful to put roommates Piccolo and Sayers in bedrooms as large as a football field with fifty feet of space between their beds. Whatever strangely flirtatious looks James Caan's Piccolo give Sayers, it's all manly camaraderie. These are athletes—real men. It is said that grown men cried over this movie, offering them an ideal of masculine friendship plus the kind of death scene that is usually the staple of chick flicks. Violence and competition are stronger, purer bonds than sexual attraction.

Nowhere is this notion of the ideal sexless male friendship critiqued more sharply than in Tennessee Williams's *Cat on a Hot Tin Roof*. Brick Pollitt is a former college football star who had what he calls an "an exceptional friendship, *real, real, deep,* deep friendship" with his teammate and best friend Skipper. After college the men played together on a minor pro football team partly so they could stay together. Unfortunately, while Brick was proud of the fact that the friendship was deep and pure—his words—for his friend Skipper, the friendship involved sexual attraction. When Skipper drunkenly calls Brick in the middle of the night and admits he loves him, Brick hangs up and cuts off his friendship with Skipper who subsequently drinks himself to death because of Brick's rejection and his own inability to deal with his sexuality. Brick can celebrate his "ideal friendship"—"that one great true thing"—with Skipper as long as there is no hint of sexual attraction on either side. He can even believe that only men can truly understand each other and women are purely for sex—that a man and a women can get no closer than "two cats on a fence humping." For Brick, men are for companionship and emotional intimacy and women are for sex, and to revise these boundaries would be to unseat masculine authority. Brick ends up in a qualified relationship with his wife—"I do admire you, Maggie"—which is less than the profound feelings he had for Skipper, but adjustment to a normative heterosexual relationship was the law of the land in the 1950s even for gay playwrights who wanted Broadway success. The United States is one of the very few Western countries that still believe this. Early on in *Cat on a Hot Tin Roof*, Maggie calls her husband Brick an "ass aching Puritan," but such ass-aching Puritanism is part of the American cult of masculinity. Sex somehow sullies any meaningful relationship and the purest relationships, the ones that must transcend sex, are those between men. Thus a relationship between a man and a woman is inferior and a sexual relationship between two men is a violation.

Throughout twentieth-century American drama, the athlete hero has not been seen as the embodiment of a masculine ideal, but rather an icon of the false values of American culture. Brick Pollitt, like many of these characters, is a failure as an adult male, living in an alcoholic haze that allows him to forget that he has lost the only thing that made him important, his athletic ability and forget as well the fact that sexual desire was not kept out of his relationship with Skipper, thus tainting his ideal of friendship. In Clifford Odets's *Paradise Lost*, Olympic track star, Ben's trophy becomes a sign of his failure to adapt to the values of a capitalist economy. Boxer Joe Bonaparte in Odets's *Golden Boy* loses his humanity in becoming a champion and boxing itself becomes symbolic of the brutality at the heart of American capitalism. In *Golden Boy*, homosexuality becomes another expression of the corrupting force of capitalism. Homosexual gangster Eddie Fuseli owns the majority share of Joe Bonaparte. His one-sided love for Joe is based on possession, the love can only be expressed by buying commodities for Joe who has become a commodity. Eddie showers Joe with gifts and binds him with obligations:

Eddie: You're in this up to your neck. You owe me a lot—I don't like you to forget. You better be on your toes when you step in that ring tomorrow night.

Joe: Your loyalty makes me shiver.[5]

For Eddie, who only owns possession, Joe is not only a boxer in whom he has 70% ownership, but a personal possession, and Joe begins to feel cornered: "I see a crowd of Eddies all around me, suffocating me, burying me in good times and silk shirts." He also realizes that to Eddie he is an appendage: "You use me like a gun! Your loyalty's to keep me oiled and polished," but what does Eddie love better than his gun?[6] Eddie's materialism and thwarted homosexual love must be rejected by Joe, the champion athlete, but at the end Joe and his girlfriend are dead in a car crash and Eddie survives to grieve with Joe's family. In Arthur Miller's *Death of a Salesman* the athlete hero, Biff Loman, cannot grow up and the geek, Bernard, becomes a great success. What better sign of the emptiness of the athletic ideal. Yet that ideal prevails.

No work deals with all of these issues as effectively as Richard Greenberg's 2002 play, *Take Me Out*. It is interesting to note that this American play about baseball had its first major production at London's Donmar Warehouse Theatre. Later the same year, it opened at the New York Public Theater and then moved to Broadway for a short run. It won the 2003 Tony Award for Best Play. Greenberg's play is less a dramatization on gay athletes than it is a meditation on loneliness in America where no one is really a team player. The New York Empires, the champion baseball team the play depicts is not a group, but nine individuals who have no strong bond to each other. At the beginning, Darren Lemming revels in that feeling of invincibility and security that has been part of his life as a star athlete. Always treated as special, Darren sees himself as better even than his teammates. One teammate tells him, "You have been damaged by your aura of invincible. You think that because you're all this talented or whatever that nothing's gonna get at ya."[7] When Darren decides to come out publicly, he thinks this will have no effect on anything: "I'm still me. I'm still the man."[8] When someone suggests that Darren's coming out is brave, he rejoins: "It's only brave if ya think somethin' *bad's* gonna happen. They don't . . . to me."[9] Darren has no affinity for the gay community, no political mission, no sense that his announcement will in any way change anything. He tells a teammate: "If I'm gonna have sex—and I *am* because I'm young and rich and famous and talented so it's a *law*—I'd rather do it with a guy, but when all is said and done, Kippy? I'd rather just play ball."[10] Darren's coming out proclamation, then, was less connected to a sexual identity than an assertion of self, an answer to his friend Davey's challenge: "I want my whole self known. You too, Darren. You should too."[11] Kippy, the intellectual of the team, celebrates what Darren has done: "You've named yourself, Darren—you've put yourself into *words*—which means you're free in a way you've never been before."[12] Yet we watch Darren lose his confidence and his love for his sport as he comes to understand his isolation and vulnerability. The first stage is the locker room where one player worries "that every time I'm naked or dressed or whatever you're checking out my ass."[13] Darren can parry that one—he is wittier than his teammates, but when Shane Munger (based loosely on John Rocker), an inarticulate relief pitcher from about as deprived a background as one can have joins the team and makes a public statement, things change for Darren. Asked by the press how it feels to be on the best baseball team, Shane says: "I don't mind the colored people—the gooks an' the spics an' the coons an' like that, But *every night* t'have'ta take a shower with a *faggot!?*"[14] As a result of this very publicized statement, Darren is placed in a position he hates: "Alluva sudden I'm a *victim* . . . Don't you have compassion for me, you *envy* me, this is how it is with me, how it has always been."[15] Any man used to triumphing in a competitive activity would bristle at being placed in the position of victim, which was for a long time the only positive position offered gay men in popular culture. Darren is beginning to realize what it means to be gay and he doesn't like it. After a brief suspension and an insincere letter of apology, Shane Munger is allowed to play again. When Darren protests to the coach, he discovers that his privileged position on the team has been compromised by his coming out. His invincibility is diminishing. As his accountant tells him: "He insulted you and humiliated you and you've never experienced that because four people a century are *spared.*"[16]

When his friend Davey, the very man who challenged him to make himself known, makes clear their friendship is over because of Darren's "perversion" and "ugliness," Darren loses control and assaults Shane Munger in the showers which leads to a spiral of ugly events. At the end, even after helping his team win the World Series once again, Darren Lemming is diminished: "I *liked* who I was . . . but I guess I really wasn't that then either."[17] Darren has moved from reveling in his solitary, superior status to realizing that joining the world of ordinary mortals is realizing how alone one is. Baseball may be a team sport, but there really is no team, only nine individuals. Greenberg seems to be saying that no one really is part of a team or a community. Everyone is a "free agent." And even the best athletes aren't really invincible. They don't really offer the example of manly men American men seem to need.

The story of Darren Lemming, like the story of every athlete in American drama is one of loss, of the emptiness of athletic success (these plays obviously weren't written by successful athletes). Yet the other story in *Take Me Out* is of a nerdy, 40-ish gay accountant who, like Darren, doesn't feel part of the gay community, but through his acquaintance with Darren Lemming falls in love with baseball which gives him an emotional high he has never felt before:

> All of a sudden I'm having *memories*.
> Playing catch with dad. Going to games over summer vacation.
> They're not even *my memories* but I'm having them.[18]

Mason knows that the nostalgia he is feeling is false, but it offers emotions rare in his world. For Mason, baseball—watching his new friend Darren Lemming play— is almost religious: "Life is so tiny, so *daily*. This . . . you . . . take me out if it."[19] This has nothing to do with sex and—here is another reason for homophobia in sports—sex should have nothing to do with pure masculine activity which is about competition and winning. Yet at the same time, baseball now has meaning for Mason because he knows a gay baseball star. The world of sports is no longer alien to him.

At the end of the play, some kind of bond is forged between the loner gay athlete and the loner gay accountant, neither of whom feels a link to the gay community or, for that matter, any other community than the people who love baseball. The bond takes us back to those asexual male relationships. Yet it is the only friendship either of these men has. As they stand outside the stadium after Darren's team has won the World Series, the athlete gives the accountant one of his world series rings and invites him to the celebration party. This is not the beginning of a romance, but of what is for these men something rarer, a friendship, an odd variation on those asexual male bonds that are so much a part of our culture. Here two loners make some kind of connection.

Richard Greenberg, who is something of a recluse, is not one to offer his characters the kind of friendship and support celebrated in many gay dramas and films. After all, those inept baseball players in the film, *The Broken Hearts Club*, have their own kind of team, a loving supportive community of gay men. Greenberg's play, like many classic American dramas about athletes, offers us sad, solitary men, supposedly objects of worship by many in American society, but aware of the hollowness of the ideals they supposedly represent. Yet the ideals remain and are strictly policed by many.

There's no romance in Greenberg's play, the most successful theatrical work about a gay athlete. Nor is there a boyfriend in John Amaechi's memoir, which is quite chaste for a confessional volume. Yet in popular fiction, the idea of a romance between gay athletes has been around for some time. Not only *The Front Runner* but Peter Lefcourt's best seller, *The Dreyfus Affair*, a variation on *Brian's Song* in which a heretofore straight baseball player falls in love with an openly gay Black teammate. Michael Downing's *Breakfast with Scot* tells of two closeted hockey players who decide to raise a boy who turns out to be much more openly gay than they are. Mark Richard Zubro penned a successful series of murder mysteries in which the sleuths are a schoolteacher and his lover who is an openly gay baseball star. Though *Breakfast with Scot* has just been filmed in Canada, there is little hope that Hollywood will tackle this subject soon. It is to television that one looks for acknowledgement of the existence of gay athletes—not on the playing field, of course, but in fictional programs which are always looking for something sensational on which to hook their plots and with which they can hook an audience until the next commercial. We shouldn't be surprised at the fact that gay athletes are more likely to appear on programs aimed at a female audience.

Toward the end of John Amaechi's memoir he writes: "In the end, I asked myself why I bothered to hide at all." Perhaps he should read Scott Anderson's book, *In the Game*, in which he tells his own story. Anderson was a high school track coach in Southern California. When he came out, fellow student athletes decided that if the coach was gay, the entire track time must be gay. Thus began a campaign of terror against the boys on the track team because their coach was gay. Suddenly they were "the other team." As Anderson tells it, "We had been moved from one locker room to the next in order to protect my team from football player harassment." The team finally ended up in a small locked bathroom, "effectively segregated away from the rest of the athletic community." Yet the harassment did not end. One football player brutally attacked one of the runners, screaming "It ain't over until the faggot's dead." The runner got away with four broken facial bones and other injuries. The police and school administration recorded the event as "mutual combat" rather than aggravated assault. Anderson notes: "Such homophobia is, of course, not surprising, especially when one considers that the assailant had been socialized into the homophobic language of masculinity embedded in combative team sports."[20] Like Anderson, I am fascinated by this topic because the very values that are central to American athletics are the values that are espoused by many of the men who run our country.

NOTES

1. Brian Pronger, *The Arena of Masculinity: Sports, Homosexuality, and the Meaning of Sex* (New York: St. Martin's Press, 1990), 19.

2. Eric Anderson, *In the Game: Gay Athletes and the Cult of Masculinity* (Albany, New York: State University of New York Press, 2005), 22

3. John Amaechi, *The Man in the Middle* (New York: ESPN Books, 2007), 268.

4. Anderson, 65.

5. Clifford Odets, *Golden Boy* (New York: Dramatists Play Service Inc., 1998), 271.

6. Odets, 271.

7. Richard Greenberg, *Take Me Out* (New York: Stage and Screen Books, 2002), 19.

8. Greeberg, 21.

9. Greenberg, 38.

10. Greenberg, 7.

11. Greenberg, 28.

12. Greenberg, 12.

13. Greenberg, 18.

14. Greenberg, 54.

15. Greenberg, 57.

16. Greenberg, 87.

17. Greenberg, 141.

18. Greenberg, 89.

19. Greenberg, 89.

20. Anderson.

Chapter Eleven

"Mestiza Feminisms and Julie Taymor's *Frida*"

Geetha Ramanathan, West Chester University

Recent feminist film criticism has shown that women filmmakers have been extraordinarily successful in using a range of cinematic strategies to overcome the curtailment embedded in the filmic apparatus' inimical representation of women.[1] Third world women filmmakers have also contested inaccurate and distorted imagery of subaltern women and have articulated a new visual aesthetic, variously called "diaspora," "black feminist," or "third world feminist aesthetic."[2] Films such as Gurinder Chadha's *Bhaji on the Beach* (1993) and Julie Dash's *Daughters of the Dust* (1991) deflected "white looking power," and questioned the metropolitan viewer's supremacy over the visual field, and its positioning of subaltern female subjects. Julie Taymor's *Frida* (2002) could putatively said to be part of this genre of films that seek to write difference in ways that don't collude with the cinematic apparatus' intransigence regarding subaltern female subjects. The attempt to bring to mainstream audiences the biography of an artist who served as a modernist feminist icon, further one who was a leftist, has been seen as an intrepid endeavor.[3] The cinematographer and the metteur-en-scène were crucial for the aesthetics of the film, and both Rodrigo Prieto and Felipe Fernández have stated that they were proud to have participated in working on Kahlo's life and bringing "Mexico" as it were, to a larger audience.[4] The film has come in for some favorable press on its feminism, on its virtuosity in bringing Kahlo's art to metropolitan audiences, and on its aesthetic.[5] My focus in this paper is to explore the extent to which the film critiques metropolitan frameworks of understanding third world female subjectivities, and more specifically mestiza feminisms.

Cultural studies critics have over the last many years been arresting in their claim that a radically different racial or ethnic sensibility expressed in popular culture contests received discourses in ways that even when appropriated still alter dominant perceptions.[6] Film critics, fond of talking about the difficult negotiations of specific films where gender, race, ethnicity, or sexuality is concerned, have not made the same large claims for Hollywood's resistance of received discourses on ethnicity. Suggesting that representations of third world subjects vary, film critics nevertheless note that the liberation of new ethnic or gender identities are contained for a variety of reasons.[7] Although the term "construction" of subjectivity is current in many semiotic interpretations of mass culture, I wish to use the term "translation."[8] Translation captures both the sense of attachment to the original /originary and its substitution by a supplement which I want to forward as one way to think through metropolitan representations of third world alterity, both ethnic and gendered.

Hollywood films obviously serve as only one of the cultural translators of gender in Latin America. Latin American films then, for instance, are marked by vernacular discourses that distinguish themselves from US productions that increasingly render it difficult for "Hollywood " to retain its role as primary translator of "foreignness" or "difference." However, the easy readability of the master code, and the use of the "imperial" tongue, sanctioned by the institutional reach of the film industry, makes these "translations" more authoritative than other renditions of difference.

Part of the metropolitan culture's understanding of "otherness" in the Mexican context, and more loosely the Latin American, is based on an inevitable forgetting of the epistemic violence that characterized the relationship with the other, or as Todorov would have it "the conquest."[9] The "forgetting" enables a domestication of the Latin American that allows metropolitan elites to appreciate other cultures in art, film and literature, whether indigenous to the culture or metropolitan in origin. Foreign culture can then be remapped to produce subjects for metropolitan consumption, subjects who in order to retain their appeal as "different" to sophisticated elites must signify difference, not in any inchoate, incomprehensible script, but in the very same script that metropolitan elites have defined as different.

This process of identifying difference through legibility is repeatedly effected by associating dominant items in each category; people, music, art, food, clothes. Here, the very difficult engagement groups of metropolitans have with other cultural subjects serves the purpose of "familiarizing." Used as a strict opposite of the Russian formalist concept of "ostranenie" or defamiliarisation, familiarisation sets the stage for popular understandings.[10] Culture and persona are conflated, as is culture and its popular imagery. The iconic status of Mexican painter Frida Kahlo is a case in point. Literary historians see her as a progenitor of artistic feminist modernism; boutiques in Center City Philadelphia sell Frida Kahlo handbags and purses. The airport

store in Mexico City sells handsomely bound books on Frida, and Frida' s relationship with the revolutionary muralist Diego Rivera in an effort to "sell"
the Mexicanness coveted abroad. An English language film for a general audience on Frida would then bring her biography to a North American audience in a context where Frida was recognized and familiar, but still largely
unknown, lending the film an opportunity to "perform difference" in rich and
complex ways.

The prospect of a biographical picture on a Latina woman artist, and her
political/intellectual circle would also seem to depart from traditional Hollywood topics on Latin America. Prior film depictions of Latina women were
exoticised to present an aura of sexuality that differentiated them from European-American women in a reprisal of the history of white and black women
in North America whereby the "cult of true womanhood"[11] positioned white
women as virtuous, and black women as sexual. Ana Lopez argues that most
studies of the portrayal of ethnic groups in Hollywood have a moment of transcendence that works as a breakthrough for that particular group. A spate of
films on Latin America during the world war when American films could not
be exported to Europe and Latin American markets were eagerly sought
showed an ethnographic inclination that depicted of Latin American topics
with greater nuance. They also carried messages of democracy and friendship
to Latin American audiences in an attempt to "translate" a variety of organs'
current thinking on Latin America, including the official; the Roosevelt administration, the State department, and the unofficial; the Rockefeller foundation.[12] The "translation" of US foreign policy on policing its backyard operated at the political level. Interestingly, the codes that presented Latin
American female sexuality as "other," and as dangerous, is deemed unsuit-
able during this time period, and women too are fitted into the new ethnographic model whereby they function as fetishes for Latin American female
ethnicity and sexuality and hence are more manageable. The plots of these
films were simple and relied on anti-narrative moves to fetishise the female,
certainly a strategy Hollywood had used for its female stars, such as Dietrich
or Garbo.

Frida, in its genre, would seem to have an ethnographic impulse, but perhaps one that would not be contaminated by the policy imperatives of The
Good Neighbor policy. Film culture today would preclude the possibility of
those early stereotypes raising their ugly heads.[13] The focus on a woman
artist, known for her self-portraiture, would also suggest that the film would
be feminist in inflexion by virtue of the artist's discovery of the self, her claim
to subjectivity, an Ur-feminist theme. In that sense, the film would challenge
metropolitan assumptions on the "machismo" culture of Latin America, and
more generally, the notion of Mexican women's subservience.

The film does follow the outlines of Frida's life, and makes feminist gestures. Her race, her gender and her modernity feature as signifieds when the
historic Kahlo is invoked. While the value of Taymor's film does not lie in
the extent to which she is able to capture the "real" Kahlo, some contextual-
ization of how these signifiers were coded in the world she lived in offers us
an approach to "difference" outside of a hermetic metropolitan narrative. In
her consideration of race as important to modernity, Tace Hedrick argues that
early twentieth century poet Cesar Vallejo was among the first artists on the
continent to have played the role of the European intellectual and then rejected it decisively. He developed a mestizo consciousness, a complex inter-
weaving of both the European and the Latin American, of the "indigenous and
the modern," not just in his writing, but in his very persona. In Paris, where
he lived for a few years in the 1920s, he fashioned himself as indigenous very
deliberately and carefully; in clothes, in emphasis on ancestry, and in his ability to reconcile the modern with the ancient. In this new space that was being
crafted for a modern Latin American aesthetic, the racial and "organic" nature
of women was still invoked. Such was the context in which the Mexicaan
painter Frida Kahlo emerged as an artist. Kahlo too, although middle-class
and "white," influenced by the post-revolutionary investment in indigenous
culture, and its conscious foregrounding of folk art as a vital part of the modern nation, fashioned herself as a modern mestiza.[14] The ethnic identity that
Kahlo's metro public assumes then has its origin in a shift in Latin American
consciousness at that time period. Ethnicity is foregrounded as innately or inherently "different"; however, we note that it was historically produced as a
function of entering the modern metro scene, not as an "ariel," but as a "cal-
iban"; i.e. as proudly resisting assimilation, as speaking a different language,
and as indigenous. If the intellectual movement produced a "hybrid modernity" in Kahlo, it also revealed the contradictions of that mestiza modernity
in its constriction of women's roles, specifically in its ascription of indigenous qualities to the woman.[15] Kahlo perforce had to graft this quality to her
modernity through modeling her clothes and appearance after the Tehuante-
pec people in Oaxaca.[16]

Taymor's film translates this mestiza modernity through the clothes, and
jewelry that Salma Hayek wears, essentialising a specifically constructed mestiza identity as irreducibly ethnic.[17] The pictorial quality of the film, the poses
that Hayek strikes make of each mise-en-cadre a photograph, rather than a
moving image. The stills arrest the movement of the narrative, congeal the diegesis, and present the artist in static terms. While the film was received warmly
for its feminist bent, the feminism itself is a translation of what Taymor's audience might consider feminist. The story of the realization of the female self
is arguably feminist in and of itself. However, the film's juxtapositionings of

sequences of Frida's trials with Rivera with the creation of her paintings ob-
scure the thematics of the discovery of the self. More subtly, this technique of
narrating the teleology of Frida's biography, separates her feminism from her
mestiza identity, thus making both readable to metropolitan audiences. The
mestiza component is presented as always already present, while the feminism
involved in assuming a non-European modernist identity is subsumed by the
strictly personal. To argue that the personal is the political in this context,
would be to misread the complexity of the public role Frida had in attempting
to build a modern Mexico which interpolated the Indian as a component of the
historical moment.[18]

In presenting the narrating self through the paintings in a self-consciously
static movement to draw attention to both similarity and difference between
art and life, and in arranging lived experience in terms of the art to be, the film
translated feminism as a universal; i.e., a woman's self-expression is resolved
as feminist. An extraordinary achievement for mainstream film,[19] the delin-
eation blurs the specificity of the feminism by pictorialising the modernity of
Kahlo's self-fashioning as distinct from narrating it. Kahlo's feminism lies in
her participating in the new narrative of modernity in the nation as being in-
clusive of the indigenous, and insisting on the modernity of the indigenous as
central to her feminist world view. When the narration of that modernity is
pictorialised, its hierophantic quality works to substitute "romantic feminism" for "mestiza feminism."

The essentialisation of ethnicity as difference is not here primarily injuri-
ous, it is the translation of difference as *sameness* at the ontological level, but
its performance as *difference* at the visual level is disconcerting. Translation
serves to reify the differences metro audiences know and accommodate.
Drama critic Augusto Boal has developed the notion of how Aristotelean patterns of identification structured in the text can force the viewer's allegiance
to the ideology of the play. He terms such identification "coercive." *Frida* offers a late capitalist variation of the theme. Patterns of identification are inscribed in recognizable formulae to reinforce the ideology of the viewer. Thus
the film's coercion involves the "consent"[20] of the viewer, and difference is
reinscribed "coercively."[21]

Part of Kahlo's biography lends itself to the mythical narrative of feminism, particularly her claim to sexual autonomy, a struggle for a mestiza
artist, who was not automatically granted the privileges of the male bohemian
artist of the time. Taymor's film addresses these very irreducible signifiers of
difference through the trope of performance. The elaborate mise-en-scéne,
the stylized sets would appear to stage the life of Kahlo in chapters that
clearly follow a rehearsed script. The opening sequence which shows Frida,
dressed in the way she might be in a self-portrait, lying on a bed and being

taken to her exhibit emerges as a theatrical metaphor for her penchant for performance, and foregrounds her imminent death dramatically. Had Taymor used a voice-over narration and unfolded the scene, the distancing effect could not have been greater. Yet, the film remains sentimental, inviting viewers later in the film to suffer with Frida, "assimilating" her in ways that contaminate the very story being narrated.

Paradoxically "performing difference"[22] is effected at the aesthetic level with extraordinary subtlety at every juncture, but the emplotment of the cultural narrative overwrites the visualization to [re]perform the journey of the hero.[23] The iconicity itself is troubling because of the transcendence it implies of the universal over the historical specifics, more disconcerting than an appropriation, it serves as a translation, thus implying that the performed text is true to the subject. Commentators have remarked on the curiosity of any mainstream format in the US welcoming the story of a committed leftist.[24] Interestingly, the difference in politics too has been "translated," and "displaced." Where Brechtian *Verfremdung* techniques allowed for a sharper self-questioning, the temporal difference through the universalisation deletes the performative, in Judith Butler's use of the concept, and does what I would like to term "negative performative." If the performative through the iterative can reconstitute socially constructed identities, the negative performative refers to performance without the power of the "performative."[25]

The negative performative impinges many dimensions of the film, primarily parsing the intersecting categories of race, ethnicity, gender, sexuality and disability. Femininity as a category invites separate interpretation. It is important to note here that femininity does not occlude the other two, but that there are gaps between each of them. Although not hierarchised, the issue of femininity assumes a place so atavistic, that a category used usually progressively to mark difference, here functions as a universal; the essential woman. The narrative follows the "tragedy" of Frida's life, her "sacrifice,"[26] her inability to have children, and her apotheosis through her death.

The story and discourse are in variance with each other.[27] The basic feminist story of the woman finding herself, her voice, her subjectivity, inserting her desire in narrative are assumed as realized because of the paintings, the self-portraiture being central. However, Julie Taymor says that the "love story was what was important. [28] The issue here does not lie in my over-investment in a model of western bourgeois liberal individualist feminism but that heterosexual love stories inevitably spell universality, and become about a woman and a man. Further, the patriarchal emplotment cannot but hedge female desire.

Frida's expressiveness is wonderfully, luminously clarified by the butterflies she starts painting on her cast. This opening invites us to witness the birth of the artist. It stings the female viewer, however, that the first butterfly is a reaction to her boy-friend Alex's departure to Europe, while Frida herself, opening her eyes in a hospital room, had been overwhelmingly concerned about him. Regardless of whether or not this is biographically true,[29] and of the value of therapeutic art, my point is that it puts Frida in women's space, in a mise-en-scène that confines her. I am not referring to physical, but ideological constraints. Frida is *metaphorically* put in women's space, and the physical space she inhabits, the bed, is *metonymic* of that confinement. The originary impulse to paint tacitly works as a "negative performative"; she paints, but it does not permit her to alter her identity, change her destiny but allows her to express herself. The discourse is feminist, the story is not.

Paradoxical as it seems, Julie Taymor and the very talented crew of the film, counter many dominant stratagems associated with a masculinist cinematic apparatus. The narration of Kahlo's story presents a *double challenge*. Given that the history of art, more specifically western modernist art used the female as model, the representation of the female *artist* in a visual medium where her role perforce would be a reprise of the female model, poses special difficulties. The film attempts to side-step this seeming impossibility through the technique of portraiture, grafting the medium of painting on the art of the film.

Women's emotions, usually painfully exposed in melodrama through extreme close-ups, are conveyed through portraits. Pioneering feminist filmmaker Dorothy Arzner had chosen to protect her female hero from violating eyes by using goggles and dark glasses to screen her. *Frida* uses what Kahlo herself was willing to reveal: her paintings. Rachael K. Bosley argues that "*Frida* literally brings a number of Kahlo's distinctive paintings to life onscreen through a subtle blend of cinematography and digital effects." Bosley quotes Taymor to make the connection between the animation of the paintings and the story of Frida's life, "'I find that it's impossible to completely understand and expose what it is for an artist to create, but Frida was actually an autobiographer in her paintings.'"[30] The idea undergirds the overall visual depiction of Frida in the film. The credit sequence itself shows an extreme close-up of Hayek, conjuring up the aura of a still life. Thus, the deliberately posed look of the film very cleverly moves from art to the life. However, the uneasy relationship between the two aspects of the seer and seen, the painter and the painting, warring in each frame translates into an emphasis on the seen. The reversal in depiction from the portrait to the painter foregrounds the figure (read artist's model) in the painting. Consequently, the discursive gestures do not compose feminist meanings.

One group of feminist critics has insisted that without changing the language or grammar of cinema, feminist meanings can not be created.[31] Others have argued that avant-garde techniques, or radical changes in film form are not necessary for challenging myths.[32] Taymor's film tests the proposition that subverting mainstream masculinist techniques to represent feminist subjects produces feminist meanings.[33] It doesn't.

Costuming is of some significance in either creating or dispelling feminist meanings in the action of the film. In the early flashbacks, we see Frida entering from off-screen space, dressed as a man, for the family portrait. This sequence, augmented by shots of the photograph itself, suggest that traditional gender roles are under erasure.[34] A later shot, canonized in the Rivera painting, shows Frida posing for Diego, but in men's clothes, not nude like the other models that he paints. Further, she is posing as a revolutionary, giving arms to the people, and we see both the painter, the model and the painting in this shot. Yet these early indications are belied by the later scenes of Frida in the company of women, when a women's community is not evoked. [35] Curiously, the women's community is organized around the male figure of the great sexual adventurer and muralist, Diego Rivera. Frida has a very real bond with Diego's ex-wife, Lupe, who encourages Frida to be self-sufficient after her divorce from Diego. In this conversation, we actually hear of the radical feminist edge to Frida's art. Frida has a painting of a woman who had been "stabbed by a man 22 times." The painting which frames her conversation with Lupe, is graphic in the impress of violence against the woman.

The sequence featuring the conversation between the two women is preceded by one of the most dramatic sequences in the film that reveals the role of costuming in Frida's self-fashioning. Frida starts wearing men's clothes again after Diego decides to divorce her. This sequence shows Frida sitting in a dark empty room, a bottle of liquor in her left hand, her hair loose. She looks into the easel in front of her and then starts hacking her hair off to a popular tune that underscores both the betrayal and the significance of cropping her hair. The shot dissolves into an elliptical montage sequence of Frida's desperate drinking and casual love-making, interspersed with shots of her in the chair chopping her hair. The sequence ends with a medium close-up of Frida wearing a red shirt, blue jacket and looking at her reflection in the mirror. The camera pulls back to establish the space in the room and follows Frida's look to the left of the frame where the reflection appears as a finished painting with her hair lying on the floor. The suturing is between Frida, the mirrored reflection, and the painting. The camera takes in the entire space as Frida gets up and exits into off-screen space, just as the image in the painting lets her head fall. Two things occur in this sequence which connect themes of feminist identity to costuming. Frida's departure insinuates the defeated exit of a woman who is no longer required now that the painting has emerged; thus signaling an emptying out of her rage and passion, and more dangerously, her self. The dropping of the head in the painting is less ambiguous in conveying the defeat of the artist as suggested by the painting. The clothes, once signaling a rebellion against the boundaries between male and female space, now leave her in women's space, the timeless space of betrayal.

The progressiveness involved in crossing gender boundaries is recuperated when Frida, suffering from Diego's abandonment, cuts her hair. Metaphorically, this excises her femininity, but metonymically it suggests that she has failed as a woman *because* she has crossed boundaries. Screen histories of cross-dressing have noted that women are often able through the performative as in Leontine Sagan's *Madchen in Uniform* (1931)[36] to reshape identities. Costuming becomes another index of the negative performative; its association with loss and despair question the feminist meanings

The power of gaze is given to Frida early in the flashback sequences when she is shown with her schoolmates voyeuristically looking at Diego. Unlike female voyeurs who are punished for such transgressions, Frida is not. Another early sequence shows Frida admiring her father's photographs, and a little later, an overhead shot shows her gazing at some murals in rapt attention with her boy-friend who seems less compelled by the work than she is. Yet again, we see her at a party, surveying both the scene, and Tina Modotti's photographs in an absorbed way.

The tango sequence, pausing to take in Diego's look a couple of times, nevertheless renders the relay of male looks impotent. The suturing should have mastered Frida, but doesn't. While classical Mexican Golden Age Cinema (1940s) used male point of view shots to suture the sequence to display the female, more contemporary films such as Novaro's *Danzón* (1992) reverse this template. *Frida*, in evoking the earlier format, reveals how it departs from it. Frida wins a dance with Tina. The camera establishes the quarrel between muralists Siqueiros and Rivera and then shifts to Frida and Tina Modotti filming the sequence frontally, iconographically. This mimics the retablo art Kahlo was so fond of and leaves the viewing field open. Although the crowd surrounds her and we watch them watching her, we are solicited, not the male viewers in the diegesis. In this iconic effect, we are asked to wonder at the scene, much as we would with religious retablos.

Notwithstanding the male Cartesian viewer's position stumbling, the iconic imagery, augmented by the paintings that are shown through the film, do serve to halt narrative momentum, which in and of itself is not necessarily a difficulty. However, in the telling of a feminist artist's life, the halts on the visual, (the eye on the female icon recalling the male artist's female model) suggests an arresting of the feminist story and its meaning.

Danzón by Maria Novaro also hearkens back to the ubiquitous cabaratera sequence. Julia, the protagonist, insists that when the danzón is performed, the male and female can not look at each other, but must gaze into space. By the end of the film, these rules are broken, so too are patriarchal traditions. In comparison to this context, Taymor's film, which has a cosmopolitan inflexion,[37] is even more radical; two women dance, the women look away, they look into each other's eyes. *And* the sequence ends with Frida kissing Tina on the mouth. The actions are outrageously out of the context of the traditional cabaratera, and seem to break with any kind of macho double standard. The metro audience functions here as implied readers,[38] and hence the actions are extreme. Notwithstanding the audience's metrosexual horizon of expectations, the performative in this sequence is resoundingly a "positive performative," Frida, the character "performs" an identity that is more masculine, risky, sexy than either Siqueiros or Rivera.

The thematics of performance in Dana Rotberg's *Angel of Fire* (1992) (also from Mexico) as a general point of comparison may be instructive. Both films are not realist, and use some elements of magical realism. Performance, in *Angel of Fire* where Alma, the 13 year old protagonist, performs as "an angel of fire" (acrobatic dance routines through fire), a prostitute, a subject for divine apocalyptic imagery, proves to be totally hollow, and does not allow her to be heard. Rotberg is successful in showing that the visuality, the drama of performance, here doubling as the magical real,[39] impedes the young Alma's voice from being heard. The magical realist moments in Taymor's film, when we see the painting of Kahlo animated[40] similarly accentuates the visual to the exclusion of speech. The critical opinion on Frida's diegetic dialogue is that it's flat.[41] The paintings are a primary visual mode of communication and expression. The iconicity of the paintings, in the example of the Two Fridas, is disrupted by the magical real in a moment of pure transcendence, the painting reveals the woman behind. Neither woman speaks.

Paintings, however, don't literally speak.

The techniques of the film were carefully orchestrated to present Frida as a speaking subject in the Kristevan sense of the term.[42] Taymor's animation sequences are contrived quite brilliantly to provide "focalisation" for Frida.[43] Focalisation makes a distinction between the narrator and the focaliser, or the person who tells the story, and the person who sees the event unfolding. As focaliser, Frida does not have narrative authority. One instance when female focalisation does, is in Marleen Gorris' *Antonia's Line* (1995) where it helps develop the narrative. The Madonna in church winks at one woman character when she persuades the priest to stop his attack on lesbian and other alternate life styles. The woman character is ratified in her transgressions.

The focalisation thematises the trope of the divided self in patriarchy, a theme whose genealogy can be traced back to Maya Deren's *Meshes of the Afternoon* (1943). Cutting emphasizes the many selves under patriarchy, and the long shots with expressionist lighting and shadows dramatise the confrontation with either death or the other self. In the barroom scene in *Frida*, the effect of the doubleness of the protagonist is apparent, evoking the richly ambiguous notion of the figure Frida sees after drinking as either her other self, or death, and more completely the other self as being Death. Shot in darkness, rapid disorienting high angle cuts from either side of the frame, before the camera finally rests on a medium close shot of Frida now on the left side of the frame, disposition the viewer. As the music starts, we see the death mask hanging close over Frida's shoulder, emerging for a second from the darkness and then receding into it. Frida then walks over to the source of the sound, to an old woman, who offers her a drink that she accepts. The song is extremely poignant, giving expression to the grief of Latin American women. One of the many versions of La Llorona tells of a woman, angry and hurt by betrayal, killing her children. The diegetic song by Chavela Vargas functions powerfully both at the visual and aural levels as an objective correlative, a fully realized aesthetic design, of a continuous component of Frida's interiority. The auditory is a positive performative here in advancing Frida's subjectivity. Frida's auditory subjectivity is this sequence is however overshadowed by the iconicity of the other sequences.[44]

Paradoxically, the iconicity which I have argued has provided extraordinarily powerful aesthetic effects without producing mestiza feminist meanings has been an immensely popular public "translation." As this article goes to press, the Frida Kahlo exhibit in the Museum of Art in Philadelphia is being used to solicit new members for the museum, Kahlo banners stream from the Parkway belt canonizing the icon. Hayden Herrera and Christina Kahlo are lecturing to capacity audiences on Kahlo. The film will be shown, along with two others. Lectures on modern Mexican art, and exhibitions by contemporary Latina women artists are also part of the program. The effect of the "translations" thus is incalculable and can not be totally appropriated by metropolitan culture. Philadelphia, for instance, is using Kahlo to draw attention to other non-iconic artists and their work. If they succeed to some degree, it would seem that the iconicity has been pierced.

I have argued that many popular texts perform difference as translation. The film *Frida*, directed by Julie Taymor translates modern mestiza feminism coercively. An array of techniques in the film counter the mainstream paradigm, but the "performative negative," and the visual aesthetic create an iconicity that militates against mestiza feminist meanings. Nevertheless, the success of a particular film in popular culture may have an impact that far exceeds its textual limitations.

NOTES

1. Geetha Ramanathan, *Feminist Auteurs: Reading Women's Films* (London: Wallfower and New York: Columbia University Press, 2006).

2. See Gwendolyn Audrey Foster, *Women Filmmakers of the African and Asian Diaspora: Decolonising the Gaze* (Carbondale, Illinois: Southern Illinois University Press, 1997), Diana Robin and Ira Jaffe, *Redirecting the Gaze: Gender, Theory, and Cinema in the Third* (Albany, New York: State University of New York Press, 1999) and Geetha Ramanathan, ed., *Third World Women's Films* Special Issue of *Deep Focus: A Film Quarterly* January 1999.

3. Joan M.West, and Dennis West, "Frida" in *Cineaste,* Volume 28 (Spring 2003): 39–41.

4. *Frida* the DVD Miramax Detailed description of the production of the film, including explanations for some of the many innovations.

5. Deborah Young, "Frida," *Variety,* 9–15 September, 2002, 29; Stephanie Zacharek, *"Frida," Salon,* http://dir.salon.com/story/ent/movies/review/2002/11/01/ frida Date of access February 10, 2008, and A.O.Scott *Frida (2002),* "Film Review: A Celebrated Artist's Biography, on the Verge of Being a Musical," *New York Times,* 25 October 2002, http://movies.nytimes.com/movie/review?res+9502E4DC133CF93 Date of Access, Febraury 19, 2008.

6. Stuart Hall, "What is this "Black" in Black Popular Culture" in *Representing Blacknesss: Issues in Film and Video,* ed. Valerie Smith (New Brunswick, New Jersey: Rutgers University Press, 2003), 123–135.

7. See Gina Marchetti, "Contradiction and Viewing Pleasure: The Articulation of Race, Class, and Gender Differences in *Sayonara*" and "Portrait(s) of Teresa: Gender Politics and the Reluctant Revival of Melodrama in Cuban Film," in *Multiple Voices in Feminist Film Criticism,* ed. Diane Carson, Linda Dittmar, and Janice R. Welsch (Minneapolis, Minnesota: University of Minnesotta Press, 1994), 243–254 and 305–318.

8. Increasingly used, the American Comparative Literature Association's annual conference in 1998 in Austin, Texas sported this title to discuss cultural encounters.

9. See Tzvetan Todorov, *The Conquest of America: The Question of the Other,* trans. Richard Howard New Edition (Norman, Oklahoma: University of Oklahoma Press, 1999), 3.

10. See Victor Shklovsky, "Art as Technique" in *Russian Formalist Criticism: Four Essays* reprinted in *Modern Literary Theory: A Reader,* ed. Philip Rice and Patricia Waugh (London: Edward Arnold, 1989), 17–21.

11. Hazel Carby, *Reconstructing Womanhood: The Emergence of the Afro-American Woman Novelist* (New York: Oxford University Press, 1989), 21–27.

12. See Ana M. López, "Are All Latins from Manhattan?: Hollywood, Ethnography, and Cultural Colonialism," in *Unspeakable Images: Ethnicity and the American Cinema,* ed. Lester D. Friedman (Urbana, Illinois: University of Illinois Press, 1991), 407.

13. Not always a given. Consider the debate around Spike Lee's *Bamboozled* and on t.v. comedians' comments on black people.

14. Tace Hedrick, *Mestizo Modernism: Race, Nation and Identity in Latin American Culture, 1900–1940* (New Brunswick, New Jersey: Rutgers University Press, 2003),165.

15. See Laura Mulvey, "Frida Kahlo and Tina Modotti" in *Visual and Other Pleasures* (Bloomington, Indiana: Indiana University Press, 1989) 81–107 both for Kahlo's assumption of the "'Historicist aspect of modernism" and for an early appropriation of her style as cosmopolitan 95 and 94.

16. For a fascinating discussion of how Kahlo's modernity is different from what Dolores del Rio, the Mexican star specified, see Hedrick, *Mestizo Modernism,* 178. Kahlo was not the only artist intellectual faced with these contradictory imperatives. The Chilean poet Gabriela Mistral also emerged at this time.

17. Manohla Dargis of the Los Angeles Times was harsh: ". . . it's that Taymor is incapable of getting past the flamboyance and layers of peasant skirts." http://www .calendarlive.com/movies/reviews/cl-et-dargis25Oct Date of access, 12 February 2008.

18. My comments here simplify the many elements of the layered modernity. For a more complete discussion, see Hedrick, *Mestizo Modernism,* 160–198.

19. Box-office receipts show $25 million in the US and $16 million worldwide for a $12million movie. See Isabel Molina Guzmán "Mediating *Frida*: Negotiating Discourses of Latina/o Authenticity in Global Media Representations of Ethnic Identity" in *Critical Studies in Media Communication,* Volume 23, No. 3, August 2006, 233.

20. See Antonio Gramsci, *Pre-Prison Writings,* ed. Richard Bellamy, trans. Virginia Cox (Cambridge: Cambridge University Press, 1994), xxxvii

21. Augusto Boal, *Theatre of the Oppressed* (London: Pluto Press, 2000), 1–48.

22. Judith Butler, *Gender Trouble: Feminism and the Subversion of Identity* (London: Routledge, 1999), 163–181.

23. Bill Moyers interview in *Frida* the DVD Miramax on the hero narration. The story of the singular hero is difficult for many feminists who see the "rara avis," the exception, as a patriarchal product.

24. Marty Moss-Kovaine, in a conversation with Hayden Herrera, Kahlo's biographer.

25. Judith Butler, *Gender Trouble.*

26. Hayden Herrera discusses this in her interview with Marty Moss-Kovaine, "Radio Times" National Public Radio, Wednesday, 13 February 2008, 11–12pm. See also her book, *Frida: A Biography of Frida Kahlo* (New York: Harper and Row Publishers, 1983).

27. I am using here Gérard Genette's notion of a story as distinct from the order of events (récit and histoire) and Emile Benveniste's "discourse," or Genette's "narration." Terry Eagleton explains discourse "as involving language grasped as *utterance,* as involving speaking and writing subjects and therefore also, at least potentially, readers and writers." See *Literary Theory: An Introduction* (Minneapolis, Minnesota: University of Minnesota Press, 1983), 105 and 105–115.

28. Bill Moyers interview in *Frida* the DVD

29. It was indeed very accurate. Based on Hayden Herrera's biography. Paul Julian Smith states that "Frida, then, suffers from an overdose of reverence," but that it's "faithful" without being "loyal." *Sight and Sound*, Volume 13, No. 3 (March 2003): 41–42.

30. Rachael K. Bosley, "A Dynamic Portrait," *American Cinematographer,* Volume 83, 7.

31. Teresa de Lauretis, *Technologies of Gender: Essays on Theory Film and Fiction* (Bloomington, Indiana: Indiana University Press, 1987), 133.

32. Clare Johnston, "Women's Cinema as Counter-Cinema" in *Notes on Women's Cinema* (London: Society for Education in Film and Television, 1973) reprinted in Bill Nichols, ed., *Movies and Methods: An Anthology* (Berkeley, California: University of California Press, 1973), 211.

33. The piece on Lizzie Borden in Multiple Voices.

34. Jacques Derrida, *Of Grammatology,* trans. Gayatri Chakravorty Spivak (Baltimore, Maryland: Johns Hopkins University Press, 1998), ix–lxxxix. The term suggests that we look for traces of another signifier beneath the one we are looking at.

35. Judith Mayne on Dorothy Arzner is illuminating in this context. See *The Woman at the Keyhole: Feminism and Women's Cinema* (Bloomington, Indiana: Indiana University Press, 1990), 103.

36. Richard Dyer, *As You See It: Studies on Lesbian and Gay Film* (London: Routledge, 1990), 37.

37. Taymor makes the claim for Rivera and Kahlo. Cosmopolitanism is an ambiguous term, signifying positively or negatively, depending on one's slant.

38. See Gerald Prince, "Introduction to the Study of the Narratee" in *Narrative/Theory,* ed. David H. Richter (New York: Longman, 1996), 226–243. Defined as "the reader whose expectations are addressed within the text, this term incorporates both the prestructuring of the potential meaning by the text and 'the reader's actualization of this potential through the reading process' (Iser). The implied reader is also the audience of the implied author," 327.

39. See Fredric Jameson, "On Magic Realism in Film," *Critical Inquiry,* Volume 12, No.2 (1986): 311.

40. Bosley, "A Dynamic Portrait," 6. Hayek was made up to look like a painting.

41. Manohla Dargis, ibid.; Paul Julian Smith, *Sight and Sound.*

42. Julia Kristeva, *The Kristeva Reader,* ed. Toril Moi (New York: Columbia University Press, 1986), 24–33.

43. Mieke Bal, "Focalisation," in Richter, *Narrative Theory*, 152–160.

44. For the concept of auditory subjectivity see Geetha Ramanathan, *Feminist Auteurs: Reading Women's Films*, 111–119.

Chapter Twelve

"The Problematic Ethnic and Sexual Discourses of Eytan Fox's *The Bubble*"

Jonathan C. Friedman, West Chester University

The cover of the September 2007 issue of *The Advocate* featured two smiling, bare-chested men (actors Ohad Knoller and Yousef Sweid) with the tagline "Can love between a Jew and an Arab heal the Middle East? It couldn't hurt!" Such happily naive language introduced to the American gay consumer the Israeli film *Ha-Buah*, *The Bubble* in English, written and produced by Gal Uchovsky and directed by Eytan Fox, the latest installment in his body of gay-themed cinema. When the film premiered in Israel in late June 2006, it received the kind of criticism from the religious and nationalist right that Fox's team expected. The context was the outbreak of hostilities between Israel and Hezbollah, and according to Fox, "the atmosphere was terrible . . . there was one article in a newspaper that was actually like 'OK, we know you do these things, but why do we have to see them on the screen?'"[1] Fox intended to challenge this mindset and undo negative discourses about gay men and Palestinians, leaving audiences with something that, in his words, "irritates their conscience for days."[2] Yet even sympathetic circles have taken issue with *The Bubble's* representations, and while the film has won a number of awards at international festivals,[3] it is not only tonally uneven, it is also, consciously or not, trapped by the very signs and codes which it seeks to destabilize.

The idea of using cinema to ameliorate ethnic conflict is a noble, albeit a credulous one, and *The Bubble* is not the right piece for such an effort, unless we see a film described by costar Sweid as "fun," with a "light touch and laughter" that ends with a gay Palestinian suicide bomber as advancing that end.[4] At a time of increasingly vicious delegitimization on both sides, and given the sensitive terrain of imagery of Israeli Jews and Palestinian Arabs that can be mined, cinematic mediation can do more harm than good if awareness and caution are not the watchwords. This is precisely Fox's problem in *The Bubble,* and it is a problem on an axis of physical space and content. There are actually four problematic discourses going on in the film—one about ethnicity in Tel Aviv, and one about sex in the city, one about ethnicity in the Palestinian Authority (PA), and one about sex there.

Many of Fox's previous films, such as *Time Off* from 1990 and *Yossi and Jagger* from 2002, situate their gay narratives within a forbidden heterosexual zone, the Israeli Defense Forces (or IDF), but, as in the productions of the late Israeli filmmaker Amos Guttman,[5] these men remain lonely, if not doomed creatures, whose expression of their sexuality has to be kept hidden lest they risk being ostracized or killed. In *Yossi and Jagger,* it is the latter who meets this fate, the more submissive, feminine of the two, the one who wants to be out about their relationship, the only sexual depiction of which is a fleeting romp in the snow ending in a kiss.[6] In *Walk on Water,* Fox's film from 2005 about an Israeli assassin tracking down a Nazi war criminal, the gay character does not die, but he is also not the lead, nor, as the grandson of the old Nazi, is he Israeli. With *The Bubble,* Fox has moved back into his operating zone of fragility, very much like the title of the film itself, a delicate bubble of protection that is easily shattered by its environment but does not itself impact its surroundings.

The Bubble is set in Tel Aviv's bohemian Sheinkin district, located between Allenby and Rothschild Avenues. The area is to Tel Aviv what West Hollywood, Greenwich Village, and the "gayborhood" are to its respective sister cities of Los Angeles, New York, and Philadelphia. One could regard this setting as a classic liminal space in which rites of passage of separation, transition, and integration play themselves out. *The Bubble's* main characters, Knoller's Noam, a gay reservist in the IDF who works at an independent record store in Sheinkin, and Sweid's Ashraf, the gay Palestinian who begins a sexual relationship with Noam, move through two of these three stages, separating themselves from their heterosexual and ethnic worlds, the IDF in the case of Noam, the Palestinian Authority for Ashraf, and then insulating themselves in the liminal bubble of Sheinkin where their relationship develops. It is their move towards the third or postliminal phase of integration which the film problematizes and to which I will return. Accompanying Noam and Ashraf on their journey are Noam's friends Lulu (played by Daniela Wircer) and Yali (played by Alon Friedman), who share an apartment with Noam. Lulu works in a store which sells luxury soap, while Yali manages a café across the street. They, too, make their rites of passage, although here again, they do not necessarily wind up in a place of acceptance or integration.

The film begins at a checkpoint between Israel and the PA, depicting the degradation which Palestinians have to endure at the hands of the IDF. It is also the beginning of Fox's conversation about sexuality in such a charged environment. Noam is a part of the patrol, and Ashraf and a dozen or so other Palestinians wait to cross the border. What is a negative, and a sexualized negative at that, becomes the opening for Noam and Ashraf's relationship. Checking for bombs, Israeli soldiers demand that the Palestinian men raise their shirts, and as Ashraf does so he catches Noam with his "queer gaze." The sexual subtext of the opening sequence continues as a pregnant Palestinian woman, also humiliated by the soldiers, goes into labor after the group is cleared. As the Palestinian men break out into panic, Ashraf runs to Noam to get help. His immediate reaction is characterized by fear, and he shoots his machine gun in the air, but once he moves past his conditioning and realizes that a human life is at stake, he rushes to help. Noam stabilizes the woman until a doctor arrives to deliver the baby, but the effort is unsuccessful; the baby dies shortly after birth, leading to a near riot on the part of the Palestinian men, who blame the Israeli soldiers for the baby's death. This event, and the almost too obvious message about sexuality, life, and death which it offers, foregrounds the state of affairs to come between Noam and Ashraf.

In the ensuing title sequence, the film follows Noam as he returns home to the ostensibly safe confines of Tel Aviv. Ashraf winds up on Noam's doorstep (on the pretext that he is returning his lost ID), and the two quickly begin their torrid affair. While both Noam and Ashraf occupy a liminal space through their marginal coupling, it is the latter whose journey is the more radical break, and Fox's comparison between Tel Aviv and the Palestinian Authority reveals this: The two places could not be more different in terms of their acceptance of gay sexuality, but neither region can break free from its visible hostile ethnocentrism. Hostility towards the "other" might be more latent in Tel Aviv, but it is easily brought to the surface. Patrons of Lulu's store make racist remarks about a piece of soap, declaring that it looks and smells bad—"like an Arab," and a passerby later confronts Lulu as she distributes leaflets advertising a "rave" against the occupation. Both incidents prompt angry rejoinders from Lulu, but in the end it is the group of four—Noam, Ashraf, Lulu, and Yali—that removes itself from the situation, rather than refusing to be cowed.

This tentativeness amidst greater acceptance in Tel Aviv is set against an environment (the PA) that is presented as simply repressive. Sweid, an Arab who grew up in Haifa and is therefore an Israeli citizen, maintains that this kind of film would be devastating in Israeli Arab and Palestinian circles:

> I'm a bit apprehensive about the Arab reaction, mostly from distant relatives. There are very intimate scenes there, and in our society we're not yet at the point where we're fighting for gay rights. I'm not sure that older Arabs will accept

such a love story. It's not a question of good or bad. It's just a question of a certain culture.[7]

Early on in the film, Yali agrees to hire Ashraf as a waiter in the café, but his identity as a Palestinian is exposed, and Ashraf flees back to the West Bank, at which point Noam and Lulu disguise themselves as French reporters and make their way to Ashraf's home, under the guise of doing a story about weddings in the PA. Ashraf is mortified by the intrusion, but he is nevertheless overcome by desire and kisses Noam in private. This action morphs from a positive embrace into a transgression in the blink of an eye, as Ashraf's future brother-in-law, a Hamas member with the stunningly uncreative name of Jihad, witnesses the deed and threatens to expose Ashraf unless he agrees to marry Jihad's cousin Samira. Jihad later on engineers the suicide bombing that sets in motion the film's ill-fated ending. With the journey to the PA, Fox and Uchovsky's Manichean contrast is complete. Tel Aviv is a den of hedonists and closet racists, while the PA is a medieval theocracy, filled with hateful terrorists. Undoubtedly this portrayal reflects a difficult social reality, but the question is, is this the only reality?

I hesitatingly refer to Edward Said's *Orientalism* on this point: The way in which Fox and Uchovsky have constructed the dichotomy between the two physical spaces might play into the "positional superiority of the west" even if this is not their intention, or if their intention is to do the exact opposite.[8] While Fox has said that "without this pleasant, international and cool retreat called Tel Aviv, many Israelis would leave the country," he goes to great lengths to cast the city as maddeningly contradictory and dysfunctional.[9] In the evening of their first encounter, Noam takes Ashraf out on the balcony and muses: "The European idiots who built the city in the 1920s didn't know much about the Mediterranean. They built it with its back to the sea, meaning the streets run parallel to the sea and block the breeze. Later came the big hotels that block everything. That's why there's no air."[10] Fox's use of western imagery similarly problematizes a claim of Israeli superiority. The Israeli characters quote Judith Butler with irony and wear T-shirts emblazoned with clashing images of American culture (like the New York Yankees and Barbara Streisand), and throughout the film, the soundtrack is punctuated by songs from George Gershwin and the doomed sixties folksinger Tim Buckley. Ironies abound as Ivri Lider, who composed the bulk of the soundtrack, sings "Loving that Man of Mine" and Knoller hums "Here I am. Waiting to hold you" from Buckley's "Song of the Siren." This imagery is a sign of a culture without a culture, a state left only with the ironic reworking of images and tropes of a place that Israel can never become. Despite all of this—the cynicism, sense of naïve denial, aimlessness, and fleeting glimpses of racism, viewers will hardly conclude that the PA is somehow a better place to live. It very well may not be, but it is Israel that emerges not only as the preferred space, but, as the last physical space to be seen in the film, also the place of greater calamity.

Above all, Tel Aviv represents a flawed yet tragically heroic political narrative, and *The Bubble's* relationship story is inseparable from the characters' political activism so that politics and sex mark a singular commentary throughout the film. Noam, Lulu, and Yali are young leftists leading alternative lifestyles who are opposed to Israeli policy towards Palestinians and who spend the bulk of their free time planning for a rave against the occupation of the West Bank. Their numbers and tactics reflect their marginalized status not only in the film but in reality; during the filming of the rave scene, one of the actors in an interview quipped, "what am I doing here with these crazy leftists?"[11] Theirs is an idealism, which, however lofty, is fringe and bordering on childish. In fact, the rave which they hold, and which Ashraf attends, is a small affair on a beach where the interest revolves around music, sex, and drugs, and not politics. This is again a retreat inward, an escape rather than an effort to mobilize a movement, and the songs which blare English language lyrics like "I wanna lie next to you . . . No one can save me from this life" suggest defeatism and withdrawal more than anything else. The T-shirts with the ever-present slogan "I Love Tel Aviv" subliminally add to the irony. When images of escalating tensions in the West Bank appear on the television or internet, punctuating intimate moments between Noam and Ashraf, the two frequently sweep their political differences aside in favor of common personal discourse about family, love, and loss. It is not clear to me if Fox is saying that this is the wrong thing to do because love doesn't necessarily conquer all, but if we remember that this is about life in a bubble, then the best sentiment we can muster is pity for all that the characters do and say.

The scenes of sexual intimacy between Noam and Ashraf offer additional insight into the conflation of the political and sexual, in addition to foreshadowing the demise of the two characters. After their first lovemaking session, Noam says "it was awful," which Ashraf mistakes as Noam's description of the sex, when he intended it as a comment on what transpired at the checkpoint. Their discourse quickly polarizes around Israeli and Palestinian tropes about the current state affairs, but the two back off and agree to forget politics for the time being. Noam then describes the sex as explosive, which takes Ashraf by surprise because of his literal understanding of the word. Comparable references to suicide bombings pepper conversations between the four friends on a couple of occasions. The references come from Yali, who, as we come to discover, is jealous of Ashraf. Upon Noam's return from the border, Yali asks Noam if he saw any sexy suicide bombers; once Noam and Ashraf start dating, Yali makes a joke about what awaits a gay Muslim suicide bomber (70 virgin boys? Or 70 muscle dudes?); and while working at the café, Ashraf considers hiding his identity by adopting a Hebrew name, Shimi, or Samson, whom Yali describes as the first suicide bomber. The omens are too apparent, and, like the characters' politics, their sexual affair is similarly destined to end in ruin.

The actual scenes of sex between Noam and Ashraf are not in and of themselves path-breaking, as Amos Guttman offered a similar representation in his 1983 film *Drifting.* Here, the main character, Robby, befriends two Palestinian men, and asks one to "fuck him," at once symbolizing in his feminized, passive state, a collective loathing for Israel's treatment of Palestinians and a racist construction of the Palestinian male as hypersexual and almost animalistic.[12] Fox does not offend on nearly as many levels, and Noam and Ashraf even assume versatile roles as top and bottom at different points during the film, thus avoiding Guttman's portrayal of Israeli-Arab sex as an act of self-loathing. Yet Fox elevates Noam and Yali's non-sexual friendship to a somehow more special level, as Noam admits as much to Yali during his recuperation in the hospital from injuries suffered during the suicide bombing engineered by Jihad. Then, too, as in Ang Lee's *Brokeback Mountain*, whose straight actors playing gay characters publically and repeatedly emphasized their heterosexuality, the leads in *The Bubble,* Knoller and Sweid, initially had difficulties with the scenes of gay lovemaking, which angered Fox. He claims that he was "offended as a gay man and a director that he [Knoller] was finding it so difficult to perform."[13] I am not suggesting that only gay actors can and should play gay characters, merely that there is a pattern in Fox's films of discomfort with gay sexuality and identity. This could be criticism of Israeli society or a reflection of Fox's own process of "working through." Like his presentation of Tel Aviv and its politics, it might be both, but I am less inclined to see it that way because of Fox's consistent use of tragedy to frame his gay narratives.

Death is the overarching reality in *The Bubble* as it is in *Yossi and Jagger.* Abstract attacks and reprisals work their way closer into the personal lives of Noam and Ashraf. The two even attend a staging of the play, *Bent,* Martin Sherman's piece about two gay men incarcerated in a Nazi concentration camp who are ultimately murdered. Ashraf identifies with the character of Horst, and on two key occasions, before fleeing back home to the PA after his identity is revealed and then again at film's end, Ashraf mimics the simple wipe of the brow which Horst uses to symbolize his forbidden love for fellow prisoner, Max. The *Bent* sequence, although another on-the-nose exercise in foreshadowing, also provides Ashraf with an opening to tell Noam about his childhood. Both men apparently grew up in Jerusalem, but Ashraf's family was forced to leave the city after Israeli forces bulldozed his house for no reason other than to claim his property. Later on, Ashraf asks about a picture of a woman taped to the wall of Noam's bedroom, and Noam tells Ashraf that it is his mother and that she is deceased. This is all that the audience knows until at the rave, in another moment that depicts the Israeli as sorrowfully noble, Noam talks at greater length about his mother, saying that she tried but failed to bring Jewish and Arab families together for a party in their neighborhood when he was a child.

> My father was our neighborhood committee president. There were complaints about Arab kids scaring the other kids. So he got an order from preventing the Issawiya kids from playing there. My mother had a terrible fight with him about it. She invited all the mothers and kids from Issawiya to come to a reconciliation party at the playground. My father laughed at her attempt at world peace. He said no one would come. And on the day of the party, no one did. Not even the Israeli mothers. Later we found out they were scared off. We sat there drinking juice and eating cake. She pushed me high on the swings. Back home, my father and brother were watching soccer on TV. Later, in the bath, I noticed my mom had tears in her eyes. She was trying to wipe them away, so I pretended I didn't see them. I know it sounds crazy, but I think that was the day the illness began in her body. Somehow I'm sure of that.[14]

Love and death converge in the climax of the film in an ever widening spiral of violence. For Ashraf, the first thing to die in the context of a ritual of love, is his sexual identity. When Ashraf returns to his home for the wedding of his sister, Rana, to Jihad, he comes out to her and reaps a torrent of rejection. His only option in this setting is to marry Jihad's cousin Samira. Jihad, meanwhile, organizes the suicide bombing which injures Yali, leading to the IDF's botched assassination attempt against Jihad that results in the death of Rana. Without anything left to live for, Ashraf volunteers to carry out a bombing in Tel Aviv in response. Finding Yali's café, and catching Noam's glance, Ashraf moves to the street to detonate the bomb. Noam, sensing what is about to transpire runs out to him. As he does, in slow motion, with the scene spinning in a surreal way, Ashraf wipes his brow as Horst does during the fateful climax of *Bent,* the two nearly kiss, and in a flash of white, there is nothing. At the end of the film, the audience sees Israeli rescue crews tending to wounded passers-by and cleaning up the rubble around Noam and Ashraf, whose corpses are covered on the ground. Narration from a news-reporter suggests that the toll could have been worse had the "bomber [not blown] himself up in the middle of the empty street." Noam's disembodied voice then narrates:

Come Hubi, my love, let's fly away. Maybe beyond the smoke and the fighting there is a better place. Maybe there really is a paradise where we can just love each other. I don't know. I wonder if we ever really had a chance . . . Lulu and Yali will probably give the paper a picture of us two. Maybe the one from the rave, where we look all high and happy. Maybe people will see how beautiful we look, and understand how stupid these wars are. No . . . they probably never will.[15]

When Fox has responded to the outcry over this ending, he has said that the film is a modern day *Romeo and Juliet,* but the analogy does not hold up on closer analysis. The ending of the play is heartbreaking not only because the two protagonists cannot be together given the hostilities of their respective families, but also because their suicides are unintended and the result of gross misperceptions. In *The Bubble,* Ashraf's decision to become a suicide bomber, despite being borne out of desperation, is a willing act, and even if he did not have murderous intentions, his action has murderous results. Here is where Fox's narrative sets back his message of healing and moving forward from his 2004 film, *Walk on Water.* The positional superiority of the Israeli victim is evident again, with Noam uttering the lyric of hope, which Ashraf, the Palestinian, has destroyed.

What were the alternatives, then, to this conclusion? "Alive and apart" would have been one possibility, with Ashraf considering and then rejecting the bombing, agreeing instead to marry Samira and lead a life that is a metaphorical suicide, while Noam could have resumed his duties on the border with only the memory of his initial connection to Ashraf through his "queer gaze" as comfort. Such an ending would have felt less exploitative, although this, too, would have mirrored a number of Fox's previous efforts which have ended with unrequited love. A redemptive conclusion, with Noam and Ashraf somehow able to continue their relationship, would have been difficult to swallow as well, but it might have been the more radical option. Perhaps at the last moment, instead of detonating the bomb, which the audience expects, Ashraf could have embraced Noam. The film could still have cut to black to the sounds of Tim Buckley's "Song of the Siren," although now the lyrics would offer more tenderness than melancholia. None of this, of course, would have fit with the sense of hopelessness which Fox seeks to convey, but it would have broken out of existing Israeli tropes of gay and Arab cinematic representation. With all of the recent films on suicide bombers (from *Paradise Now* to *Zaka: Living with Death*), and all of the films with gay themes which end in disaster, there is a crying need for a different resolution. Maybe this is impossible in Israel and Palestine, but one could argue that, as much as American films are weakened by their knee-jerk happy endings, the relentless nihilism and problematic balance of Israeli films such as *The Bubble* might actually be undermining their social criticism

NOTES

1. Kyle Buchaman, "The Boys in the Bubble," *The Advocate,* 11 September 2007, 38.

2. "IndieWIRE Interview: *The Bubble* Director Eytan Fox," http://www.indiewire .com/people/2007/09/indiewire_inter_102.html, 2.

3. These awards include two awards for director Fox at the 2007 Berlin International Film Festival, an award for best screenplay at the 2007 Durban International Film Festival, and awards for best picture at LA Outfest (2007) and the 2007 Torino International Gay and Lesbian Film Festival. http://www.imdb.com/title/tt0476643/ awards.

4. Rona Kuperboim, "A Genuine Ashkenazi," http://www.ynetnews.com/articles/ 0,7340,L-3272023,00.html., 1.

5. Examples of dystopic gay-themed cinema from Israel include Guttman's *Safe Place* (1977), and his *Drifting* films (1979, 1983), as well as Yair Hochner's disturbing *Good Boys* (2005). For the best analysis of Guttman, see Raz Yosef, *Beyond Flesh: Queer Masculinities and Nationalism in Israeli Cinema* (New Brunswick, New Jersey: Rutgers University Press, 2004)

6. Some critics have implied that Fox accepts all-too-readily the existing Israeli social and ideological narrative, the result, in the words of Shai Ginsburg, of the "ever-growing influence of American commercial cinema and television on Israeli media." Raz Yosef has suggested that *Yossi and Jagger* "represents an attempt on the part of its director to join the national heterosexual collectivity and to attach himself to the myths that constitute it, at the price of depoliticizing and desexualizing gay male identity." Shai Ginsburg, "Between Sex and Country: The Films of Eytan Fox," *Tikkun*, May/June 2005, 78, and Raz Yosef, "The National Closet: Gay Israel in *Yossi and Jagger,*" *GLQ: A Journal of Lesbian and Gay Studies* 11/2 (2005): 286.

7. Kuperboim,1.

8. In Said's words, "Orientalism . . . is rather a *distribution* of geopolitical awareness into aesthetic, scholarly, economic, sociological, historical, and philological texts; it is an *elaboration* not only of a basic geographical distinction (the world is made up of two unequal halves, Orient and Occident) but also of a whole series of "interests" which, by such means as scholarly discovery, philological reconstruction, psychological analysis, landscape and sociological description, it not only creates but also maintains; it *is,* rather than expresses, a certain *will* or *intention* to understand, in some cases to control, manipulate, even to incorporate, what is a manifestly different (or alternative and novel world.) See, Edward Said, "From Orientalism," in *The Norton Anthology of Theory and Criticism,* ed. Vincent E. Leitsch (New York/London: W. W. Norton & Co, 2001), 1999

9. "Interview with Eytan Fox: Falling in Love with the Enemy," www.qantara.de/webcom/show_article.php/_c-310/_nr-399/i.html, 3.

10. *The Bubble,* directed by Eytan Fox (Strand Releasing, 2006), 0:16:00–0:16:39.

11. "The Making of *The Bubble,*" in *The Bubble* DVD, 0:16:00–0:17:00.

12. Yosef, *Beyond Flesh*, 137.

13. "The Boys in the Bubble," 37. There is the added dimension here that nearly all of the actors, including Sweid, are Israeli, not Palestinian—although Fox did use Palestinian extras from Gaza for the checkpoint scenes in an important act of bridge building. One of the actors had to return to the Gaza Strip upon hearing news that his house had been bombed.

14. *The Bubble,* directed, 1:19:00–1:20:27.

15. *The Bubble*, 1:53–1:53:55.

THE HOLOCAUST, WAR, AND GENOCIDE

Chapter Thirteen

"Time and Representation: Generic Transformations and Historicist Interpretations of Holocaust Films"

Ilan Avisar, Professor of Film, Tel Aviv University

In one of the earliest studies of Holocaust representation, *The Holocaust and the Literary Imagination*, Lawrence Langer made the following claim: "To establish an order of reality in which the unimaginable becomes imaginatively acceptable exceeds the capacities of an art devoted entirely to verisimilitude; some quality of the fantastic, whether stylistic or descriptive, becomes an essential ingredient of *l'universe concentrationaire*."[1] Langer argued that the extreme horrors of the Holocaust require formal disfiguration, and he mentioned Picasso's *Guernica* as a model for artistic representation of the Shoah. *The Holocaust and the Literary Imagination* was published in 1975. Twenty-five years later, Lawrence Langer published a study of survivors' video testimonies. The book, *Holocaust Testimonies: The Ruins of Memory,* contains a motto written by Aharon Appelfeld: "By its very nature, when it comes to describing reality, art always demands a certain intensification, for many and various reasons. However, that is not the case with the Holocaust. Everything in it already seems so thoroughly unreal . . ."[2] Thus, Langer's scholarship on Holocaust texts displays a radical change, from a call to artistic formal disfiguration in any representation of the event to appreciation of the avoidance of any artistic intensification of the Shoah.

I wrote my book, *Screening the Holocaust*, about twenty years ago.[3] I tried then to consider the special claims of the Holocaust on artistic texts in ethical and aesthetic terms and to analyze cinematic representations of historical atrocities. It seems to me today, that from the perspective of nearly six decades, scholars need to apply critical discourse to the history of Holocaust movies. By historicizing the Holocaust film, we can identify principal paradigms of representation and comprehension. These paradigms have been modified by the historical moment, by their position in time in relation to the event and by the accumulative relationships of Holocaust texts since the rise of Nazism until the present time. Changes in the domination of one mode of registration over another are also the result of historical developments in different spheres of human activity, like national and international affairs, technological innovations, altering life styles, or shifting cultural moods. More significantly, these changes testify to the actual unfolding of the Holocaust in time and history, and the place of Auschwitz in contemporary culture and in collective memory.

Beyond historicist considerations that place the Holocaust in historical context, it is the dimension of time, or the duration of the catastrophe that account for the unique character of the Holocaust. The twelve years of the Third Reich, or the six years of World War II, or the four years of the genocide process, mark a very long period for the occurrence of a monumental crime. The years of Hitler's power allowed the various agencies of the modern state to conceive the plan of genocide and to prepare the necessary tools for its implementation. These tools included propaganda and brainwashing, developing scientific solutions for mass murder, or preparing meticulous and efficient apparatus for the identification of the victims, the transport of the victims, the murder of the victims, and the disposal of the victims' bodies in order to enable the continuation of the killing and the concealment of the crimes of genocide. The many months and years of executions of millions produced unprecedented vistas of atrocities and indeed another planet—the concentration camp universe. In the planet of Auschwitz, moral character and existential possibilities were tested beyond the limits of known human faculties. The time and duration of the Holocaust compelled impossible adjustments and impossible decisions, the victims in their extreme predicament, the executioners with their adopted "life style" as murderers, and the bystanders, neighbors of the deported Jews, farmers who continued their living next to the camps, or what George Steiner called the scandalous contemporariness of the horrible crimes in Europe and the continuation of normal life in most parts of western civilization.[4]

After the liberation of the camps, the Holocaust continued to exist as the trauma of the victims and an indelible scar in humanity's collective memory. However, its perception and apprehension underwent significant changes in the course of our cultural history. In the thirties, during the years of the world war and even in the immediate aftermath of the war there was little realization of the Holocaust in the terms of the attempted genocide of the Jewish people. During the war years, the concentration camp was regarded as the ultimate horror of Nazi menace. At the end of the war, there was a growing realization that the Jews may have suffered more than other victims in the crimes against humanity, but no clear apprehension of the genocidal policies and that the Holocaust might have been humanity's crime against the Jews. The identification of the Holocaust as a watershed event in human culture developed in the sixties. In the seventies and eighties various societies of the western hemisphere came to grips with the Holocaust and its specific implications for their own political history. Recently we witness how organizations like the United Nations or the Council of the European Union officially recognize the Holocaust as a universal event that must be remembered and venerated.[5]

Cinema has been a special agent in the unfolding of the Holocaust, both in the historical narrative during the years of the Third Reich and in the postwar years that established the place of the Holocaust in collective memory and cultural consciousness. In terms of film theory, cinema has recorded the instaneity of the historical moment and has served also as the archival site for historical events.[6] These two functions operated in the context of the development of cinema, its development in terms of technology, its place in society, and its cultural status. The Holocaust and cinema have a shared history. It's a shared history in the sense that films played a role in the history of the Shoah, and the subject of the Holocaust played a role in the evolution of cinema as an art form and as a major medium of cultural discourse. Thus, the examination of the Holocaust film in the context of time should take into consideration the historical unfolding of the attempted genocide of the Jews in the Nazi era, the social and political history of the Holocaust in the post war period, and the historical narrative of Holocaust film representation as an evolving art form.

After the advent of sound, the economic crises of the early thirties, and the rise of totalitarian regimes in Germany, Russia, and Italy, cinema was recognized by political leaders as a potent medium for spreading ideology and controlling the masses. The first years of Nazism displayed the use of cinema for propaganda, mobilizing the medium for what Propaganda Minister Joseph Goebbels regarded as the fourth army of the war. The first national rallies of the ruling Nazi party in Germany were documented by film crews headed by Leni Riefenstahl. *Victory of Faith* (1934) on the 1933 Nuremberg party convention was followed by *Triumph of the Will* (1935), a film designed to transform ordinary viewers into impassioned Nazis by stunning spectacles, fiery speeches by the *Führer*, and a musical soundtrack based on national and party anthems, military marches and Wagnerian tunes. After the outbreak of the world war, the notorious Nazi anti-Semitic films, *Jud Süss* and *Der ewige Jude,* revealed genocidal intentions as early as the fall of 1940, nearly a year before the beginning of the actual systematic killing of the Jews.[7] These extraordinary hate films were shown to German troops charged with carrying out the Nazi genocidal program. Conversely, Charlie Chaplin's *The Great*

Dictator and other Hollywood war time movies tried to warn the free world against the dangers of Nazism and the need to fight and win the war. The few films that addressed the predicament of the Jews revealed the contemporary difficulty to express support for and aid Jewish victims; indeed there was a near universal abandonment of the Jews during the Holocaust.

The initial phase of film propaganda was followed by the use of cinema as documentary medium. The years of World War II displayed the full potential of the photographic image. Since many of the Nazi atrocities were literally unbelievable, the photograph became an indispensable testament of their truth. There is a rich body of photographic heritage of World War II that is immediately evoked in any reference to the period. Wartime photographs of barbed wires, watchtowers, barracks, chimneys and smoke, evoke the most hideous products of Nazism, the concentration camps and the death camps in eastern Europe. The most graphic images of the Holocaust are those of the victims at the liberated concentration camps. Upon entering the camps in Germany, shocked commanders of the Allied forces ordered that the atrocious conditions unfolding before their eyes be captured on film. Although pictures of decimated bodies and wretched living skeletons were taken in liberated concentration camps and not in the extermination centers of Poland, they have become the ultimate images of genocide and dehumanization.

The next phase of the development of Holocaust films feature postwar narrative movies, realistic dramas motivated by the desire to inform, to remember, and to learn the lessons of the past while asserting a commitment to a better world. The idea of "a better world" took many political forms. In the communist regimes of eastern Europe, national cinemas treated the Nazi horrors as the crucible for the ideological triumph of Russian-inspired socialism. Postwar Zionist productions showed survivors recovering from their traumas in the society of the emerging Jewish State. In the United States, Hollywood followed years of ignoring the Jewish genocide with films that addressed the problem of anti-Semitism and the need to eradicate racism and prejudice from postwar American society. The first American film on the experiences of Jews in the Holocaust was *The Diary of Anne Frank* (1959). The Hollywood production sentimentalized the Holocaust, promoting shallow forms of optimism associated with American popular culture. The final message is of hope, and the legacy of the Americanized Anne appears in her words that "in spite of everything" she believes in human goodness. The discomfort with the transparently simplistic sentimentality of the Hollywood presentation of Anne Frank may easily apply to other productions of the fifties in other parts of the world; all are usually national narratives that celebrate heroic and self-justified national ideology.

In addition to being ideologically transparent, the national films of the fifties embraced realistic codes of representation. *The Diary of Anne Frank* was filmed in a replica of the original attic, and included exterior pictures of the original site in Amsterdam. Other films were shot in the camps of the war years or other authentic sites. The ideology informing the realistic approach was the need to describe and inscribe the unsettling truth of the concentration camp universe. Alain Resnais' *Night and Fog* offers a special case. Its dualistic structure and double perspective serve two purposes. On the one hand, the film contains powerful documentary pictures of the camps and other aspects of the genocide system. On the other hand, the brooding camera in the present shots of Auschwitz, accompanied by a cryptic narration and probing flute melodies express the modernist anguish of the epistemological gap with the universe of atrocities, questioning the very possibility to represent the ultimate horror.

The fourth stage of Holocaust cinema emerged in the sixties, featuring modernist reflections on the war years. Existentialist philosophy generated visions that regarded the concentration camp universe as the incarnation of the angstful human condition, an extreme reality that offered insights and metaphors for the understanding of the human predicament. Modernist films like Luchino Visconti's *The Damned* (1969), Bob Fosse's *Cabaret* (1972), or Josef Losey's *Mr. Klein* (1976) explored the salient tenets of the civilization that created Nazism and the Holocaust. Distinguished filmmakers like Ingmar Bergman (*Serpent's Egg*, 1977) and Francois Truffaut (*The Last Metro*, 1980) explored the complexity of character in light of the experiences under Nazi menace. American movies like *Judgment at Nuremberg* (1961) and *The Pawnbroker* (1965) addressed the ethical dimension of social behavior vis-a-vis injustice and racism.

In Europe, the critical attitudes of modernism led to the abandonment of simplified patterns of valiant national memory for the sake of new, harsh reckoning with the past. In France, *The Sorrow and the Pity* (dir. Marcel Ophuls, 1969) prompted a new wave of "retro" films that subverted the heroic historical narratives fostered during de Gaulle's years in power. A young generation of German filmmakers emerged in the seventies with quality films known as the "New German Cinema." One of their central themes was dealing with the history of their country from the perspective of a personal confrontation with the burden of Nazism. Israeli filmmakers also began to examine the legacy of the Holocaust in the national psyche and the effects of the historical trauma on the political behavior of the Jewish State.

In 1973, Claude Lanzmann produced a film entitled *Why Israel?* Lanzmann's cinematic investigation of Israeli society led him to years of work on the Holocaust. The completion of *Shoah* in 1985 marked the appearance of a canonical text in the discourse of the Holocaust as well as a unique film masterpiece. Lanzmann presented the Holocaust as a watershed historical event, a singular human experience, and a unique challenge to the possibilities of artistic expression. In *Shoah*, the dramatic content occurs in two levels that interact with each other—the excruciating accounts of the past and the painful recounts in the present. Lanzmann declared: "The film that I have made is . . . an inquiry on the present of the Holocaust or at the very least on a past whose scars are still so fresh and so inscribed in places and on mind that it appears with hallucinatory timelessness."[8] Although it appears as a "lean" documentary, supposedly limited to interviews and pictures of the sites of the genocide, avoiding narration, music or any sound effects, *Shoah* is a highly artistic text, rich with significant aesthetic decisions of sophisticated modernist poetics. Most remarkably, Lanzmann avoids any inclusion of the historical photographs or archival footage from the war years. Several years ago, while speaking of Spielberg's "Schindler's List," Lanzmann commented on the fact that:

> There is not one second of archival material in *Shoah*. . . . If I had found an existing film—a secret film because that was forbidden—shot by an SS and showing how 3,000 Jews, men, women and children, were dying together, asphyxiated in the gas chamber of Krema 2 in Auschwitz, not only would I have not shown it, but I would have destroyed it.[9]

This is undoubtedly an extreme position, probably more polemical than practical. Lanzmann underscores the argument that the Holocaust's heart of darkness is beyond representation. It also discloses a curious distrust in the value of the documentary images. Their presence might suggest that there are images of the unimaginable, that the unrepresentable can be shown. Furthermore, in the transition from the documentary phase of the war years to realistic narratives, the initially unsettling and alarming pictures became all too familiar, saturated, eroded by time. *Shoah* was the ultimate modernist text on the Holocaust, complex in its expression, ambitious and conscious of its intention to reach out to the unspeakable and the unimaginable. Lanzmann's opposition to a spurious realistic approach has become a rage in a postmodernist culture that engages in the endless, and often mindless, recycling of images. Moreover, Lanzmann's cautious approach to the visual image as a record and index to extraordinary reality, has been replaced by postmodernist celebration of spectacle and the power of images.

As the fundamental aspects of the Holocaust have been established and familiarized through numerous texts, (most notably the American TV series *Holocaust* and also Lanzmann's *Shoah*), the cultural discourse has shifted from the core of the horrors to other aspects of the concentration camp universe and its aftermath in contemporary culture. The postmodernist challenge to the notion of grand narratives combined with the new technologies of computer and video characterize the post-*Shoah* production of numerous works on the multiple and diverse aspects of the Holocaust. Space now exists for inexpensive film productions by many members of the second generation who wish to explore their family roots and the special predicaments of their parent survivors. Large scale collections of video testimonies by survivors, like the USC Shoah Institute, Spielberg's repository at the University of Southern California, make possible this diffusion of narratives.

Schindler's List marked the shift from the engagement with victimizers and victims to saviors and survivors. Postmodernist treatment of the Holocaust withdraws from anguished reflections on the tragic aspects of existence. Put differently, in spite of everything, *Life is Beautiful* (1999). Roberto Benigni was ready to claim this postmodernist assertion in the face of the ultimate horrors, and Holocaust comedy, an impossible oxymoron, has become a popular option, with films like *Train of Life* (1998), and *Jakob the Liar* (1999). Rather than irreverence or mockery, these works attempt to offer the life-enhancing vision of comedy in connection with the Holocaust. As such, they echo numerous post-*Shoah* documentary films, celebrating life and human virtues in film titles or review titles like *Weapons of the Spirit* (1987), *Daring to Resist* (1999), and *They Risked their Lives* (1991). This list curiously includes Lanzmann's most recent film, *Sobibor, 14 octobre, 16 heures* (2001), which focuses on the prisoners' revolt in Sobibor that put an end to the functioning of the death camp.

The evolution of the Holocaust film has involved both internal and external factors. The most significant external frameworks include the cultural moods of realism, modernism, and postmodernism. In the first phase, of realism, the Holocaust was a demanding reality, demanding to be recorded, documented, transmitted, and then demanding to be recognized as a moral or political lesson of catastrophic dimensions. In the second phase, that of modernism, Auschwitz became a metaphysical dissonance of supreme implications for the assessment of the human condition. The Holocaust was featured as an elusive reality, unrepresentable and incomprehensible, suggesting the limits of representation and the edges of human faculties. In the third phase, that of postmodernism, the Holocaust has become a familiar element in the culture of images and popular stories. The abundant presence of the Holocaust in contemporary dramas of adolescent development, stories of family crises, political thrillers, science fiction fantasies, and crime stories has reduced the event to Woody Allen's postmodernist title, *Anything Else.*

The internal factors effecting Holocaust cinematic representations refer to intertextual influences of Holocaust films. More specifically, Holocaust films display the characteristics of a film genre, formulating a stock of narratives, characters, and iconography. In particular, the genre's diachronic dimension, as explicated by Christian Metz in his analysis of the internal evolution of the Western, accounts for significant changes in representation.[10] Henri Focillon's *The Life of Forms in Art* set out a fundamental observation: "Forms obey their own rules—rules that are inherent in the forms themselves. . . [they] behave throughout the phase which we call their life. The successive states through which they pass are . . . : the experimental age, the classic age, the age of refinement, the baroque age."[11]

Thomas Schatz applied this passage to the study of film genres in the following terms: "At the earliest stage of its life span, a genre tends to exploit the cinematic medium *as a medium* (sic). . . ."[12] In Holocaust representation this applies to the stages of propaganda and war time documentaries in which film served as a medium to convey political messages or a medium that transmitted the visual horrors of the liberated camps. The next stage, which Schatz also calls the classical stage, is "one of formal transparency. Both the narrative formula and the film medium work together to transmit and reinforce that genre's social message—its ideology or problem-solving strategy—as directly as possible to the audience."[13] This stage corresponds to the realistic Holocaust dramas of the fifties, characterized by both formal transparency and messages of national ideologies. When the genre evolves into what Focillon dubs the age of refinement, the premises and codes are "reexamined, grow more complicated formally and thematically, and display, moreover, stylistic embellishment."[14] This age, in our discussion, is the phase of modernism in the representation of the Holocaust, the adoption of sophisticated aesthetic strategies mostly in the so-called European art cinema of the 1960s. Finally, what Focillon calls the baroque age, is in the evolution of the genre the stage of parody and subversion. This stage describes a central strain of postmodernist consciousness or self-reflective treatment of earlier texts, including the appearance of Holocaust film comedies.

Any periodization runs the risk of overgeneralization and inaccuracy. But the historicist reading of Holocaust movies reveals both a significant evolution and the principal paradigms in Holocaust representational discourse. Thus there are five stages to the Holocaust film and five fields of reference to Holocaust texts. The five fields are: propaganda, documentation, realistic national narratives, modernist probing of philosophical issues, and postmodernist deconstruction and textualization. Propaganda is the principal tool and concern in the discourse of Holocaust deniers, neo-Nazis, Islamic radicals, anti-Zionists, and other types of anti-Semites. The issue of evidence is important for the exposition of little known or even unknown aspects of the historical event, and documentation is valuable to record direct consequences of the historical experience, or legacies of the Holocaust like post traumatic syndromes. The theme of national narratives plays a role in the continuous reckonings of different societies with the Holocaust and its place in national politics and culture. Modernist ideas inform the critical discourse with the challenges of artistic representation and philosophical comprehension. The postmodernist intellectual challenge to the notion of grand narratives, combined with the new video and computer technologies, characterize the post-*Shoah* production of numerous works on the multiple and diverse aspects of the Holocaust, assimilating the Holocaust or textualizing the event into multiple facets of postmodernism.

The five paradigms of Holocaust discourse—propaganda, documentation, realistic ideological narrativization, modernist philosophical reflection, postmodernist textualization—may serve as a critical assessment of any text. For example, Leni Riefenstahl's *Triumph of the Will* was first and foremost a propaganda film, designed to consolidate Hitler's power in the Third Reich in a critical moment of Germany's history. As evidence, Riefenstahl's film displays salient aspects of Nazism, like the cult of the leader, or the militarization and regimentation of German society, and it also reveals the political needs and strategic decision of Adolf Hitler at the moment that the film was made, particularly the critical transition from SA-dominated party to the new, deadlier style of the SS. *Triumph of the Will* is an extravagant demonstration of German nationalism, in speeches, flags, symbolic locations, and musical themes. Its ideological excess testifies to the unbridled forces of extreme nationalism that eventually led to the world war and the "total war" for German citizens. Several critics regarded a few moments in *Triumph* as foreshadowing the disastrous images of ruined Germany ten years after the film's completion.[15] A modernist search for deeper symbolism in the film's sounds and images may uncover the themes of death wish, twilight of the gods, romantic flirtation with the edge—the divine and the devilish. Finally, a postmodernist attention to the film as spectacle may result in a complex reaction to the grand symphony of images and sounds, as one may find in the 1993 documentary *The Wonderful Horrible Life of Leni Riefenstahl* (whose original title was *Die Macht der Bilder: Leni Riefenstahl*).

The public discourse of some recent films displays the confusion of the paradigms of criticism outlined here, ignoring the meaning of temporal and cultural context. Without acknowledging its postmodernist context, critics of *Life is Beautiful* condemned the film for its distortion of concentration camp realities and claimed that it opened the possibility of exploitation by Holocaust deniers. *Schindler's List*, although a realistic presentation, was marred by the failure to acknowledge the special problematics and specific limits of Holocaust representation. Spielberg offered the project as a work of a modernist artist, burdened by personal angst and tragic recognitions. Ultimately, though, *Schindler's List* was a postmodern media event, and a postmodernist text celebrating life saving, capitalism, and the power of the medium, nearly blurring the distinctions between film images and real horrors.

The Holocaust—the attempted genocide of the Jews, the industrial mass murder, the unimaginable trials and horrors of the concentration camp universe—in its scope, methods, and details poses a special challenge to any act of representation, expression or comprehension. Any Holocaust text is determined by the rules of its discourse, by the codes of its artistic form, and by the technological possibilities, cultural norms and socio-political ideologies of its time. Any text is therefore inevitably limited in its claim for truthful account or transmission of the unique "unreality" of the other planet. At the same time, the representation of the Holocaust is necessary to inform and to enlighten, to pay homage to the victims and their sufferings, to warn against the dangers of ideologies of hatred and doctrines of destruction. The anguished recognition that the universe of atrocities is beyond representation yields to the moral command to present the incomprehensible facts and tell the unbelievable stories. In Elie Wiesel's words, any text on the Holocaust is "a Mitzvah and a Matzeva," a moral commandment and a reverent commemoration.[16] Given the uniqueness and enormity of the Holocaust, the unresolved problems of truthful representation, ethical presentation, and meaningful comprehension call for critical vigilance that requires theoretical lucidity, sound morality and understanding of time and historical context.

NOTES

1. Lawrence Langer, *The Holocaust and the Literary Imagination* (New Haven, Connecticut: Yale University Press, 1975), 43.

2. Langer, *Holocaust Testimonies: The Ruins of Memory* (New Haven, Connecticut: Yale University Press, 1991).

3. Ilan Avisar, *Screening the Holocaust: Cinema's Images of the Unimaginable* (Bloomington, Indiana: Indiana University Press, 1988).

4. "Precisely at the same time in which Mehring or Langer were being done to death, the overwhelming plurality of human beings' two miles away on the Polish farms' five thousands miles away in New York, were sleeping or eating or going to a film or making love or worrying about the dentists. This is where my imagination bulks. The two orders of simultaneous experience are so different, so irreconcilable to any common norm of human value . . ." In George Steiner, *Language and Silence* (New York: Atheneum, 1967), 156.

5. On December 14, 2006, the General Assembly of the United Nations adopted by consensus a resolution that "decided that the United Nations would designate 27 Jan-

uary, the anniversary of the liberation of the Auschwitz death camp, as an annual *International Day of Commemoration to honour the victims of the Holocaust*. See http://www.un.org/holocaustremembrance/emainpage.shtml.

6. Mary Ann Doane, *The Emergence of Cinematic Time: Modernity, Contingency, the Archive* (Cambridge, Massachusetts: Harvard University Press, 2002).

7. Ilan Avisar, "The Historical Significance of *Der ewige Jude*," *The Historical Journal of Film, Radio and Television*, vol. 13, no. 3 (1993): 363–365.

8. *New York Times*, 2 May 1985, C21

9. Claude Lanzmann's review of *Schindler's List* was published in *Le Monde*, 3 March 1994.

10. Christian Metz, *Language and Cinema* (The Hague: Mouton, 1974): 148–161.

11. Henri Fucillon, *The Life of Forms in Art* (New York: George Wittenborn, 1942), 10.

12. Thomas Schatz, *Hollywood Genres* (New York: McGrow-Hill, 1981), 38.

13. Schatz, *Hollywood Genres*.

14. Schatz, *Hollywood Genres*.

15. Leif Furhammar and Folke Isaksson, *Politics and Film*, (New York: Praeger, 1971), 104.

16. Elie Wiesel, *Legends of Our Time*, (New York: Holt, Rinehart and Winston, 1968), 10.

Chapter Fourteen

"The Bystander and the 'Other' in Holocaust Films"

John J. Michalczyk and Susan A. Michalczyk, Boston College

Sonia Weitz, a Holocaust survivor of three concentration camps, poet, and director of the Holocaust Center of the North Shore (in Peabody, Massachusetts), observed during an interview for our documentary, *The Cross and the Star: Jews, Christians and the Holocaust* (1992) that she has reconciled the roles of the perpetrator and the victim. She cannot, however, understand the position of the bystander.[1] In her poem "Where was Man?" she describes her private challenge to God after experiencing his silence. Her concluding line shifts the focus from blaming God for the tragedy of the Holocaust, to placing the blame squarely on the human bystander:

> I called on You in torment wild
> And desperately cursed Your name
> Then I was nothing but a child
> And there was no one else to blame
> But now I feel God wasn't dead
> And *where was man* I ask instead?[2]

In Holocaust studies, there have been countless analyses of the psychology of the rescuers, attributing to these courageous individuals many positive, and at times, even heoric characteristics. These individuals faced lethal danger from government forces, threats to themselves and their family, financial losses, and rejection by their peers, some of the reasons for which they could have closed their eyes to the persecution and annihilation of the Jews. Yet, the rescuers who normally came from nurturing families and neighborhoods which had more open relations with diverse groups, and were often engaged risk-takers, acted with courage for reasons of altruism, compassion, and sheer desire to do the right thing. One of the first examples of this altruism viewed in the United States came in the form of the feature film *The Diary of Anne Frank* (1959), wherein the Dutch rescuers of Anne Frank, including Miep Gies, take great risks in occupied Amsterdam to create a secret hiding place for the Frank family. Some of the personal stories of the rescue are recalled in Jon Blair's documentary *Anne Frank Remembered* (1995). The film, *Imaginary Witness: Hollywood and the Holocaust* (2000), addresses the issue of softening the message of the horrors of the camps and indicates how *The Diary of Anne Frank* focuses on the goodness of the rescuers and Anne's faith in humanity. George Stevens, the director, had experienced the death camps in his filming at the close of the war and did not wish to present this graphic image, according to the director's son, George Stevens, Jr.[3]

Among the more celebrated rescuers documented in film, we find André Trocmé the charismatic Huguenot clergyman in France portrayed in Pierre Sauvage's *Weapons of the Spirit* (1989);[4] Oskar Schindler seen in *Schindler's List* (1993) as the Nazi entrepreneur who valiantly rescued over a thousand Jews in Poland to work in his factories; Wɫadysɫaw Bartoszewski, one of the key players in the rescue of some four thousand Jews in Poland, witnessed in *Żegota* (1998), the codename for the Council for Aid to Jews; Kaj Munk, the courageous Protestant minister who preached against Nazi oppression in Denmark, viewed in *The Cross and the Star*; Raoul Wallenberg the Swedish diplomat who rescued anywhere from 30,000 to 100,000 Hungarian Jews, featured in *Good Evening, Mr. Wallenberg* (1990); and Chiune Sugihara, often labeled the "Japanese Schindler," the focus of the documentary *The Conspiracy of Kindness* (2000). Each had a personal rationale for rescue. Yet these more memorable individuals serve as only the tip of the iceberg because the whole system of rescue depended on the courage of those altruistic persons committed to rescue Jews, who were also willing to lay down their lives for "The Other." Most say that they had never thought of being courageous but acted out of impulse when the opportunity presented itself.[5] They became "accidental heroes," yet, as in *Weapons of the Spirit*, Pierre Sauvage's interview with an elderly Huguenot couple who rescued many Jews reveals that they did not honestly believe themselves to be heroes because they simply responded out of necessity and naturalness.

The bystander, diametrically opposed to the rescuer, perceived "The Other" in a very negative fashion. "The Other" was a threat to the "normality" of the situation, for these targeted individuals brought attention to the local area of the "Occupation," attracted danger and violence, influenced the financial status of the region, and above all, "were not like me"—in terms of religion, ethnicity, or class. The underlying question thus for the bystander was "Why should I endanger my life or that of my family for the likes of this Jew?"

As scholars and witnesses examined the motivations of the rescuers in the service of "The Other,"[6] it is also noteworthy to analyze the psychology of the "innocent" bystander who can in no way be called "innocent." The bystander can be a country such as the United States with a long-standing history of anti-Semitism, as viewed by historian David S. Wyman in *The Abandonment of the Jews*.[7] In the American Experience documentary for PBS, *America and the Holocaust* (1994), Wyman shows the intricate paper maze set up by the American government to keep out the Jews, even though it knew of the Nazi threats against them following the actions of Kristallnact in November 1938. In the religious arena, some critics say that the Vatican played the role of the bystander in Pope Pius XII's refusal to challenge the Nazi policies of extermination of the Jews. Following the death of Pope Pius XII, once viewed as a friend to the Jewish community, Rolf Hochhuth's controversial play *The Deputy: a Christian Tragedy* (1963) dramatically raised the issue of a silent Vicar of Christ while the Holocaust raged right under his window in the Vatican. Costa-Gavras' film *Amen* (2002) used the essence of the play to portray the Pope as reluctant to confront Hitler, especially in his Christmas address of 1943 when the Final Solution was well underway. The Catholic Church objected to the film's presentation of the Pope as a weak and spineless bystander, and was also critical of the advertisement of the film with a poster showing a cross intertwined with the swastika.

On a personal level, all of the individuals and institutions portrayed in the above films had to make the private choice of rescuing their endangered neighbors, persecuting the Jews whom they saw as non-human, collaborating with the Nazis, or being the bystander. It all came down to how each perceived "The Other." Sander L. Gilman, in *The Longest Hatred: The History of Anti-Semitism* (1993), describes the paradoxical image of the Jew in contrasting images:

> All Jews are clannish. All Jews are loners. All Jews look like everybody else. All Jews look absolutely different from everybody else. All Jews are communists and anarchists. All Jews are bankers and capitalists. All Jews love money. All Jews despise worldly goods. In other words, the image of the Jew is a protean one; it shifts. That's what's so nice about this image. It isn't just that the Jews are "X". The Jews are everything you don't want yourself to be. The Jews are everything that threatens you.

The image of the Jew as other, as the scapegoat, through the Christian era is dark and troubling. David P. Barash discusses the victims of "transferred aggression" in an enlightening manner:

To understand how and why people engage in redirected aggression is to gain insight into seemingly disconnected events. For example, the power and ubiquity of scapegoating are revealed afresh: from Old Testament accounts in which the transgressions and sins of the people were placed upon the head of a goat, which was then slaughtered or driven away, to current psychological theory whereby families often establish a "designated transgressor" who is blamed for any dysfunction.[8]

This scapegoating became very obvious as the Nazis chose the Jews as their target of aggression. One would often see at Nazi gatherings a banner which read, "Die Juden sind unser Unglück" (The Jews are Our Misfortune). This attitude has its roots, however, in biblical times, dating even as far back as Egypt as depicted in the book of *Exodus.* It can be perceived in the Christian gospels of Matthew and John where the Jews are the betrayers of Christ and the "Christ killers," guilty of deicide.[9] Mel Gibson's controversial film, *The Passion of the Christ* (2004), brought to the fore many criticisms of insensitivity and anti-Semitism, showing Gibson's film a quasi-literal interpretation of the gospel narrative of the death of Jesus. The Passion narrative read during Holy Week just prior to Easter, reinforced the image of the Jew as "Christ killer." (The pogroms against the Jews in Eastern Europe in the early 20th century provide dramatic evidence that the Jews were persecuted especially after Christians heard the Passion narrative on Good Friday.[10] The government stood by allowing the persecution, for it took away the attention from the government's many failures, especially financial.) The Church Fathers, especially John Chrysostom, saw the Jew as a wild beast and the synagogue as a brothel and den of scoundrels. During the Crusades in the Middle Ages and the 15th–16th century Inquisition, the "perfidious" Jew faced forced conversion, expulsion, or death.[11] The reformer Martin Luther saw the Jew as the devil incarnate and suggested burning synagogues.

With this historical background, a deep negative image was already latent in the minds of those Germans and also the Poles who saw their Jewish neighbors as different, threatening, or racially impure. Given this tainted image of the Jew, the bystander during the Holocaust found little motivation to help rescue a Jew in danger. The bystander in essence allows an evil or an injustice to occur without taking a stand. Daniel Goldhagen's provocative book, *Hitler's Willing Executioners: Ordinary Germans and the Holocaust*, raises the issue that the Holocaust could not have happened without the total participation of the German people.[12] Goldhagen sees the Germans as most complicit. Given their cruel indifference and their strong antipathy and jealousy of the Jewish community, he notes, it did not take much to elicit their cooperation in the Final Solution. According to Goldhagen, the Germans were willing, even eager, to do their part in the removal of the Jews from their Aryan society.

Examining the psychological mindset of the bystander, we can determine several factors that played a principal role in his or her decision not to come to the defense of the vulnerable and threatened individual Jew or Jewish community.

One of the foremost reasons for not taking a stand, not challenging the status quo of anti-Semitism, was fear. The threat of reprisals struck at the heart of every German and Pole who attempted to speak up or harbor a Jew. A rescuer once caught would be made an example of, demonstrating to would-be rescuers the lethal repercussions of such an action. Dr. Maciej Kozlowski, Polish Ambassador to Israel (from 1999 to 2003), described the ultimate risks to a Pole rescuing a Jew as more aggressive than anywhere in occupied Europe. The individual rescuer could be killed with his family, and even those who knew of the situation and did not denounce him or her could be placed in extreme danger. [13] More than two thousand Polish rescuers lost their lives for their heroic deeds of rescue. The fear of being taken to prison or a concentration camp loomed high in the mind of someone who would think twice of taking a risk to help someone in danger. Any possible altruism would be offset by fear of tragic consequences. This was always in the mind of Sefania Podgorska, as witnessed in *The Other Side of Faith* (1991), seen rescuing thirteen Jews. In general, the bystander was most hesitant when contemplating acting in the defense of a Jew, fearing danger for himself or herself or the entire family. In the groundbreaking NBC television mini-series *Holocaust* (1978), Poles were seen as unwilling to get involved, while some were eager to help Jews in the resistance, but for an exorbitant price for arms. The bystander was even afraid of being found guilty by association; hence the Jews were often isolated in a community where they once lived and worked in relative peace prior to the Third Reich.

The upbringing of a non-Jew shaped in great part the decision to help or not to help another in danger. Were the parents passive themselves politically? What was their attitude toward the Jews? Samuel P. Oliner and Pearl M. Oliner offer a concrete example of a Polish resister's attitude toward Jews:

'I wanted to fight the Nazis, but I had no interest in Jews.' His perception of Jews' irrelevance had begun early in life, when his parents had emphasized that Jews were rich and shrewd and, above all, how different they were from Poles. The attitudes and experience of this active non-rescuer underscore that how one perceives the victims is an important element in making a decision to help, and that parents play a major role in shaping such perceptions.[14]

The scene of the young Polish girl in the Krakow street screaming "Goodbye, Jews" at the traumatized cortege of Jews in *Schindler's List* reinforces the anti-Semitic views of the parents passed down to their children.

In Louis Malle's semi-autobiographical film, *Au revoir, les enfants* (1987), it is most apparent that the young male students of Petit-Collège d'Avon, a religious boarding school, have learned their view of the world from their parents. As they walk in line with their teacher, we can hear comments now assimilated as their own personal politics, especially derogatory of Jews and communists. In the local restaurant, a motley group of collaborating militia harass a Jewish client, wanting to evict him. Some of the diners look on, helpless, while others make anti-Semitic remarks, suggesting that the Jews should be sent back to Moscow. It is only when a German officer in the restaurant disapproves that calm returns. At the close of the film, as the Gestapo searches for the three Jewish boys hidden by Père Jacques, the scullery boy Joseph changes from bystander to collaborator, taunting the young Julien (Louis Malle persona), that the boys taken by the German soldiers "are only Jews."[15]

Ignorance, too, played a key role in the decision not to help a Jew in trouble. They were often used either as excuses or as coping mechanisms. Most Christians knew nothing about the religious or cultural background of Judaism. What they learned was primarily from the gospels, which created a negative image of the Jew. Why would the bystander risk danger for someone so different, so foreign? Unless a personal connection or communication existed, the risk became too enormous. With awareness and understanding comes change. For example, Oskar Schindler, though completely unaware of Jewish culture, evolved from being a business-oriented bystander to a rescuer by grasping the seriousness of the Nazi threat in Krakow during the liquidation of the ghetto. In Steven Spielberg's *Schindler's List* (1993), this is depicted in his view overlooking the city of the little girl in a crimson coat. It is his moment of conversion.[16] Samantha Powers would say that he became an "up-stander" as a result of his experience of viewing the plight of the Jews.[17]

Claude Lanzmann's *Shoah* (1985) uncovered a wide range of behavior during the Nazi occupation of Poland, from a German officer clandestinely filmed discussing the extermination process to ignorant bystanders and to rescue and resistance efforts of Jan Karski. Poles object strongly to their harsh stereotypical image presented on screen ever since the *Holocaust* television miniseries, and this holds true for their depiction in *Shoah.* Besides being portrayed in films and historical texts as bystanders, they see themselves unjustly represented as collaborators or mercenary, turning in Jews to save themselves or their family, or to make a profit. The Polish press at the time of the release

of the film *Shoah* viciously attacked Lanzmann for the revival of the stereotypes of Poles as bitterly anti-Semitic.

In an allegorical way, Albert Camus' novel *The Plague*, can also be inter-
preted as an image of World War II and the Holocaust.[18] Here, the journalist
Raymond Rambert states that he is not supposed to be in plague-ridden Oran
and initially wants to flee the unfortunate circumstance he has unexpectedly
fallen into as the plague rages. He later evolves to become a strong witness to
the tragedy and commits himself to helping others. Near the close of the
novel, the words of visitor to Oran Jean Tarrou as he speaks with Dr. Rieux
can be taken symbolically: "The good man, the man who infects hardly anyone, is the man who has the fewest lapses of attention. And it needs tremen-
dous will power, a never ending tension of the mind, to avoid such lapses.
Yes, Rieux, it's a wearying business, being plague-stricken. But it's still more
wearying to refuse to be it."[19]

Another factor is indifference. The Jewish community was seen as culturally, religiously, and ethnically different from the rest of society, be it in Germany or Poland. Except for commercial interaction, the Jewish community in
its customs and daily life were explicitly cut off from the Christian world.
Anything positive or negative happening to the Jews had no impact upon the
lives of others in the larger community. Cynthia Ozick writes:

> Indifference is not so much a gesture of looking away—of choosing to be
> passive—as it is an active disinclination to feel. Indifference shuts down the hu-
> mane, and does it deliberately, with all the strength deliberateness demands.
> Indifference is as determined—and as forcefully muscular—as any blow.[20]

Determined to fight such indifference, the young members of the White Rose
Movement in Bavaria, Germany risked their lives to bring to light the plight
of the Jews. Their second pamphlet reads:

> (B)y way of example do we want to cite the fact that since the conquest of
> Poland *three hundred thousand* Jews have been murdered in this country in
> the most bestial way. Here we see the most frightful crime against human dig-
> nity, a crime that is unparalleled in the whole of history. For Jews, too, are
> human beings—no matter what position we take with respect to the Jewish
> question—and a crime of this dimension has been perpetrated against human
> beings.[21]

Further on, the leaflet shames the German people for being so indifferent to
such cruelty and slaughter, not ready to awaken to the tragedy playing out before their very eyes:

Why do German people behave so apathetically in the face of all these abominable crimes, crimes so unworthy of the human race? Hardly anyone thinks about that. It is accepted as fact and put out of mind. The German people slumber on in their dull, stupid sleep and encourage these fascist criminals; they give them the opportunity to carry on their depredations; and of course they do so. Is this a sign that the Germans are brutalized in their simplest human feelings, that no chord within them cries out at the sight of such deeds, that they have sunk into a fatal consciencelessness from which they will never, never awake? It seems to be so, and will certainly be so, if the German does not at last start up out of his stupor, if he does not protest wherever and whenever he can against this clique of criminal, if he shows no sympathy for these hundreds of thousands of victims. . .[22]

Another leaflet shows how the German bystander allows for and is guilty of the government's evil actions:

He [the German] must evidence not only sympathy; no, much more: a sense of *complicity* in guilt. For through his apathetic behavior he gives these evil men the opportunity to act as they do; he tolerates this "government" which has taken upon itself such an infinitely great burden of guilt; indeed, he himself is to blame for the fact that it came about at all! Each man wants to be exonerated of a guilt of this kind, each one continues on his way with the most placid, the calmest conscience. But he cannot be exonerated; he is *guilty, guilty, guilty.*[23]

Several films have captured the efforts of the White Rose students to combat fascism and alert the world to the destruction of the Jews, notably Michael Verhoeven's celebrated *White Rose* (1982). More recently, *Sophie Scholl: The Final Days* (2005), provides a very good insight into the imprisonment, pseudo-trial, visit with her parents, and death by guillotine.[24] The students take the ultimate risk with their lives and are beheaded to serve as an example to others who dare to challenge the power of the Nazi state. The various publications, feature films, and documentaries on their resistance have given a vivid image of role models who were socially conscious and who could have put their studies before their activism.

In the film *Żegota*, which deals with the Polish-Catholic rescue organization of that name (in English, the Council for the Aid of Jews), Władesław Bartoszewski admits openly that it was the indifference of some Poles that prevented them from helping Jews. In Les Goldman and Paul Julian's allegorical film *The Hangman* (1964), based on Maurice Ogden's poem, the same indifference is manifest. In this animated film, each citizen in the town avoids getting involved when the Hangman executes someone else, as long as it is not the individual himself. After the Hangman executes a foreigner, critic, black, and a Jew, he hangs the narrator, a bystander, the last man standing, who did nothing while the others before him went to their deaths.

Acceptance of or accommodation to German policies seemed very natural to those who did not wish to get involved in the Nazi occupation. Some non-rescuers or bystanders felt they had much to gain from the Nazis, and consequently they had high financial hopes for themselves. As Samuel and Pearl Oliner, who have done detailed studies of the psychology of rescuers point out, personal gain was frequently a motive for compliance:

> Acceptance of or accommodation to Nazi authority helps explain why some by-standers engaged neither in general resistance nor in helping Jews. But, for most bystanders, failure to act appeared to have other causes. Despite their hostility toward Nazis, the majority of bystanders were overcome by fear, hopelessness, and uncertainty. These feelings, which encourage self-centeredness and emotional distancing from others, provide fertile soil for passivity.[25]

In an early sequence of *Schindler's List*, as the Jews in the Krakow ghetto are presenting their papers to the Nazi controllers, Polish Jews in police uniforms assist in the process. Arrogant and condescending to those Jews who are being jostled in the long queues waiting to be registered, they illustrate the painful truth that many sold out to the Nazis and comfortably watch the procession of the distraught from a superior vantage point. Even a young Jewish boy, no more than ten years old, is ready to alert the German soldiers during the round-up that he located a Jew in hiding.

In Ján Kadár and Elmar Klos' *The Shop on Main Street* (1965), the Czech protagonist Antonin Brtko is a hapless soul who does not want the Nazi occupation to impact upon his simple life. His conniving wife sees how well the other side of the family lives after making accommodations with the Nazis and landing fine jobs, so she pushes her husband to do the same. In order to maintain peace, he becomes an Aryan supervisor for an elderly Jewish woman who keeps a run-down sewing shop, and in the end silently watches the roundup of Jews in front of the store. He awakens from his stupor too late, unable to save the shopkeeper or himself.

Paralleling the career of German actor Gustaf Gründgens, Hungarian director István Szabó creates the protagonist Hendrik Höfgen in *Mephisto* (1981), based on the novel by Klaus Mann. Little by little the actor accepts one offer after another to accommodate those presumably interested in his acting and to bolster his own career. He finally ends up a puppet of the Nazis as director of the State Theatre. Only too late does he come to understand the high price that has been paid for his soul.

At the heart of a bystander's rationale for not becoming involved is the notion of accountability. In *Genesis*, when the Lord asks where is Abel, Cain flippantly replies, "Am I my brother's keeper?" (Gen. 4: 9) His curt reply follows his stoning of his brother Abel. He is the perpetrator here, but echoes words of a bystander as well, not accountable for his fellow man, in this case, his own brother. He disclaims any responsibility for his murderous action. Immanuel Kant discusses responsibility for the other and puts it very clearly in presenting several examples of the categorical imperative or law of morality:

> A fourth man finds things going well for himself but sees others (whom he could help) struggling with great hardships; and he thinks: what does it matter to me? Let everybody be as happy as Heaven wills or as he can make himself: I shall take nothing from him nor even envy him; but I have no desire to contribute anything to his well-being or to his assistance when in need.[26]

Reasserting the significance and value of all individuals, Kant stresses that others are to be treated as the *end*, and not the *means* to an end.

In Markus Imhoof's film *The Boat is Full* (1981), the viewer finds a wide range of reactions of the Swiss towards the Jewish refugees crossing into their country. The Swiss couple, the Flückinger's, at first are fearful of the refugees. They are the traditional bystanders who do not wish to get involved; however, they reluctantly do so, first by offering them food, and then by feeling most responsible for them. In this way they defy the Swiss law concerning illegal refugees in Switzerland.[27]

The population of Nazi-occupied countries most often felt helplessness. Once a large mechanized force makes threats to a community or individuals, the weaker or smaller group backed down seeing that they would readily be overpowered, and any resistance would be foolish. One of the purposes of distributing Leni Riefenstahl's documentary *Triumph of the Will* (1935) in many languages to various European countries was to show the mighty, state-of-the-art military force that Germany possessed. The not-too-subtle message read: This is a force to fear! Institutions and individuals alike would feel helpless to contend with this military might. It would take courage and fearlessness to join a resistance movement against a powerful country such as Germany. Marcel Ophuls' documentary *Le Chagrin et la Pitié* (*The Sorrow and the Pity*, 1969), shows the complete gamut of reaction to the occupation of France from those who were cowardly and backed out of the picture, to the collaborators, and finally to those who fought their feeling of helplessness by joining others, as we learn elsewhere, that Jean Moulin did in creating a large, sophisticated network of resistance. There is strength in numbers, something a bystander has a moral obligation to consider.

At the close of Imre Gyongyossy's film, *Revolt of Job* (1983), the slow-moving cortege of horse-drawn carts transports the Jews from the Hungarian countryside to the central train station, as musicians play to accompany the displacement of the Jewish villagers. When the local clergyman tries to protest this deportation, the Hungarian police roughly push him aside, admonishing him, "Pastor, you have no business here." Ironically, the business of the pastor was certainly here, standing up to an injustice, even though the police then forced all the neighbors inside, relegating them to the status of unwilling bystanders, powerless and unable to stand up to this armed force.

During World War II, everyone especially worried about personal survival, so anything apart from the family would be outside of one's personal parameters, not meriting interest or action. The Nazis put severe controls on every aspect of life, especially food supplies. Following a Darwinian principle of survival of the fittest, the bystander chooses to preserve his own safety, rather than jeopardize his welfare for the sake of a Jew in hiding. David P. Barash, in his work *Selfish Altruists, Honest Liars and Other Realities of Evolution,* insists that we are hard-wired to take action to survive, to save ourselves before we save others.[28] In the Italian film, *La Finestra di Fronte* (*Facing Windows*, 2003), the aged protagonist Simone/Davide Veroli, a homosexual, painfully recalls his complacency during World War II and lives with profound regret at having been a bystander and allowing his partner to be taken by the Nazis.

Films dealing with the Holocaust have been able to chronicle, at times graphically, the behavior of the perpetrators and the victims, the rescuers and the collaborators, and in the above case, the bystanders. For a plethora of reasons, the bystanders chose to see the Jews as "Other," and refused to take action on their behalf against an injustice. Pastor Martin Niemoeller (1892–1984) criticized the Germans who stood by as civil liberties and human rights were taken away by the Nazi regime, leaving this vivid image of the bystander:

> They came for the Communists,
> And I didn't speak up because I
> Wasn't a Communist.
> Then they came for the Jews,
> And I didn't speak up because I
> Wasn't a Jew.
> Then they came for the trade unionists,
> And I didn't speak up because I
> Wasn't a trade unionist.
> Then they came for the Catholics,
> And I didn't speak up because I
> Was a Protestant.
> Then they came for me,
>
> No one was left to speak up.[29]

NOTES

1. John J. Michalczyk, *The Cross and the Star: Jews, Christians and the Holocaust* (New York: First Run Features, 1991). This documentary traces anti-Semitism from the various indifferent governments to the Catholic Church, shown as institutions guilty of being a bystander during the Shoah, and chronicles it from the Gospels through the end of World War II.

2. Sonia Schreiber Weitz, *I Promised I Would Tell* (Brookline, Massachusetts: Facing History and Ourselves, 1993), 86.

3. This documentary by Daniel Anker depicts Hollywood's approach to the production of Holocaust films with eyewitness accounts by Hollywood directors and producers concerned about how to present the tragedy of the Holocaust to American viewers.

4. See a very solid analysis of this film and other French films by Louis Malle, Marcel Ophuls, Claude Lanzmann, etc. in André Pierre Colombat's *The Holocaust in French Film* (Metuchen, New Jersey: Scarecrow Press, 1993).

5. Telephone interview with Sonia Weitz, 21 January 2008.

6. See Pearl M. Oliner, Samuel P. Oliner, Lawrence Baron, Lawrence A. Blum, Dennis L. Krebs, and M. Zuzanna Smolenska, *Embacing the Other: Philosophical, Psychological, and Historical Perspectives on Altruism* (New York: New York University Press, 1992).

7. David S. Wyman, *The Abandonment of the Jews; America and the Holocaust 1941–1945* (New York: Pantheon Books, 1984). Wyman captures here the anti-Semitism and the lack of interest in helping in the US government at the time. Martin Ostrow's documentary, *America and the Holocaust: Deceit and Indifference* (1994), utilizes Wyman's research as a pivotal point in showing America's lack of support of the endangered Jews.

8. David P. Barash, "Targets of Aggression," *Chronicle of Higher Education*, vol. 54, no. 6, 5 October 2007, B6.

9. Matthew and John's Gospels are replete with images of the Jews calling for the death of Jesus, as especially seen in Matthew 27:25: "Then the people as a whole answered, 'His blood be on us and on our children!'"

10. Our documentary, *Of Star & Shamrocks: Boston's Jews & Irish* (1995), shows the relationship of the Catholic liturgies to the violent pogroms during Christian holydays with graphic images of the Jews killed because they were a religious and political threat.

11. Prior to the Second Vatican Council (1963), during the Good Friday orations, Catholics prayed for "The perfidious Jews," a prayer now changed to "our brothers and sisters who first received the covenant. . . ."

12. Daniel Jonah Goldhagen, *Hitler's Willing Executioners: Ordinary Germans and the Holocaust* (New York: Vantage Books, 1996). Goldhagen shows the full gamut of assaults on the Jews by the Nazis and the German people starting immediately at the beginning of the Third Reich. See pp. 135–136 for the policies and actions of the Nazis in the steps toward the Final Solution. The author also states that for the

extermination of the Jews to take place, "They [the Nazis] had to induce a large num-ber of people to carry out killings." (p. 9)

13. Dr. Maciej Kuzlowski, remarks, Boston College, 25 January 2008. Dr.Ku-zlowski also offered a sharp critique of Jan T. Gross's *FEAR: Anti-Semitism in Poland* for its lack of sensitivity about Jewish-Christian relations and its harsh, acerbic tone.

14. Samuel P. Oliner and Pearl M.Oliner, *The Altruistic Personality: Rescuers of Jews in Nazi Europe* (New York: The Free Press, 1988), 149.

15. In *Lacombe Lucien* (1974), Louis Malle shows Lacombe, a Joseph-type young man, failing to enter the resistance, taking up a new life working with the French fas-cist police. His political tendencies then shift one more time as he falls in love with a Jewish girl.

16. In a more contemporary setting, the film *Hotel Rwanda* (2004) shows Paul Rusesabagina, the manager of the Hotel des Milles Collines, at first shying away from helping a Tutsi neighbor in trouble with the Hutus and then becoming a rescuer of a thousand Tutsis in the hotel.

17. See Samantha Power, *"A Problem from Hell:" America and the Age of Geno-cide* (New York: Basic Books, 2002).

18. In his *Carnets,* Camus drew a strong parallel of the plague to the war as the German occupation, stripped away basic rights and at times life itself. His novel un-derscores the fact that each person, when confronted with a crisis, acts differently.

19. Albert Camus, *The Plague* (New York: Vintage International, 1991), 253.

20. Cynthia Ozick, "Bystanders," *A Teacher's Guide to the Holocaust* (Miami: Florida Center for Instructional Technology, College of Education, University of South Florida, 2005).

21. The six leaflets are found on the website: http://www.jlrweb.com/leaftwoeng.html.

22. http://www.jlrweb.com/leaftwoeng.html.

23. http://www.jlrweb.com/leaftwoeng.html.

24. These scenes were thoroughly documented from the archives of the former East Germany following the end of the Cold War.

25. Samuel P. Oliner and Pearl M.Oliner, *The Altruistic Personality: Rescuers of Jews in Nazi Europe* (New York: The Free Press, 1988), 146.

26. Immanuel Kant, *Grounding for the Metaphysics of Morals*, Translated by James W. Ellington. (Indianapolis/Cambridge: Hackett Publishing Co., 1981), 32.

27. Annette Insdorf, *Indelible Shadows: Film and the Holocaust*, 2nd Edition (Cambridge: Cambridge University Press, 1989), 109–113.

28. See David P. Barash, *Natural Selections: Selfish Altruists, Honest Liars and Other Realities of Evolution* (New York: Bellevue Literary Press, 2008).

29. There are several variations of Niemoeller's poem. This one is located on the New England Holocaust Memorial located in Boston. All stress the notion that apa-thy can eventually lead to one's own personal downfall.

Chapter Fifteen

"Fiend, Foe and Friend: The German Image in American World War II Films"

Christopher Thomas, Texas A & M University

Films—like coins, stamps, ornamental pottery and sculpture—should be preserved in museums or special archives as "slices of public and national life"[1]

Why people are so attracted to war films is something best left to Freudian scholars, but the value of films as a mass communication and propaganda tool was not absent from the minds of American politicians and general officers upon America's entry into the Second World War. Films have the ability to affect both the mental attitude and social behavior of the audience.[2] A study of expatriated Nazi youths in America in 1946 showed that, regardless of social backgrounds, those that viewed the film, *Tomorrow the World* (an anti-Nazi film adaptation of a play by the same name), shifted their attitudes towards the Nazi regime in a manner coinciding with those expressed by the film.[3] Similar studies involving adult subjects' attitudes toward war and ethnic minorities also found similar results. If films can adjust the way in which former "enemies" viewed America it is only reasonable to conclude that films could also influence the way Americans viewed their former (or current) enemies. Such is true of Hollywood's depiction of Germans in World War II films.

The relationship between films and society, and using films as historical documents has not escaped modern scholarship. In 1996 the Rutgers Center for Historical Analysis published a group of essays that collectively argued that "visual representation of past wars is itself a cultural construction, reflecting social, political, economic and cultural dynamics of the time."[4] Numerous books have been written about the American World War II film and its relation to society.[5] Many of these works, however, focus primarily on the films produced *during* the war (or shortly thereafter) and the people and organizations that wrote, produced, directed, and above all, censored the films.

These works are a social and cultural history *of* film. This study is a social and cultural history *through* film. Using films as historical documents is not a new concept. Peter Paret and Denise Youngblood have both written papers about, respectively, the Third Reich and post-Stalinist Russia using popular films as historical documents. Youngblood's essay is particularly relevant to this study because by analyzing how post-Stalinist films altered the public attitude toward the war and actually challenged current paradigms, (what she refers to as the "myth of World War II") Youngblood has demonstrated the feasibility and value of making broader, culturally specific conclusions based on film evidence.[6] This study analyzes the changes in an American World War II "myth" based on film sources and how those changes not only reflected the social and political conditions of the time, but also how these films have successfully altered the American perception of a former enemy.

The depiction of "the other" has received some attention, but there is still much to be studied. Thomas Doherty, in *Projections of War*, devoted a chapter to "Properly Directed Hatred" and discussed the depiction of Germans in American films made during and shortly after the war. Bernard Dick has a chapter in *The Star Spangled Screen* entitled, "Nazis, Germans and GIs" that also addresses the subject of how "the other" is portrayed. Both these studies, however, limit their film sources to the war era and do not include films made after the late forties and early fifties. From America's entry into the war, (and even a little before) until the present, Hollywood's portrayal of Germans in World War II films has gone through a number of significant stages and has identified them as enemies, friends, and everything in between. These stages do not correspond to definite blocks of time and often overlap, but they are nevertheless distinct and relevant to history.

On 11 December 1941, Nazi Germany declared war on the United States. With America's entry into the war, Hollywood slid into an uneasy partnership with the government and began producing war films.[7] The emerging genre of the "war film" both motivated and educated millions of Americans in their roles as citizens of a belligerent nation. One of the most important lessons in this education was teaching the masses how to view "the other." After the war, the genre was so popular that Hollywood continued to produce war films that necessarily involved German characters, but Germany was no longer the enemy. In fact, Germany was now America's ally against a new enemy; the Soviet Union. Hollywood had to reevaluate its portrayal of Germans in war films to re-educate the masses and undo what it had done during the war, but at the same time not go so far as to demean the lives of Americans who died fighting Nazi Germany.

The solution was the creation of the German/Nazi myth. By differentiating between the average German and the more sinister Nazi, Americans could retain both their enmity and their pride. As the Cold War developed and German-American relations became more important, Germans were depicted either as equals that just happened to be on the wrong team when the big game started, or simply as "guys like us." When the war in Vietnam turned sour, American World War II films turned inward and German characters were marginalized to make room for other, more pressing political and social statements. With the end of the Cold War, films shifted again, this time wiping away many of the apologetic trends (the German/Nazi myth among them) and appealing to a more philosophical definition of "the other," that is to say, Nazi is as Nazi does, regardless of nationality. These revisionist films blur the difference between "friend" and "enemy" altogether.

When Germany declared war in 1941, the only "education" that Hollywood had produced in regards to the Germans is demonstrated best by films such as *Confessions of a Nazi Spy* and Charlie Chaplin's *The Great Dictator*. Chaplin's satire of the Nazi regime pulled few punches, making fun of the German language and problematizing the physical similarities between the *Führer* and Chaplin's character of the Jewish barber. The film's ability to keep the viewer laughing continues right up until the last five minutes at which point the movie tone takes a dramatic turn for the serious. Chaplin steps out of character and makes an impassioned speech to the people of Germany to fight against the tyranny of the Nazis and to fight for the cause of "freedom" and "democracy."

Chaplin released *The Great Dictator* in October 1940, over a year before the formal declarations of war and over two full years before American and German soldiers met in combat for the first time. Although Poland, France, Denmark and Norway had fallen and Britain was suffering under the Blitz by the time of the film's release there was little in the film that portrayed German military strength in any form. The German people as a whole were completely absent and the film focused only on the leaders, suggesting that the deeds and crimes of the Nazis were to be attributed solely to the politicians, exonerating the masses from any blame. Chaplin's plea to the masses at the end of the film further created this rift between Nazi and German. This film is among the first in which we see the appearance of the Nazi/German myth. This myth perpetuates the idea that there was a difference between a German and a Nazi and that the average German citizen was an unwilling participant under the iron-fisted Nazi regime. Other early war films such as *Once Upon a Honeymoon* and *To Be or Not to Be* also make light of the Nazis in an attempt to perpetuate the myth. *The Great Dictator* was nominated for five Academy Awards and although it did not win any (under curious circumstances), the film was well received by the public. The New York Times Film Review said it was a "truly superb accomplishment by a truly great artist."[8]

Such lucrative returns at the box office may not prove that the American public wholly bought into the myth immediately, but it does demonstrate that the public was not averse to it. At the very least the average American movie-goer had been exposed to the myth, something that Hollywood and the government worked hard to reverse once the war broke out.

When Germans became "the other," Hollywood began to experiment with different molds in which to cast them. By the time American soldiers first saw combat against Germany the Third Reich had expanded its territory in the Balkans, the Aegean, North Africa, and the Soviet Union. The German military was a formidable force whereas the American army had not seen large-scale combat since 1918. American filmmakers had the difficult task of answering two crucial questions; who is the enemy and how do we portray him? The enemy could not be identified as individual leaders nor the country as a whole. If the blame was placed solely on the shoulders of Hitler, what happened if he died in the middle of the war? Would the country lose its war fervor? In 1943, President Franklin Roosevelt announced that the Allies would accept nothing less that the unconditional surrender of the Axis powers, meaning that the war must go on whether Germany was led by Adolf Hitler or Santa Claus. At the same time the blame could not be placed on the German people. How then would the US government deal with the millions of German Americans then living in the United States? Were they the enemy too? The solution was "properly directed hatred" designed to lay the blame with the total sum of the parts. The enemy were not the Nazis, but Naz*ism*.[9] If the enemy was the ideological system then anyone associated with the system was also the enemy.[10] Conversely, as important as it is obvious, anyone not associated with the system was not an enemy. The first question, "who is the enemy?," had found its answer.

To motivate and educate the public in regards to the second question, "how do we portray the enemy?," the government assigned Frank Capra the dubious honor of creating America's first series of government sponsored propaganda films. Produced in conjunction with the Army Signal Corps, theaters across the nation screened his seven-part documentary series, *Why We Fight*. The armed forces required all men in the armed services to view it. The first film, *Prelude to War*, established the war as a crusade against the "slave world" by the forces of the "free world." Hitler was referred to as the murder of the newborn German Republic, the boss of a "gangster" government, and even the Antichrist, a far cry from Chaplin's comical dictator. The religious aspect was hammered home further at the end of the film with parades of American soldiers marching under a superimposed Liberty Bell while "Onward Christian Soldiers" booms in the background.

But what of the masses? Chaplin appealed to them as though they were yearning to break free and still had "democratic" hearts and minds. Capra takes no such liberties and places the masses in the same boat as Hitler. According to the film, the Nazis were not humans, but machines, trained and willing to follow any order given to them, but praise be to the system as the enemy. Even with Capra's heavy accusations towards all Germans, Naz*ism* allowed him to pay obeisance to the myth. In part two of *Why We Fight,* Capra differentiates between those Germans living in Europe and German Americans residing in the United States. By highlighting prominent politicians and military officers (such as Eisenhower), Capra, like Chaplin, maintains that there are still differences between Germans and Nazis. Unlike Chaplin, however, Capra asserted that by 1943 (the year *Why We Fight* was released) all Germans in Germany had become Nazis under the system.

The next step in portraying the Nazis was in reference to their military might. This presented another problem to filmmakers. The first war films came out while the war was still being fought. If they portrayed Nazis too weak, Americans might become sloppy or complacent, resulting in a prolonged war with more casualties. On the other hand, portraying them too strong could foster defeatism.[11] In *Sahara,* director Zolton Korda found the middle ground by portraying the German's as worthy opponents, but not overly difficult. The film gave the feeling that America would not roll over Germany the way Germany had rolled over Poland and France, but in the end America would be victorious nonetheless. In *Sahara,* a small, but conspicuously representative, group of Allied soldiers has to defend an oasis against a vastly outnumbering German force while one member of the group makes a desperate break to the British lines for help. The small band, numbering no more than a dozen men, successfully holds off the German advance until finally, driven by thirst to desperation, the entire German force, numbering in the hundreds, surrenders. The fight was difficult and only two of the original group survived, but two holding out against over two hundred sent a definite message.

Hangmen Also Die, produced in 1943 as well, tells the moral boosting story, though woefully inaccurate, of the Czech assassination of Reinhardt Heydrich, the architect of the Final Solution, which is referred to in the film as the "blood bath loosed by Hitler's hordes."[12] The Nazis are further demonized by a gigantic banner conspicuously hung in the SS main office which states; "He who serves Hitler serves Germany, He who serves Germany serves God." The assassination occurs in the first five minutes of the film. The remainder of the film is a cloak and dagger story in which the German police and inspectors try to find the assassin. The German inspector is portrayed as an alcoholic womanizer, but a very clever one. At the end of the film

he actually has the killer cornered at gunpoint in a hospital, but the timely in-
terruption of a doctor stumbling into the locker room gives the assassin, and
his accomplice, a chance to overpower the inspector and kill him too. As in
Sahara, the Nazis are depicted as crafty people who should not be underesti-
mated, but at the same time they are not invincible and can be defeated.

Within the films themselves Hollywood had another paradox to tackle. The
"face of the enemy," so to speak, had to be seen in combat scenes so that
viewers would not be caught up in myths of German supermen (owing to the
substantial German victories throughout the war) but at the same time keep
the American public aloof and prevent any recognition of common bonds
(they're normal people who look "just like us"). The problem was to bring
them down to the level of ordinary men while continuing to distinguish them
as "the other." They could not be faceless, but at the same time they had to be
denied identities. This problem was solved by three men and a machine gun.

The German MG42 operated as a three man team and was a trademark
weapon of the German Army. Nicknamed "Hitler's Buzzsaw" due to the
sound it made when fired, the MG42 was feared and respected by American
soldiers. The beauty of the squad, at least for American filmmakers, is that it
represented German strength, power and myth while remaining far enough
from the camera to avoid close-ups. *A Walk in the Sun* provides a classic example of the use of the MG42 squad. The big battle scene, of course, takes
place at the end of the film when a platoon of GIs has to assault a farmhouse
held by the Germans. When the platoon attacks, the camera shifts to a position inside the farmhouse, looking out from behind the German gunner. Only
the back of his helmet and the barrel of the gun are visible. He fights valiantly
and kills several GIs, but the audience never sees his face, despite how close
the camera is. The paradox has been satisfied; the Germans have fought
bravely, and the audience still hates them. One of the most heroic scenes in
To Hell and Back shows Audie Murphy single handedly taking out three of
these faceless machine gun nests that have the rest of Murphy's unit pinned
down. Other films such as *Sahara, Battleground,* and *Hell is for Heroes* use
the machine gun squad. Even the comedy *Stalag 17* makes use of the faceless
machine gun squad for one of its only serious scenes; two prisoners escape
the POW camp and are immediately shot when they emerge from their tun-
nel into the nearby woods. Although it is not present in every war film without exception, the three-man squad makes appearances in many films made
during, and shortly after the war. It is not necessarily a signature of the early
American war film but rather it is a symbol of the era. Once America went to
war it had to identify and describe "the enemy." By appealing to the Ger-
man/Nazi myth, American filmmakers were able to use as broad or as narrow
a brush as necessary to paint the enemy. By depicting them as worthy, but not

invincible, Americans viewers were given healthy doses of both motivation to fight, and respect for, their new enemy.

On 2 September 1945, Japanese and American officials met onboard the USS Missouri to sign Japan's formal surrender and officially end the Second World War. In less than a decade, however, the United States was again at war. This next war was a curious one. Lacking grand offensives, strategic withdraws, and the heat of battle, this new "cold war" turned former allies into enemies, and more importantly, former enemies into allies. The once hated Germans became the first line of defense in Europe against the communist behemoth of the Soviet Union. In the tense atmosphere American moviegoers were drawn even more to World War II films about American victories over tyrant, dictatorial enemies, but in those films the enemy, Germany, was a current ally. World War II films during the Cold War had to maintain American patriotic spirit while not insulting Germany. Hollywood had to back-paddle.

In its efforts to overcorrect for years of throwing Nazis and Germans in Europe (thanks to Capra) into the same bowl, Twentieth Century Fox released, amid some controversy, *Desert Fox: The Story of Erwin Rommel*, a biography of one of Hitler's finest generals. Twentieth Century Fox made the film for three closely related reasons. First, Rommel was a highly accomplished military figure and had earned the respect of the American and British forces that fought him in Africa. The screenplay was based on Desmond Young's book of the same title. During the war, Young, a Lieutenant Colonel in the British Army, referred to Rommel with praise and admiration. Second, Rommel never joined the Nazi Party and was therefore free of any "taint" that the film would have to somehow wipe away or minimize. Finally, and most importantly, he was an instrumental accomplice in the failed plot to assassinate Hitler, a role that cost him his life. As a brilliant, non-Nazi German officer willing to sacrifice his life to kill Hitler, Rommel became the poster child of the German/Nazi myth. Rommel's position as a pillar supporting the myth has become so high that in a recent biography, *Knight's Cross*, British officer-turned-historian David Fraser asserts that Rommel may not necessarily have been involved in the assassination attempt. Assassination and murder are awful things, beneath the dignity of one so accomplished as Rommel, but let us not forget who their target was! The fact that such an assertion exists, and that the book has been a great success, is stunning proof that Americans have wholeheartedly accepted the myth and have adopted Rommel as its mascot.

Even though *Desert Fox* is one of the pinnacle films of the Nazi/German myth, it is not the first. One of the earliest examples of blatant distinction between German and Nazi (as opposed to Chaplin's implied distinction) is in one of the most famous films in American cinema, *Casablanca*. Amidst the love stories and immortal one-liners, director Michael Curtiz included one very peculiar character. The mâitre d' of Rick's nightclub is a German; a balding, obese, but clever German. This mâitre d', Carl, represents the "good" German and is put in the film as the antithesis of the "bad" Nazi Major Strasser. Carl's character is not only the physical opposite, but his aid to Rick in the escape of Czech underground leader Victor Lazlo, makes him the moral and ideological opposite as well. With the clever use of the myth in *Casablanca* it is no surprising that the film was re-released in the United States in 1949, just as the Cold War was developing.

Only a year later, George Seaton released *The Big Lift*, not only a success at the box office, but a monumental film in terms of the perpetuation and manipulation of the German-Nazi myth. The film, which begins more as a documentary than a feature film, tells the story of two Air Force sergeants stationed in Berlin during the Berlin Airlift. One of the sergeants, Hank Kowalski, a Pole and former POW, hates and belittles the Germans around him throughout nearly the entire film, including Gerda, a young German woman whom he courts but verbally abuses. The other, Danny MacCullough, falls in love with Frida, a Berlin widow, and desperately tries to get the necessary military clearance to marry her and take her back to America. As the love story progresses, Danny discovers that she has been lying about her past. Her husband was in the SS (she claimed he was not), her father was associated with the Nazi Party (she claimed he was an ardent opponent) and the dénouement comes when Danny learns that she does not love him at all, but is using him to get to America where her true love has been waiting for her. Kowalski's girlfriend on the other hand, begins to study the Constitution and ask questions about "democracy." When Danny walks away after Frida's treachery is unveiled, Gerda chases after him to try and explain how the Third Reich and the war have ruined German lives and values, and that Germans had to learn to lie just to survive.

In *The Big Lift*, Kowalski and Danny represent the dialect confronting America. The Germans were our enemies, but now they are not. Some were ardent Nazis, but others were not. Cold War expediency necessitated the cultivation of friendly relationships between America and Germany, but at the same time America could not simply forget what Germany had done in the 1930s and 1940s. Kowalski was too bitter and unwilling to forget, Danny was too naive and unwilling to remember. The lesson that American viewers were to take from the film was expressed at the end by Kowalski, who after recognizing his bitterness and Danny's naiveté states, "the answer lies somewhere in between."[13]

The Big Lift is one among many films that address another important aspect of post-war Germany that contributed greatly to the German/Nazi myth;

the growing number of American GIs marrying German women and bringing them back to America. During wartime, "fraternization with the enemy" is strictly forbidden, but after the war, such restrictions were no longer in place. *A Foreign Affair*, released two years prior to *The Big Lift,* is another film dealing with the relations between women of occupied-Germany and their American occupiers. These unions, out of necessity called for a reassessment of how American films treated Germans, many of whom were now living in the United States. Films such as *A Foreign Affair* and *The Big Lift* helped redefine American attitudes toward German civilians and war-brides.

In order for the myth to fully compensate for the way it had portrayed Germans in wartime; however filmmakers could not limit the separation to civilians versus the military as they had in *Casablanca*. Hollywood also needed films applying the myth to the military. Hollywood accomplished this application of the German/Nazi myth in several subtle ways. The separation of the Wehrmacht from the SS and the Gestapo, the creation of a moral dilemma in German characters regarding the orders and behaviors of superior and more blatantly Nazi officers, and the development of a rift between officer and subordinate all serve to widen the gap between Germans and Nazis and further the myth. The separation between army and SS is easily visible in films such as *The Guns of Navarone*. When the allied commando unit is captured and taken to German headquarters for questioning they are initially interrogated by a Wehrmacht officer. He is dignified in his interrogation, never physically abuses the prisoners, and appeals to logic and reason to try and extract information. Another officer enters and identifies himself as a member of the SS. Less than five seconds after his entry he slaps one of the prisoners across the face twice and starts tapping on the broken leg of another with his pistol while threatening, "I want an answer now or I will personally rearrange this officer's splints." The Wehrmacht officer bolts up from his desk in outrage and is rebuked by the SS officer with a terse "Halten Sie, Hund!" (Silence, dog!) Shortly thereafter, the prisoners manage to wrestle control from the Germans and make their escape. Before leaving, Captain Mallory (Gregory Peck) informs the Wehrmacht officer that Major Franklin, the officer with the broken leg, is being left behind and that as an officer he is entitled to proper medical attention. The Wehrmacht officer replies, "We don't make war on wounded men. We are not all like Hauptman Zessler."[14] Later in the film, Hauptman Zessler is again challenged by an army officer for his "interrogating" methods on the wounded Major. The challenging officer, a general, calls for the more humane use of scopolamine, rather than torture, to extract information.

The Young Lions, aptly demonstrates the other two methods of applying the German/Nazi myth to the military. In the film, Marlon Brando plays Christian Diestl, a patriotic German civilian who is "taken in" by Hitler's promises of a brighter, richer, more respectable future for Germany. Early in the film he mentions to an American tourist, that he is willing to fight for these great ideas. A willingness to fight for a better life is not wrong. A handful of British colonists in the Americas in the late eighteenth century thought it a worthy cause. The parallels could not be lost on the American viewer. When the war breaks out, Diestl joins the army as an officer and serves with distinction, but throughout the film his loyalty and morals are questioned by repeated clashes with his superior officer. The first instance is over the brutal interrogation tactics of the Gestapo (much like the SS in *Guns of Navarone*). The superior officer has no qualms about it while Diestl questions the use of violence to extract information. His commanding officer tells him that it is not his place to question authority. The job of the army is simply to carry out orders, regardless of their moral implications, and he even threatens Diestl with a court-martial should he ever question orders again. This altercation sets Diestl's foundation for questioning both the regime and his role in it.

The conflict is pushed further when Diestl is sent to North Africa to fight the British. After a successful ambush he is ordered by the same superior officer to shoot the wounded British. He again refuses and would have been court-martialed and shot had not a British counterattack prevented it. The episode leads Diestl to further question how one can perform such awful atrocities under the guise of duty and obedience to orders. At the end of the film, Diestl reaches the breaking point when he stumbles into an extermination camp (the purpose of which is initially unbeknown to Diestl) and asks the commandant for food. While Diestl eats, the commandant talks about how he has always met his killing quotas and kept right on killing even after all the other officers in the camp fled from the advancing Americans. He clasps Diestl on the shoulders and says "The German officer, our kind of officer, does what he is ordered to do . . . at least we know what is important, the courage to stay and face the enemy, and the honor to be able to say, 'I have done my duty for the fatherland'" at which point Diestl snaps, shocked at the degree of barbarity Germany has sunk to because of "orders" and "duty."[15] For the rest of the film, after trying to smash his machine gun against a tree stump, Diestl wanders through the nearby forest, in mental agony over what he has become a part of. Two patrolling GIs spot and shoot him, allowing Diestl to atone for crimes he never wanted to commit.

That Hollywood would even make a movie that centers on a German character is proof enough that severe backpedaling was the order of the day, but to go the next step and portray that main character as a human being, duped into following the regime, marks a complete turn around from films made during and shortly after the war. Even the title, *The Young Lions*, is in the plural and groups Diestl with his American counterparts in the film. The American GI and the German Landser are both elevated to the same status, opponents but equals. The moral dilemma in *The Young Lions* convinced the viewer that not every citizen of Germany in the 1930s and 1940s was a member of the Nazi party or even agreed with Hitler's policies. It also asserted that many who did join tried to get out later when the full horrors of the regime became known. Films like *The Guns of Navarone* and *Attack!* introduced the SS or the Gestapo as the embodiment of the true-blue, dyed-in-the-wool Nazi, while officers and soldiers in the Wehrmacht represented individuals like Diestl; good Germans caught up in Hitler's lies. The final step in fully establishing the myth was to create a visible, on-screen confrontation between the "good" German and the "bad" Nazi. This was accomplished through the conflict between officer and subordinate.

This conflict was first established, and forcefully at that, with *The Desert Fox*. Rommel's relationship with Hitler degenerates from friendship to a willingness to assassinate, but Rommel was a field marshal, not an "average" German. The conflict had to be developed from the ground up. It was developed briefly in *The Guns of Navarone* and even more so in *The Young Lions*, but the film that demonstrates this conflict most brilliantly is *The Battle of the Bulge*. Throughout the film the relationship between Colonel Hessler and his batman Corporal Conrad shifts from one of admiration and trust to one of contempt and disgust.[16] At the beginning of the film close camaraderie is expressed between the two. They have fought together on the Russian Front and have now been assigned to spearhead Operation Wacht am Rein, Hitler's last desperate offensive designed to drive to Antwerp and cut the Allied armies in two.

All is well between the two until a monumental confrontation erupts three-quarters into the film. Conrad walks into the command post just as Hessler finishes a call to headquarters. Hessler cries "We have done it, Conrad! We have done it!" With a hopeful expression, Conrad asks, "We have won the war?" "No," Hessler replies. Conrad's expression changes to one of confusion, "Then we have lost?" Again Hessler replies in the negative. The good news, Hessler explains, is that the offensive has guaranteed that the war will go "on, and on, and on!" Hessler adds, "In 1941 we knew we could never win," but, according to Hessler, for Germany to keep an army in the field, for he and Conrad to remain in uniform, is a victory. Conrad asks, "What about my sons?" to which Hessler replies that they too will became soldiers and fight for the fatherland. Upon hearing this, Conrad verbally lashes out at Hessler. He calls Hessler a murderer and accuses him, and all the warmongers in Berlin, of "*murdering my country*" [emphasis added]. "You would sacrifice my sons . . . you would murder the world to stay in that uniform" he cries. Conrad then requests to be transferred. At the end of the film, as the defeated

German army is retreating, Conrad, transferred to a rifle division, begins to sling his rifle over his shoulder, pauses, then throws it to the ground and starts walking back to Germany.[17] The ambiguity of what will happen next (will he be court-martialed? Will he keep fighting so that his sons will not have to be called up in his place? Will he desert?) is unimportant. He has made his stand. The moral conflict within him reached its capacity and the German has turned on the Nazi. What an incredible statement this makes to the American movie viewer! Not only was the average German a moral being, but given enough prodding and an opportunity they would have come out in open defiance to the Nazis. The "Hitler Gang" so vehemently rejected at the beginning of the war was now wholly embraced.

The conflict between officer and subordinate is utilized in many other movies although not always restricted to lower army echelons. At the beginning of *The Longest Day* Field Marshall von Rundstedt refers to Hitler as "that Bohemian corporal," a derogatory term first used by former Weimar President (and Field Marshall) Paul von Hindenburg.[18] During a scene in *Where Eagles Dare* an army officer, although a member of the SS, is interrogating prisoners. When a fellow officer mentions that the Gestapo wants to be in charge of interrogation the SS officer comments, "We don't need the Gestapo cluttering up things with their torture chambers. This can be a strictly army affair."[19] The opening scene of *The Big Red One* portrays a German soldier in the *Afrika Korps* refusing to fight. When ordered to move out he confronts his commanding officer and says "I want no more. I'm no damn Nazi fanatic like you. Germany is through singing for Adolf Hitler," at which point he is shot by the officer.[20] The soldier's comment is crucial. Not only does he distinguish German from Nazi, but his statement also implies that the Germany as a whole was against the war and fought only by force of compulsion.

The last tactic of pre-Vietnam or early-Vietnam era films involved presenting "good" Germans as American equals both individually and on the battlefield. The epic recreation films like *The Longest Day* and *A Bridge too Far* both pay homage to the German military's fighting prowess, reversing the "worthy but not overly difficult" message sent by films like *Sahara*. Additionally, they serve to reconcile the former enemies on the Western Front and unite them against the new enemy, Soviet Russia.[21] In fact, *A Bridge too Far* is unique in that it is a film that ends with a German victory. *Kelly's Heroes* makes a non-military comparison and contains the scene that best portrays the individual German as being just like an American. When Kelly's platoon is kept out of the bank they plan to rob because a German Tiger tank guards the entrance, Sergeant Crapgame suggests that they try to "make a deal" with the crew. When asked what kind of deal, Crapgame responds, "a deal deal!" then sarcastically adds, "maybe he's a Republican."[22] When Kelly approaches the tank, he emerges from inside rather than opening fire. His orders are to protect the bank from "zee Ameriken Ah-mee" (because the Germans cannot be *completely* like the Americans, that is to say, without accents), but when Kelley offers him a share of the money in return for his help, he takes a whole three seconds to decide. That American soldiers would hold a civil conversation with the enemy on the battlefield is odd enough, but to invite him to become "one of the gang?" The message is clear; the "good" Germans were not so different after all.

The separation of army and SS, the creation of moral dilemma within German soldiers, the rift between officer and subordinate, and the portrayal of German's being "just like us" solved the problem of how to apply the myth on the battlefield, when American and German faced each other on relatively equal terms. There was another situation, American prisoners of war in Germany, that had to be handled differently. *Stalag 17, The Great Escape,* and *Hogan's Heroes* depict German soldiers, not as duped patriots or good people blinded by Hitler's subtle lies, but as complete fools and objects of mockery. *Stalag 17* is a comedy, make no mistake about it. Of course there is suspense and action among other components of the war film genre, but first and foremost, *Stalag 17* makes the viewer laugh. From the imbecilic prison guards opening the front gate, allowing two POWs to get out of the camp in order to paint lanes in the dirt, to the camp commandant putting on jackboots so he can click his heels when saluting during a phone call, *Stalag 17* portrays German soldiers in a manner that might make the viewer ask "How in the world did these guys conquer Europe?"

The Great Escape, though leaning towards action, suspense and a more serious attitude towards life in the POW camps in Germany is not totally devoid of humor either. Corporal Werner, a prison guard, is an honest but somewhat dimwitted liaison officer. Werner is easily fooled, manipulated and even pickpocketed. One almost feels sorry for him. Captain Hilts, "The Cooler King," provides other instances of comic relief. He escapes and is recaptured so many times that it almost becomes a game. In addition, every time he is returned to the cooler for escaping, the music on the soundtrack is light, staccato flutes, creating a lighter tone. The movie ends on one of these scenes, making the film's last impression less dramatic considering the escape was largely a failure.

Starting in 1965, CBS produced *Hogan's Heroes,* a television sitcom based on *Stalag 17* and *The Great Escape. Hogan's Heroes*, however, take its comedic portrayal of Germans far in excess of *Stalag 17*. The inmates of the camp, in addition to acting as the hub of the Allies main POW escape effort, manage to conduct impossible military operations (such as stealing a Tiger tank and hiding it in the barracks or building an airplane to help a defecting

German noble to escape) on a regular basis and with little difficulty. The Germans in the camp are so easily controlled that the inmates literally run the camp. For example, the prisoners, although constantly breaking camp regulations, are never punished and essentially hold their guard, Sgt. Schultz, hostage. If Schultz were ever to report the prisoner infractions he would be blamed for failing in his duties as a guard and would be sent to the Russian front. The prisoners constantly remind Schultz of this and consequently whenever Schultz stumbles upon any item or action that is against camp rules he shuts his eyes, and keeps repeating, "I see nothing, I see nothing."

The prisoner population itself offers important insights. The prisoners are lead by an American, with a British soldier acting as his second. The camp also includes a Frenchman and an African-American. In fact, the premiere episode of *Hogan's Heroes* even included a Russian prisoner, but his character is only in the first episode and is absent from the show for the rest of its six years on the air. The political necessities of the Cold War mandated that Americans attitudes toward the Soviet Union needed to be hostile and a Soviet "fellow prisoner" did just the opposite.

In addition to the laughable circumstances with which the Allies dominate their captors, the German characters themselves are privy to some of the same separations between German and Nazi that were presented in combat films. Klink, although a patriotic German who loves Wagner, is not a very staunch Nazi (separating the regular military and the SS). A running gag throughout the film occurs whenever Klink finishes a phone call. Just as he is about to hang up the receiver he says, "What was that?" After a short pause he mutters in an apathetic tone, "Oh, yes. Heil Hitler" and weakly raises his arm in salute. The prisoners laugh at Klink and Schultz behind their backs but take on a more serious attitude when a member of the SS or the Gestapo visits the camp.

This curious shift in the portrayal of German characters becomes less puzzling when one looks at these films (and episodes) in context. Combat films often end with an American victory over the German army on the battlefield. The Germans may have got the upper hand at different points in the film, the American's may have suffered severe casualties, and the situation at one point most likely looked hopeless, but at the end of the day the American GI came off conqueror. POW films, on the other hand, start off with the assumption of an American defeat on the battlefield. In order for American soldiers to be in a prison camp they had to have somehow fallen short on the battlefield, thus in the POW film the initial atmosphere is one of unquestioned German dominance. By portraying the German camp guards as weak, foolish and easily controlled, filmmakers were compensating for the initial portrayal of German dominance. In *The Great Escape, Stalag 17,* and especially *Hogan's Heroes,* it is the prisoners who actually run the camp. The Germans are left only think-ing that they are in charge.

The ability of the inmates to essentially run the camp under their captor's noses hints at the Hitler Gang stereotype of the early war years. If the Ger-mans are so easily controlled by others, even when in positions of authority, perhaps they *really were* duped by Hitler and the Nazis. If the viewer can laugh at the *Hogan's Heroes* episode in which Schultz hands his rifle to one of the inmates while he lights a cigarette, perhaps the viewer will also be will-ing to accept that the German people handed Hitler power in order to secure the comforts and necessities of life. During the war the idea of the Hitler Gang was condemned because it absolved all of Germany from responsibil-ity for the war. In these prison films it is embraced for the exact same reason. With the Germans no longer as enemies, but allies against the Soviet Union, Hollywood fostered the German/Nazi myth as a means of undoing the atti-tude created by films made during and shortly after the war. Through moral dilemma, separating the army from the SS and the Gestapo, and creating the superior-subordinate rift, war films reinvented America's former enemy. But as the Cold War progressed and the war in Vietnam affected American poli-tics and society, the image of the German soldier in World War II films shifted yet again.

There are very few films about the Second World War produced from the late 1960s through the 1980s. During these years, filmmakers were more con-cerned with displaying and interpreting the war in Vietnam, and films like *Platoon, Apocalypse Now,* and *Full Metal Jacket* set new standards for the war film genre. The few World War II films that were produced take on sim-ilar themes and messages as their fellow Vietnam films. The tagline of Samuel Fuller's *Big Red One* is "The real glory of war is surviving." The glory of fighting the Nazis and freeing the world form tyranny has been re-placed with hopes of simply being alive the next day, a clear crossover from Vietnam. The characters of *Big Red One* talk, dress and act like Grunts rather than GIs. The dialogue among the men becomes cruder and the attitude to-ward the war becomes indifferent. As far as the Germans in such films are concerned, they are not enemies, nor friends, but simply obstacles in the GI's path back home.

There are no more films revolving around (or even including for that mat-ter) German characters. The viewer seldom even encounters a German char-acter with a face and name. The three-man machine gun squad reappears, and dialogue about the war's larger purpose is as rare as the German main char-acter. The combination of these two trends marginalizes the Germans. The previously mentioned scene in *Big Red One* in which the officer shoots his subordinate is the only scene in the film where the Germans are on camera as the primary focus for more than a few seconds. Other films like *Hell is for Heroes* and *The Dirty Dozen* also focus more on the darker side of war and less on the need to free Europe from dictatorial rule. In *The Dirty Dozen,* killing Germans has nothing to do with patriotism, freedom, or any other catch-word, rather it is simply what must be done if the 12 soldier-prisoners of Major Reisman's squad want their sentences commuted. In *Hell is for Heroes*, Private Reese is a rebellious, former non-commissioned officer who would just as easily kill an American as a German if he thought it prudent. Through Vietnam era war-films (whether set during the Vietnam or Second World War), the enemy becomes internal. Chris Taylor, the main character in *Platoon*, best summarizes this shift at the close of the film when he asserts that "we were fighting ourselves" rather than the Vietnamese.[23] In another scene near the end of the film a squad of men scouts the area of the previous night's attack to look for survivors. The armored personnel carrier accompanying them is flying a small, though noticeable Nazi battle-flag. Where would American boys that are a generation removed from World War II and fighting on the other side of the world find a Nazi flag? This seemingly trivial prop makes an unmistakable statement; "We (America) have become animals like the Nazis." The German soldier had been marginalized because his role as "the enemy" was transferred to the American public that now had to make similar "good" and "bad" distinctions among its own population. Did the Grunts at My Lai represent all Americans in the way Landsers at Malmedy represented all Germans? Were they just following orders too?

With Vietnam more or less taking over the genre, the river of World War II films dries to a trickle until the end of the Cold War in 1989. With the release from having Soviet enemies and German allies, World War II films re-remerge, but with definite Vietnam-film influences. This revisionist era attempts to wipe the table of all previous paradigms, German/Nazi myth included, and start over. There is no longer a political need to pigeonhole German atrocities and portray Germans favorably, but at the same time, American soldiers can no longer be depicted as the standard bearers of freedom and justice. The Holocaust, for example, is inseparable from World War II and Nazi Germany, yet because of the necessities of the Cold War, very few war films even mention it. In fact, of all the movies surveyed in this study, only one pre-1989 film, *The Big Red One* includes any significant reference to the Holocaust. *The Big Red One* actually ends with the liberation of an extermination camp. The coward of the squad, who has never been able to shoot another human throughout the entire film, empties two full clips (16 bullets) into a single German soldier after he discovers him hiding in an oven in the crematorium.

Post-Cold War and post-Vietnam films blur the lines between friend and enemy, leaving the viewer without the nice and tidy "us" versus "them." In the opening scene of *Saving Private Ryan*, American soldiers purposefully shoot Germans who have thrown down their weapons, held their hands up, and surrendered. At the end of the film it is the Germans turn to act dishonorably when the captured German soldier who exclaimed "f—k Hitler," returns to his unit instead of surrendering (as he had promised) and ends up killing some of the Americans who earlier held him captive. Neither side is "the hero." Even the film's plot is ambiguous in terms of right and wrong. The selected platoon is not trying to kill Hitler, end the war or save the day. They are just looking for Private Ryan. At several points in the film members of the platoon question their mission. One such discussion almost leads to a mutiny. Scenes such as these have a strong, Vietnam influence.

Where Eagles Dare was produced in 1968 and provides a truly mind-boggling example of blurring the lines between enemy and friend. For three-quarters of the movie the viewer is led to believe that British Special Forces are on a mission to rescue a captured American General. In actuality, the mission is designed to flush out a horde of German spies that have infiltrated British Intelligence. At the film's climax, all the major characters are seated around a conference table. They (and the viewer) are thoroughly confused as to who is on whose side. Major Smith, the team's leader, turns out to be a dou-ble-double agent, who must constantly pretend to switch sides in order to obtain the necessary information about the suspected spies. Viewers might even have to watch the film several times before it all makes sense. For several years Smith worked for Germany in order to gain the trust of high-ranking German officials and collect information that he turned over to British Intelligence. Even though he came out on the British side in the end, is he not a traitor for what he did for the Germans?

In *The English Patient*, a caring army nurse sets up a makeshift hospital in the Italian countryside to look after a severely burned patient who is days away from death. The mystery of the man's identity unfolds throughout the film and reveals that he was a Hungarian noble, surveyor and cartographer who sold secret maps of the African desert to the German's in order to save his lover's life. The maps gave the German Army the necessary information to capture the British stronghold at Tobruk. The question is unspoken but posed nonetheless; is he the enemy? The man was not a spy, nor was he a subject of the British Crown. He did not care much for the Nazis and provided valuable information for the British throughout the war. Does his one misdeed, motivated by love, justify lumping him in with the Nazis?

Mother Night provides another such moral dilemma. The film, based on Kurt Vonnegut's novel, tells the story of Howard W. Campbell, Jr., an American living in Germany when the war breaks out. He is approached by an American CIA agent and asked to be a spy for the United States. Campbell's role is simply to make propaganda speeches for the Nazis (yes, *for* the Nazis). Without knowing how, Campbell's speeches are edited by another agent in the German Propaganda Ministry so that when delivered over the radio they convey troop movements, officer locations, army supply status and other crucial information that helps the Allies to win the war. But this information came at the cost of serving the German war effort through propaganda. As in *Where Eagles Dare* and *The English Patient*, is the main character a hero or a villain?

Saints and Soldiers blurs the distinction between "us" and "them" in a somewhat different way. When a German soldier is captured by a small squad of American GIs he turns out to be an old friend of Corporal "Deacon" Greer, one of the members of the capturing squad. As a missionary in Germany before the war, Greer developed a strong bond with the captive and his family. In *A Bridge too Far*, the Germans were shown as equals. In *Kelly's Heroes*, they could possibly even be friends, but in *Saints and Soldiers* they are depicted as brothers. Portraying one's enemy as one's brother is strange enough, but the film takes the blending of friend and enemy even further. Shortly after the German is captured, and much to the dismay of his fellow soldiers, Greer allows his old friend to escape. This act of treason threatens to tear the tiny band apart. At the end of the film, the German soldier repays the favor and saves the lives of the group by betraying his own officers. With the American betraying his comrades for his German friend, and the German in turn betraying his duty as a German soldier and saving the lives of the Americans later in the film, the distinction between ally and enemy is shattered.

The effect of the Vietnam War on the German/Nazi myth is clear. What formerly could be depicted in clear black and white terms (good vs. evil, democratic vs. totalitarian, American vs. Nazi) had been dismantled. The Vietnam War brought the realities of American war atrocities into American living rooms. As a result, the German/Nazi myth was placed on the back burner as Americans wrestled with their own identities. When a World War II film was produced, the former distinctions between characteristics of German, Nazi and American had to be reassessed. The result was the abandoning of the myth and the rejection of "us" and "them" rhetoric. Any individual, no matter on which side they fought, who participated in atrocious actions in wartime became the enemy.

From the creation of the genre to the present day, filmmakers have struggled with portraying the "enemy." The depiction of Germans in World War II has gone from hated foe to brother-in-arms, hitting every point in between as social and political events shaped, and were shaped by, public opinion. But that is not all. By altering how Germans were depicted, Hollywood changed how society remembers the war and how future generations will be taught to understand the war.[24] Almost all of the films contained in this study were highly successful films, proving that society is accepting the new history that Hollywood is writing. The full implications of this blending of "us," "them," Axis, Allies, enemy, and friend is something for sociologist, psychologists and possibly even psychiatrists, but the fact remains that post-Cold War and post-Vietnam era World War II films which have eliminated the German/Nazi myth are rewriting history through the lens of Vietnam. The Rutgers study observed, films offer a "new reality" of history and have become "a vehicle for shaping historical consciousness" among the public.[25] The German has ceased to be "the enemy" of American World War II combat films. It will be interesting to see how they are portayed if American society comes to terms with its recent past and once again begins making distinctions between "us" and "them."

NOTES

1. Quoted in John Whiteclay Chambers II and David Culbert, *World War II, Film, and History* (New York: Oxford University Press, 1996), xiv-xv.

2. Franklin Fearing, "Influence of the Movies on Attitudes and Behavior," *Annals of the American Academy of Political and Social Sciences* 254 (November, 1947): 70.

3. Fearing, "Influence of the Movies," 74.

4. Chambers and Culbert, *World War II Film*, 10.

5. Many of the foundational works include Koppes and Black, *Hollywood Goes to War* (Berkeley, California: University of California Press, 1990); Shindler, *Hollywood Goes to War, 1939–1952* (New York and London: Routledge, 1993); Dick, *The Star-Spangled Screen: The American World War II Film* (Lexington, Kentucky: University of Kentucky Press, 1985); Doherty, *Projections of War: Hollywood, American Culture, and World War II* (New York: Columbia University Press, 1993); Basinger, *The World War II Combat Film: Anatomy of a Genre* (Middletown, Connecticut: Wesleyan University Press, 2003).

6. Both Paret's and Youngblood's essays were published in Chambers and Culbert, *World War II, Film and History*.

7. Lewis Jacobs, "World War II and the American Film" *Cinema Journal* 7 (Winter, 1967–1968): 1.

8. New York Times Film Review, Oct 15, 1940.

9. Thomas Doherty, *Projections of War: Hollywood, American Culture, and World War II* (New York: Columbia University Press, 1993), 122.

10. Doherty, *Projections of War*, 122.

11. Doherty, *Projections*, 125.

12. *Hangmen Also Die*, directed by Fritz Lang (Dick Arnold Productions, 1943).

13. *The Big Lift*, directed by George Seaton (Twentieth-Century Fox, 1950).

14. All dialogue taken from *The Guns of Navarone,* directed by J. Lee Thompson (Columbia, 1961).

15. *The Young Lions*, directed by Edward Dmytryk (Twentieth-Century Fox, 1958).

16. As an ironic side-note; the "bad officer" is played by a British actor while the "good subordinate" is played by a German.

17. All dialogue taken from *The Battle of the Bulge*, directed by Ken Annakin (Warner Brothers, 1965).

18. *The Longest Day*, directed by Ken Annakin, Andrew Martin, Bernard Wicki, Darryl Zanuck (Twentieth-Century Fox, 1962).

19. *Where Eagles Dare*, directed by Brian G. Hutton (MGM, 1968).

20. *The Big Red One*, directed by Samuel Fuller (Lorimar, 1980).

21. Stephen Ambrose, "Blockbuster History," in *World War II Film, Society and History*, ed. John Chambers and David Culbert (New York: Oxford University Press, 1996), 105.

22. *Kelly's Heroes*, directed by Brian G. Hutton (MGM, 1970).

23. *Platoon*, directed by Oliver Stone (MGM, 1986).

24. Chambers and Culbert, World War II Film, 6.

25. Chambers and Culbert, World War II Film, 148.

Chapter Sixteen

"Representations of Genocide in Recent Films"

Edward C. Hanes, West Chester University

In the films *Ararat, Hotel Rwanda, Killing Fields, Sometimes in April* and *Welcome to Sarajevo*, several trends are common to the direction of the story line. Because of the visually overwhelming content, emotional engagement becomes an effective device in holding the attention of viewers, which all of these films incorporate. In telling the story of genocide, the question of "what is truth?" becomes synonymous with the emotional and physical struggle to survive or remember. Portraying the experience of a specific family or individual allows the viewer to more closely identify with the struggle for truth, allowing the viewer to become a witness to genocide. When placed in the context of historical recording, the human story represented on film becomes a powerful image of testimony to the memory of those who died. Complemented by historical facts, a concrete story develops within each film to provide the viewer with a better understanding of the unfolding genocidal events.

The Killing Fields is the account of three journalists—a Cambodian, Dith Pran, an American, Sydney Schanberg, and an Englishman, Jon Swain. Each reporter witnesses the genocide perpetrated by the ruthless regime of Pol Pot and the Khmer Rouge, implicating American foreign policy in Cambodia and Vietnam as an aggravating factor. *Welcome to Sarajevo*, meanwhile, involves a British reporter who attempts to save a child during the Bosnian civil war. Similarly, *Hotel Rwanda* involves rescue in the context of genocide as the story of hotelier Paul Rusesabagina, a moderate Hutu who created a safe zone for over 1200 Tutsis. Through the use of metaphor and analogy, *Ararat* depicts the complications of not knowing, remembering, or even denying genocide and the force of emotions arising in the wake of such denial. *Sometimes in April* is also about coming to terms with loss ten years after genocide; here, the story is refracted through the experiences of a man who lost his entire family to the Hutu militias. The first three films represent genocide as it is happening, providing critical evaluation of the international community, while the latter two represent genocide in the context of memory and the effects trauma can have after the event. Taken together, all five films demonstrate the characterization of genocide from classification of the victims to the implementation of mass murder to denial after the events.[1]

Filmmakers have a responsibility to portray, as accurately as possible, the historical events that created conditions for genocide. *The Killing Fields* provides such a prologue by documenting the impact of the Vietnam War and its spillover into Cambodia. The film literally demonstrates the danger and physical cost of attempting to document the truth. Early on, Schanberg and Pran are shown attempting to avoid U.S. forces in order to reach a location accidentally bombed by a B-52 bomber. When the two eventually come upon the scene of destruction, Schanberg interviews residents, and the Cambodian army carries out an execution of Khmer Rouge rebels. He is arrested at gunpoint when he attempts to take pictures of the execution. This scene conflates covert U.S. actions and the murderous policies of its surrogate in the Cambodian army, setting up citizen support for the Khmer Rouge. For Pran, the difficulty is balancing a multilevel allegiance—to his profession, his homeland, his family, and to Schanberg. His bond to the latter is strong enough to risk death itself. This is evident when Pran saves the team of American reporters from the Khmer Rouge, persistently negotiating for their release, risking execution at every turn.

Similar to *The Killing Fields, Sometimes in April* provides us with the prologue of genocide through the experience of a moderate Hutu military captain, Augustin Botera. Yet it provides this in the context of memory. The time is 2004 and Botera must deal with the memories of his dead family and the guilt of his "incite to genocide" accused brother, Honore. Through the use of flashbacks, not only does the film piece together in a post-traumatic way the historical events leading to genocide, but it allows the viewer to become intimately involved in the grieving process. In one flashback, Botera realizes that the extremist Hutu militia (or Interhamwe), were being trained by the Hutu regime not to combat the Tutsi rebels but to kill Tutsi civilians. Suspicion falls on Botera because he is married to a Tutsi, a common reason for being placed on the traitor's list and justifying execution. (Hutu paramilitary forces drew up these lists prior to the beginning of the genocide suggesting premeditation.)[2] Finally, Botera recalls the event that set the genocide in motion, namely, the shooting down of the Rwandan President's plane on 6 August 1994.

As the film progresses, Botera meets other victims of genocide who must confront the past, facing their oppressors in a court of law. Here, the tension is balancing justice with the need to move past a cycle of violence. Without an outlet to process their memories of trauma, victims may resort to more destructive means of "settling a score," therefore setting conditions for future genocides, and yet inadequate or absent prosecution also impedes the healing process. The film posits no easy answer to this dilemma. As the victims recount their story in court, they face their past as an action of justice. They have a forum in which to process and work through their memories. In one scene, a woman concealing her identity faces her oppressor as she recounts her memory of being raped. As Botera hears this, he understands that he is no longer alone in the traumatic experiences he remembers, and he realizes he must finally face his brother to find out the truth of the death of his family. Botera, more so than others, has the chance to know the truth, a luxury for many survivors of genocide searching for knowledge of their family's death.

In depicting the effectiveness of a *court* prosecuting the agents of genocide, *Sometimes In April* advances the position of "no violence, but no healing without justice." It is within the framework of the law and reason, in establishing the truth, that the court gains both legitimacy and victory over trauma. Without either, and bearing the open wound of genocide, succeeding generations might internalize the hatred of their oppressors. This is no more apparent than in the film, *Ararat*. Central to its story is the assassination of a Turkish diplomat by an Armenian father and husband. In the wake of his death, he leaves behind the legacy of the Armenian genocide to his family. They must come to terms with why he would commit such an act and how it affects their relationships. In *Ararat*, we learn how unresolved issues and denial perpetuates a cycle of violence both literally and in the subtle expression of one's memory, which is used to manipulate individuals into accepting a specific paradigm of truth.

Similar to *Sometimes in April*, *Ararat* provides the context of history in the form of flashbacks, but it also operates as a film within a film. The character of Edward Sarayon, an Armenian director, comes to Canada to shoot a film based on the stories of his mother and an American Red Cross Doctor, Usher. The film within a film provides the contextual background for the metaphorical representation of genocide, depicted by the present day characters dealing with their own emotional issues of passion for absolute truth and denial. In its entirety and similar to *Sometimes in April*, *Ararat* reveals the importance of re-connecting to source, from the testimonies of witnesses and victims, in helping survivors move on from the past.

The historical analysis of genocide relies heavily on the availability of direct evidence to corroborate circumstantial evidence. With the exception of Rwanda and the Holocaust, many genocides have only eyewitness testimony as direct evidence. Because of the frailty of memory, eyewitness testimony is only as effective as the ability to recall particular details and maintain internal consistency. One's memory is not restricted to any timeline and therefore requires a thoughtful interpreter to analyze what is said and to place testimony in the context of history. Yet *Ararat* asks the questions, "How do successive generations interpret the memory of genocide, and is absolute truth even possible, desirable, or necessary?" Interpreting historical events in the paradigm of a society that incorporates ideas on many different levels, *Ararat* weaves a non-linear chronology of genocide, effectively discerning important aspects as they pertain to the remembrance of events.

Ararat deconstructs and then reconstructs the Armenian genocide through a conversation between the character, Raffi, and a customs agent known as David, using metaphor as a vehicle of discovery. The dialogue also reveals the troubles survivors have in getting people to believe. In Raffi's personality there exists the reality of experience but the naivety of suffering. He represents the significance of truth only as far as his equal but opposite (David) chooses to explore. David, who is much older, embodies the strong skeptic, a characterization important in his position as a customs agent. David also represents the capacity in all of us to search deeper into the meaning of actions, important to understanding the complexity of human suffering.

On suspicion of smuggling drugs in from Turkey, Raffi is adamant that what he is carrying is actually exposed canisters of film for a major studio production (the film within a film). Taking pity on him, the customs official (David) decides to allow Raffi to tell his story. In revealing the reasons behind his trip and why he has the film, Raffi tells him the story of the Armenians struggle against Turkish oppression. Raffi tells this story in a way that depicts the current ongoing struggle for recognition of the genocide. Providing analogy to the skepticism of the unimaginable events of genocide, David responds, "What are we going to do? There is no one I can contact, there is no way of confirming that a single word of what you say is true." Raffi responds with a solid conviction, "Everything I told you is exactly what happened." There is no doubt in Raffi's mind that what is in those canisters is exposed film. For Raffi, the canisters develop into a metaphor for the absolute truth, a truth that can never be exposed. For David, the canisters represent his own awakening, that there is a greater truth at work than the truth of the canisters' contents. Ultimately, both David and Raffi must rely on the pivotal character (Raffi's mother) of the film to decide a course of action.

Raffi's mother is a metaphor for the memory of the survivors, as well as an expression of the power of denial. As the stepmother to Raffi's girlfriend, she holds the truth to her second husband's death. As the wife of Raffi's father, she epitomizes the blind acceptance of revenge as a means of justice and harboring the cycle of violence. Her own denial of the actions of her first husband provide the motivation for Raffi's search for the truth but when faced with the consequences of smuggling drugs, Raffi must ultimately rely on her denial to save him. In her denial there is a connection she has to Raffi. In order to save him from the absolute truth (the contents of the canisters), she must confirm his story. She is a metaphor for the denial of genocide the Turkish government provides for its own people, a consequence of passing a legacy from one generation to another. Faced with her own issues of truth and denial as an analogy to the continuation of memory, she represents the necessary link in connecting the past with the present for the customs official. In the process of asking her about the validity of Raffi's story, David comes to understand the complexity of Raffi's search and the power of denial to save oneself. David begins to awaken from his own issues of denial concerning his gay son. *Ararat* conveys the process of inquiry into any historical event and the responsibility each of us hold in maintaining the memory of those events.

Denial, the last stage of genocide, is the attack on the memory of those who suffered. It is the lasting insult to a generation of people nearly destroyed because it reveals the level of hate that continues, unabated, in some cases, years after the event of genocide. In the film *Ararat*, the director of the film within a film (Sarayon) describes the insidiousness of denial as the component of hatred that fueled genocide. Although not a survivor himself, he is well aware of the level of hate from the architects of genocide as it passed down from one generation to another. The actor portraying the genocidal architect, Captain Jevdet Bey, feels revulsion and guilt in accepting the role. He may fear reprisals from the Turkish community because he is half Turkish. He asks the director, "You cast me in this role because I am Turkish?" The director assures him that he cast him because he could make the part believable. A one-way conversation ensues about the Armenian genocide. The actor, justifying his ancestral guilt by blaming the Turkish response on militant Armenians, receives only a passive nod from the director. After this short conversation, Raffi approaches the director and asks him why he didn't confront his denial. The director answers with a pensive look, "Do you know what still causes so much pain? Not the people we lost or the land. It's to know that we could be so hated, who are these people that they hate us so much, how can they still deny their hatred and so hate us, hate us even more?" Of these five films only *Ararat* and *Sometimes in April* introduce the concept of denial as the last stage of genocide.

While *Ararat* deals with the struggle of memory and the effect of memory on subsequent generations, *Sometimes in April* evinces the importance of defining and prosecuting the criminals responsible for genocide. Since the murdered are unable to speak on their behalf, the international community must rely on the survivors to tell the story of genocide. The survivors are left with a legacy of conveying their experience to a skeptical and often ambivalent or hostile international community. Much of this reaction to genocide resides in the disbelief that murder can happen on such an immense scale; therefore it becomes vital that filmmakers represent the killing with utmost clarity and precision.

Welcome to Sarajevo, like *Ararat,* relies more on intimation rather than exposition of the graphic horror of genocide, but it explores a less well-known aftereffect of collective murder of adults—the creation of legions of orphans.[3] In the film, scenes of UN diplomats are shown feigning concern. Only when the plight of orphans is revealed does any action happen and only on the part of a non-governmental organization called "orphans r us?" Set against an international community unwilling to act against genocide, the film depicts how a few individuals can overcome the indifference of international diplomats to rescue potential victims.

Similar to *Welcome to Sarajevo, Hotel Rwanda* portrays the true story of one man who saved civilians facing certain death. Yet the latter is also about an individual who could also have easily been a victim as well. Married to a Tutsi woman, and initially a-political, Paul Rusesabagina struggles to provide refuge in his hotel to over a thousand people, all the while fearing for his own and his family's life. The film shows the mounting casualties of the Interhamwe's brutal actions, but its main thrust is redemptive, concentrating on the heroism and hope of survival against incredible odds and in the face of, once again, an ineffective international community. Like Dith Pran's survival story, too, the film reveals that much of one's survival of genocide is based in large part on luck. At a certain point in the story, Paul's only source of support from the outside world is from the Belgian company that owns the hotel. By influencing the French government (who have clout with the Hutu guards), the company is able to buy time for Paul and the refugees. Ultimately, though, it is the advancement of the Tutsi led Rwandan Patriotic Front (without the help of anyone) which defeats the extremist Hutu government and the Interhamwee and allows for the survival of those trapped in *Hotel Rwanda.*

The trends and techniques used in the portrayal of genocide in these five films cover a variety of issues. Common to all of them is the device of emotional engagement to allow the viewer to view what is almost fundamentally unrepresentable. Most of us cannot comprehend how anyone could orchestrate or implement genocide. Given that, and given the risk of trivializing murder through restaging it in a forum as problematic as mass marketed film, artists have often relied on personal stories for exposition. The most salient link between the films, however, is not their heroic or redemptive thrust, and I would argue that none of the five features leave audiences with much in the way of uplift. Their shared effectiveness comes in the form of a multilayered critique. On one level, the films condemn international inaction towards genocide, while at the same time decrying the suppression of memory or outright denial of genocide by subsequent generations. Underlying the assumption of each work is an almost Freudian warning about the perpetuation of trauma (and the possibility of future atrocities) in the absence of a process of "working through" the loss.

NOTES

1. The stages of genocide include the following: Classification (creating "the other"), Symbolization (labeling, marking "Jewish Star", i.e.), Dehumanization ("Cockroaches," "Jews like Rats," Organization (formation of militias), Polarization (hate speeches), Preparation (death lists, camps, ghettoes), Extermination, and Denial. Recognition of each stage of genocide implies a responsibility for international authorities to step up to prevent genocide from continuing.

2. "Leave None to Tell the Story: Genocide in Rwanda." *Human Rights Watch.* http://www.hrw.org/reports/1999/rwanda.

3. The UN definition of Genocide includes the fate of orphans. This definition defines the taking away of children from their original heritage as genocide.

Chapter Seventeen

"Genocide and Redemption in the Modern Western"

William L. Hewitt, West Chester University

A recent Australian "western," *The Proposition* (2006), makes oblique references to that continent's genocidal past. Singer-song writer Nick Cave wrote the script for the film, and promoted it in several interviews, comparing what he sees as a basic difference between American and Australian historical viewpoints: "We see our history not in terms of good guys and bad guys. We don't see our history heroically at all. There's this sense of shame that permeates the Australian psyche, about what happened back then, the colonizing of Australia and the near-genocide of the Aboriginal population."(*IFC News*) *Rolling Stone* promoted the film in this vein in an advertisement reading, "Nick Cave and Australia's Bad Deeds: Rocker's screenplay for *The Proposition* considers Australia's *open wounds*." A couple of live Aboriginals are depicted in bit parts working with whites in the film, and more are shown massacred in an act of revenge. Yet there is no coherent attention paid in the film to racism or the genocide Cave alluded to in interviews. A brief scene showing an Aborigine's head blown off, and the few actual pictures of naked and chained aboriginal people shown during the end credits seemed merely gratuitous and trivial exploitation of a recent controversy over judging the extent of Australia's genocidal past. A brief warning at the beginning of the film states that: "there are images in this film that aboriginal people may find disturbing and pictures of real dead people," seemingly alerting the audience what to look for rather than a warning.

Recent Hollywood westerns have paid attention to representing flawed main characters, which often are showing human nature's dark and destructive side witnessing or even committing genocide themselves. Brief insights into the psychology of those who witness, collaborate in, and are complicit with atrocities, uncover some disturbing common elements—tribal hatred, blind adherence to ideology, diminished personal responsibility—as well as denial and redemption in the aftermath. The irony is that the perpetrators often find redemption by adapting, to one degree or another, the "primitivism" of the noble savage targeted for genocide. The civilization that sanctions genocide is fatally flawed, since the audience is led into the world of the "noble savage," a romantic concept of humankind unencumbered by a destructive civilization, and nurtured by a natural essence of harmony with one's human and physical environment.

Common threads of representation and interpretation run through seven films including: *A Man Called Horse* (1970); *Little Big Man* (1970); *Dances with Wolves* (1990); *Quigley Down Under* (1990); *Thunderheart* (1992); *The Last Samurai* (2003); and *Hidalgo* (2004); and *The Proposition* (2006). These films, although showing different locales, time periods, and cultures, depict white characters who regret the genocide of Native Americans or indigenous peoples, and find redemption in embedding themselves in the cultures of the *others*. They cleanse themselves of the corruption of European-American imperialism, thus exhibiting profound ambivalence about America's past, as well as about modernity, and adopt the best of the *other* culture resulting in their regeneration and redemption. In all of these movies, white society is in some way seriously flawed, and the white hero immerses himself in the exotic other society emerging cleansed to what had tarnished his character in American society, realizing himself in another society in a way he never could in America. These films, moreover, comprise a genre that might be called "white messiah movies." In a two-way exchange, the white gives as good as he gets, not only giving advanced technology and tactics to the *other*, but usually saving the culture as well.[1]

The end of this stream of movies leading Americans to conclude that their imperialism is something of which they need not be embarrassed, but in fact can be proud, is *We Were Soldiers*, showing Lt. Col. Harold Moore's unit, the 1st Battalion, 7th Cavalry Regiment, 1st Division, which was Custer's unit. This movie depicts the point of view of the United States' military in a three-day battle in the Ia Drang Valley in November 1965 that resulted in the deaths of dozens of U.S. soldiers and enemy casualties that numbered over 1,000. There is little sympathy generated for the Viet Cong who become just a faceless enemy mob to be killed. *We Were Soldiers* countered a spate of previous movies about The Vietnam War that, according to movie critic Michael Medved, "almost always show American GIs perpetrating ghastly atrocities against innocent civilians—despite the painstakingly plain and well-documented historical record that shows that only a tiny minority of our troops engaged in such brutalities."[2]

In 1941, Hollywood set out to supplant isolationism with right thinking about the war in Europe by sweetening the bitter memory of World War I. Hollywood released *Sergeant York* (1941), a stirring tale of a pacifist who makes the correct choice to fight in World War I, and becomes a hero. Similarly, following this precedent and to portray and then to erase the negative images of the Vietnam War for a wounded generation of Americans, Hollywood employed the Western genre as surrogate to show the trauma and heal the wounds of an American generation. In a scene at the beginning of *We Were Soldiers*, Moore is shown thoughtfully leafing through an illustrated account of the Battle of Little Big Horn, along with a French book describing what is called the 'Massacre' of French troops in a battle along Route 19, near where he will soon find himself and his men fighting for their lives.[3] In this scene of Vietnamese soldiers slaughtering French prisoners—and Custer's ill-fated men—there is a reversal of victimization. Historian Richard White also sees the ethos of white westward expansion with the settlers seeing *themselves* as victims of savage Indians. For example, according to White, "Americans had to transform conquerors into victims." As early as the second decade of the twentieth century, a delegation of Lakota to Chicago mayor Big Bill Thompson, "had him posing in a headdress as part of their campaign to change the portrayal of the Battle of the Little Big Horn in Chicago schoolbooks from an Indian massacre of whites to an American attack on Indians."[4] Moore, and his men in *We Were Soldiers*, besieged and attacked, fight shoulder to shoulder suggesting that they were the victims of Vietnamese imperialism.

A MAN CALLED HORSE

The hardened conventions and themes of the Western genre were examined, criticized, dismantled, and refined in the late 1960s and 1970s. The conventional Western's traditional thematic myth of whites attacked by Indians, or seeking revenge against Indians became outmoded. New attitudes toward Native Americans included seeing them as proto-environmentalist victims of white progress and technology, not as opposition to white progress. *A Man Called Horse* (1970) provides a good example of the revisionist Western of that era. Jack DeWitt wrote the screenplay for *A Man Called Horse* (1970), based on a short story by Dorothy M. Johnson, but he turned Crows into Sioux, their ancient enemies. Asked why he had changed so much of the original story, showing the Sioux sun dance ceremony as being the Okipa ceremony of the Mandans (the Sioux did not practice elevation the way the Mandans did), and why he had Horse, played by Richard Harris, teaching the Sioux British military tactics. In response to this last question, he stated he had based the teaching episode on *Lawrence of Arabia* (1962) and as for the rest, at this date, who cares? When this conversation was repeated to Dorothy M. Johnson, she replied that if one thought *A Man Called Horse* was a bad film, one should see the sequel.

In Johnson's novel the protagonist is a Bostonian, but a British substitute in the film provides more insulation for American viewers, thus reducing their discomfort by only indirectly addressing their genocidal past through the British surrogate. "Rather than a tale of INDIAN LIFE," Dave Georgakas wrote in an essay titled "They have not spoken: American Indians in Film," *A Man Called Horse* is "really about a white nobleman proving his superiority in the wilds,"[5] offering what Philip DeLoria calls "a deep, authentic, aboriginal American-ness."[6] As Horse assimilates into Sioux culture he saves a group of children from an enemy war party gaining the respect of the Sioux. His epiphany occurs when he has his initiation into tribal manhood by having his flesh pierced and skewered by eagle claws, which are attached to thongs that hoist Horse in excruciating pain. The final battle scene—*á la Lawrence of Arabia*—makes Morgan the primary warrior and the one most responsible for saving his adopted culture, using the white's own military tactics. Through a strange turn of events, he absolves the guilt of the audience by having the Indians massacre the invaders who are bent on annihilating them, thus giving white audiences the eye-for-an-eye justice that muddles issues of ethnicity, violence, and genocide.

Early in the story, John Morgan's (Richard Harris) guides are killed and he is captured by a band of Sioux warriors. He is beaten and mocked by the warriors who put a saddle on his back and call him Horse, before dragging him to their village where he is given to an elderly woman (Judith Anderson) as a servant. His attempts to escape end when he meets Batise, a captive feigning insanity to be spared by the superstitious Indians, and who educates Horse in Sioux culture. This film framed Morgan's experience in anthropologically detailed daily Indian life of the Sioux in the Dakotas in the early 1900s, offering what Philip Deloria calls, "rituals earnestly copied from a George Catlin painting."[7] It inverted the traditional captive narrative by focusing not on how someone will be rescued from their Indian captors, but rather how he is drawn to prefer their way of life to that of "civilization." Focusing on the white character makes Indians strange and exotic props, foils for his criterion of westernized civility.

LITTLE BIG MAN

Director Jack DeWitt ends *A Man Called Horse* with a massacre, and Arthur Penn's "progressive" Western *Little Big Man* begins with one.

However, the film, and Thomas Berger's 1964 book upon which it is based, cannot exhaust the psychic energy and mythic trauma of the massacre with this single bloodletting. Therefore, throughout *Little Big Man*, Penn gives the audience another slaughter of Cheyenne at the Washita, and by inverting the conventions of the massacre, concludes with Custer's infamous "Last Stand," this time the Indians do the massacring.[8] In this attempt to highlight American racism that supported genocidal "Manifest Destiny," Penn simplistically reverses the dichotomy of good whites and bad Indians.[9] Besides lacking analytical sophistication, it portrayed a maniacal Custer, thus diluting the association with the event by white audiences, and absolving them of the negative consequences of racism since the insane racist in the film in no way represented them or their government.

Penn's comic-ironic Western portrays another white character living among Indians. A 121 year old curmudgeon named Jack Crabb (Dustin Hoffman), through a series of flashbacks, recalls that when he was a ten year-old, after the massacre of his family, he was taken by a Cheyenne war party and given to a chief named Old Lodge Skins (Chief Dan George). Crabb is raised Cheyenne, who refer to themselves as "human beings." Old Lodge Skins articulates the dichotomy of white and Indian worlds when he says to Crabb, "The Human Beings, my son, they believe everything is alive. Not only man and animals. But also water, earth, stone. And also the things from them. . . . That is the way things are. But the white man, they believe EVERYTHING is dead. Stone, earth, animals. And People! Even their own people. That is the difference."

During an ill-fated battle with the cavalry, Crabb uses his whiteness to save himself and is returned to "civilization." But the dominant culture is lampooned during a series of misadventures with a religious family, the Pendrakes, revealing the hypocrisy of white civilization in stark contrast to the wholesome and honest Sioux way of life, thus asserting that the two cultures have been portrayed, in the past, inversely by the dominant culture's triumphal myth history. This inversion of the traditional interpretations of dominant and Indian cultures is termed a "gigantic distortion of the American Past," by traditional history defender and film critic Michael Medved.

The Battle of the Little Big Horn, in *Little Big Man* in effect, with a blustery egomaniacal Custer (Richard Mulligan), stands for American treatment of Indians in explaining genocide by attributing it to the whims of a few unbalanced people, i.e., General Custer and exonerates the settler-state system of responsibility for the very process on which its founding myth of expansion has been so resolutely based.[10]

DANCES WITH WOLVES

Almost twenty years after *Little Big Man*, the even more sympathetic *Dances With Wolves* (1990) re-employs the shoreline of whites living among the exotic *other* and the massacre themes. The story had antecedents from the early twentieth century. In 1907, J. W. Shultz published *My Life As An Indian*, for example, telling a story that anticipates the one told by Kevin Costner in *Dances With Wolves* decades later, and marks a transition in the representation of Native peoples in American culture. Set in the mid-nineteenth century, just before the European-American invasions into the region reached their highest point, Shultz's book celebrates his years on the frontier living as a member of the Blackfoot tribe.[11] By identifying with the Blackfoot, who conveniently "vanish" at the end of the narrative, Schultz concealed his complicity in the conquest,[12] and by indicating that progress (rather than European-American acquisitiveness) conveniently deflected difficult ethical questions about centuries of slaughter of Native peoples and usurpation of their resources.[13]

Because of the shared colonialist themes in *Dances with Wolves* and *Lawrence of Arabia*, embattled writer Ward Churchill calls the movie "Lawrence of South Dakota."[14] *Dances With Wolves* reworks themes previously covered in *Broken Arrow, Run of the Arrow*, and as described in *Little Big Man*. In those earlier films, James Stewart, Rod Steiger and Dustin Hoffman (respectfully) had each married Indian women, an integral part of their assimilation within the larger Indian society. *Dances With Wolves* sidesteps a suggestion of miscegenation by conveniently having a white woman (Mary McDonnell) as a ready-made romantic interest living among the Sioux. Thus, at heart, *Dances With Wolves* was not so much a repudiation of WASP America as a paean to an alternative (and ecologically harmonious) culture in which a nice young WASP couple may find a home in an ode to a mythical bucolic suburbia.[15] The union of Dunbar and Stands-With-A-Fist implies that these two characters, cleansed of the corruption of European-American life by adopting Indian ways, hold the promise of a new and better white society that proves the ultimate goal of Dunbar's journey into the primitive.[16]

Theorist Claude Levi Strauss maintains that, "myths and narratives reconcile cultural contradictions and bring opposing forces and values together."[17] Dunbar goes to the Garden of Eden and has the opportunity to start over, to redress the wrong headedness of his people in the past. R.W.B. Lewis, in *The American Adam*, describes the historical development of the idea of a new American hero who would be "emancipated from history, happily bereft of ancestry, untouched and undefiled by the usual inheritances of family and race."[18] Film historian Richard Grenier asserts that this new characterization of the hero allows him to "violently reject 'evil America' and its diseased values without appearing patently disloyal" precisely because he chooses to join our own "Indigenous Aborigines."[19] By the end of the film, *Dances With Wolves* and Stands-With-A-Fist have donned buckskins, spoken the Sioux language, and adopted Sioux ways.[20]

Like Dunbar, Stands-With-A-Fist is redeemed after suffering a violent trauma which she recalls as a massacre told as a flashback, described by psychologist Robert Baird as the most:

> distilled and powerful an embodiment of the massacre trauma as has ever been presented by Hollywood. Shot in soft focused at sunset, [dawn?] the scene begins slow-motion, as an idyllic view of a rustic farm and cabin; two frontier families are eating outdoors on a large table when ominous looking Pawnee warriors ride slowly in on horseback, their faces painted in bilious blues and bloody reds. At first it seems a peaceful meeting of two cultures, but then a tomahawk flies through the air, and the scene takes on added poignancy as the edit returns us to the horrified gaze of the young witness and, by a film dissolve, to the still-haunted Stands-With-A-Fist.[21]

The movie industry claimed with pride that *Dances with Wolves* was Hollywood's attempt to render justice to Indians through Kevin Costner's sympathetic telling of their proud history. Encountering the carcasses of bison skinned and left to rot on the prairie, for example, Costner's disillusioned cavalryman wonders, "Who would do such a thing? It must be people without values, without soul." He is, of course, talking about whites. By contrast, among the Sioux, "Everyday ends with a miracle." The message is clear; to act Indian is to transcend oneself, to be reborn. It suggests as well that being Indian is not merely an ethnic or physical fact, but, in essence, a spiritual condition.[22] This self-actualization is bitterly ironic, as Ward Churchill opines, since Indians live "today, in abject squalor under the heel of what may be history's most seamlessly perfected system of internal colonization," an observation likewise apropos regarding Australian Aborigines. *Dances with Wolves* and *Quigley Down Under* both divert attention to their reinterpretations of the past relegating problems facing Indians and Aborigines to yesteryear.[23]

This attempt to totally negate traditional Western themes, showing Euro-Americans almost without exception as sadists, thugs, or lost souls, did not sit well with Conservative film scholar Richard Grenier:

> In the 1860s, the period of Dances with Wolves, some of the greatest generals of the Union Army (Sherman, Sheridan, Custer) led American troops against the bloodthirsty Sioux, who erupted in the midst of the Civil War in one of the most

savage Indian uprisings in history. Along the western frontier, the Sioux massacre. They pillaged. They raped. They burned. They carried women and children into captivity. They tortured for entertainment by converting these Sioux Indians into gentle, vaguely pacifist environmentally responsible bucolics, Kevin Costner, in a state of holy empty-headedness, has falsified history as much as any time-serving Stalinist of the Red Decade.[24]

Grenier represents the side of an argument led by historian James Axtell who cautions that we use the word genocide sparingly and with extreme care, avoiding the fallacy of applying it wholesale to every Indian death in colonial American history. Anthropologist James A. Clifton extends Axtell's disclaimer to the entirety of United States history arguably claiming that, "In the over two hundred years it has existed as a nation, no U.S. administration from George Washington to Ronald Reagan has ever approved, tolerated, or abetted a policy aimed at the deliberate systematic termination of Indians."[25] On the other side of the argument is Churchill, who asserts on the contrary that: "The American holocaust was and remains unparalleled, both in terms of its magnitude and the degree to which its goals were met, and in terms of the extent to which its ferocity was sustained over time by not one but several participating groups."[26] *Dances with Wolves'* hero presents the revisionist point of view making Dunbar the center of consciousness, and he is re-named, at first, without his knowledge and without dialogue so that viewers, knowing the title of the film, rename the character his Sioux brothers will name him. In this scene without dialogue, the audience also renames him, knowing the title of the movie, and thus participates in his reconstruction. A new name enables Dances with Wolves to shed the culpability associated with his official army duties as an "Indian fighter". Significantly, because his perspective provides the film's narrative center and thus the white audience's point of identification, it also symbolically purges white America of its responsibility for the terrible plights of Native Americans—past and present. It thus assures contemporary European Americans of the legitimacy of their power and possessions. Because real Indians were destined to disappear anyway, European Americans are the proper heirs of *Indianess,* as well as the land and resources of the conquered Natives.[27]

Although he has just recently attained the status of a Sioux warrior, Dunbar has the entire tribe depend upon him for their welfare as a skillful buffalo hunter and superior warrior." *Dances With Wolves,* in other words, actually reinforces the racial hierarchies it claims to destabilize, and it thus serves another primary function of going native, reinforcing a regeneration of racial whiteness and European-American society.[28] In a scene depicting the first social interaction between the Sioux and Dunbar, he serves them coffee, shows them how he grinds beans, and sweetens their cups with sugar. They depart, after reflecting naiveté for innocence, displaying new tin cups obviously impressed by their introduction to Dunbar's products. Throughout the twentieth century, going native in movies has served as an essential means of defining and regenerating racial whiteness and a radically inflected vision of Americanness. While those who go native frequently claim benevolence toward Native peoples, they reaffirm white dominance by making some (usually distorted) vision of Native life subservient to the needs of the colonizing culture.[29]

The third massacre in *Dances With Wolves* transforms the horror associated with that depiction into the Hollywood-sanctioned celebration of dispatching the badman-the U.S. Cavalry. Dunbar has been captured by the cavalry as a renegade and is being taken by wagon in shackles to a frontier prison. When the Lakota attack and kill Dunbar's tormentors, one realizes that—even with ninety years of Hollywood history turned on its head—we have here the same cheer for the good guys; the skillful and precise application of violence in order to right the world; the promise of 'regeneration through violence,' which Richard Slotkin has so eloquently elaborated.[30] Weapons go to those opposing genocide—we are willing to turn our technology over to the Sioux so that they can defend themselves from their enemies—the less civilized Pawnees,[31] just as the U.S. needed to identify the good to help fend off the bad, an imperative in the wake of American expansionism. Dances with Wolves implements vicariously America's post-Vietnam desire to not become directly involved in struggles elsewhere, but instead support friend against enemies. Dances with Wolves knows the implacable truth as the audience sees the truth as the murderous, cruel Pawnees emerge from the horizon bent on destroying 'our' home (the Sioux village). With punkish haircuts and fierce facial paint jobs, they are not Native Americans but the treacherous Indians of movie history, and Medved and Grenier's history. What had changed here—and it indicated the limits the Vietnam era still imposed—was that whites, constrained from killing directly, gained that right vis-à-vis the people central to the spectacle.[32] *Dances With Wolves* appears to embrace, what Annette Hamilton calls the "national imaginary;" it seeks to contest, pitting the Pawnee (bad Indians) against the Lakota (good Indians) in ways that play-out the western paradigms that the film strives to counteract.[33]

The film leaves the power of European-American society unchallenged at the end of the story. The Sioux (like virtually all other movie with Indians) disappear, thus eliminating any threat their presence poses to white privilege. In the film's closing scenes, the military redirects its efforts to the conquest of Indians. An epilogue instructs audiences about the fate of Dunbar's noble companions in the years following the end of the Civil War: "Their homes destroyed, their buffalo gone, the last band of free Sioux submitted to white authority at Fort Robinson, Nebraska. The great horse culture of the plains was gone, and the American frontier was soon to pass into history." The film's end then, is elegiac. Though regrettable, the Indian's fate, it seems, is inevitable in the face of white settlement.[34] As Ward Churchill laments, "fate closes upon Indian and Arab alike, despite the best efforts of well-intentioned white men like the two lieutenants *in Dances with Wolves* and *Lawrence of Arabia.*" Predictably, though, Dances with Wolves does not share the fate of "his" tribe. The final scene shows him leading his probably pregnant wife on horseback, ascending into the mountains. The scene carries heavily Biblical overtones. It recalls illustrations of Joseph leading the mule bearing a pregnant Mary, in search of a place for the birth of Christ, redeemer of a fallen world. Redemption for whites plays a key role in *Dances With Wolves*, since the audience cheers the good against the bad Indians.[35]

THUNDERHEART

Thunderheart is an allegory of race denial and redemption seen in the dilemma of a half-Sioux FBI agent, Ray Levoi (Val Kilmar). Because of his heritage, hoping to improve the image of the FBI on the Pine Ridge Reservation, the Bureau calls on Washington, D.C. based Levoi, to help investigate the murder of an Oglala Sioux. Levoi nevertheless avoids any reference to his half-Indian heritage, but tribal policeman Walter Crow Horse (Graham Green) challenges his circumspection. Grandpa Sam Riakes (Chief Ted Think Elk), a medicine man tells Levoi that the spirits of the Ghost Dance and Wounded Knee Massacre summoned him to the Badlands. Through a series of visions and the idealistic charms of the local schoolteacher Maggie Eagle Bear (Sheila Tousey), Levoi's religious epiphany redeems him.

In its narrative patterning and visual design, *Thunderheart* draws substantially on what Mikhail Bakhtin calls the "genre memory" of the Western, one of the most enduring and important vehicles of national ideology in the United States.[36] Native America, in these new Westerns, reshaped the *national imaginary* and acquire a different status and meaning within what Annette Hamilton calls the *national imaginary*—the collectively held images circulating within the dominant culture that aim to distinguish the "national self" from "national others." In place of the disfiguring stereotypes of the past, Hollywood films and documentaries have recently visualized Indian nations as desirable alternatives to the nation-state, imaginative substitutes for a state order that, as one writer says, "has largely lost the ability to confer an adequate sense of identity upon its people."[37] *Thunderheart* invites a kind of imaginary identification with Native Americans, a tendency Churchill says "empower(s) the non-Native to begin to view himself as a new hybrid, embodying the 'best of both worlds.'"[38] [Once distinguished, the individual redeems himself and remedies the flawed aspect of his character. This is accomplished as Richard Slotkin says, by regeneration through violence.][39]

Rather than emerging from concrete experience, the national imaginary is formed from the circulation of national others against the national self.[40] Figures of national imaginings for centuries, Indians have emerged in contemporary films as agents of a powerful counter narrative of nation, bearers of an alternative historical consciousness molded and shaped by centuries of incessant war, a message especially apparent in films such as *Thunderheart* and *Geronimo*. The theme of continuous struggle against the nation-state defines many recent films and documentaries of Native American life, can be seen as a legitimate expression of the antagonism toward the corrupt omni-present nation state that has become such a pervasive motif in contemporary American society, and decidedly ambiguous and troublesome for Americans now engaging insurgents in Iraq.[41] Blurring this realization, however, *Thunderheart* fails utterly to explain the complex social chaos wrought on the Pine Ridge Reservation in the aftermath of Wounded Knee 1973. By dream-like reference to Wounded Knee 1890, as well, both events are relegated to a fuzzy past, and thus the United States government and contemporary the FBI are not associated with disturbing events. Americans are saved from troubling self-scrutiny.

QUIGLEY DOWN UNDER

Quigley Down Under (1992) returns to the comfortable conventions of the Western formula, transporting the American West to the Australian Outback. Matthew Quigley is a throwback to the old Western hero, ever popular as shown by the history of the project. Tom Selleck points out that Steve McQueen "Had his fingerprints all over the script. But it never got made," until another super-star produced it. Quigley, sporting a Buffalo-Bill-like goatee comes from 1880s Wyoming, travels from America to the Australian Outback, responding to an invitation for the world's greatest long-distance marksman, where Elliot Marston hires him. He sets up a traditional western dichotomy of good versus evil, or the iconoclastic white hat versus black hat. When Quigley is told the real purpose to which his skills will be used, he demurs by throwing his would-be employer through a window, prompting his ex-employer to have him severely beaten. Cora (Laura San Giacomo), a young woman hired at the same time as Quigley to be a prostitute for the men at Marston's ranch, defends Quigley, and is also beaten. The two are taken deep into the Outback where they are abandoned to die.

They witness the genocide of Aborigines, driven over a cliff like Indians drove bison, by whip-wielding men on horseback, which Quigley stops with his prodigious marksmanship. This scene sets up a situation to allow audiences to exercise their modern bourgeois sensibilities by protecting moral interest against degenerate behavior. Less strident than in the late nineteenth century due to politically correct sensibilities, seeing white men herd helpless Aborigines over a cliff, to be killed with as little thought as an animal, contemporary audiences feel no less moral sanction prescribing appropriate retribution. Psychologist Dolf Zillamn concludes, "displays of monstrous gratuitous slaughter and the distress they evoke are a necessary prelude to the portrayal of righteous maiming and killing that is to spark euphoric reactions."[42]

Quigley exacts revenge at the end of the film, killing Marston and his men. When a small detachment of British troops threaten to arrest Quigley, hundreds of Aborigines line the surrounding hills intimidating the troops into withdrawing without Quigley. They disappear ghost-like but have sanctioned Quigley's retribution on their behalf. *Quigley*, like *A Man Called Horse*, *Dances with Wolves*, and *Thunderheart,* makes an association between primitivism and weaponry. The Aborigines have weapons, but only for hunting. The expertise of Quigley with firearms represents the superiority of European-American technology to solve or resolve the primitive's dilemma, which is also the premise behind *The Last Samurai*.

THE LAST SAMURAI

Tom Cruise plays Captain Nathan Algren, a Civil War veteran who is enlisted at the end of the Civil War to fight Indians. Haunted by his subsequent involvement in the massacre of innocent Indian men, women, and children, an alcoholic Algren[43] is soon successfully recruited by his former commander, a slimy opportunist Col. Benjamin Bagley (Tom Goldwyn) who tries to recruit Algren to join him in Japan where the Emperor (Scichinossuke Nakamura) is intent on modernizing his army. In Meiji Japan, Algren learns that his purpose is to train the Japanese peasant army to fight the last of the Samurai, loyal warriors and protectors of the Emperor for 900 years. They are in revolt against what they perceive to be the wrong course taken by the Emperor following the intrusion of Westernization in Japan.

Katsumoto (Ken Watanabe) who despite being targeted as an outlaw leads the Samurai by the Emporer, and remains loyal to the office. Director Edward

Zwick took as a point of departure the story of Saigo Takamori's support of the rebellion against the Emperor. The Emperor sends his army to eradicate the Samurai, much as the U.S. government did with the Indians. Algren and his troops are defeated in their initial battle and the Samurai capture Algren, and take him to the Samurai village, where Katsumoto intends to learn from the enemy whose life he spared. The simple uncorrupted life of the village stands in stark contrast to the modernizing bustle of Tokyo.

As if the parallelism between America's destruction of the Indians and the Japanese government's war against the Samurai was not obvious enough, Algren makes it explicit when he explains his willingness to side with the Samurai saying: "The white men have come to destroy what I have come to love." The problem here is not the negative judgment of the American treatment of the Indians or of the Japanese attacks on the Samurai. The problem, as is often the case, is that simplistic moralism replaces dramatic nuance and political complexity. Algren can achieve redemption only in Japan because the film's America is utterly devoid of honor and nobility.

Algren is redeemed from his dissolution finding solace and meaning in Samurai traditions. The mercenary and cynical alcoholic Algren is detoxed, learns eastern philosophy, and falls for the Japanese widow of a man he killed in battle. Katsumoto (Ken Watanabe) engages in philosophical conversations with Algren similar to the exchanges between Dances With Wolves and Kicking Bear. Adding to the drama and reflecting her own way the Samurai code is Taka, Algren's chief caretaker during his recovery and the wife of the man he killed in battle. Soon Algren converts to the Samurai way of life and finds himself opposing not only the Japanese government but the American representatives as well.

The Last Samurai follows the formula of putting the disaffected American in the other's culture paralleling the isolation of Japan and isolation of the Plains Indians and Aborigines. Katsumoto acknowledges Algren's transformation after they kill Ninja assassins. They ride together to face the corrupted dominant culture and reinforce the inevitability of superior technologically to vanquish the primitive.

HIDALGO

Hidalgo has much in common with Edward Zwick's *The Last Samurai*, as both are set near the end of the nineteenth century and are about troubled Americans resentful of their government's treatment of Native Americans who find personal redemption in cultures of the East. Tom Cruise's Nathan Algren goes to Japan with the intention of modernizing the Emperor's army, but instead embraces and learns the ways of the honorable Samurai. In *Hidalgo*, Viggo Mortenson's Frank T. Hopkins travels to the Middle East to compete in "The Ocean of Fire," a 3,000-mile horse race across the Saudi desert. Disney Studios purported *Hidalgo* to be "based on a true story," and the actual life of Frank T. Hopkins, who allegedly had been born at Fort Laramie, worked for Buffalo Bill, witnessed the massacre at Wounded Knee, and rode in the legendary long-distance horse race across Arabia called the "Ocean of Fire;" none of which was true.

In the Middle East setting for the film, the Arab world is presented as desolate and primitive similar to the Great Plains and the Outback. Hopkins enjoys the other's culture as a spectator, and is renamed by the other as Dances with Wolves was. But Hopkins, called the "Cowboy," "impure animal," and "infidel," remains an outsider reflecting recent American experiences at nation building. Screen writer John Fusco, who also wrote *Thunderheart,* turns Hopkins' fictions into an allegory of race and redemption. In order to ameliorate the racist notion of white American superiority over darker skinned challengers, the movie foregrounds Hopkins' mixed race heritage. His mongrel of a horse, metaphorically representing a polyglot American society, inverts strength and nobility by competing against thoroughbreds and nobility.

The differences between East and West are highlighted in other ways. A wealthy *Sheik* Riyad (Omar Sharif)[44] admires Hopkins' firearm (technology), but he would have Hopkins castrated for cavorting with his daughter, Jazira (Zuleikha Robinson), a proto-feminist who detests her second class status. An attack by the *Sheik's* rivals delivers Hopkins from mutilation. Jazira's potential power is weakened, however, when she is kidnapped by one of the Sheik's evil, dark, Arab rivals, Prince Bin Al Reeh (Said Tagmaoui), but Hopkins' superiority is reaffirmed when he saves her.[45] The Prince wants to force her to "become his fifth wife. The youngest of his harem. No more than a slave in his house."[46] Film historians Matthew Bernstein and Gaykyn Studlar, in *Visions of the East: Orientalism in Film*, observe that, "In this sense the narrative of Western women in the Third World can be read as a projected didactic allegory insinuating the dangerous nature of the uncivilized man and by implication lauding the freedom presumably enjoyed by Western women.[47] The white hero by his actions, denounces the sexism with which the film imbues traditional non-western cultures; thus Hopkins civilizes the other in an enlightened masculinism.[48] Thus Princess Jazira stands in for submissive and mistreated Arab women wearing burkas, liberated by the American forces in Afghanistan, so that she and all Arab women, may decide their own destiny and realize their full potential. The vulnerable woman, threatened by a lustful male in an isolated desert locale, similar to the imagery of Rudolph Valentino in the *Sheik* (1921) with a swooning woman lifted in his arms, gives voice to the masculinist fantasy of complete control over western, or westernized, women.

The rescue fantasy, when liberalized through the rescue of a woman from a lascivious Arab, has to be seen not only as an allegory of saving the Orient from its libidinal, instinctual destructiveness, but also as a perpetuation by contrast to the myth of the sexual egalitarianism of women in the United States.[49] Of course, the status of American women is in no way comparable to that of women living under fundamentalist male domination in the Middle East.[50] The exoticism film context, nevertheless, gives voice to antifeminist backlash, responding to the threat that women will become totally independent. Puritanical Hollywood thus claims to censure the tyranny of the harem and female adventurousness.[51]

At the end of the film, Hopkins finds redemption by returning to his heritage and inner strength. At the point of total exhaustion near the end, and apparent defeat in the race, Hopkins is within seconds of giving Hidlago the *coup de grace*; when a hazy vision of Indian Warriors miraculously instills vitality in Hopkins. Thus the shimmering influence of his synthesized heritage is what Hopkins needs to triumph. Hidalgo is a thinly disguised allegory about the Iraq invasion—in which a surrogate for the American army—encounters good and bad Arabs in the desert where he respects Arab customs and womanhood—rescuing the woman from the bad Arabs—and returns home having left the good Arab in power. All it takes is a smart American to make the difference. When Hopkins returns to South Dakota, where he enlists a few Indians to help release penned-up wild horses, a metaphor for freeing Indians, and more importantly whites, from their historically confining history.

CONCLUSION

American warriors, scared and recovering after their culture sent them where they witnessed or participated in atrocities, seek redemption emersing themselves in the culture of the other, but ironically changing only that part of themselves that allows them to redeem themselves without losing their dominant cultural identity. These films show a progression from Vietnam syndrome antiwar films, to post 9/11 pro-war films with individual Americans triumphant at center stage. Iraq may turn into a Vietnam-like quagmire, stalling the apotheosis of America, instead sending it into a retrogression of self-doubt about American imperial superiority, and refocusing individual culpability in the deaths of the other. Linda Williams suggests, in *Refiguring American Film Genres*, "The greater the historical burden of guilt, the more pathetically and more actively the melodrama works to recognize and regain a lost innocence."[52]

There is a problem inherent in America's self-image, or more accurately, false image of itself. "American Exceptionalism" is a particularly bizarre concept, according to Churchill:

> Put most simply, this is the notion that the U.S. is the "most peace-loving of nations," its populace—especially those of European descent—composed of essentially "peace-loving citizens" who go to war only when the aggressive irrationalities of other countries or peoples have left them "no choice," and then in a uniquely altruistic and humane fashion.[53]

On an individual level, the myth of the white savior bolsters the white superiority ideology while allegedly debunking it. On another level, these films depict bucolic communities of the other at peace, but threatened by genocidal adversaries that must be stopped by the intervention of a virtuous American. Using the conventions of the Western, which might be called the principal war myth of the American nation-state, to reinforce the national imaginary, these films suggest that it is the image of an altruistic and reluctant nation at war against genocidal forces that best captures the "mythological and spiritual continuity of identity" that the dominant culture desires.[54] Each of the heroes in these westerns redeems past violence with more violence, and Americans are redeemed of their troubled past, and purged of guilt and remorse, in the modern Western, ready to assist the other in a convoluted defense against victimization.

NOTES

1. Hernan Vera and Andrew M. Gordon, *Screen Saviors: Hollywood Fictions of Whiteness* (Lanham, Maryland: Rowan and Littlefield, 2003), 40.

2. Michael Medved, *Hollywood vs. America* (New York: HarperPerennial, 1992,) 228.

3. Marilyn B. Young, "Now Playing: Vietnam," *Magazine of History*, 18 October 2004, 4-25.

4. James R. Grossman, ed., *The Frontier In American Culture: An Exhibition at the Newberry Library, August 26, 1994—January 7, 1995* (Berkeley, California: University of California Press, 1994), 44-45.

5. Dan Georgakas, "They Have Not Spoken: American Indians in Film," in *The Pretend Indians: Images of Native Americans In The Movies,* ed. Gretchen M. Bataille and Charles L. P. Silet (Ames, Iowa: Iowa State University Press, 1980), 136.

6. Philip J. Deloria, *Playing Indian* (New Haven, Connecticut: Yale University Press, 1998), 183.

7. Raymond William Stedman, *Shadows of the Indian: Stereotypes in American Culture* (Norman, Oklahoma: University of Oklahoma Press, 1982), 222, 260. The

film is pronounced to be "the most accurate and authentic ever made," and "history as it really was." Ward Churchill, "American Indians in Film: Thematic Contours of Cinematic Colonization," in *Reversing The Lens: Ethnicity, Race, Gender, and Sexuality Through Film,* ed. Jun Xing and Lane Ryo Hirabayashi (Boulder, Colorado: University Press of Colorado, 2003), 52.

8. Robert Bird, "Going Indian: Discovery, Adoption, and Renaming Toward a 'True American,' from *Deerslayer* to *Dances with Wolves,*" in *Dressing in Feathers: The Construction of the Indian in American Popular Culture,* ed. S. Elizabeth Bird (Boulder, Colorado: Westview Press, 1996), 201.

9. Churchill in Xing, 46.

10. Churchill in Xing, 58.

11. Huhndorf, 19. J. W. Shultz, *My Life As An Indian* (New York: Fawcett Columbine, 1981), 9-10.

12. Huhndorf, 21.

13. Huhndorf, 31.

14. Ward Churchill, *Fantasies of the Master Race: Literature, Cinema and the Colonization of American Indians* (Monroe, Maine: Common Cause Press, 1992), 243-47, "Lawrence of South Dakota: Dances with Wolves and the Maintenance of American Empire;" Stephen Powers, David J. Rothman, and Stanley Rothman, *Hollywood's America: Social and Political Themes in Motion Pictures* (Boulder, Colorado: Westview Press, 1996), 186.

15. Michael Coyne, *The Crowded Prairie: American National Identity in the Hollywood Western* (New York: I.B. Tauris Publishers, 1997), 188.

16. Shari M. Huhndorf, *Going Native: Indians in the American Cultural Imagination* (Ithaca, New York: Cornell University Press, 2001), 4.

17. Bird, 196.

18. Bird, 197. R.W.B. Lewis, *The American Adam Innocence, Tragedy, and Tradition in the Nineteenth Century* (Chicago: University of Chicago Press, 1955), 5.

19. Medved, 225-26; Richard Grenier, "Hollywood's Foreign Policy: Utopian Tempered by Greed," *The National Interest,* Summer 1991, 76-77.

20. Bird, 204.

21. Bird, 201.

22. Fergus M. Bordewick, *Killing the White Man's Indian: Reinventing Native Americans at the End of the Twentieth Century* (New York: Doubleday, 1996), 211.

23. Fantasies, 246.

24. Medved, 225-26; Richard Grenier, "Hollywood's Foreign Policy: Utopianism Tempered By Greed," *The National Interest,* Summer 1991, 76-77.

25. James A. Axtell, *Beyond 1492: Encounter in Colonial North America* (New York: Oxford University Press, 1992), 260-63; James A. Clifton, "Alternate Identities and Cultural Frontiers," in *Being and Becoming Indian: Biographical Studies of North American Frontiers,* ed. James A. Clifton (Chicago: Dorsey Press, 1989), 6.

26. Ward Churchill, *A Little Matter of Genocide: Holocaust and Denial in the Americas 1492 to the Present* (San Francisco: City Lights Books, 1997), 4.

27. Huhndorf, 5.

28. Huhndorf, 3.

29. Huhndorf, 5.

30. Bird, 202.

31. Tom Engelhardt, *The End of Victory Culture: Cold War America and the Disillusioning of a Generation* (New York: Basic Books 1995), 279.

32. Engelhardt, 279.

33. Annette Hamilton, "Fear and Desire: Aborigines, Asians, and the National Imaginary," *Australian Cultural History* 9 (1990): 13-35.

34. Huhndorf, 4.

35. Huhndorf, 4.

36. Burgoyne, 41; Gary Saul Morson and Caryl Emerson, *Mikhail Bakhtin: The Creation of a Prosaics* (Stanford, California: Stanford University Press, 1990), 290–92.

37. Robert Burgoyne, *Film Nation: Hollywood Looks At U. S. History* (Minneapolis, Minnesota: University of Minnesota Press, 1997), 38–39.

38. Burgoyne, 41; Churchill, Fantasies, 242–43.

39. Burgoyne, 39.

40. Burgoyne, 39.

41. Burgoyne, 40.

42. Burgoyne, 54; Jon Tuska, *The American West in Film: Critical Approaches to the Western* (Greenwood, Connecticut: Greenwood Press, 1985), 204, 208, 238.

43. Eric T. Dean, Jr., *Shook Over Hell: Post-Traumatic Stress, Vietnam, and the Civil War* (Cambridge, Massachusetts: Harvard University Press, 1997). Much of the current thinking about the American veteran has been shaped over the past thirty years by the image of the troubled Vietnam veteran psychologically damaged, even deranged by the experience. "In this view, psychologists regard Vietnam veterans as having suffered serious, lingering, and debilitating mental problems, centering around the phenomenon of Post-Traumatic Stress Disorder (PTSD) a delayed stress syndrome which is caused by exposure to combat and can produce symptoms of rage, guilt, flashbacks, nightmares, depression, and emotional numbing, and lead to a variety of grave social and psychiatric problems—from unemployment to suicide.(5)"

44. Jack G. Shaheen, *Reel Bad Arabs: How Hollywood Vilifies a People* (New York: Olive Branch Books, 2001), 19, "Sheikh" means, literally, wise elderly person.

45. Shaheen, 22, Stereotypical Arab women are portrayed as "bosomy belly dancers."

46. Shaheen, 20, a prevalent stereotype has Arab men kidnap and seduce women.

47. Matthew Bernstein and Gaylyn Studlar, eds., *Visions of the East: Orientalism in Film* (New Brunswick, New Jersey: Rutgers University Press, 1997), 57.

48. Churchill, 70.

49. Bernstein and Studlar, 56.

50. Stephen J. Ducat, *The Wimp Factor: Gender Gaps, Holy Wars, & the Politics of Anxious Masculinity* (Boston: Beacon Press, 2004), 210-11.

51. Bernstein and Studlar, Visions of the East, 54.

52. Linda Williams, "Melodrama Revised," in *Refiguring Film Genres,* ed. Nick Brown (Berkeley, California: University of California Press, 1998), 61.

53. Ward Churchill, *On the Justice of Roosting Chickens: Reflections on the Consequences of U.S. Imperial Arrogance and Criminality* (Oakland, California: AK Press, 2003), 39.

54. Burgoyne, 49: Hamilton, 16, 18, 23.

Conclusion

One of the pitfalls of cross-thematic and cross-disciplinary studies is the loss of narrative cohesion. In bringing together scholars from different fields with different academic languages, it was my firm belief that the advantages of engaging in a conversation about "the other" outweighed the disadvantage of topic diffusion. This compilation has demonstrated the myriad and shared ways in which the creative endeavor has given representation to "others" in different contexts over time. A chief assumption underlying each article is the notion that life imitates art and vice versa. Although this is a cliché, composing the other through artistic performance is a powerful act; it has ramifications for how in-groups and out-groups construct their performance in "the real world." Performance about the other is fundamentally about an exchange of power, more specifically, the loss of it by an in-group and the acquisition of it by an out-group, and stage and screen have often provided a safe, public space for dialogue. The reverse has equally been true. The performing arts have been used to justify and reinforce attitudes, policies, and behaviors that have demonized, persecuted, or even annihilated society's numerous others.

One umbrella question has emerged over the course of this volume to help bring unity to the surface cacophony as well, and that is, to borrow phrases from the likes of Antonio Gramsci and Gayatri Spivak, "Can the subaltern speak?"[1] (The latter would say no, and would be highly critical of the privileged academic discourse presented here, which, although well intended, is part of the dominant discourse). We have seen on numerous occasions throughout this volume representations of, for, and to a lesser extent by the other, with each variant generating its own set of problems. Depictions of the other by in-groups have ranged from patently hateful to patronizing, and the question here is can such representation ever be effective? Two major issues stand out on this front. One is the use of in-group heroes in redemptive storylines, a tactic that wins audiences, which one may argue is a mark of effectiveness, all the while maintaining the "goodness" of the in-group. Those in power who very often perpetrate abuses against the out-group do not have to fear for their thoughts and actions and can even vicariously, if fleetingly, become heroes themselves. I would not go so far as to advocate an all-out end to the redemptive or in-group hero tropes, mostly because this would supplant one totalized vision for another, but redemption has to come at a cost. The challenge for artists in the future will be to use this track in ways that unsettle audiences and force them to look inward at unspoken and hidden biases, as well as the ways in which the dominant discourse has buried the subaltern.

The second problem has to do with money. Winning over audiences with in-group heroes not only makes the in-group feel good about itself, it also maximizes profits, which, taken in tandem with a desire to trot out productions of conscience to present a progressive front, sullies what is an artistic venture, and, since we are dealing with issues of race, gender, and class, a philosophical one as well. Clearly, studios are money making ventures, which is a good thing, because if films lost money, none would be made; however, studios are operations of the powerful, and with productions costing in the millions of dollars, even for smaller scale projects, there aren't that many pieces that ever wind up on the screen. The same is true (probably more so) for stage productions.

Here, the medium can democratize the message, meaning that we might not necessarily need more representations of the other from the others themselves, but perhaps simply a wider pool of voices. With the advent of affordable digital media technology and internet forums such as YouTube, we are beginning to experience this democratic effect, but this is not a perfect solution either, as many productions on this level often lack the quality of larger studio ventures—again primarily because of cost or a related lack of access to talent. Frequently, too, plays and films of this sort are sub-par in terms of basic writing, coming off as bad propaganda, and there is the risk of casting all members of the in-group as immutably bad. While reconstituting voices of the other involves uncovering their effacement by the powerful, that does not necessarily justify a post-colonial impulse towards hegemony on terms that would generate new prejudices and hatreds, this time of the in-group. For me, effective cinematic and theatrical representations of the other would be those in which race, gender, and class intersect; those in which in-group and out-group behavior operates on a number of levels and plays with our expectations; those that deal in the gray, liminal zones of ambiguity rather than certainty; those that ask more questions than answer; those that continue conversations about otherness in a language that assumes an intelligent audience.

Additional questions surrounding films and stage plays deal with utility. Can cinematic and theatrical productions be put to educational use? Should they? I would say yes, but again with reservations. The desire to mold a more tolerant citizenry is part and parcel of contemporary civics education, and using films can be an effective way of beginning a discussion on any number of difficult issues. Problems arise when the intellectual conversation is carried only by representations of popular culture and not other disciplines and, more importantly, when the exercise becomes one of indoctrination and group-think. There is no definitive line in the sand which cannot be crossed here, but the key is to use performance as a springboard for discourse, in tandem with any number of other branches of learning, and to maintain a framework of discussion that respects multiple viewpoints, rather than one that imposes one unalterable, monolithic vision.

The goal of performance studies such as this one should be to advance both the living, critical mind as well as a different view of world, and here the words of Martin Buber are again illustrative. We need to relate to the other, "not as a mere sum of qualities, aspirations, and inhibitions," but we must "apprehend him, and affirm him, as a whole." We can only do this if we encounter this other "as a partner in a bipolar situation:"

> . . . To give his influence unity and meaning, [a person] must live through the situation in all its aspects not only from his point of view but also that of his partner. He must practice the kind of realization that I call embracing."[2]

We would be wise to follow the guidance of Emmanuel Lévinas as well, treating the other in the realm of reality and performance in a way we would like to be treated ourselves. In his belief system, "The challenge to self is precisely the reception of the absolutely other."[3]

NOTES

1. Gayatri Chakravorty Spivak, "A Critique of Postcolonial Reason," in *The Norton Anthology of Theory and Criticism,* ed. Vincent E. Leitsch (New York: Norton, 2001), 2193–2197.

2. Martin Buber, *I and Thou,* Walter Kaufmann, trans. (New York: Touchstone, 1970), 178, and Neve Gordon, "Ethics and the Place of the Other," in *Lévinas and Buber: Dialogue and Difference,* ed. Peter Atterton, et al (Pittsburgh, Pennsylvania: Duquesne University Press, 2004), 114.

3. Emmanuel Lévinas, *Humanism of the Other* (Urbana, Illinois: University of Illinois Press, 2006), 33. Spivak does not share the *a priori* position of Lévinas towards the "other" as for her, the other is a construct of whatever discourse names it as other. See Spivak, "A Critique of Postcolonial Reason," 2195.

Index

simulacral spaces, 77, 79
Sioux Indians, 266–67, 270
Skirts Ahoy, 163
slavery, 30; Christian practice of, 54
Slotkin, Richard, 272, 274
Smith, Gerald L. K., 4
The Snake Pit, 3, 8–9
Snead, James, 125
Snickers commercial, 174
Soares, Luiz Eduardo, 66
Sobibor death camp, 219
social issue films, 3–13
social reality, 61
Sometimes in April, 257–59
song lyrics, 79, 203–4
sonnets of Shakespeare, 46–47
Sophie Scholl: The Final Days, 231
The Sorrow and the Pity, 233
"The Souls of White Folk," 22–23
Spanish invasion, fear of, 42
Special Police Operations
    Battalion, 66
spectacles, biblical, 13
Spielberg, Steven, 219, 221–22, 229
Spigner, Clarence, 129
Spivak, Gayatri, 82
sports in drama and film, 172–84
SS, German, 245–47
Stalag 17, 249
The Start Spangled Screen, 238
Steiner, George, 214
stereotypes: of Asian Americans,
    128–29; of Asian women, 129–30;
    ethnic, 114, 127–28; of Jewish
    women, 144–46; of Mexican women,
    188; of women in the armed forces,
    161–63
Stevens, George, 225
Stimson, Henry L., 158
"stock character" analysis, 113–14
Stone, John, 120
Strauss, Claude Levi, 269
Stuckart, William, 150
Studlar, Gaykyn, 277

subaltern: female subjects, treatment of,
    186; subjects, 283
"subalternity" defined, 85
Sumner, Cid Ricketts, 9
Supreme Court (U.S.) and housing
    covenants, 7
survival of the fittest, 234
Szabó, István, 232

Taboo Memories and Diasporic Visions,
    89–90
Tajima, Renee, 119, 121–22
Take Me Out, 172, 181–83
Taymor, Julie, 186–96; and love story,
    191
"Teaching Multiculturalism from the
    Movies: Health and Social Well-
    being," 129
technology, digital, 284
Tel Aviv compared to Palestinian
    Authority, 202–3
Telemaque, Adrienne, 137
television images, 79; as symbol of
    globalization, 82
Third Command *(Comando Terceiro),*
    65
third eye, 28–29
third space and cultural discourse,
    31–32
"Third-World Literature in the Era of
    Multinational Capitalism," 85
This Above All, 163
Thomas, Christopher, 237–55
Thunderheart, 273–74
Tiana (Thi Thanh Nga), 134
time and representation, 213–22
To Hell and Back, 242
tolerance, plea for, 51–52, 57–59; by
    Shakespeare, 41
tolerance in England, 173–74
Tom, Lauren, 137
Tomorrow the World, 237
Toraty, Benny, 95, 99–102
Townsend, Robert, 137

Biographies of Contributing Authors

Ilan Avisar is a professor in the Film and Television Department at Tel Aviv University. After completing his Ph.D. at Indiana University, Professor Avisar taught at The Ohio State University for five years. He is the author of *Screening the Holocaust: Cinema's Images of the Unimaginable* (1988), *Visions of Israel: Israeli Filmmakers and Images of the Jewish State* (1997, rpt. 2002), *Film Art: The Techniques and Poetics of Cinematic Expression* (1995, in Hebrew), and *The Israeli Scene: Language, Cinema, Discourse* (2005, in Hebrew).

John Clum is professor of theatre studies and English and chair of the Department of Theatre Studies at Duke University. He is the author of a number of books, including *Still Acting Gay: Male Homosexuality in Modern Drama* (2001), *Something for the Boys: Musical Theater and Gay Culture* (2000), and *"He's All Man": Learning Masculinity, Gayness, and Love from American Movies* (2002). Professor Clum has also edited two major anthologies of contemporary drama, and his own plays have been produced in theaters around America. He has twice won Duke's Distinguished Teaching Award.

Jonathan Friedman is director of Holocaust and Genocide Studies and associate professor of history at West Chester University. He has worked as a historian at both the United States Holocaust Memorial Museum in Washington, D.C. and the Survivors of the Shoah Visual History Foundation. He is the author of four books, most recently *The Literary, Cultural, and Historical Significance of the 1937 Biblical Stage Play, The Eternal Road* (2004), and *Rainbow Jews: Gay and Jewish Identity in the Performing Arts* (2007).

Edward C. Hanes, is enrolled in the Holocaust and Genocide Studies Master of Arts Program at West Chester University. He holds degrees in biology and art from Portland State University, and with his training in history, he intends to pursue his Ph.D. in Holocaust and Genocide Studies.

William Hewitt is professor of history at West Chester University. Professor Hewitt's areas of specialization include Native American history, genocide, film, and gay and lesbian studies. He has published an historical novel *Across the Wide River* (2003) and the book *Defining the Horrific: Readings on Genocide and the Holocaust in the 20th Century* (2003).

Dalton Anthony Jones is currently ABD in American Studies at Yale University.

Margarete Landwehr is associate professor of German at West Chester University. She holds a Ph.D. from Harvard University and is the author of numerous articles on literary and film analysis. She is completing a book on German memorials of the Holocaust.

Tia Malkin-Fontecchio is an assistant professor in the department of history at West Chester University. A graduate of Brown University, her area of specialization is 20th century Brazil.

John Michalczyk is co-director of film studies and chair of the Fine Arts Department at Boston College. Since 1970 in doctoral studies at Harvard University, his research has focused on fascism in art, film, and literature. Over the past 25 years, this scholarship has led to the publication of several books dealing with the Holocaust, including most recently *Confront! Resistance in Nazi Germany* (2004). In addition to his scholarship in print, professor Michalczyk is also an award-winning documentary filmmaker. He has produced and directed twelve documentaries, including *Nazi Medicine: In the Shadow of the Reich* (1997).

Susan A. Michalczyk is currently the director of senior year in the Honors Program of Boston College. Her publications include "Troubled Silences: Trauma in John Huston's *Let There Be Light* (1946/1981)," as well as essays on the autobiographical and sociological interpretations of a variety of authors and artists, including Michelangelo, Italo Calvino, James Ensor and Georges Rouault. She holds a Ph.D. from Harvard University.

Paul Pfeiffer is professor of communication and theatre arts at Salisbury University, where he has been teaching since 1980. Professor Pfeiffer has originated performance groups, directed plays, and written theatrical pieces of his own, including *Apology for the Life of an Actor*. An active scholar in international conferences, where he has presented on various aspects of the classical theatre, Professor Pfeiffer is currently working on a stage adaptation of Henry Fielding's novel, *Joseph Andrews*, and several other projects for screen treatment.

Geetha Ramanathan is professor of English and the director of women's studies at West Chester University. She is the author of *Feminist Auteurs: Reading Feminist Film* (2006).

Christopher Thomas has written extensively on the United States and World War II, contributing articles to edited volumes and encyclopedias, such as Aaron Hsiao's *United States at War: Understanding Conflict and Society* (2005), Paul Pierpaoli's *United States at War—Project 2007* (forthcoming), and Sue Moskowitz's *One Day in History Series: December 7, 1941* (also forthcoming). Mr. Thomas holds a Master of Arts degree from Texas A & M University.

Jun Xing is professor of ethnic studies and director of the Difference, Power and Discrimination Program at Oregon State University. Dr. Xing received his Ph.D. in American Studies from the University of Minnesota at Twin Cities. He is the author/editor of *Reversing the Lens: Ethnicity, Race, Gender and Sexuality through Film* (2003), *Asian America through the Lens: History, Representations, and Identity* (1998), and *Baptized in the Fire of Revolution: The American Social Gospel and the YMCA in China, 1919–1937* (1996).

Raz Yosef holds a Ph.D. in cinema studies from New York University. He teaches in the Film and Television Department at Tel Aviv University and in Sapir College, Israel. He is the author of *Beyond Flesh: Queer Masculinities and Nationalism in Israeli Cinema* (2004), and of numerous articles on issues of gender, sexuality and ethnicity in Israeli visual culture.

Melissa Ziobro holds a Master of Arts degree in United States History from Monmouth University in West Long Branch, NJ. She works as a Historian at the U.S. Army Communications-Electronics Life Cycle Management Command, Fort Monmouth, NJ.